WORKBOOK

THE MUSIC KIT
TOM MANOFF

W · W · Norton & Company · Inc · New York

WORKBOOK DESIGNED BY ELSA ANN DANENBERG

Copyright © 1976 by Tom Manoff. All rights reserved.
Published simultaneously in Canada by Geogre J. McLeod Limited, Toronto.
Printed in the United States of America.
First Edition
ISBN 0 393 09179 1
1 2 3 4 5 6 7 8 9 0

Library of Congress Cataloging in Publication Data

Manoff, Tom.
    The music kit.

    CONTENTS: [1] Workbook.—[2] Rhythm reader.—
[3] Scorebook.
    1. Music—Theory, Elementary.   I. Title.
    MT7.M267   781   76-1006
    ISBN 0-393-09179-1

FOR MY BROTHER MIKE

CONTENTS

Preface XI
Acknowledgments XIII

CHAPTER 1.   1

Pitch • The Notation of Pitch • Note Names • The Octave • Note Names on the Staff • The Treble Clef • Notes in the Treble Clef • The Bass Clef • Notes in the Bass Clef • Ledger Lines • Writing Ledger Lines • The Grand Staff • Learning the Note Names • Middle C • Suggested Activities • Terms and Concepts

CHAPTER 2.   23

The Piano Keyboard • Any Keyboard Will Do • The Construction of the Keyboard • The White Keys • The Black Keys • Notating the White Keys • Notating the Black Keys • Suggested Activities at the Keyboard • Terms and Concepts

CHAPTER 3.   34

Scales • Half Steps • The Chromatic Scale • Whole Steps • The Whole-Tone Scale • Other Names for the Half Step and Whole Step • Diatonic Semitone/Chromatic Semitone • Accidentals • Summary of Accidentals • Use of the Natural Sign • Precautionary Accidentals • Suggested Activities • Terms and Concepts

CHAPTER 4.   48

Diatonic Scales • The Major Scale • Major-Scale Construction • Constructing Other Major Scales • Adding Accidentals to Form a Major Scale • Major-Scale Spellings • "In the Key of" • Tonality • Intervals • Inversion • Suggested Activities • Terms and Concepts

CHAPTER 5.   61

Key Signatures • The Major-Scale Key Signatures • The Circle of 5ths • Transposition • Accidentals: Two Definitions • Singing Major-Scale Melodies • Syllables • Singing Melodies • Octave Relationships • Suggested Activities • Terms and Concepts

CHAPTER 6.   78

Intervals • The Quality of an Interval • Which Term of Quality Applies? • Relationships of Quality Designations • Relationships of Intervals to the Major Scale • Major-Scale Interval Relationships • Altering Major-Scale Intervals • Rule for Identifying Intervals by Major-Scale Relationships • Consonance and Dissonance • Consonant and Dissonant Intervals • Terms and Concepts

CHAPTER 7.   86

A Second Look at Intervals • Intervals Without Key Signatures • Use of the Natural Diatonic Semitone • Adding Accidentals • Singing Intervals in Familiar Songs • The Pentatonic Scale • Singing the Pentatonic Scale • Composing Melodies • Suggested Activities • Terms and Concepts

CHAPTER 8.   102

Minor Scales • Minor-Scale Key Signatures • Finding the Relative Minor Scale • Finding the Relative Major Scale • Parallel Minor/Parallel Major • Singing the Natural Minor Scale • Other Minor-Scale Forms • The Augmented 2nd • The Melodic Minor Scale • Modes • Mode Mixture • Suggested Activities • Terms and Concepts

CHAPTER 9.   120

Part Singing • Harmony with 3rds and 6ths • Canons and Rounds • Counterpoint • Chords • Triads • Quality of Triads • Singing the Triads • Difficult Triad Spellings • Enharmonic Spellings: The Reasons • Diminished and Augmented Triads • Suggested Activities • Terms and Concepts

CHAPTER 10.   131

Working with Triads • Learning the Triads • Voicing • Inversions • Harmonic Background of a Melody • Composing a Chord Melody • Nonharmonic Tones • An Aid for Spelling Other Triads • Group III: Triads on B and B♭ • The Use of Progressions in Scores • Suggested Activities • Terms and Concepts

CHAPTER 11.   147

The Harmonic System • Major-Scale Triad Quality • Practical Use of the Harmonic System • Seventh Chords • The V^7 Chord • The Sound of the V^7 Chord • Tonality • Harmonization: Methods for Harmonizing a Melody • Suggested Activities • Terms and Concepts

CHAPTER 12.   164
Accompaniments to Songs • Guitar and Autoharp Accompaniments • Piano Accompaniments • Voicing • Modern Accompaniments • Suggested Activities • Terms and Concepts

CHAPTER 13.   176
Form: Phrase Design • Words and Music • Two Types of Cadences • Cadential Design of *One Grain of Sand* • The Harmonic Aspects of the Cadence • Perfect Authentic Cadence • Imperfect Authentic Cadence • Semicadence • Plagal Cadence • Deceptive Cadence • The Design of Phrase Forms • Parallel and Contrasting Periods • The Three-Phrase Period • Composing Periods • Suggested Activities • Terms and Concepts

CHAPTER 14.   188
The Motive • Characteristics of the Motive • Identifying the Motive • Motivic Development • Popular Use of the Motive • Suggested Activities • Terms and Concepts

CHAPTER 15.   199
Melody • Melodic Shape • Melodic Goal • Motivic Development • Suggested Activities • Terms and Concepts

CHAPTER 16.   208
Texture • Elements that Affect Texture • Voice Combinations: Musical Terms • Harmony and Counterpoint • Instrumentation • Form and Texture • Terms Used in Describing Form • Elements of Form • Suggested Activities • Terms and Concepts

Appendices

Appendix I: Table of Note and Rest Values	222
Appendix II: Checklist of Notation Symbols	224
Appendix III: Major and Minor Scales and Key Signatures	226
Appendix IV: Triads and Chords	228
Appendix V: Methods of Sight Singing	230
Appendix VI: Rock and Blues Scale Patterns	232
Appendix VII: Progressions for Improvisation and Composition	233
Appendix VIII: The Guitar and the Autoharp	234
Appendix IX: Recorder Fingering	237
Appendix X: How to Read a Lead Sheet	238
Appendix XI: Glossary of Terms	242

PREFACE

My first teacher was a wonderful musician named David Labovitz. Someone once referred to his joyful and direct conducting style as "from the no-nonsense school." There are many things he taught me for which I am grateful, not the least of which was his conviction that technique must be seen as one essential element in the total musical experience. It was on this premise that I based the form and content of *The Music Kit*.

It has often been said that there are really only two kinds of music: good and bad. The idea that "good music" can be found only among the works of the great masters of the past seems both self-limiting and ingenuous in view of the incredible output of and interest in all forms of popular music today. (Included in this category would be jazz, folk, rock, electronic, ethnic, and theater music.)

Many "serious" composers admit freely that they have been influenced both in style and concept by the inventiveness and sheer energy so characteristic of popular music. And, as the technology advances and is enlisted in the service of this new music, the serious popular musician gains in stature and significance. Inclusion of popular music in the education of young people seems long overdue.

Blending all kinds of music in the learning environment presents us with some unique opportunities. The emphasis on improvisation and the freedom it engenders offers the traditionally oriented student some dynamic involvement with musical creation. For that student who is sophisticated only in the more popular kinds of music, exposure to the formal traditions of classical music can open new doors to stimulating and provocative experiences.

It is my hope that in this meeting of styles without bias, greater appreciation for all music and creativity without limitations will result. And in the sheltered environment of the classroom, the interaction may conceivably give birth to completely new musical sounds and shapes.

The Music Kit, by deliberate design, includes a very wide variety of music types. No judgments have been made on the relative merits of any style, nor are such judgments necessary for the examination of techniques and theories. Instead, the universal elements of all music are considered in the broadest sense.

preface

It would never occur to anyone to read either a great poetic masterpiece or a gripping piece of science fiction in a language he does not understand. Yet, a thorough grounding in theory and fundamental skills has never been considered a prerequisite for the performance or appreciation of music. It is an undeniable fact, nevertheless, that enjoyment will increase with understanding, that technical facility will open the doors to creativity. Let this be the point of departure for both student and teacher.

So, with this "no nonsense" approach, let us proceed to our work!

HOW TO USE *THE MUSIC KIT*

You will find four different components in your kit: the *Workbook*, the *Rhythm Reader*, the *Scorebook*, and the *Records*. All the parts are interrelated. The *Workbook* and the *Rhythm Reader* are to be used together: for example, when you are working on Chapter 1 in the *Workbook*, you should also be working on Chapter 1 in the *Rhythm Reader*. As you proceed, always study chapters of the same number in each book. References to specific selections in the *Scorebook* and the *Records* may be found in each chapter. For example (S 2, B 5) means record side 2, band 5; (SB 25) refers the reader to selection number 25 in the *Scorebook*.

Answer all questions. Even if some answers seem obvious, write them down anyway. No questions are to be considered optional.

Do all exercises described as Suggested Activities.

Proceed slowly and steadily from one section to the next. Go back and try again if a topic does not seem clear. Review periodically all terms and concepts listed at the end of each chapter.

The Music Kit will teach you to play simple melodies on the piano or other keyboard instruments such as the xylophone. Make every effort to play all examples. The playing exercises are designed to correspond to your rapidly developing skills in rhythm and your growing theoretical understanding.

Work hard—it will be worth it.

Tom Manoff

ACKNOWLEDGMENTS

I wish to express my gratitude to Leo Kraft, Professor of Music at Queens College of the City University of New York, and to Claire Brook, Music Editor, and Hinda Keller Farber, both of W. W. Norton, for their patient assistance in the editing of this text. I also wish to thank Barbara Schuster for her dedication and suggestions in the preparation of the manuscript, as well as Bob and Gayle Leaversuch and Nora Horn, for their support throughout this project. The musicians who contributed their talents to the recorded music are: Paul Anselmo, Frank Feliciano, Beth Goldstein, Richard Hoffman, Gordon Johnson, Philip Markowitz, Ted Moore, Jack Parrot, Susan Reiring, Jim Saporito, Barbara Steinberg, and Neil Waltzer. Finally, I express special appreciation to Richard Maisel for his confidence in my work.

CHAPTER 1

PITCH

If you play a few notes on the extreme right side of the piano keyboard, then play a few on the extreme left side, the notes on the right side will sound "high" and the notes on the left side will sound "low." This difference in the sound of musical tones—how high or low they sound—is called *pitch*. When a pitch is written it becomes a *note*.

THE NOTATION OF PITCH

Pitch is written on a group of five lines called a *staff*.

Staff:

———————————————
———————————————
———————————————
———————————————
———————————————

The higher a note is placed on the staff, the higher the pitch; the lower a note is placed on the staff, the lower the pitch. The direction of pitch from low to high is:

The direction of pitch from high to low is:

Notes are written either on the lines or in the spaces of the staff.

notes on lines   **notes in spaces**

1 Using 𝐨 as the note:
  1. Write a high note in a space on the staff provided below.
  2. Write a high note on a line.
  3. Write a low note on a line.
  4. Write a low note in a space.

1.   2.   3.   4.

2 Circle the lower note of each group.

Example   1.   2.   3.   4.   5.

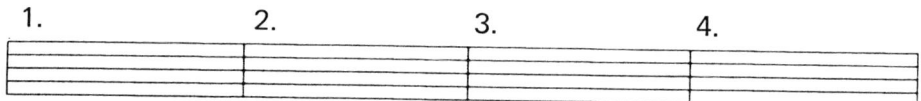

3 In each group of three notes, circle the one whose pitch lies **between** the pitches of the other two.

Example   1.   2.   3.   4.

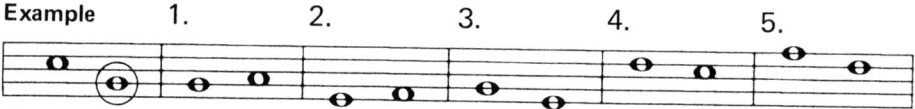

4
  1. Listen to the fourth movement of *Antiphonies* (1969) by Leo Kraft (S 1, B 1). In what direction does the pitch go at the very end of the movement—up or down? _____

  2. Listen to the Chopin *Waltz in C-Sharp Minor* (S 2, B 1). Listen for a passage that rises steadily. Does it begin or end a thought? _____

3. Listen to *How Strange* (S7, B1). Which instruments play high notes? Which instruments play low notes? Write the names of the instruments in the appropriate place. If an instrument plays both high and low notes, write its name under both headings.

Instruments	Low	High
Piano		
Bass		
Guitar		
Synthesizer		
Drums		
Triangle		

NOTE NAMES

The notes on a staff have the same names as the first seven letters of the alphabet. From low to high:

After G, we start with A again:

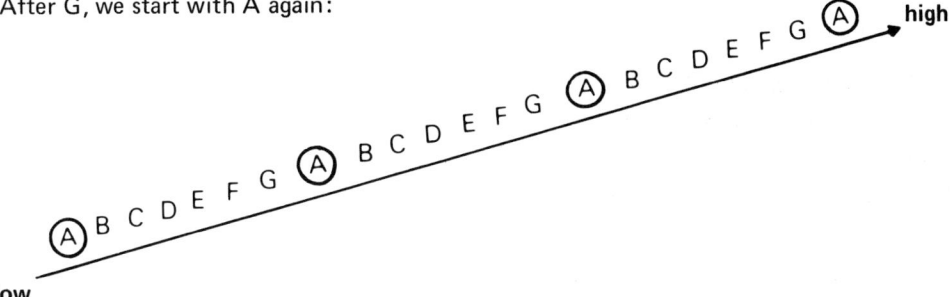

5 Starting from A, write the consecutive letter names of the notes, but with the pitch direction from high to low (the alphabet backwards). End on A.

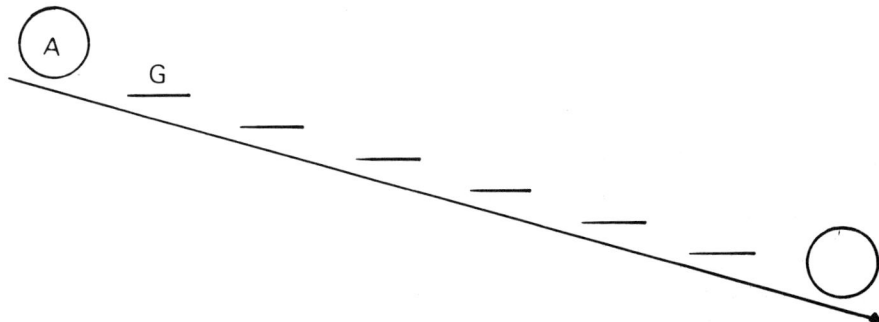

THE OCTAVE

You have just observed that letter-names are repeated as pitch rises and falls. There are high A's and low A's, but all are from the same pitch family—A. The distance between two A's—eight notes apart—is called an *octave*. One octave above a G, you will find another G.

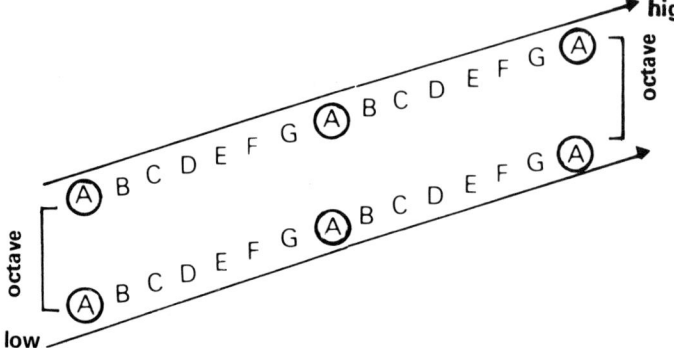

An octave below a D, there is another D. Sometimes, instead of saying that one F is higher than another, we say that it is in a higher *register*. When men and women sing the same pitch, they often sing in octaves; the men choose a lower register, while the women sing an octave above the men. Pitches of the same letter name are considered to be in the same *class*. Thus, each pitch belongs to a larger class (or family) of pitches, all having the same letter name, so that **different** versions of the **same** pitch exist in higher or lower registers.

NOTE NAMES ON THE STAFF

Consecutive lines and spaces indicate consecutive letter names. Therefore, going up in pitch:

If this line is E,   the next space is F,   the next line is G,   the next space is A.

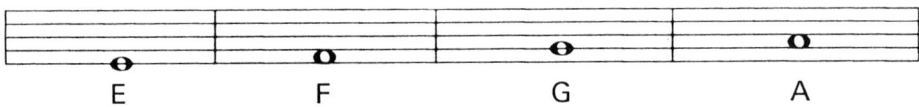

Going down in pitch:

If this line is A,   the next space is G,   the next line is F,   the next space is E.

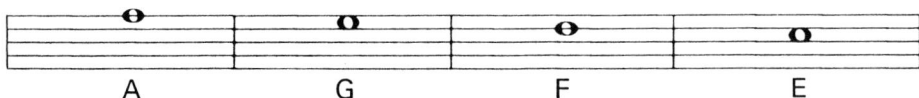

> **Rule**
> Consecutive letter names going up or down in pitch are always notated as line-space-line-space-line-space-. The sequence may start on either a line or space.

THE TREBLE CLEF

Since there is obviously not enough room on one staff to notate the pitches in all the registers, separate staffs are used for high notes and low notes. To notate the high notes, a staff with a *treble clef* is used. This symbol indicates that the second line from the bottom on the staff is G. Because of this, the treble clef is also called the *G clef*.

Treble clef or G clef

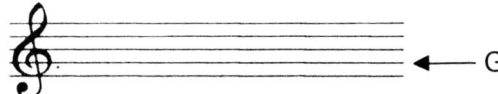

6 Draw treble clefs across this staff. Make sure that the loop wraps around the second line.

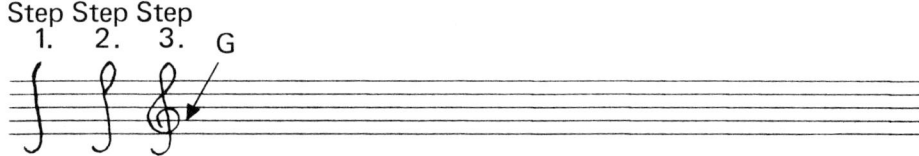

NOTES IN THE TREBLE CLEF

Study the note names in the treble clef as (1) consecutive letter names, (2) names of lines, and (3) names of spaces.

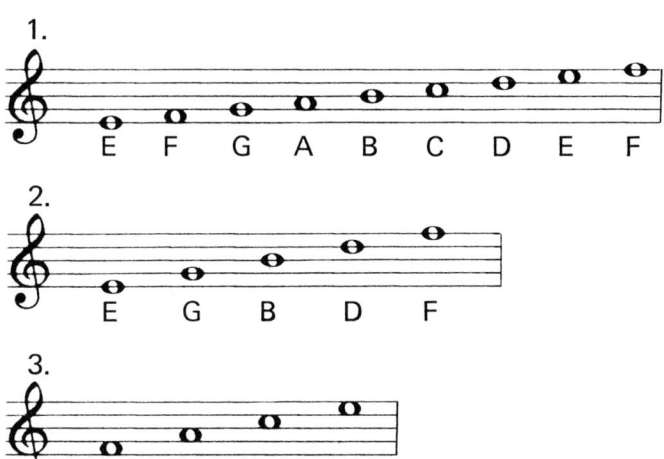

7 Identify each note:

Write the indicated note (use o):

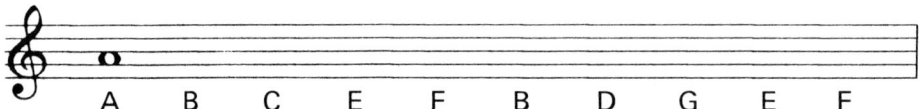

A B C E F B D G E F

THE BASS CLEF

To notate the low notes, the *bass clef* 𝄢 is used; it indicates that the second line from the top on the staff is F. It is also called the *F clef*.

Bass clef or F clef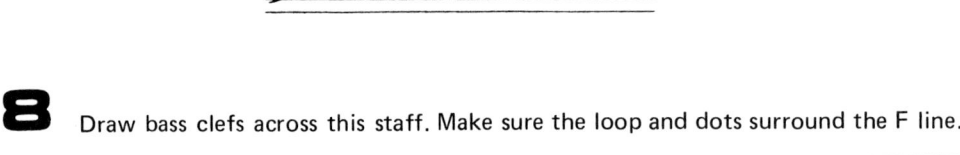

8 Draw bass clefs across this staff. Make sure the loop and dots surround the F line.

NOTES IN THE BASS CLEF

Study the notes in the bass clef as (1) consecutive letter names, (2) names of lines, and (3) names of spaces.

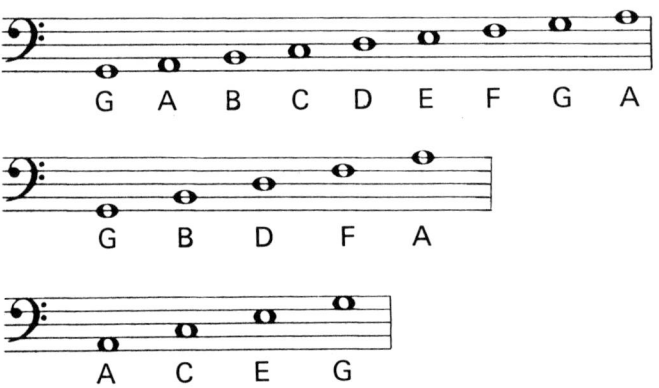

9 Identify each note:

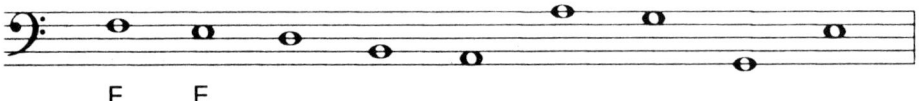

Write in the indicated note (use o):

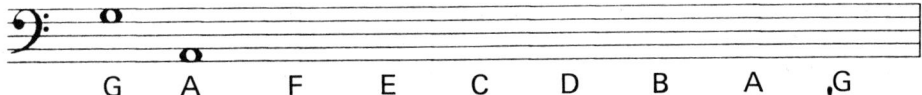

LEDGER LINES
In order to notate pitch above or below the five-line staff, the staff is extended by *ledger lines*. These lines continue the alternation of lines and spaces.

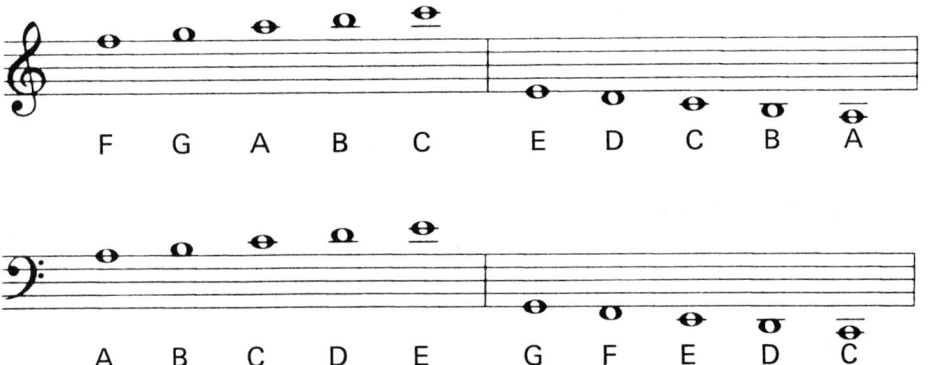

WRITING LEDGER LINES
The space between a staff line and a ledger line and between any two ledger lines should be equal to the space between any two staff lines.

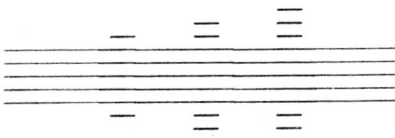

10 Write these ledger lines, being careful to space them in relation to the staff lines.

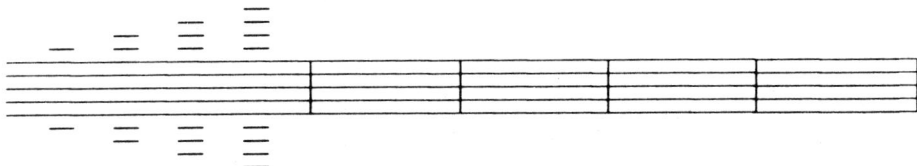

THE GRAND STAFF

In order to notate music that uses both high and low pitches, the treble clef is joined with the bass clef to form the *grand staff*. The grand staff is also called the *great staff* or the *piano staff*. The two clefs are divided by middle C, the C midway on the piano keyboard.

Grand staff

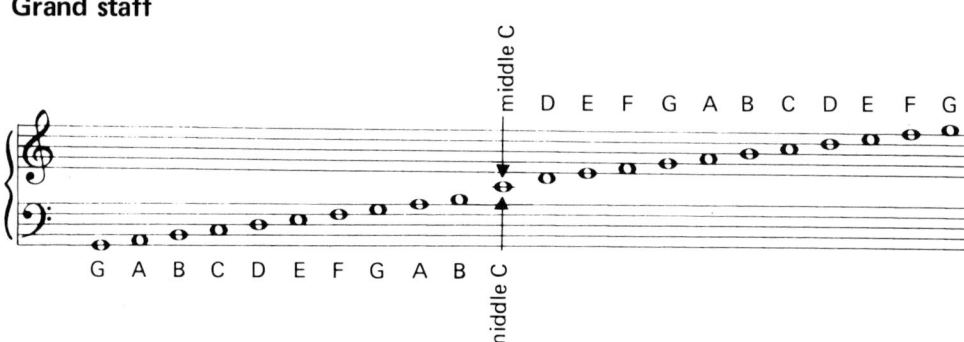

LEARNING THE NOTE NAMES

To study music you must be able to recognize note names in both clefs. As you work with the various elements of music that follow, your ability to recognize note names will increase. However, if you don't gain a secure basis in note reading now, further study will be very difficult. The following exercises will help you develop facility in note reading.

11 Rearrange, in order, from the lowest to highest. Name all notes.

4.

5.

6.

7.

12 Rearrange, in order, from highest to lowest. Name all notes.

Example

D C B A G

1.

2.

3.

13 Make note name flash cards (like the type used for studying vocabulary):

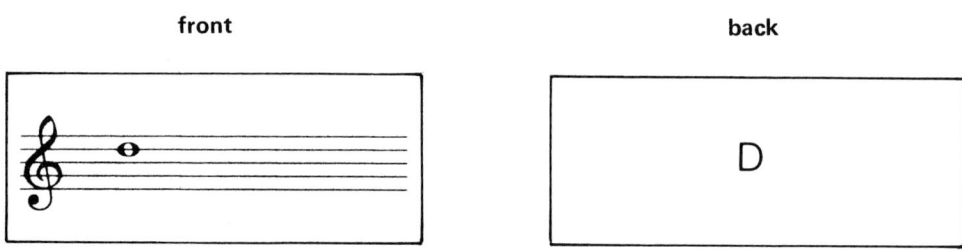

Use the cards to make up games for yourself or friends, or use the old faithful system: the ones you miss go into one pile, the ones you know go into another.

14 Study each group of notes on the left, memorizing the position of each note. Keeping an even beat, name each note on the staff at the right out loud. **Do not** write the note names. Record the time (in seconds) of your fastest accurate reading. There is space for future timings, so that you can come back to this exercise while studying later chapters.

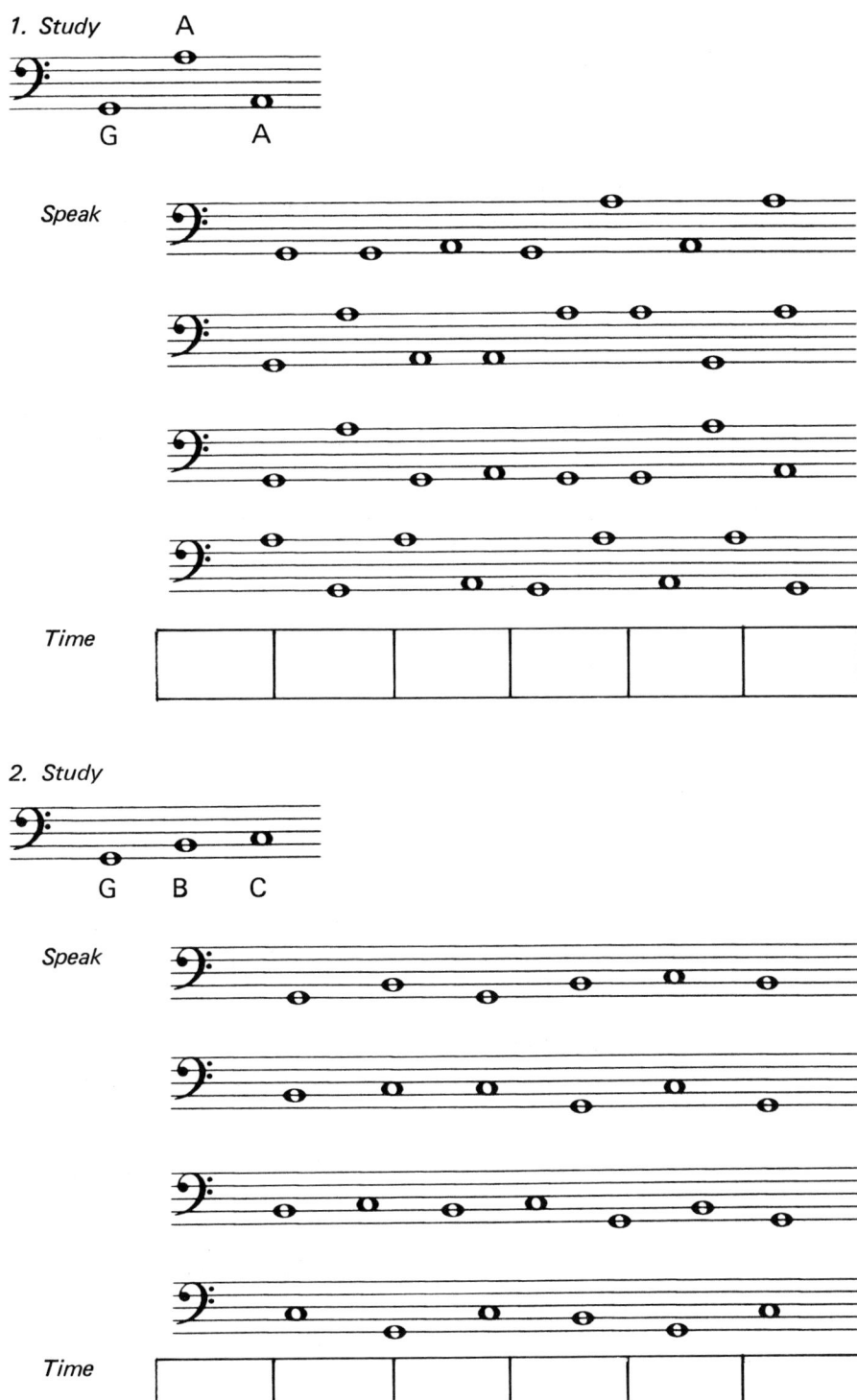

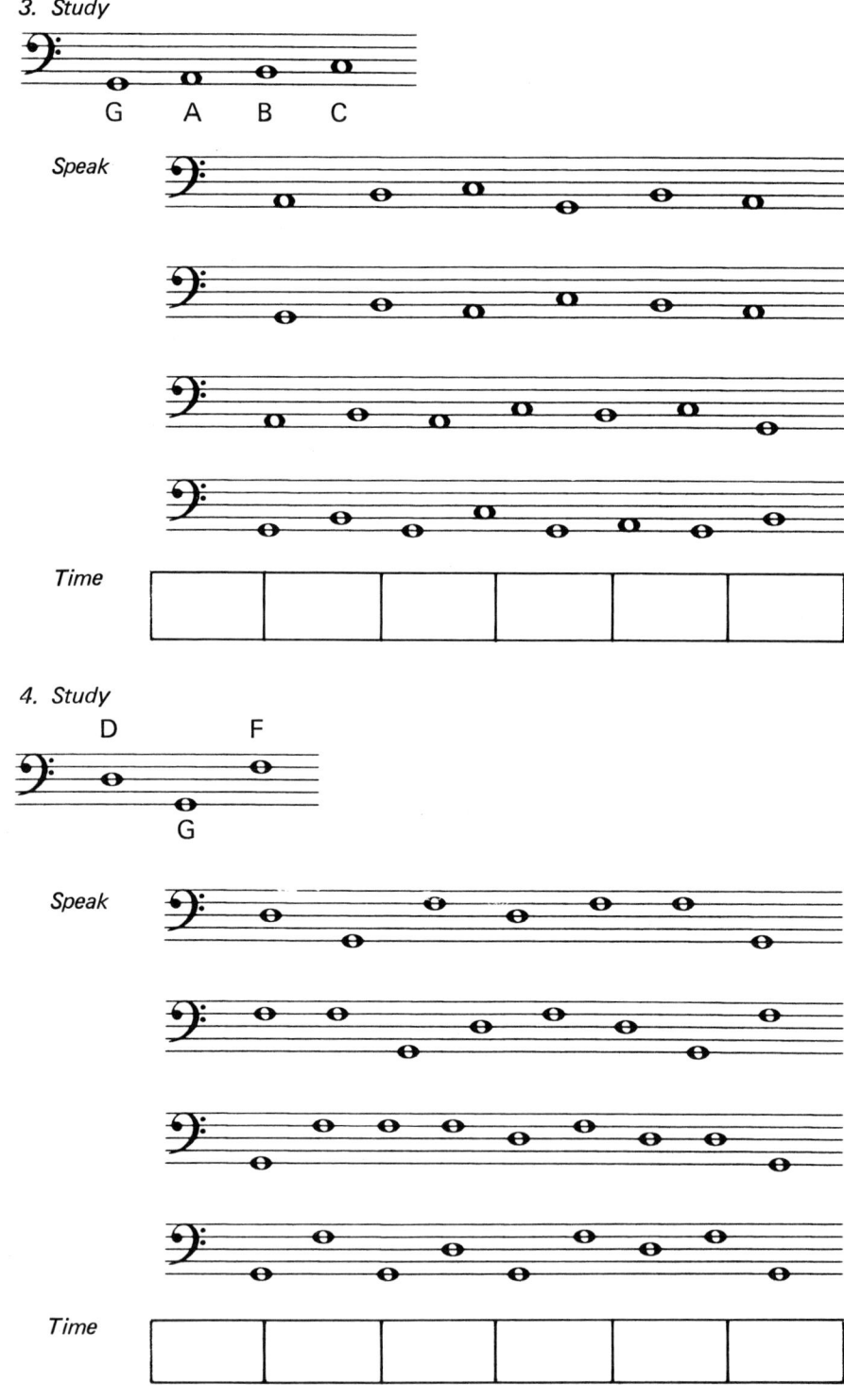

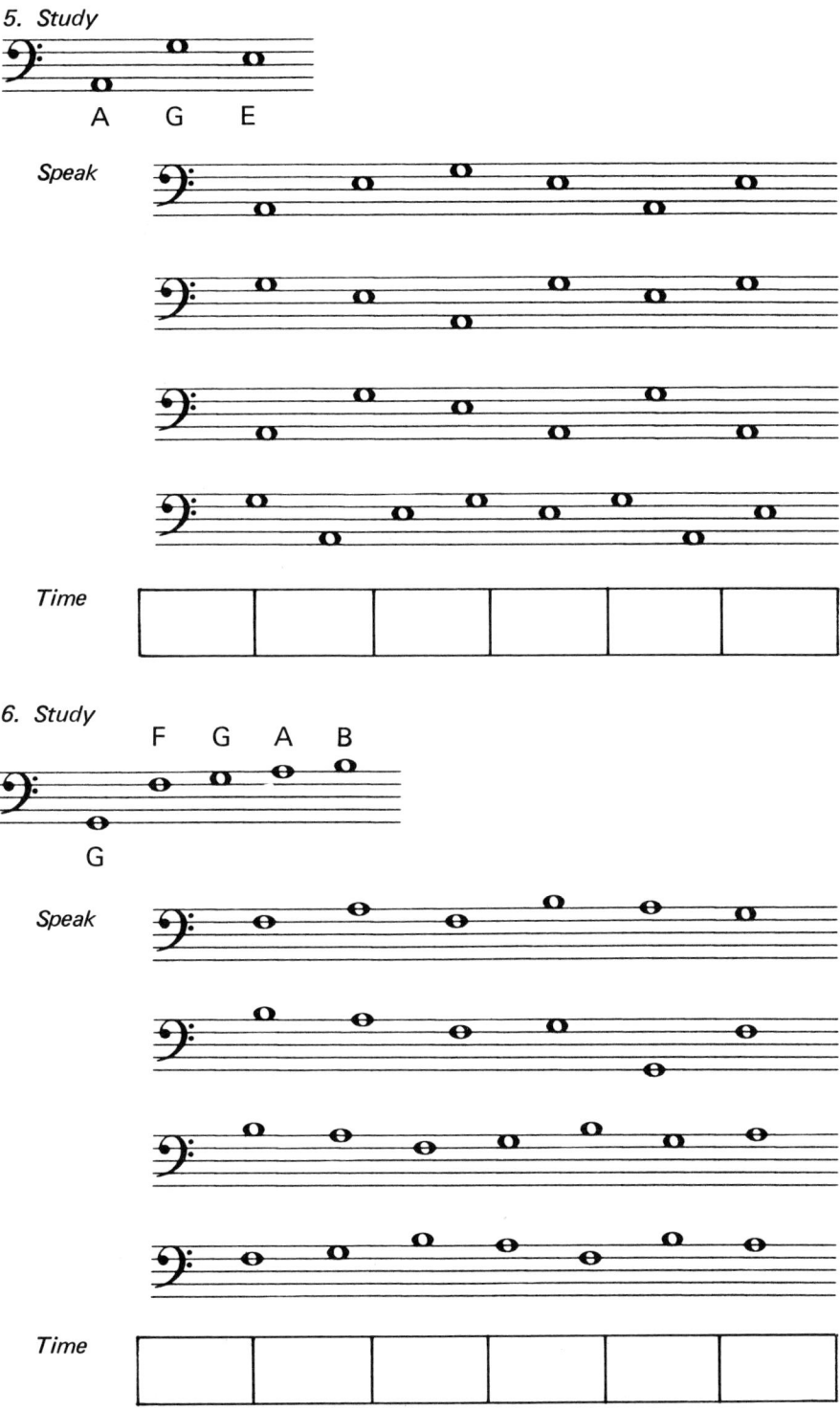

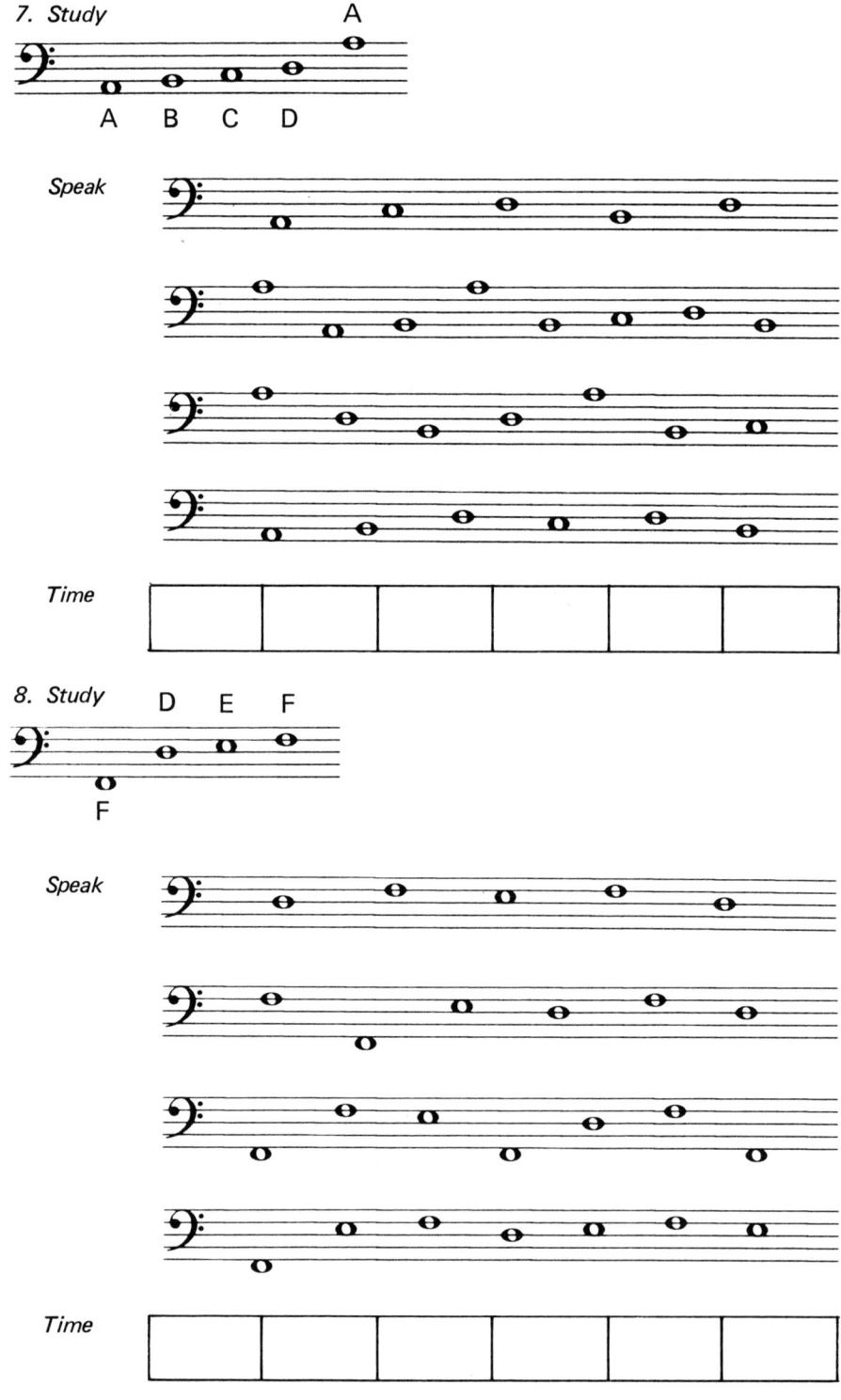

15 Write the staff around the note. The word "line" or "space" will indicate whether the higher or lower note, with the same letter name, is required. All notes in this exercise are in the bass clef.

Example
A/space

Answer:
A/space

1. C/space	2. E/space	3. F/line
4. G/line	5. G/space	6. A/line
7. D/line	8. A/space	9. B/line
10. B/space	11. F/space	12. G/line

16 Repeat instructions as in **14**.

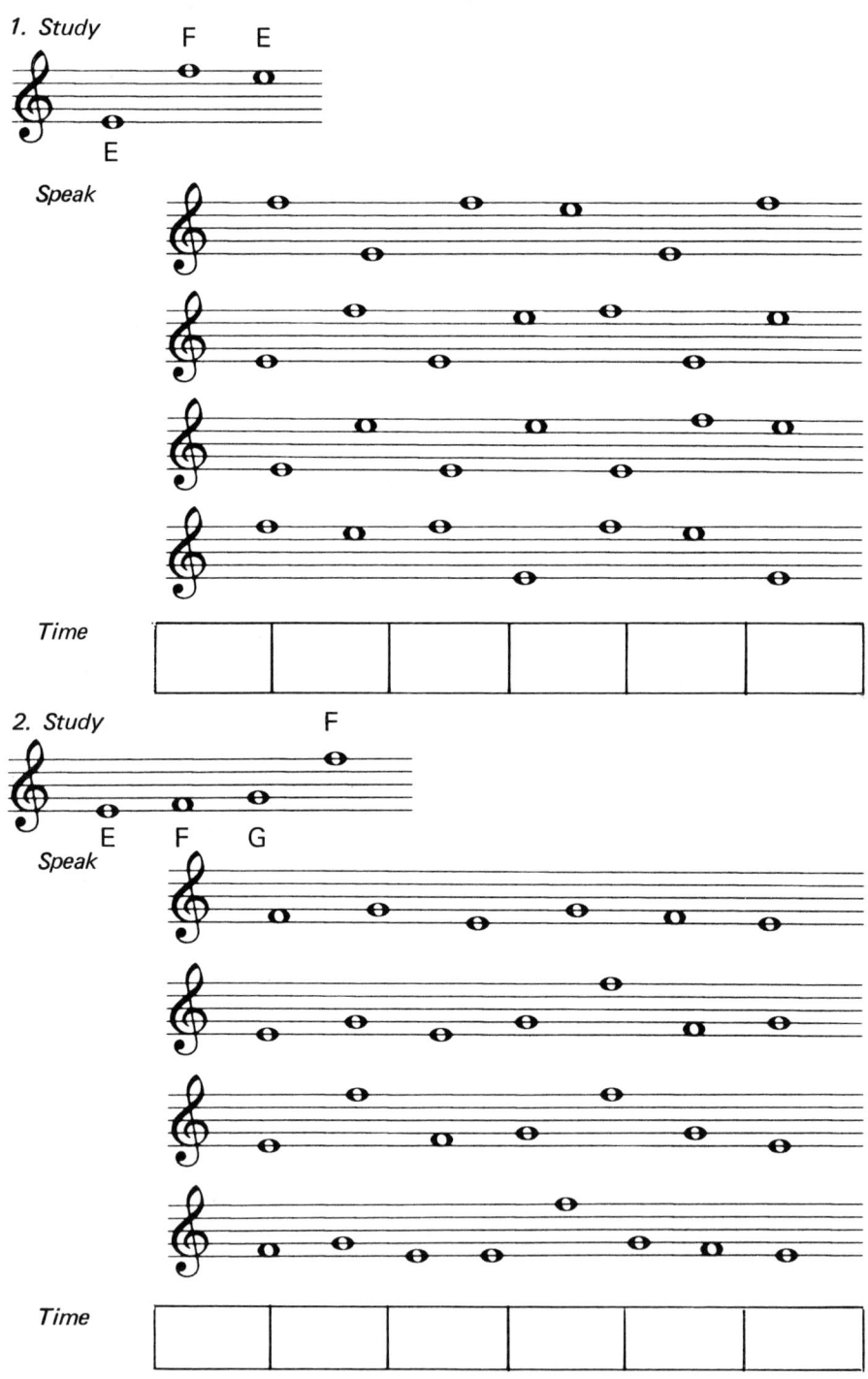

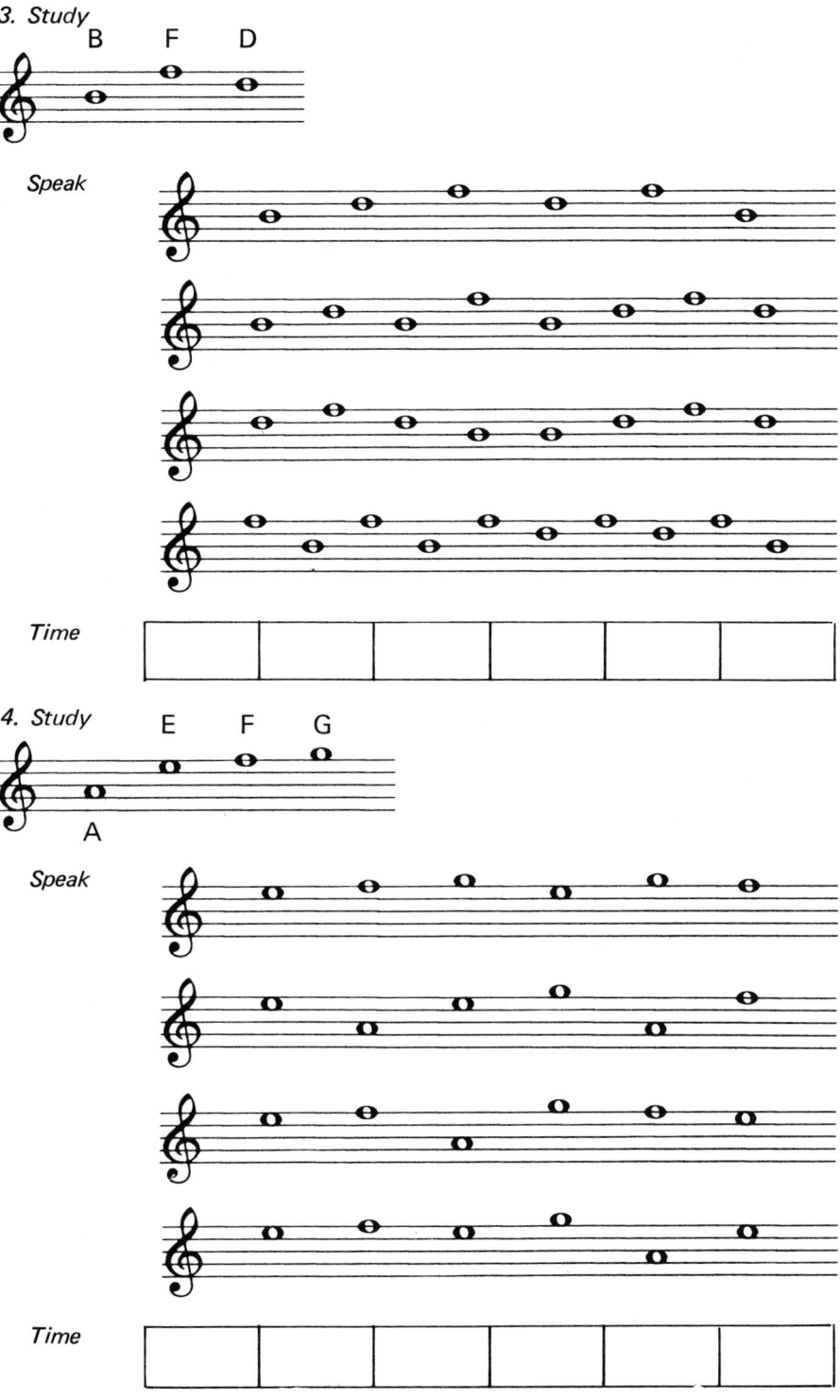

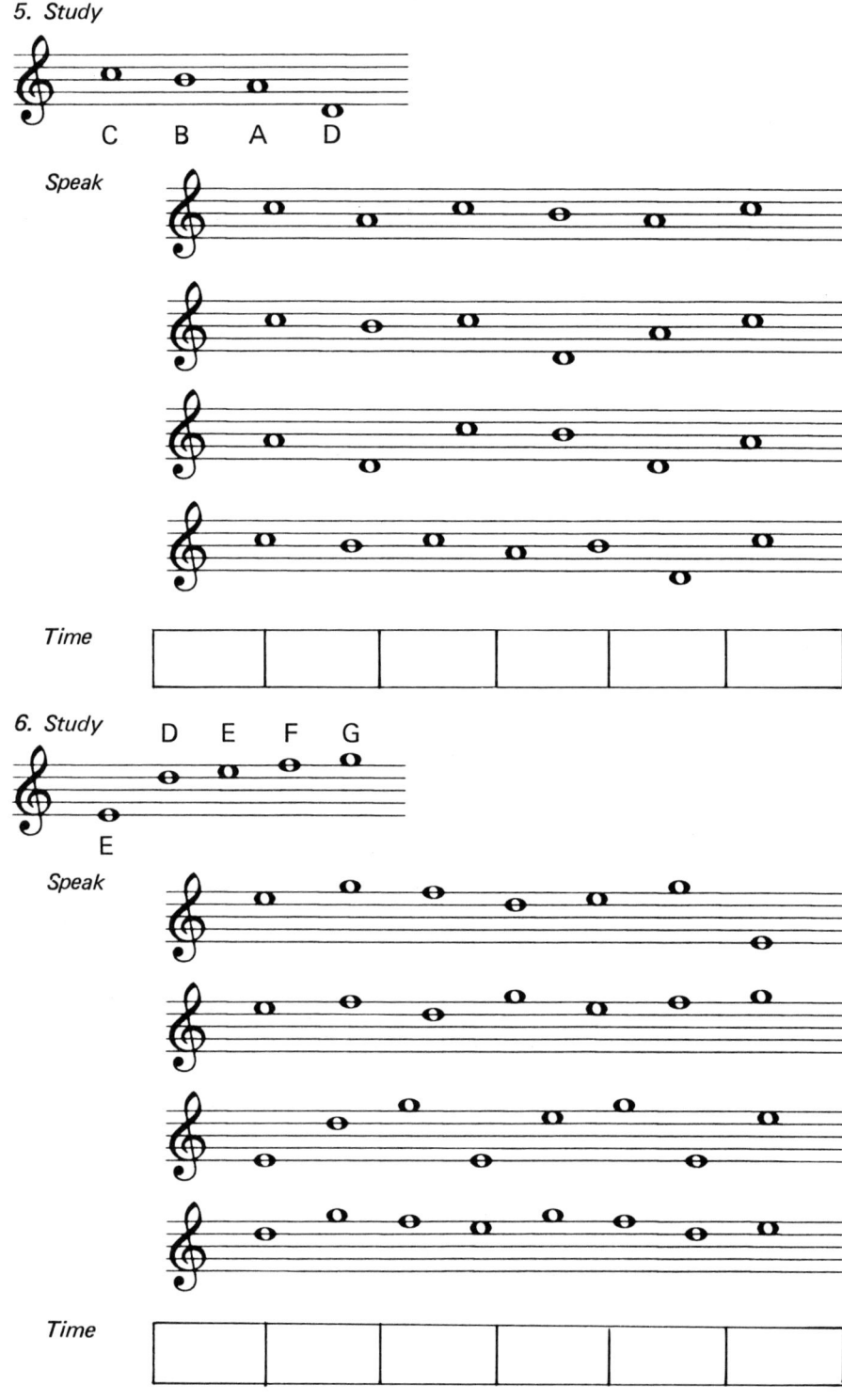

7. Study

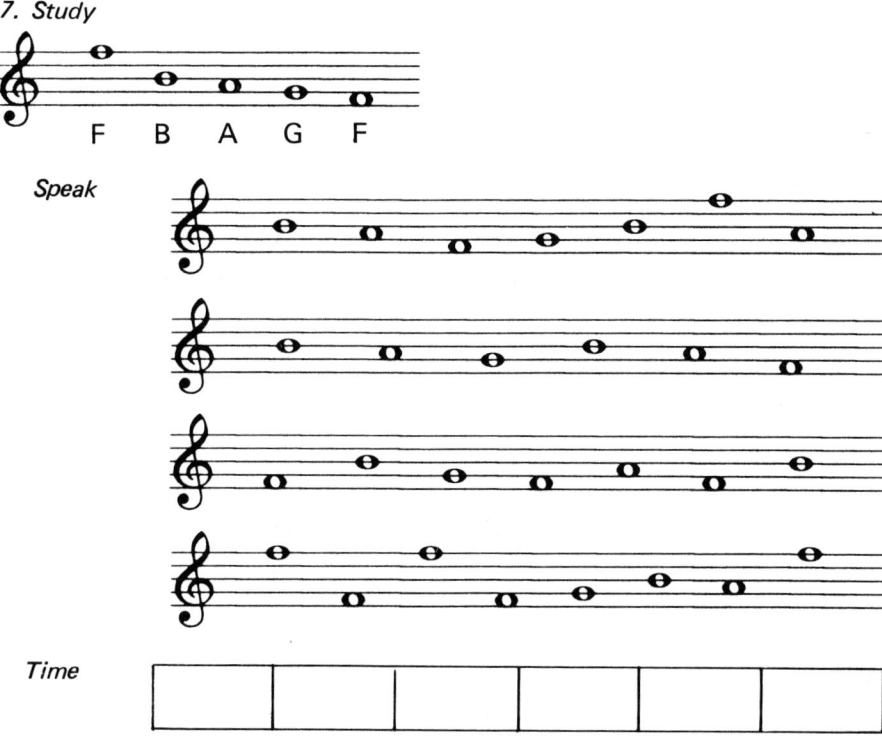

F B A G F

Speak

Time

17 Write the staff around the note (as in **15**). All the notes in this exercise are in the treble clef.

1. A/space	2. F/space	3. F/line
o	o	o
4. E/line	5. E/space	6. B/line
o	o	o

7. G/space	8. C/space	9. D/line
10. D/space	11. G/space	12. F/space

MIDDLE C

Middle C appears on the first ledger line below the staff in the treble clef and on the first line above the staff in the bass clef. Written either way, it is the same note.

Two versions of Middle C

Compare with the diagram of the grand staff on page 8.

18 Name all the notes aloud, proceeding at a moderate but steady speed. Review previous exercises as needed. Use this exercise as your goal for identifying pitches quickly and accurately.

SUGGESTED ACTIVITIES

1. Listen to *Rhythm Improvisation*, by Jim Saporito and Ted Moore (S 5, B 2). This piece is performed on rhythm instruments. Do you hear any musical pitches? _____ If you hear pitches, do they seem as definite as the sound of the piano? _____ In your own words, contrast the sound of music that is primarily rhythmic with music in which melody predominates.

_____

_____

_____

2. Secure a piece of strong string or wire between two sticks. Wind the string around each stick a few times.

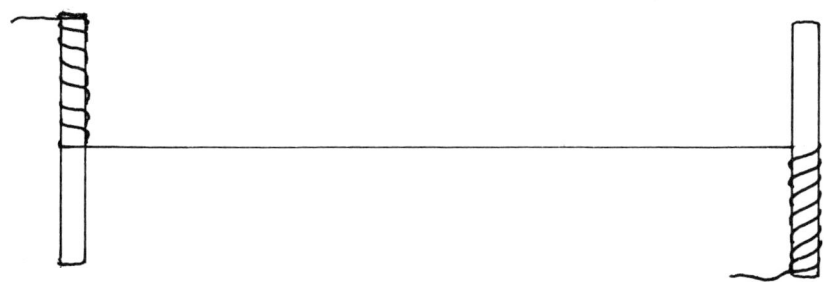

Experiment with different types of string or wire until you find one that produces a distinguishable pitch when plucked. When you have completed your "instrument," discover how the pitch is affected by these factors:

- tightening the string
- lengthening the string (unwind a few turns)
- shortening the string (wind a few turns)

3. Repeat the experiment above, using a guitar or other string instrument instead of two sticks.

4. Fill glasses with different amounts of water and then tap on them with a spoon or stick. Discover how the pitch is affected by the following factors: the amount of water in the glass, the size of glass, the thickness of the glass.

5. Compare the lengths of woodwind instruments and the highness or lowness of the pitches they produce (bassoon, flute, piccolo).

6. Look through the songs in the *Scorebook.* Sing any that you know, first with words and then using the names of the notes instead of the words.

TERMS AND CONCEPTS

Explain in your own words:

pitch

staff

octave

treble clef

bass clef

ledger lines

grand staff

CHAPTER 2

THE PIANO KEYBOARD

The piano is the basic instrument for the study of music, and a working knowledge of the keyboard is essential for musicianship. The design of the keyboard (the arrangement of the keys) parallels the system of notation. Thus the keyboard will help you understand many aspects of music notation and theory.

ANY KEYBOARD WILL DO

Throughout this book, there are diagrams to help you understand the relationship between the written note and its keyboard position. However, this cannot replace the experience of playing and hearing the music on an instrument. So when there are instructions to play a simple melody or exercise, **play**! Many types of keyboard instruments are available. Besides the piano, other instruments you might use are the electronic organ, electronic piano, chromatic xylophone, or accordion. The playing requirements in this book are minimal—no special technique is necessary. Playing simple melodies and exercises, even slowly, will greatly enhance your enjoyment and understanding of this book. Make every effort to do this! At each level, it is assumed that you will have done **all** the playing required.

THE CONSTRUCTION OF THE KEYBOARD

The first thing to notice is the way the black keys are grouped: alternating clusters of twos and threes, spanning the entire keyboard. This pattern will serve as an orientation for the location of all keys.

THE WHITE KEYS
The white keys are named from A to G, exactly like the lines and spaces on the staff.

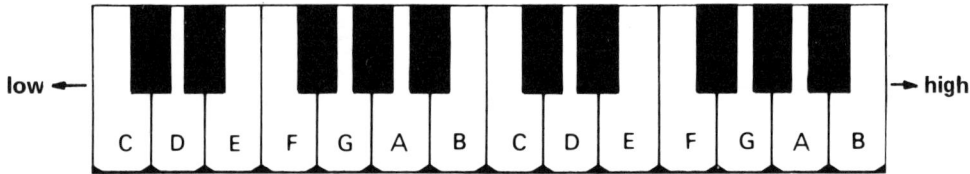

The C key is often used as the starting point for locating the other keys. It is always the white key to the **left** of each group of **two black keys**.

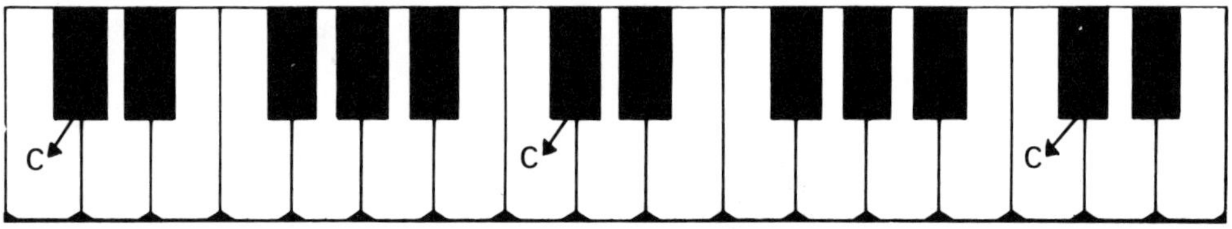

1 Write the letter D on each D key:

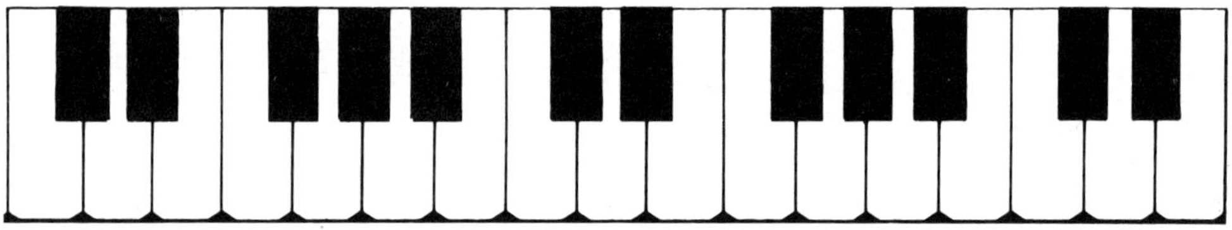

Write the letter E on each E key:

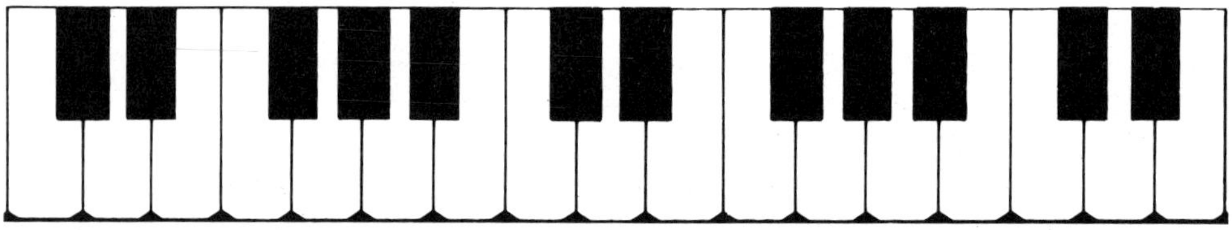

Write the letter F on each F key:

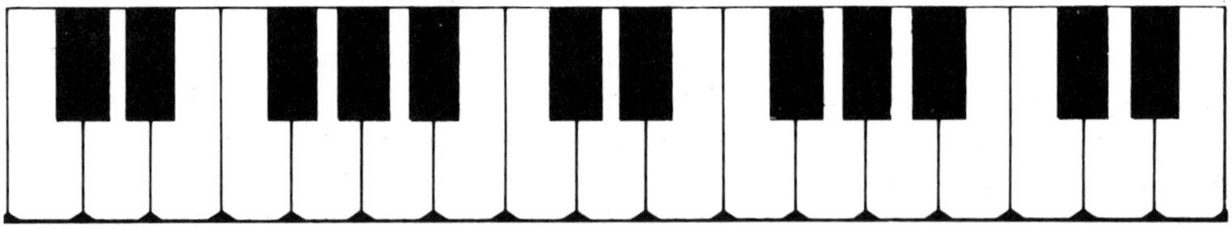

Write the letter G on each G key:

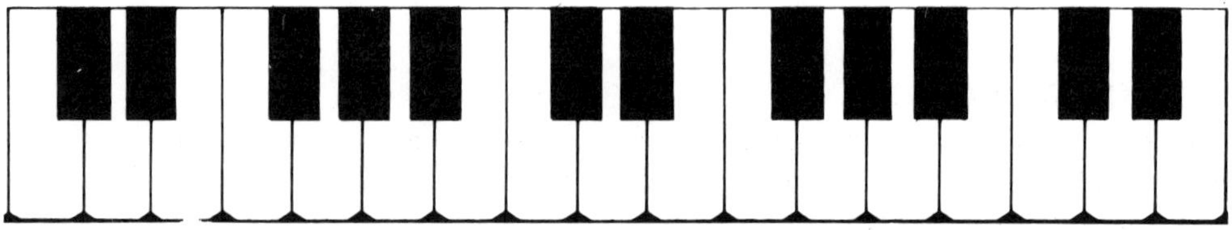

Write the letter A on each A key:

Write the letter B on each B key:

THE BLACK KEYS

Each black key lies halfway between two white keys. If you play a black key and its neighboring white keys, you will hear that the black key is also halfway in pitch between the two white keys. The black keys are named by their neighboring white keys in this way:

1. The black key immediately above a white key (to the right of it) is named by adding a *sharp* (♯) to the white key name. A sharp (♯) is the musical symbol which indicates that the note has been raised in pitch.

2. The black key immediately below a white key (to the left of it) is named by adding a *flat* (♭) to the white key name. A flat (♭) is the musical symbol which indicates that the note has been lowered in pitch.

Thus, each black key has two possible names, depending on which white key it derives its name from. Observe this in the following example:

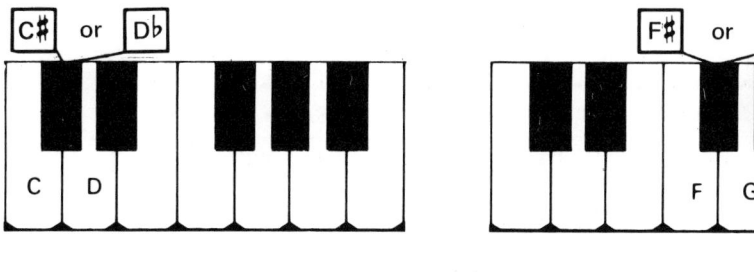

2 Name these notes in two ways (using ♯ or ♭).

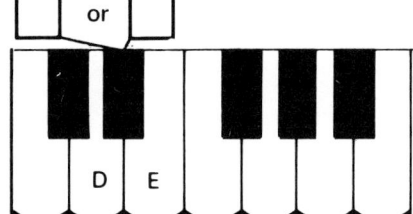 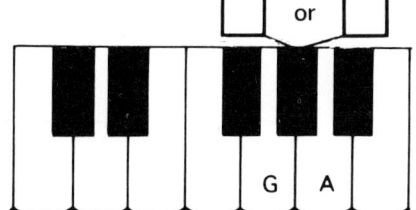

Notating the same pitch with different names (using either a sharp or a flat) is called *enharmonic spelling*. For example, an enharmonic spelling for F♯ is G♭. Both spellings indicate the same note.

3 Fill in the black key which corresponds to these note spellings:

Example:
G♭ (G flat)

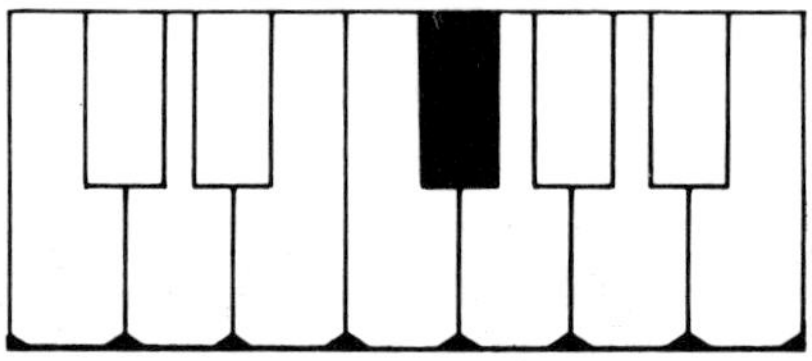

1. F♯ (F sharp)

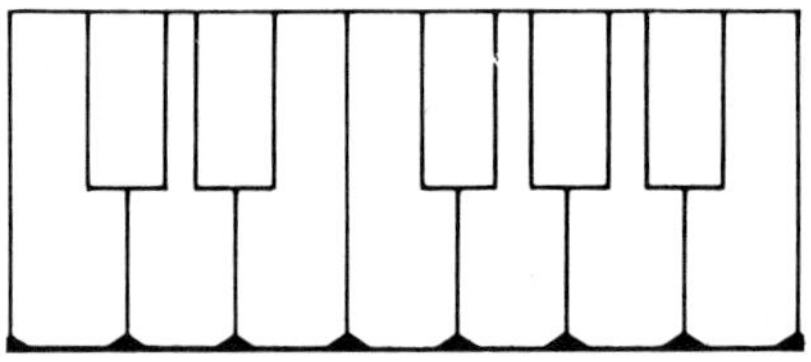

2. A♭ (A flat)

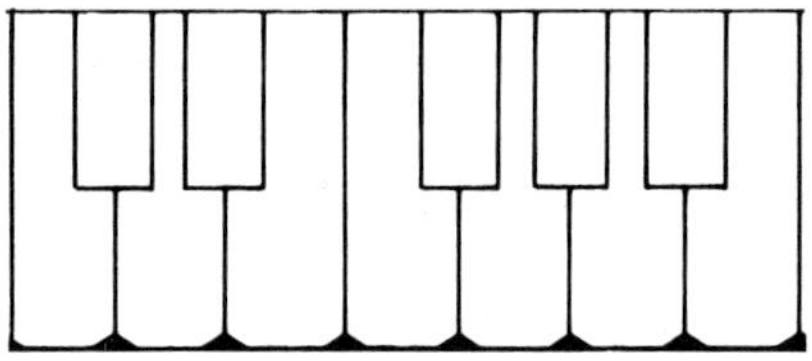

3. B♭ (B flat)

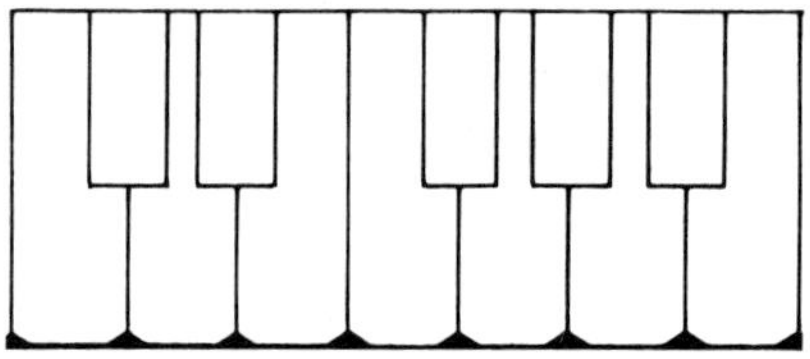

4. C♯ (C sharp)

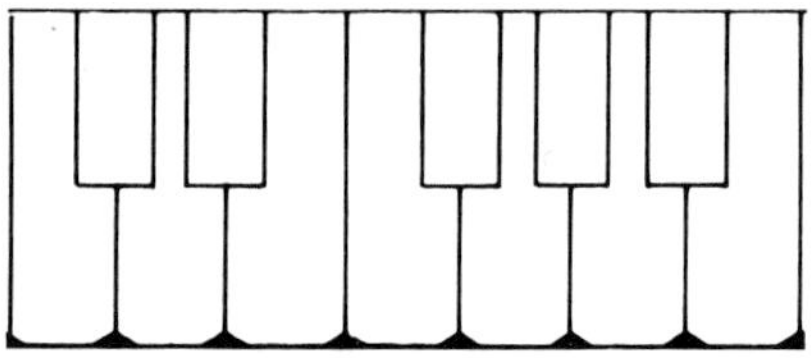

5. E♭ (E flat)

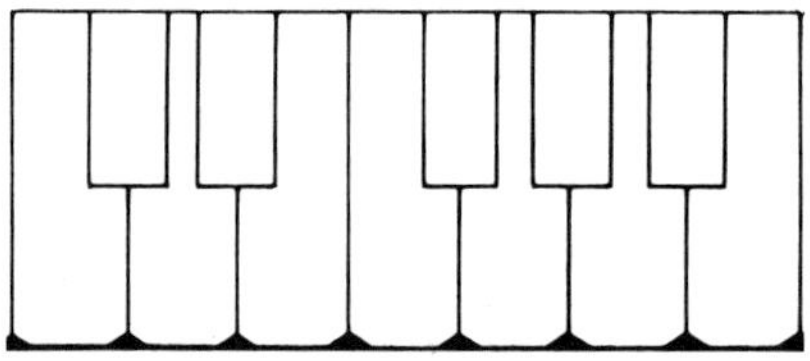

6. D♯ (D sharp)

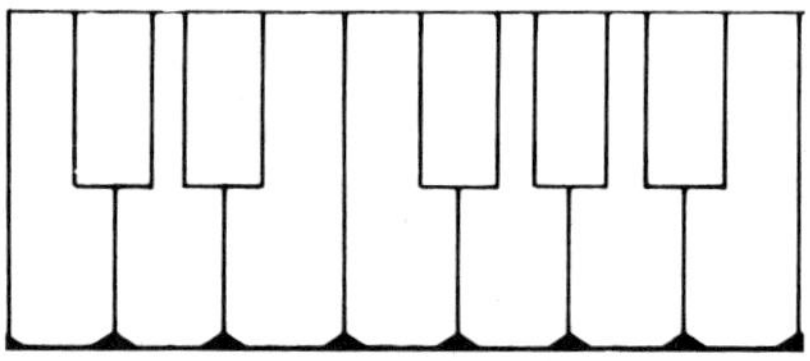

7. G♯ (G sharp)

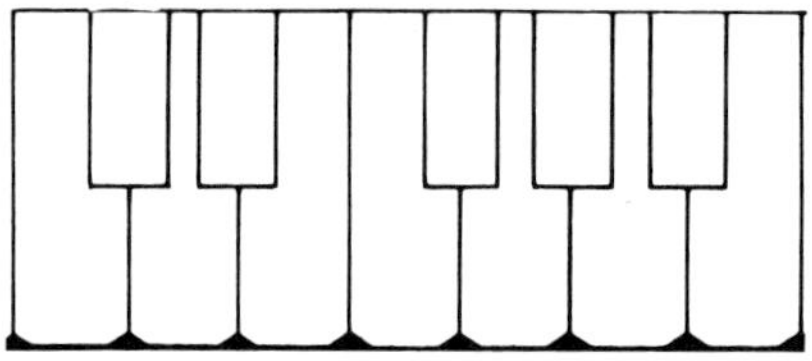

8. D♭ (D flat)

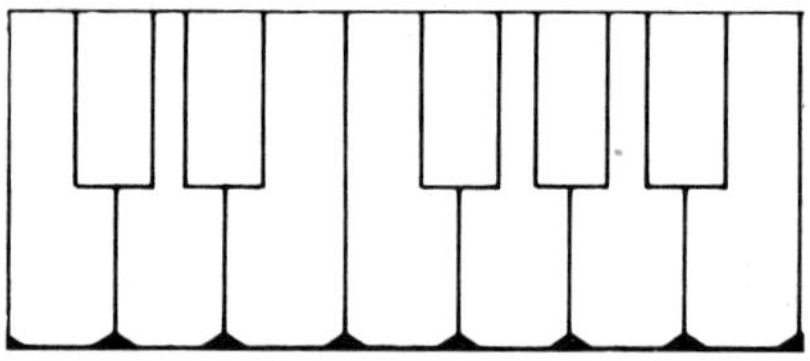

9. A♯ (A sharp)

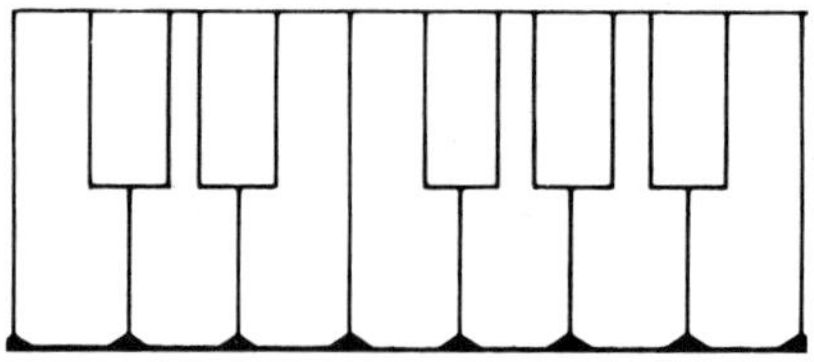

4 Describe the position of each of the following keys by its relationship either to the black-key group of 2 or the black-key group of 3.

Key	Description
C	The white key to the left of each group of 2 black keys.
C♯ or D♭	The black key at the left in each group of 2.
D	
D♯ or E♭	
E	
F	
F♯ or G♭	
G	
G♯ or A♭	
A	
A♯ or B♭	
B	

5 On each keyboard, mark each correct key with an X.

Example
D and F♯

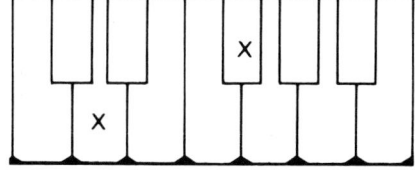

1. C and E

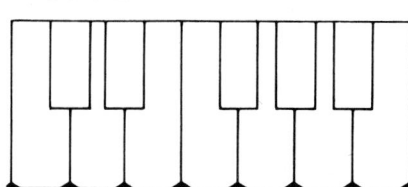

2. C♯ and A

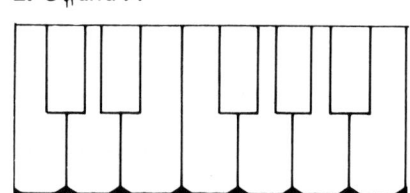

3. D♭ and A♯

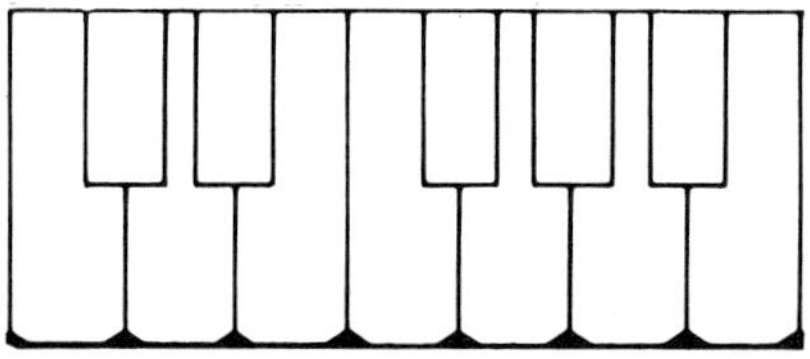

4. B♭ and E

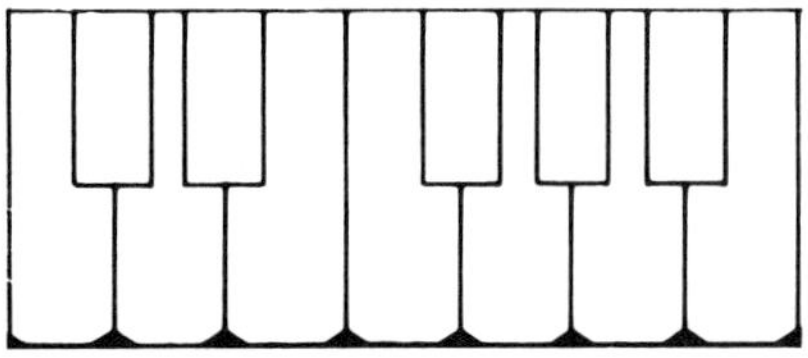

5. E♭ and B

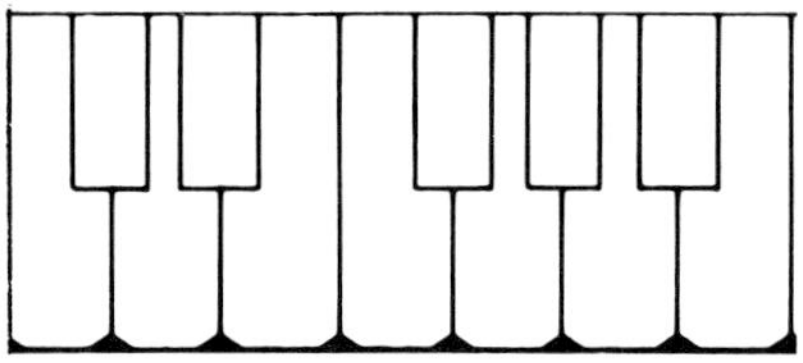

6. F♯ and G♯

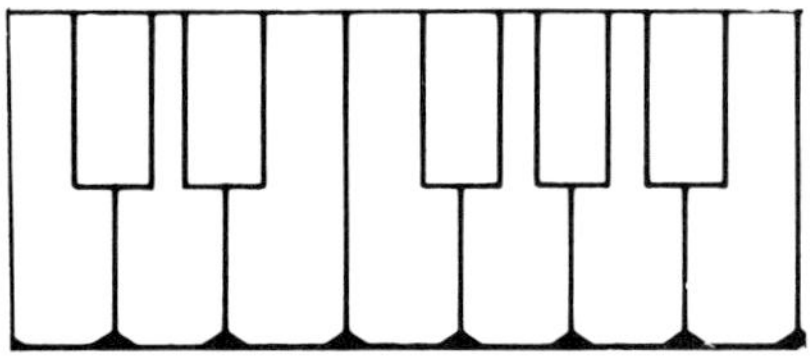

7. G♭ and A♭

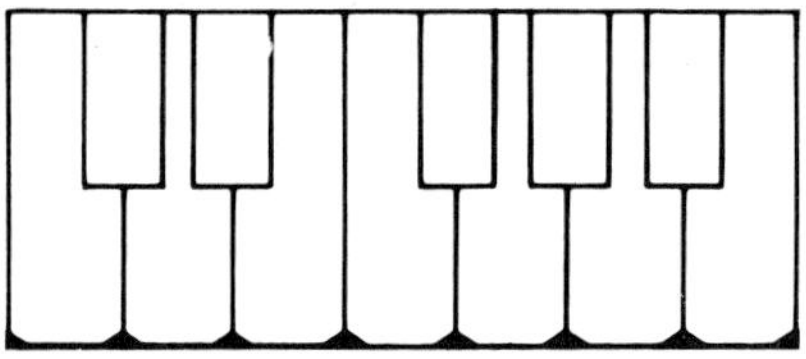

8. F♯ and F

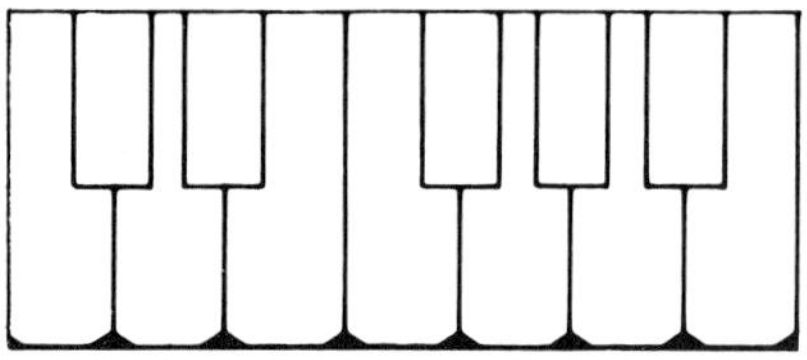

9. C and D♭

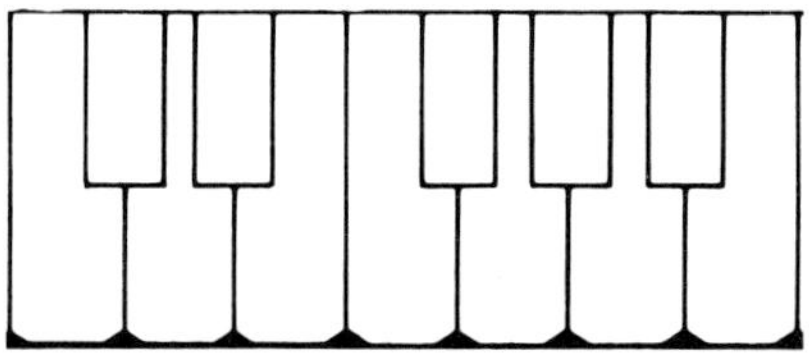

10. G and B♭

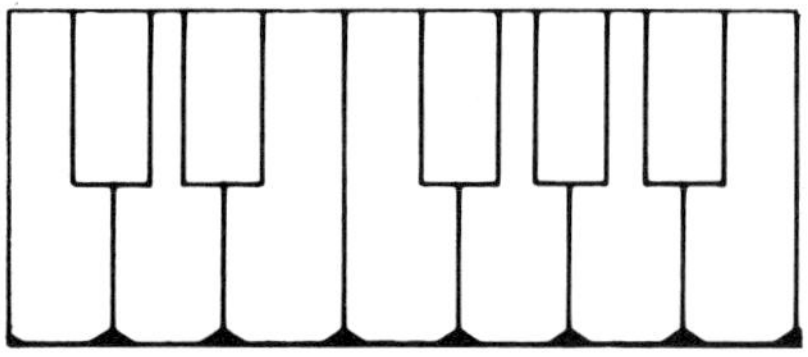

11. E and F♯

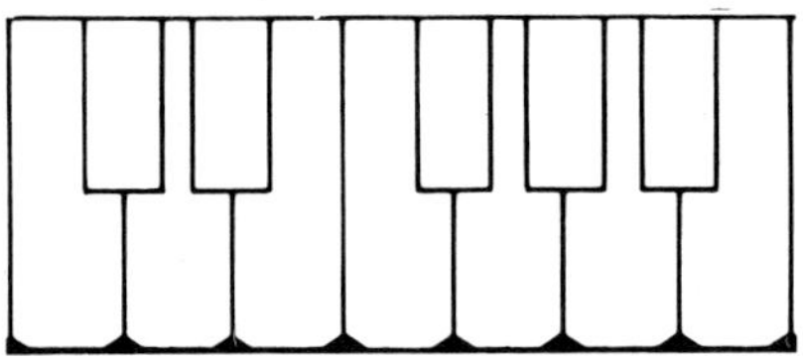

12. C♯ and E

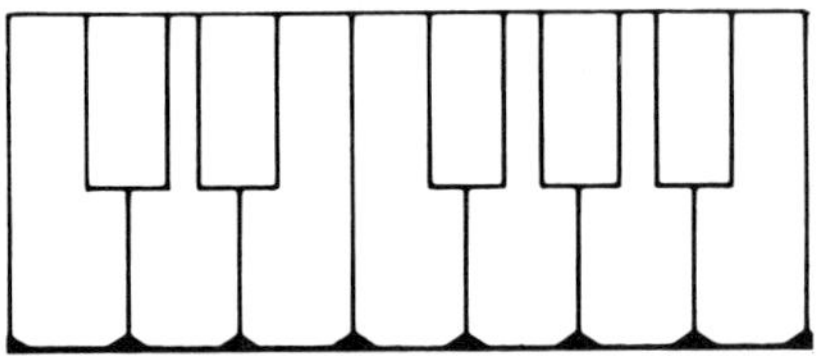

13. D and D♭

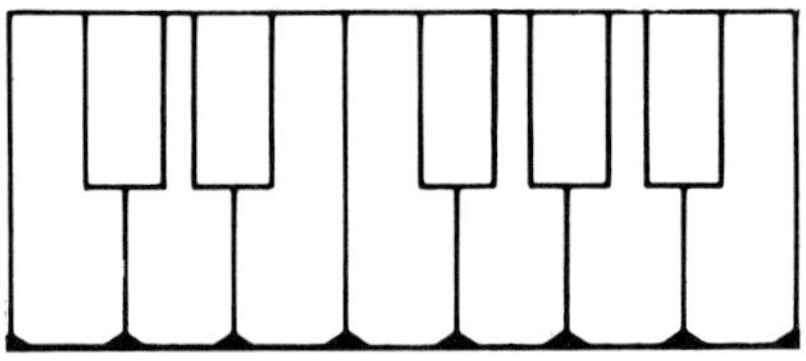

14. D and C

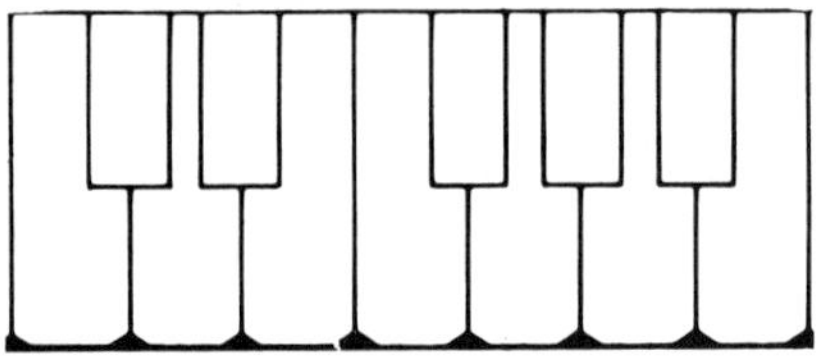

15. F♯ and B

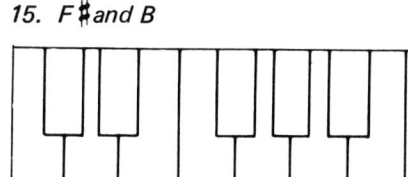

NOTATING THE WHITE KEYS
Starting from middle C, the white keys are notated as successive lines and spaces.

Treble clef

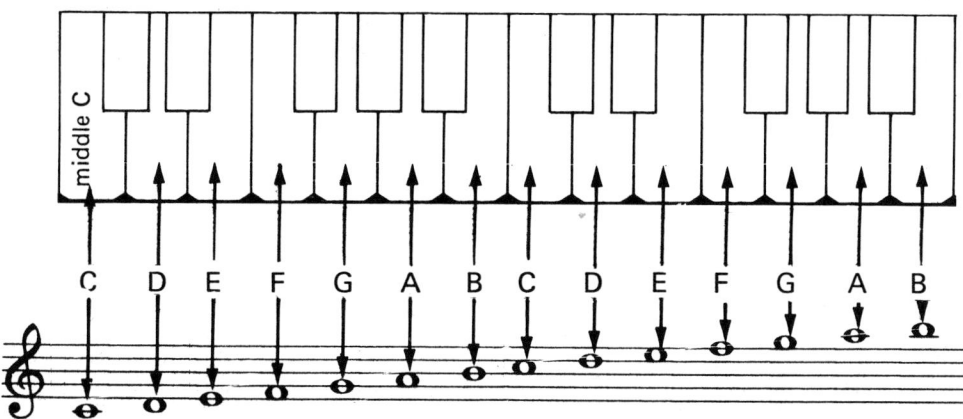

Bass clef

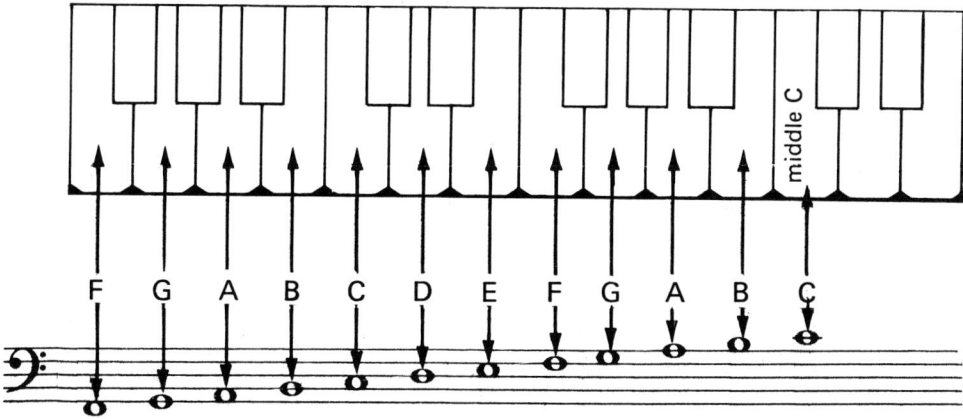

6 Name each note marked with an X on the keyboard. Then write the notes on the corresponding staff. Use the type of notehead indicated (o or ●).

Example

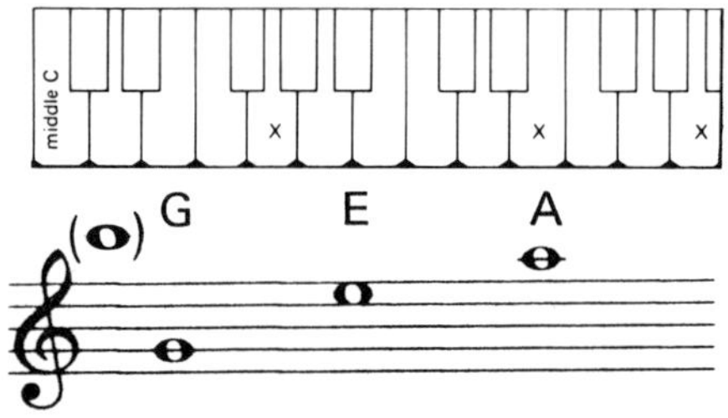

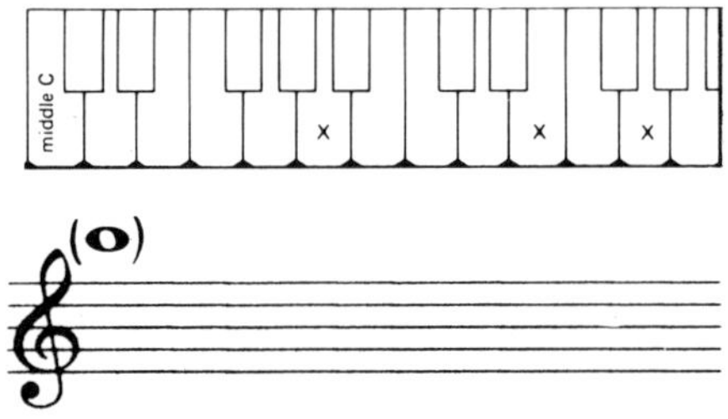

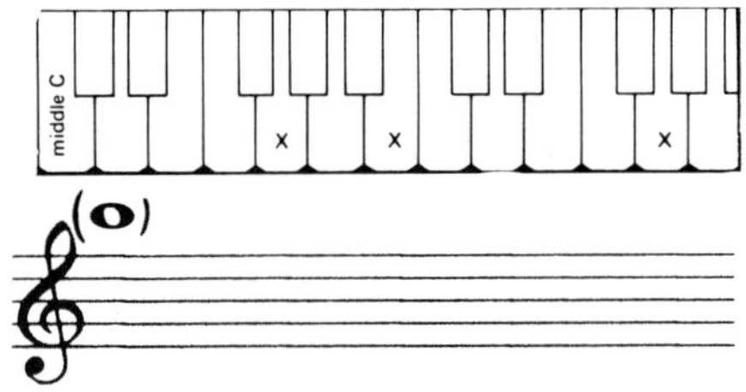

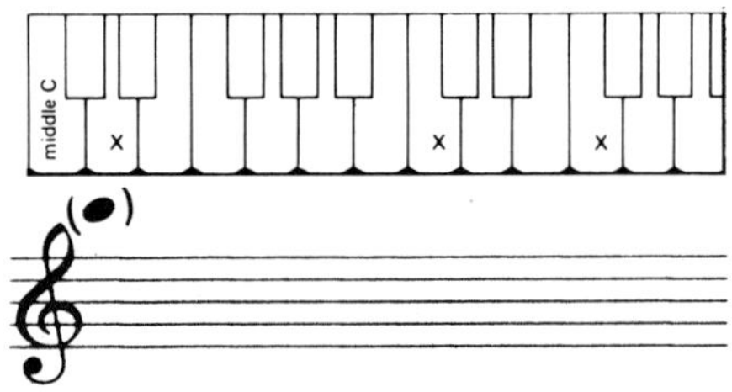

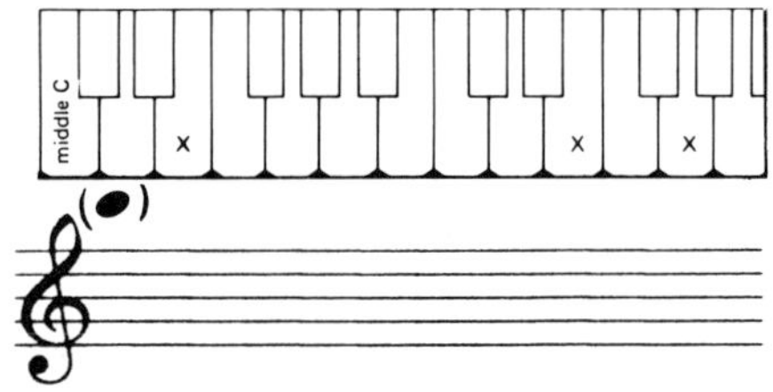

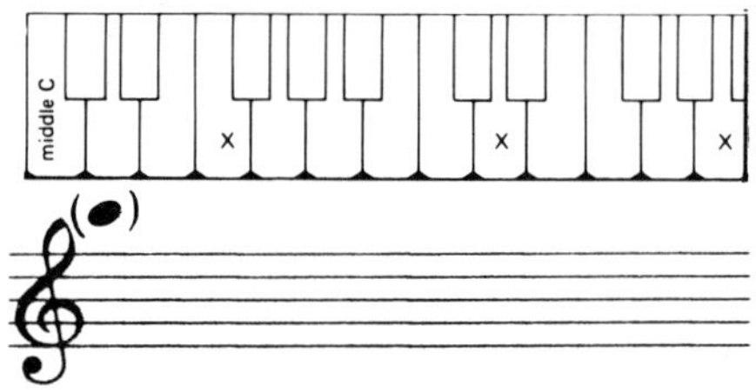

7 Repeat the same instructions as for **6.**

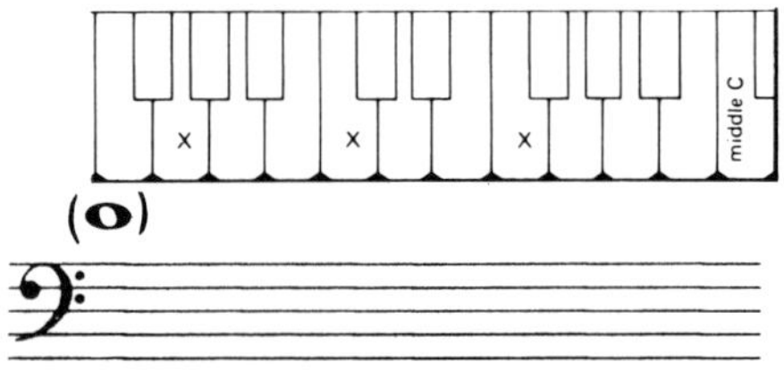

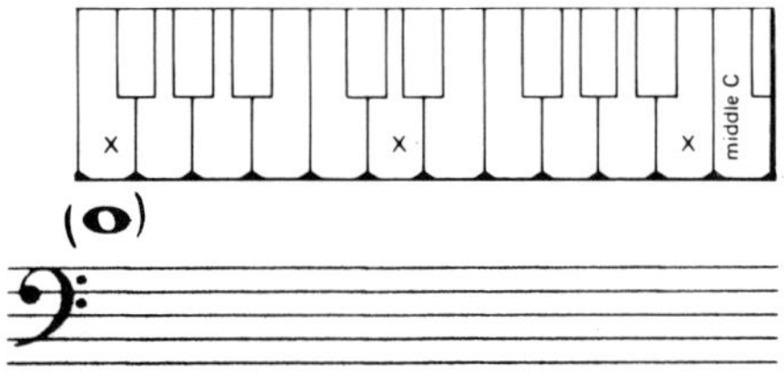

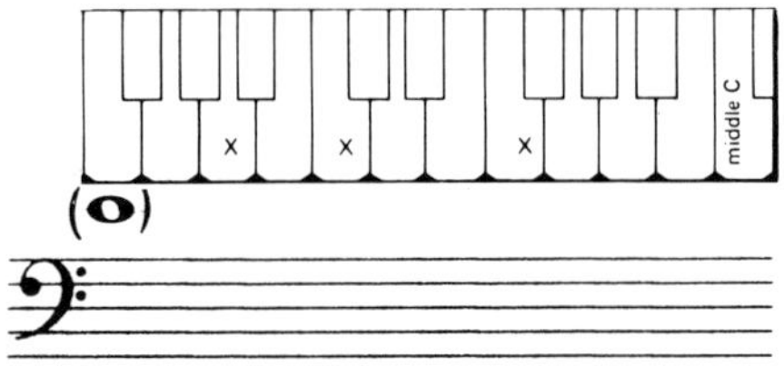

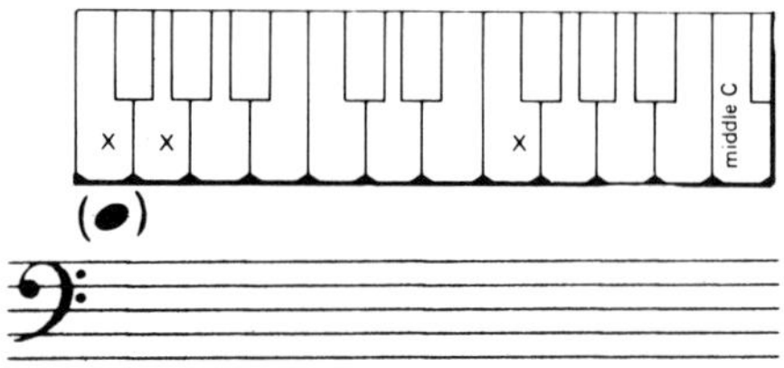

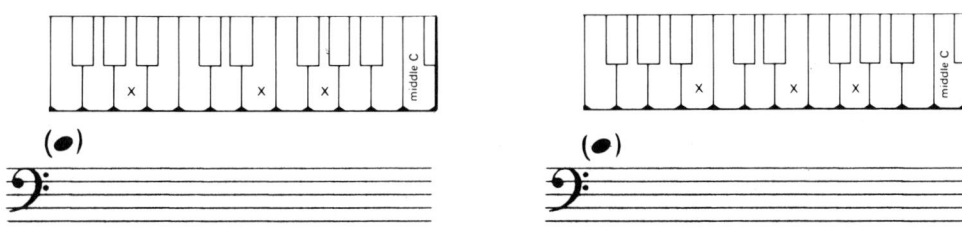

NOTATING THE BLACK KEYS

The black keys are notated on the staff by placing either a sharp or a flat before the notehead. For example,

A♯ is notated:

D♭ is notated:

Notice that the sharp or flat is placed on the same line or in the same space as the notehead:

Correct: Incorrect:

8 Notate each of these notes, first with a sharp and then with a flat.

Example

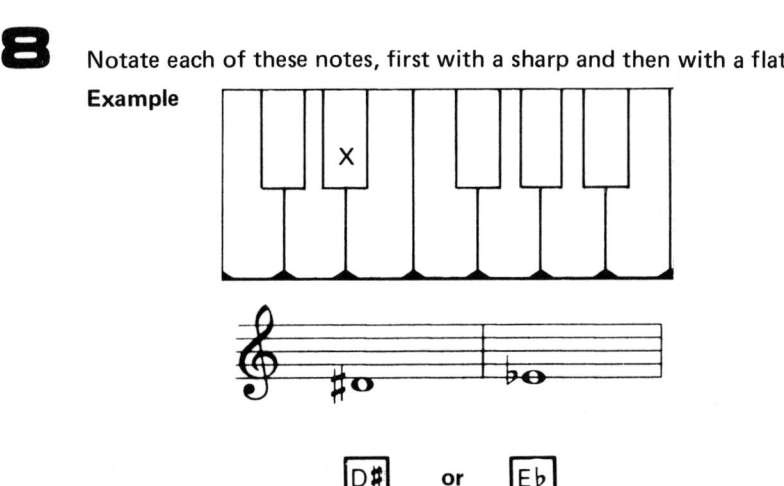

D♯ or E♭

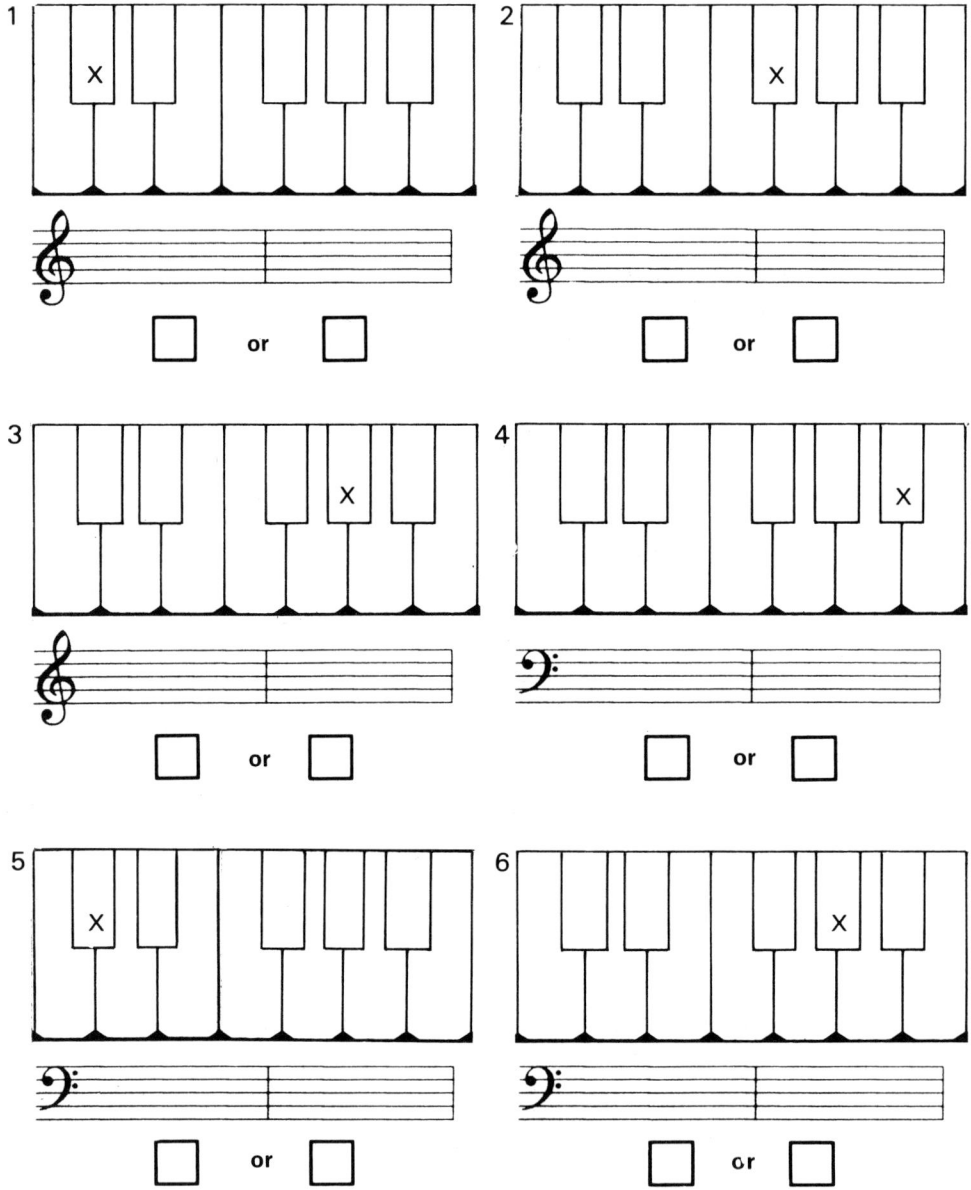

SUGGESTED ACTIVITIES AT THE KEYBOARD

1. Practice playing all the C's on the keyboard as fast as you can. When you can negotiate all the C's, proceed to each of the other keys.

2. Think of any three different notes. Visualize their position on the keyboard; then play them.

3. Draw a piano keyboard from memory (as in the diagrams). Name each note. Name each of the black keys two different ways.

TERMS AND CONCEPTS
Explain in your own words:

      the piano as the "basic instrument"
      location of the black keys
      ♯
      ♭
      enharmonic notation

CHAPTER 3

SCALES

In Italian, *scala* means ladder. If you replace the rungs of a ladder with musical pitches, you have the traditional musical scale: a series of ascending or descending pitches. On a ladder, we call the distance between two adjacent rungs a *step*; in a scale, the distance between two adjacent pitches is also called a *step*.

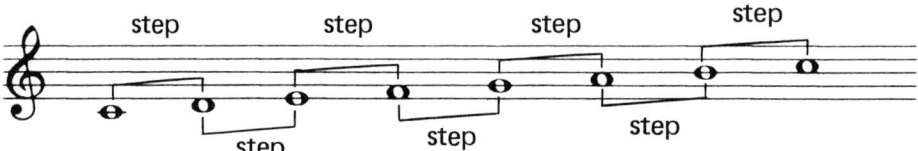

There are many kinds of scales made up of different numbers of pitches and different kinds of steps. The first scales we will study use two types of steps: *half steps* and *whole steps*.

HALF STEPS

We will first consider a scale made up entirely of half steps. A half step is the smallest measurable distance in our system of music. On the keyboard, a half step occurs between every two keys **directly adjacent**.

1 Play the following scale from one to twelve.

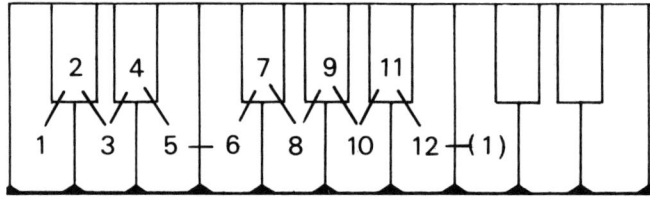

Notice especially that between **white keys**, half steps occur in **only two places**, E–F and B–C, since those are the only white keys that are **adjacent** to each other on the keyboard.

 Play E–F and B–C.

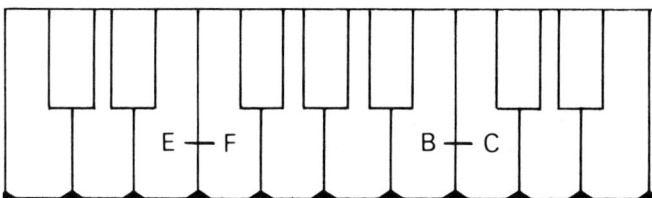

All the other half steps occur between a black key and the nearest white key, or a white key and the nearest black key. There are no half steps between two black keys.

3 Draw an arrow to the key which is one half step **above** the indicated note.

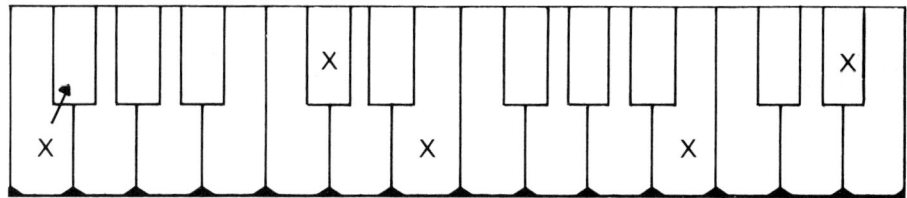

4 Draw an arrow to the key which is one half step **below** the indicated note.

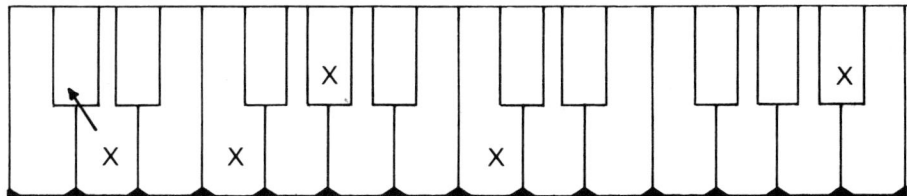

THE CHROMATIC SCALE
A scale ascending or descending in half steps and containing all twelve tones (or pitches) is called a *chromatic scale*.

5 Play and name notes.

Ascending chromatic scale using sharps

Notice that each letter name is used twice (once unmodified and once with a sharp) **except** for E and B because a half step above each of them is the adjacent white key, and has a different letter name. Since this is an ascending chromatic scale, it is usually written with sharps. A descending chromatic scale (see below) is usually written with flats. Notice again that each letter name is used twice (once alone and once with a flat) **except** for C and F because a half step below each of them is the adjacent white key.

6 Play and name notes.

Descending chromatic scale using flats

7 Finish numbering this chromatic scale, which starts on A, and notate it below. Then play and name the notes.

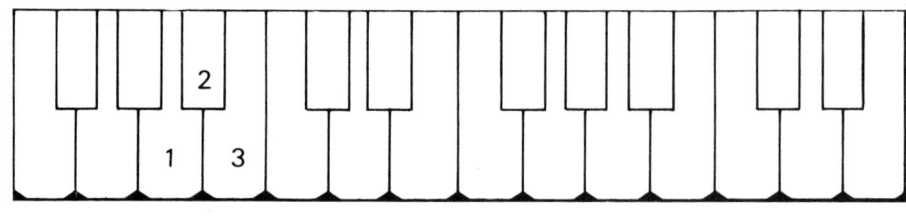

8 Finish numbering this descending chromatic scale, which starts on F, and notate it below. Play and name the notes.

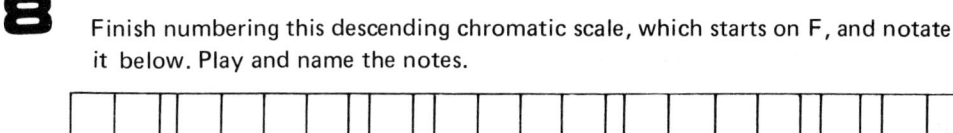

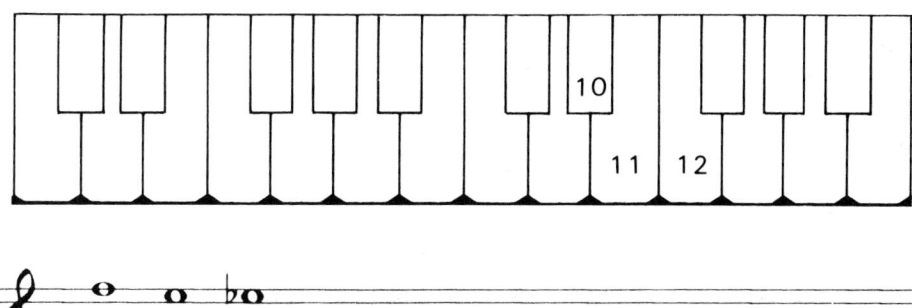

WHOLE STEPS

A whole step consists of two half steps. Observe and play the following examples of whole steps.

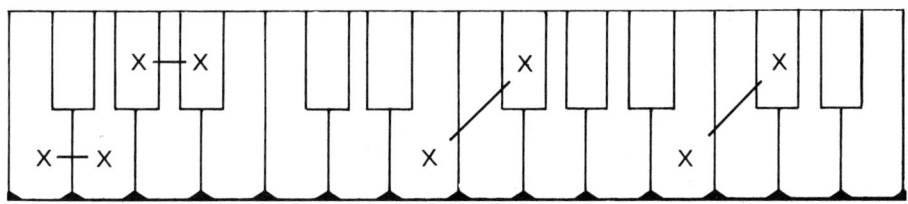

9 Draw an arrow to the key which is a whole step **above** the indicated note.

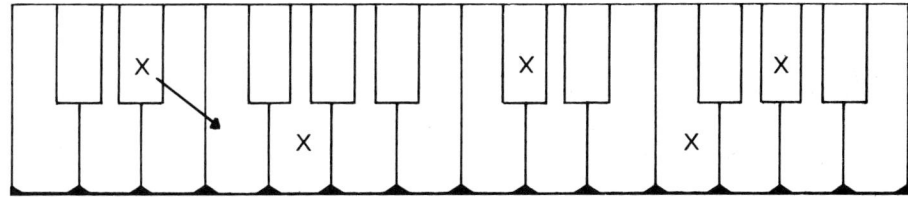

10 Draw an arrow to the key which is a whole step **below** the indicated note.

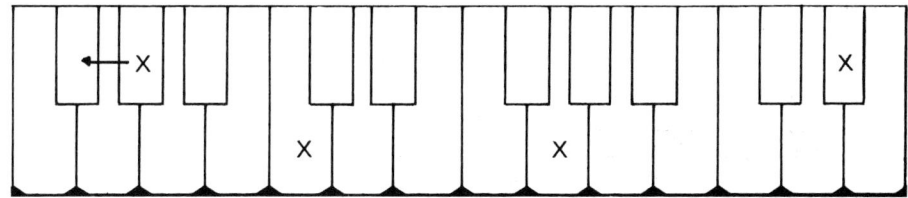

THE WHOLE-TONE SCALE

Just as there is a scale made up of half steps, the *chromatic scale,* there is a scale made up of whole steps, called the *whole-tone scale.*

11 Play and name each note in the following whole-tone scales.

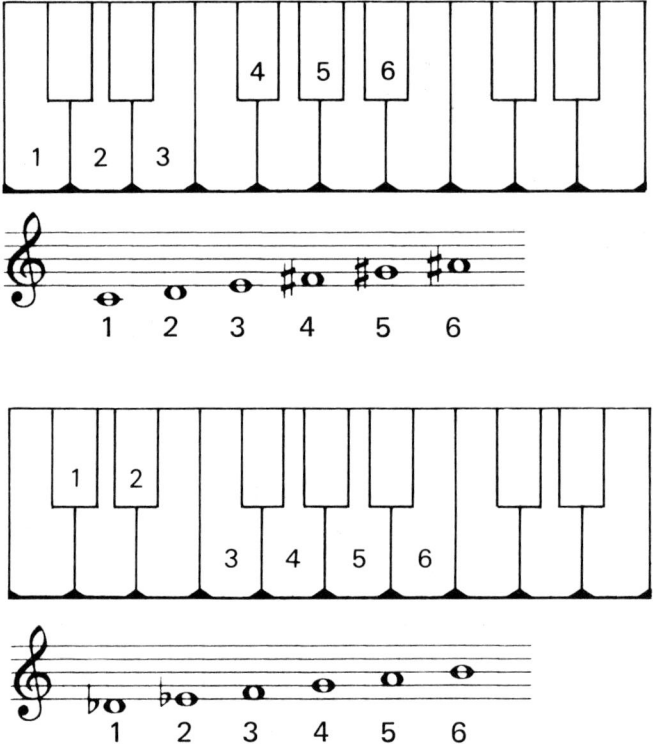

12 Notate the six notes of the following whole-tone scales on the keyboard and staff. If a whole-tone scale starts with sharps, use only sharps, not flats. If it starts with a flat, use only flats, not sharps.

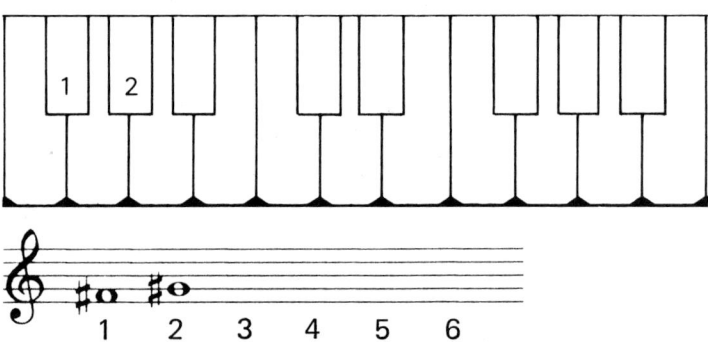

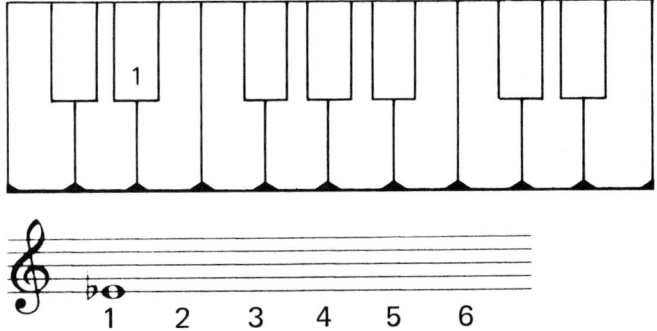

OTHER NAMES FOR THE HALF STEP AND WHOLE STEP
In music theory, there is often more than one term for a technical concept. For example, different terms exist for the half step and whole step. The half step is also called a *semitone*, and the whole step is also called a *whole tone*. These terms are used interchangeably.

1. A whole step is also called a _____.

2. A half step is also called a _____.

DIATONIC SEMITONE/CHROMATIC SEMITONE
There are two types of semitones (half steps) depending on how they are **notated**.

1. The *diatonic semitone (DST)* is notated with **two different letter names**.

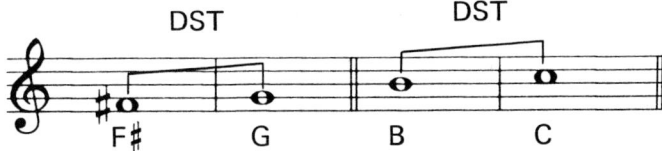

2. The *chromatic semitone (CST)* is notated with **the same letter names**.

Observe that the **same** semitone can be notated in two ways:

1. as a diatonic semitone (DST); 2. as a chromatic semitone (CST).

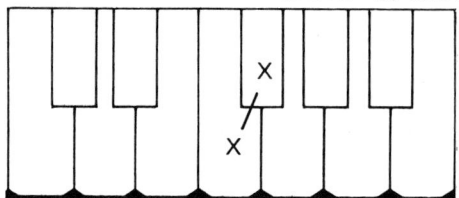

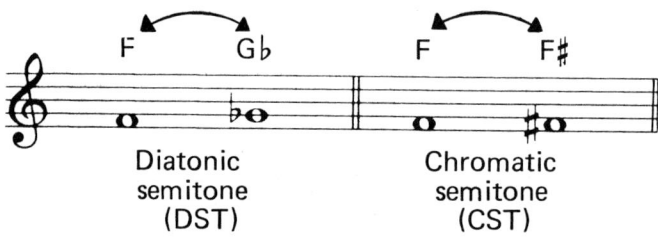

13 Answer:

1. A diatonic semitone is notated with _____ letter name(s).

2. A chromatic semitone is notated with _____ letter name(s).

3. The abbreviation for a diatonic semitone is _____.

4. The abbreviation for a chromatic semitone is _____.

5. A semitone can also be called a _____.

6. A whole tone can also be called a _____.

14 Mark each of the following semitones as a diatonic semitone (if two letter names are used) or a chromatic semitone (if the same letter name is used). Use the abbreviations DST and CST. Play and name each note.

15 Notate each semitone (half step) as a **DST** and as a **CST**. Study the example carefully. Name each note.

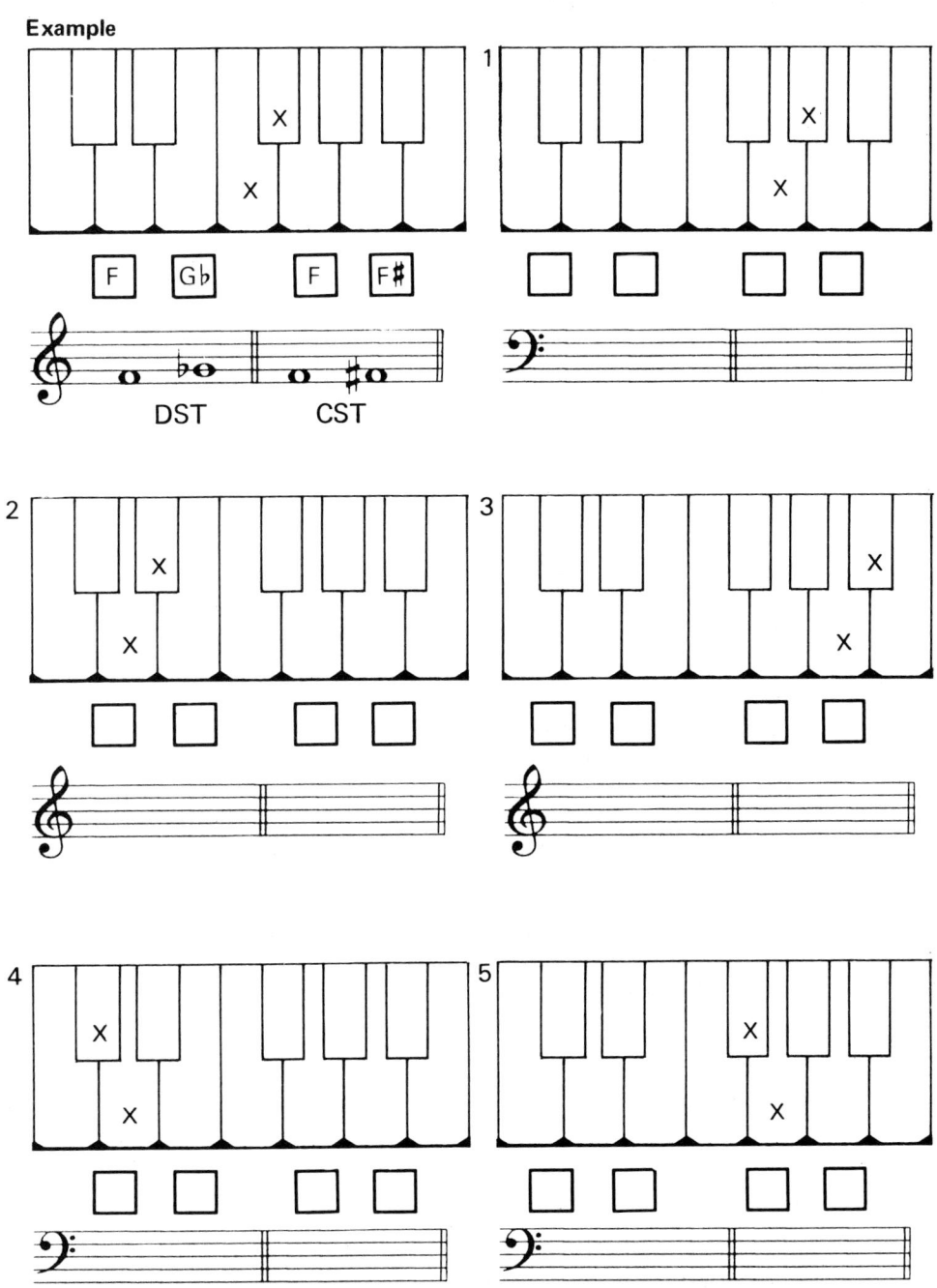

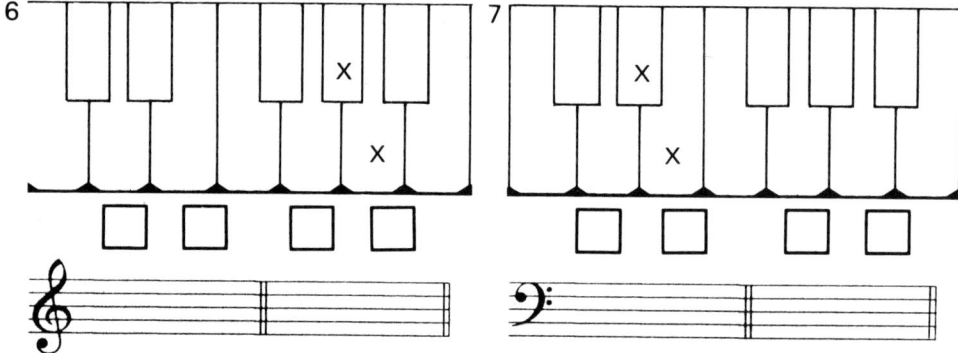

ACCIDENTALS

Symbols that alter the pitch of a note are called *accidentals*. We have used two: the sharp and flat. All together, there are five accidentals. Here are their names, symbols, and functions.

 Play

1. The *sharp* (♯) raises the pitch of a note a semitone (half step).

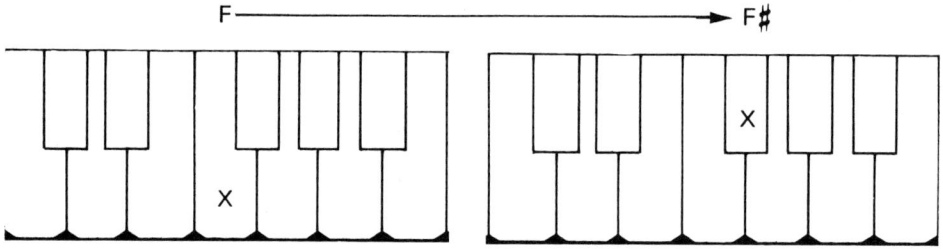

2. The *flat* (♭) lowers the pitch of a note a semitone (half step).

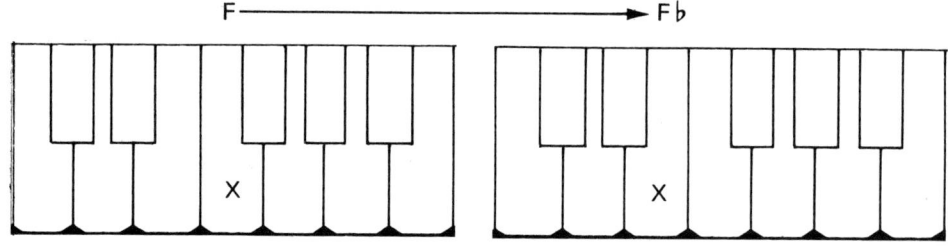

Notice that a note with an accidental is not always a black key, but can be a white key. Accidentals are indications of a **function**.

3. The *natural* (♮) cancels an accidental.

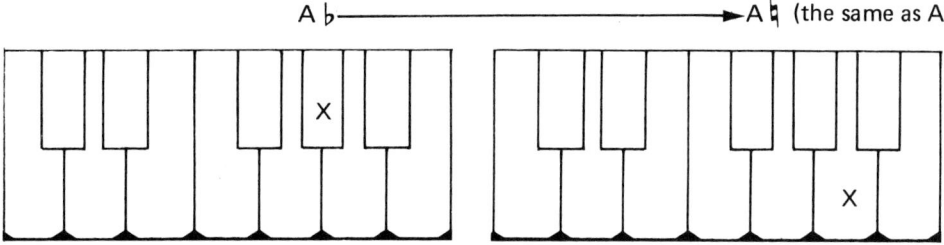

4. The *double sharp* (x) raises the pitch one whole tone (whole step).

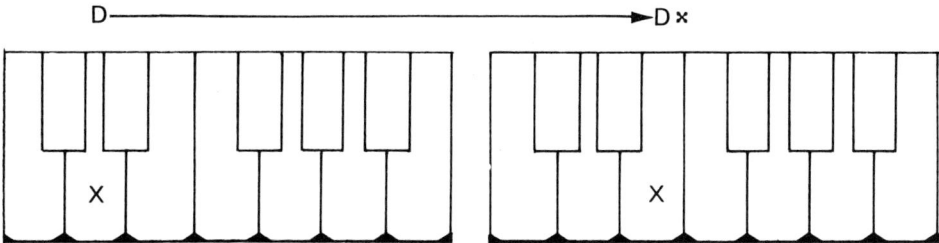

5. The *double flat* (♭♭) lowers the pitch one whole tone (whole step).

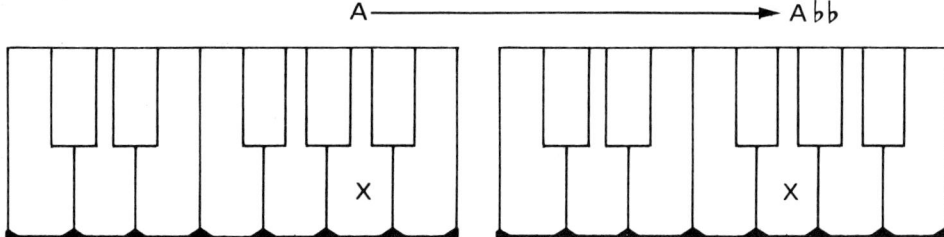

SUMMARY OF ACCIDENTALS

1. Sharp (♯) raises the pitch of a note a half step (semitone).

2. Flat (♭) lowers the pitch of a note a half step (semitone).

3. Natural (♮) cancels an accidental.

4. Double sharp (x) raises the pitch of a note one whole step (whole tone).

5. Double flat (♭♭) lowers the pitch of a note one whole step (whole tone).

17 Mark the key indicated by the accidental. When in doubt, refer to the function of the accidental listed above.

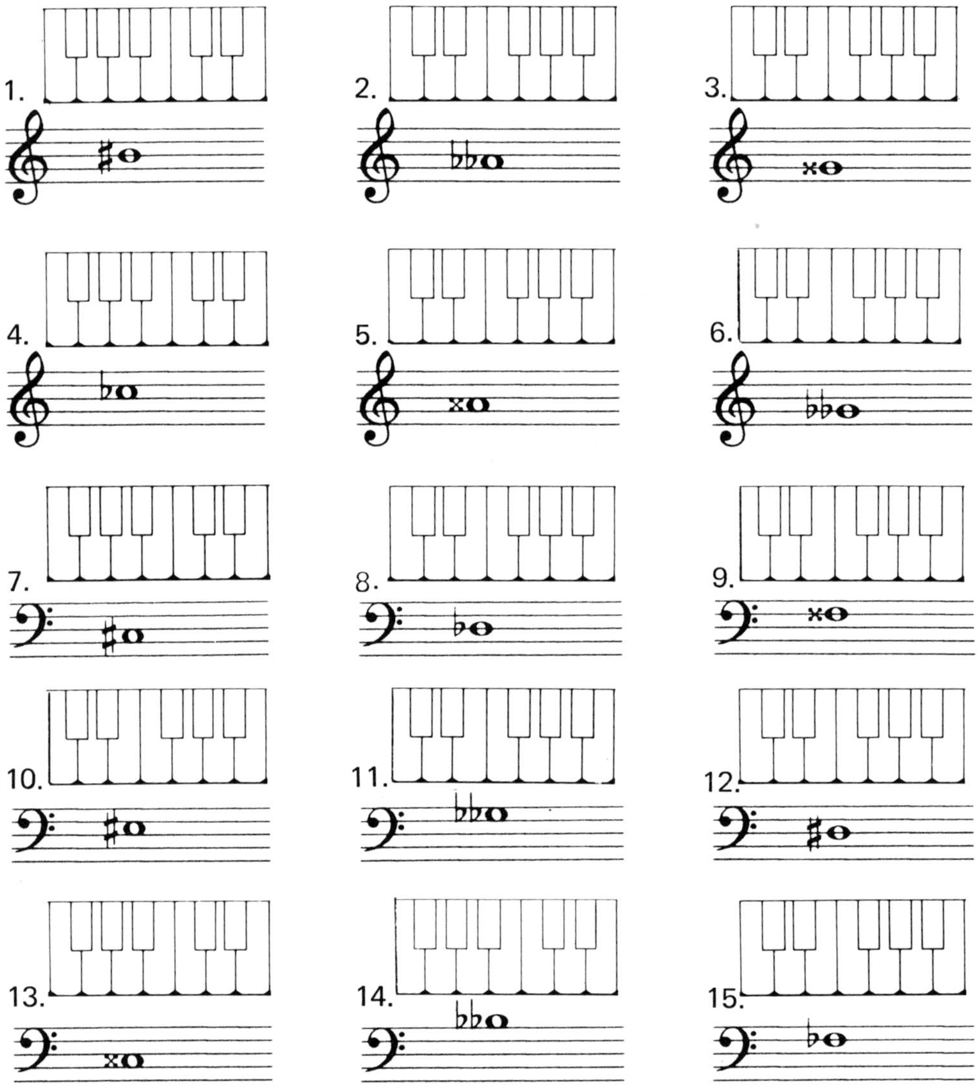

USE OF THE NATURAL SIGN
Once an accidental has altered the pitch of a note, the note will remain altered for the duration of the measure in which it occurs. For example:

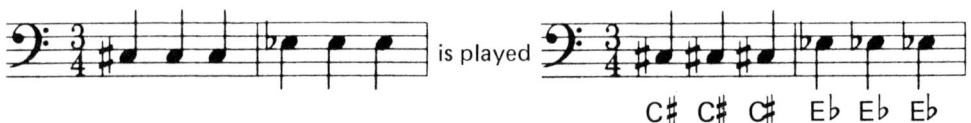

To cancel a sharp or flat, the natural sign is used. Once the natural sign is used on a note, it remains in effect for the rest of the measure. For example:

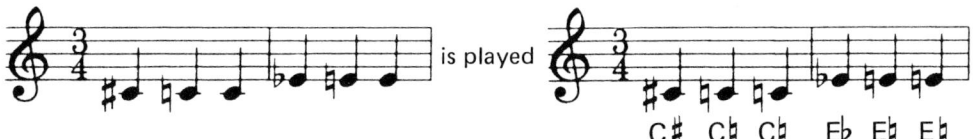

PRECAUTIONARY ACCIDENTALS
The natural sign may be used to clarify any note whose identity is in doubt because of a previous accidental. This practice is left to the discretion of the composer. For example, in the following excerpt from a Brahms piano accompaniment, notice the precautionary naturals on D and C in the second measure.

18 By **adding** a natural sign, alter each of these pitches to its original letter name. Indicate whether the addition of a natural sign raises or lowers the pitch a half step by writing either "up ½ step" or "down ½ step." Use the keyboard as a reference.

Examples:

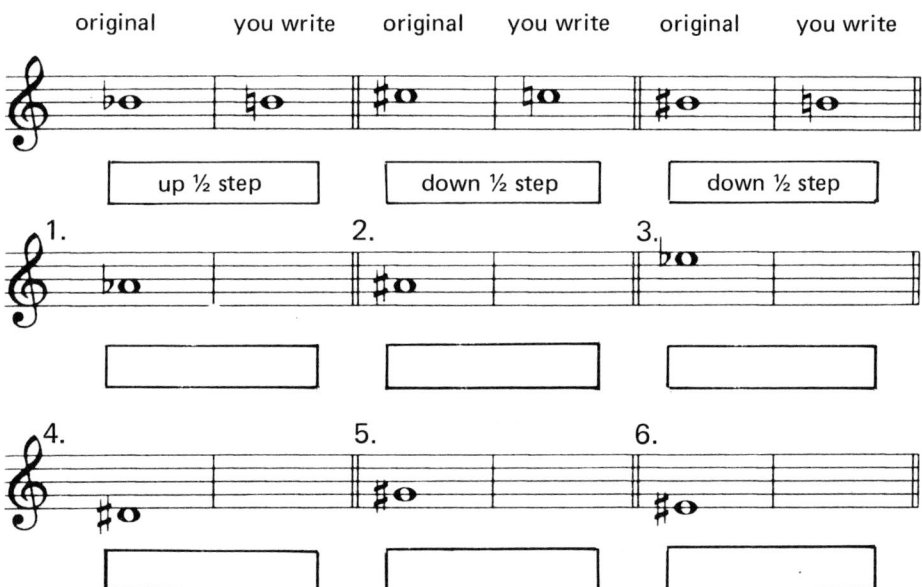

19

Write the pitch a whole step above or below each given pitch. Use the keyboard!

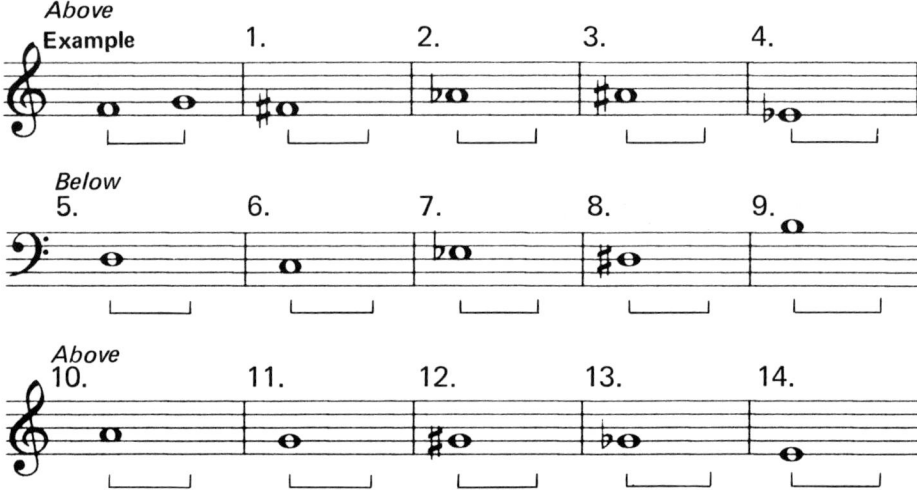

20

1. Using the keyboard as a reference, write chromatic semitones above each pitch.

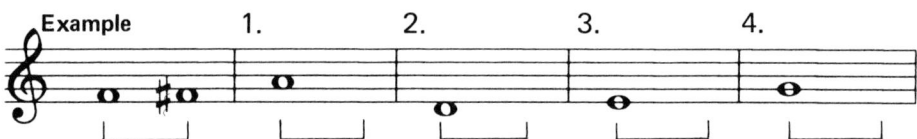

2. Write chromatic semitones below each pitch.

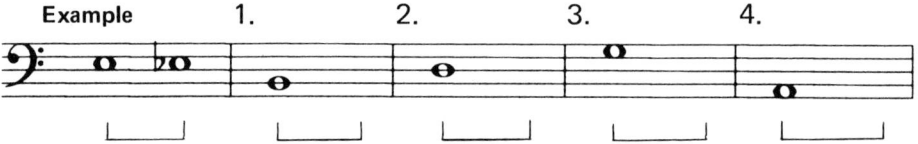

3. Write diatonic semitones above each pitch.

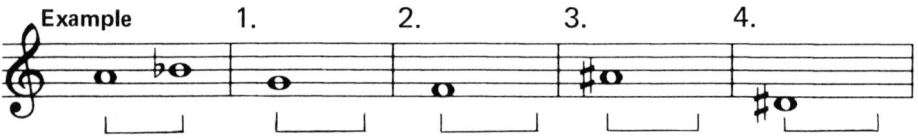

4. Write diatonic semitones below each pitch.

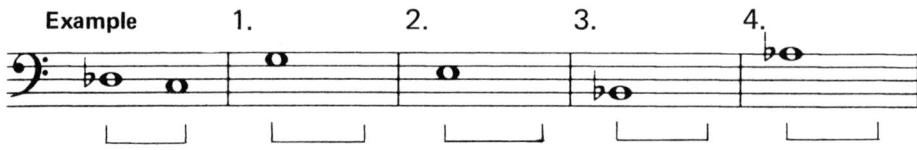

21 Write two enharmonic equivalents of each pitch. All accidentals may be used. Use the keyboard as a reference.

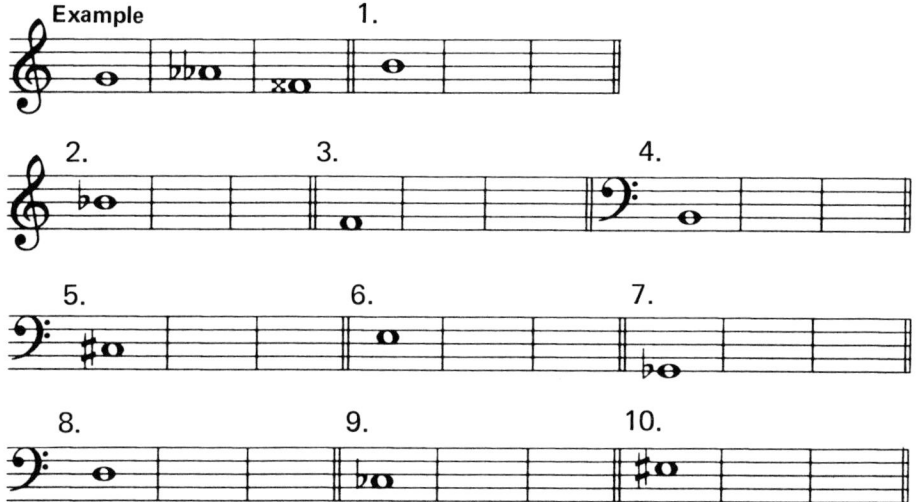

SUGGESTED ACTIVITIES

1. Listen to the sounds of the half step and whole step by playing them at the keyboard. Sing them.

2. Observe the physical attributes of the half step and whole step on a guitar, violin, or other string instrument. On a guitar, each fret is a half step, two frets a whole step. On a nonfretted instrument, like the violin, a similar relationship exists, but there is no fret to indicate the exact finger position. This is why it's harder to play a violin in tune than a guitar.

3. Listen to *How Strange* (S 7, B 1), and follow it in the *Scorebook* (SB 53). Find as many half steps as you can in the first two measures.

4. Listen to the *Waltz in C-Sharp Minor* by Chopin (S 2, B 1), and follow it in the *Scorebook* (SB 52). Circle any double sharps. How is a double sharp restored to one sharp? (See measure 3.)

TERMS AND CONCEPTS

Explain in your own words:

half step	flat
chromatic scale	double sharp
whole step	double flat
notation of half steps and whole steps	natural sign
accidentals	diatonic semitone
sharp	chromatic semitone

CHAPTER 4

DIATONIC SCALES

Western music has traditionally used a group of scales known as *diatonic scales*.
In our discussion of the diatonic semitone, the term "diatonic" indicated successive pitches with different letter names. Similarly, a diatonic scale **also** uses pitches with successive letter names. The diatonic scales in common use have seven different pitches, with the original pitch repeated at the octave—thus the diatonic scales have pitch outlines of one octave. The notes of the diatonic scale are referred to as *scale degrees*. The first (lowest) scale degree is numbered 1. The letter name of this note serves to give the scale its name. The successive scale degrees are numbered, 2, 3, 4, 5, 6, and 7; 8 has the same letter name as 1, but sounds an octave higher.

1 Play and name each note.

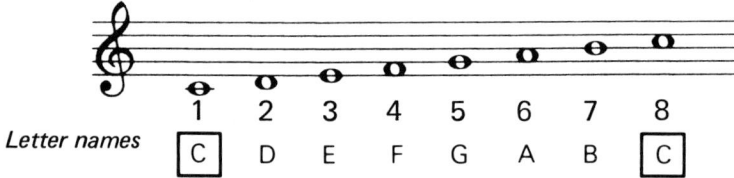

2 Write the notes and names of each of the diatonic scales as in the example above. Do not use sharps and flats. Each scale is of a different type, but they are all diatonic.

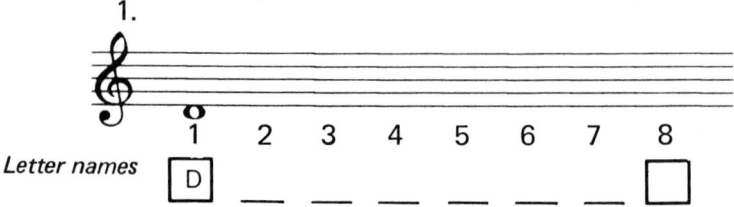

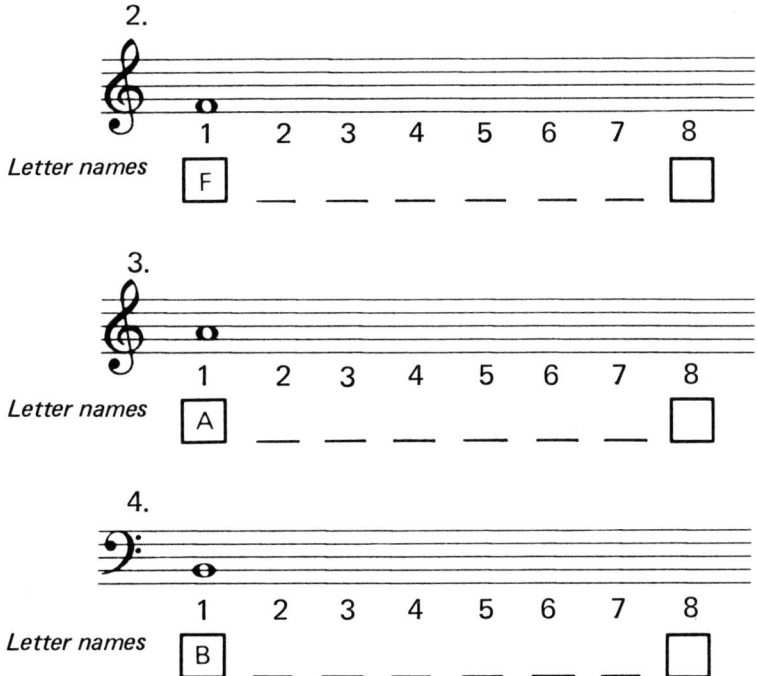

THE MAJOR SCALE
The first type of diatonic scale we will study is the *major scale*. Before we learn about it, listen to its sound in the songs *I Know Where I'm Going* (S 2 B 3) and *The Water Is Wide* (S 3, B 1).

MAJOR-SCALE CONSTRUCTION
The characteristic of the major scale which differentiates it from other diatonic scales is the placement of whole steps (whole tones) and half steps (semitones) between the various scale degrees. In the following major scale, the whole steps are labeled "1," and the half steps are labeled "½." Observe the relationships carefully:

C-Major Scale on the Keyboard

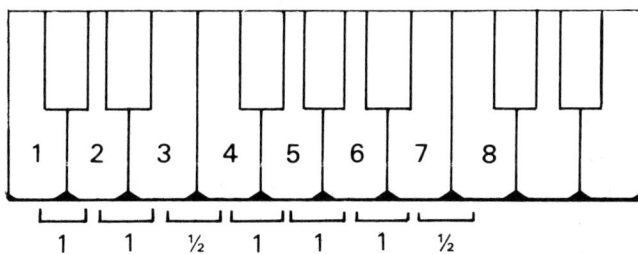

C-Major Scale on the Staff

[C-major scale notated on treble staff with intervals marked: 1, 1, ½, 1, 1, 1, ½ between scale steps 1 through 8]

3 Answer the following questions. Refer to the diagrams above.

1. Between scale degrees 1 and 2 is a _____ step, or _____ tone.
2. Between scale degrees 2 and 3 is a _____ step, or _____ tone.
3. Between scale degrees 3 and 4 is a _____ step, or _____ tone.
4. Between scale degrees 4 and 5 is a _____ step, or _____ tone.
5. Between scale degrees 5 and 6 is a _____ step, or _____ tone.
6. Between scale degrees 6 and 7 is a _____ step, or _____ tone.
7. Between scale degrees 7 and 8 is a _____ step, or _____ tone.

Rule
All major scales have the following pattern of whole steps and half steps: half steps occur **always** and **only** between 3–4 and between 7–8. All other steps are whole steps.

---

4 Restate this rule using the words **whole tone** and **semitone** instead of **whole step** and **half step**.

_____

_____

_____

_____

CONSTRUCTING OTHER MAJOR SCALES

To build a major scale on a pitch other than C, accidentals must be used. To illustrate this, observe the following diatonic scale on D without accidentals. It is a diatonic scale because it is spelled with consecutive letter names. It is not a major scale because of the positions of the whole steps and half steps.

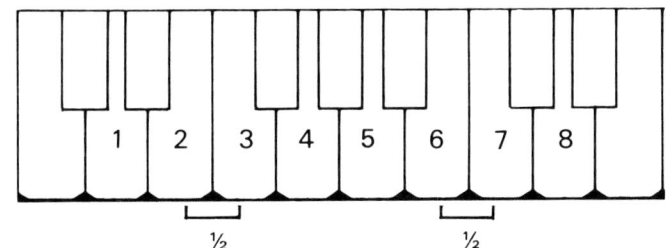

Play

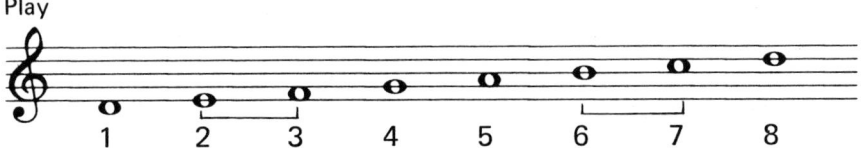

5 Answer the following questions. Refer to the scale and diagram above.

1. This scale **is** a diatonic scale because it is spelled with _____.

2. This scale **is not** a major scale because the half steps (semitones) occur between _____ and _____ and between _____ and _____.

3. In a major scale the half steps (semitones) must occur between _____ and _____ and between _____ and _____.

ADDING ACCIDENTALS TO FORM A MAJOR SCALE

We will now form a major scale on D, by the addition of accidentals to the scale shown above. In order to have a whole step between scale degrees 2 and 3, we must raise F to F♯. This also produces the required half step between scale degrees 3 and 4. Similarly, by raising C to C♯ we have the required half step between scale degrees 7 and 8, and the required whole step between 6 and 7. Observe this below and play.

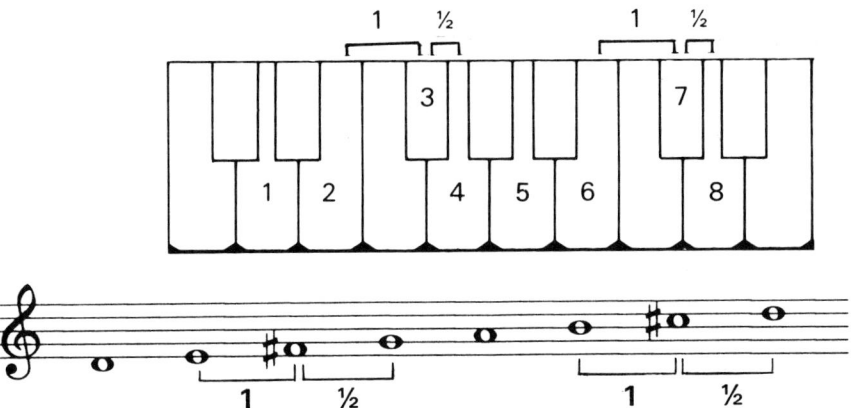

The importance of the diatonic spelling of scales can be illustrated by the following enharmonic equivalent of the D-major scale. Although it sounds the same, it looks like this:

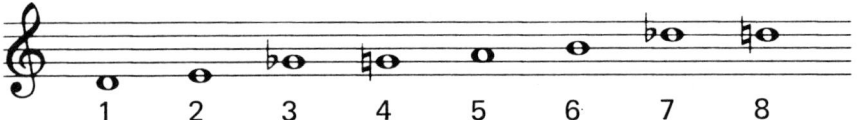

In the **incorrect** version above, scale degrees 3–4 and 7–8 are notated with chromatic semitones. In the **correct** version, scale degree 3 must be notated as some kind of F, and scale degree 7 must be some kind of C—in other words, 3–4 and 7–8 must be diatonic semitones. The importance of this simple point is not merely technical. Look at the above scale: does it look like a major scale?

6 Answer the following questions.

1. Are all diatonic scales major scales? _____.

2. To form a major scale on a pitch other than C, one must add _____.

3. The scale immediately above is incorrect because _____

_____

_____

MAJOR-SCALE SPELLINGS
Follow these steps for deriving the correct major-scale spellings:

1. Write the eight notes that have consecutive letter names on the staff, starting with the note that has the same name as the scale you are going to build.

2. If the scale starts on an accidental, place the sharp or flat **immediately** in front of both 1 and 8. Once this is done, do not change the spelling of 1 and 8.

3. Add accidentals to form the correct whole step–half step pattern (see pages 49-50). Scales with sharps do not use flats, and scales with flats do not use sharps.

Example: How to Construct the E♭-major scale

Step 1

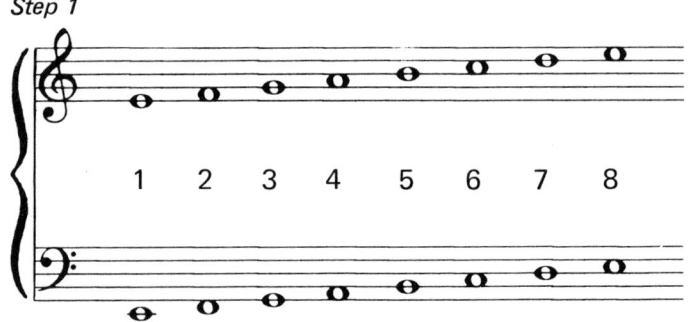

Step 2

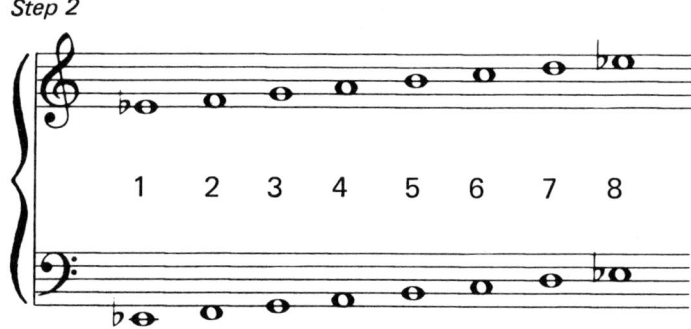

Step 3

7 Write each major scale in both treble and bass clefs. Mark the scale steps on the keyboard. Scales 2 to 5 use sharps; scales 6 to 9 use flats. Only nine scales appear here; other scales are in Appendix III.

Example: E major

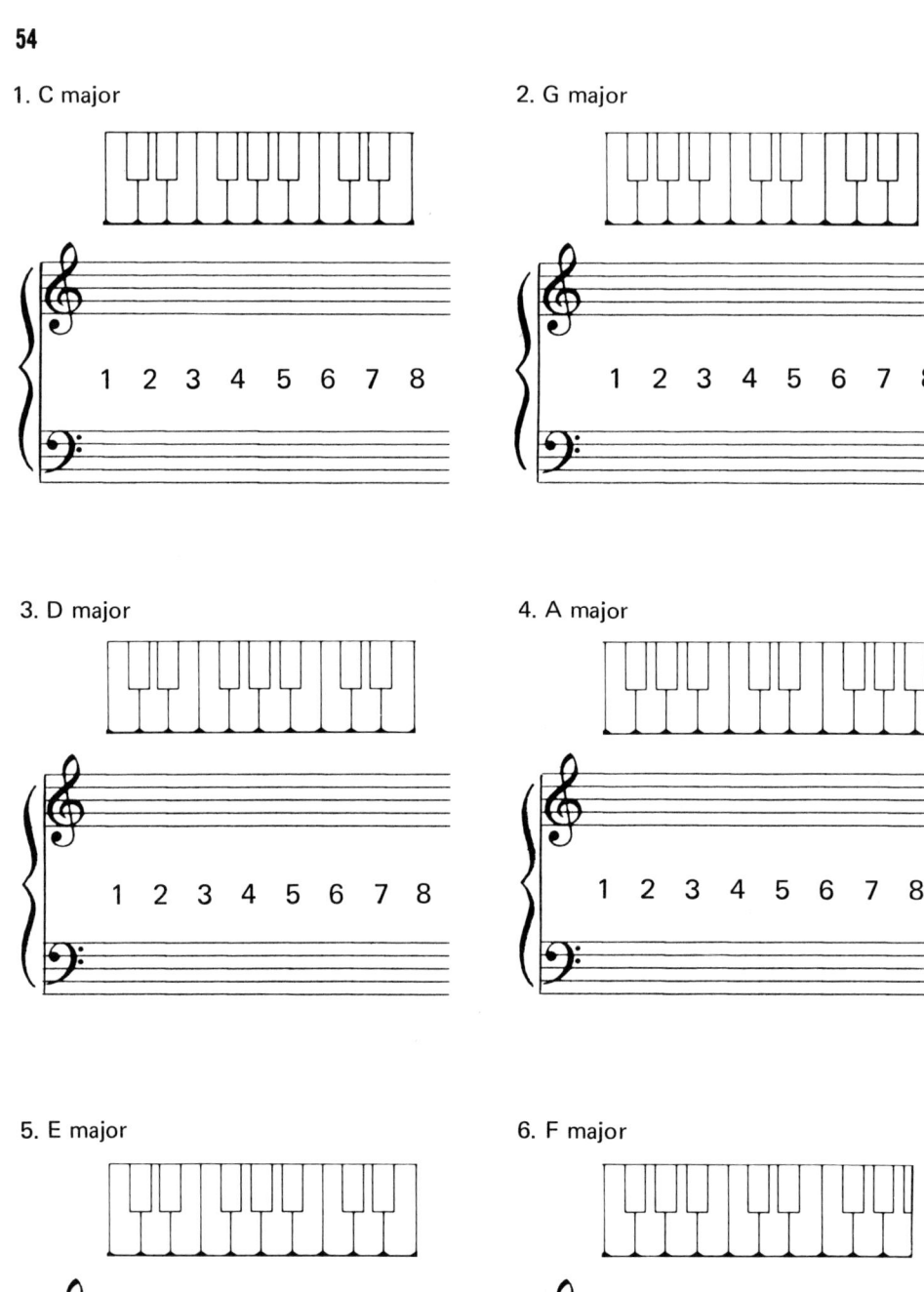

7. B♭ major

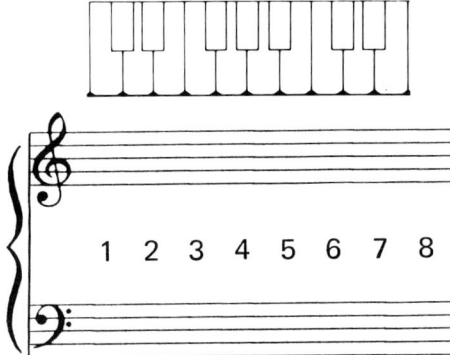

8. E♭ major

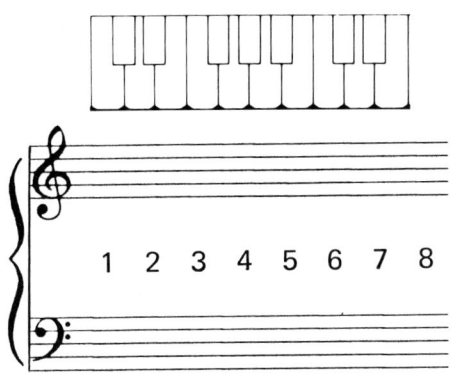

9. A♭ major

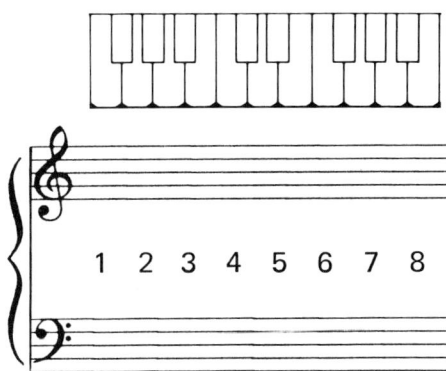

"IN THE KEY OF"
Music that uses a scale built on a particular note is said to be "in the key of" that note. It is then further identified by the type of scale (remember, there are many types of scales other than major). For example, a melody using pitches primarily from the major scale starting on D is said to be "in the key of D major."

TONALITY
The term *tonal* describes a piece of music in which all the notes are related to one central note, called the *tonic*. In a major scale, the first degree of the scale is the tonic; thus "in the key of E♭" implies that E♭ is the tonic. The tonic is heard as the strongest pitch; the other scale degrees are heard in a state of motion **toward** the tonic. We will discuss tonality in more detail in later chapters; for now, consider *tonality* to mean the relationships between the various scale degrees (other than 1) and the pitch on which they focus: the tonic.

8 In the following excerpts, determine which note is the tonic. You can do this by a combination of two means: 1) which note sounds most important? 2) to which major scale do the notes belong? (These are not complete pieces; more music follows in each case.) Play:

1.

Tonic ☐

2.

Tonic ☐

3.

Tonic ☐

4.

Tonic ☐

5.   Mozart

Tonic ☐

INTERVALS

In our study of whole tones in relationship to semitones, we have measured and compared the distance between two pitches. The musical term that describes the distance between any two notes is *interval.* There are different classifications of intervals. We will start with one: the number of steps on the staff or *staff steps* from one note to another. For example, the interval between F and B contains 4 staff steps:

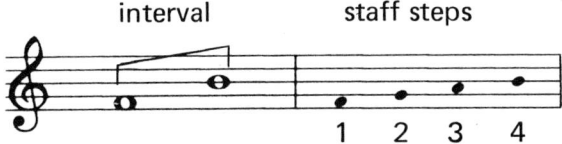

Because of the four staff steps, the interval F to B is called a 4th. Observe this procedure in the following intervals:

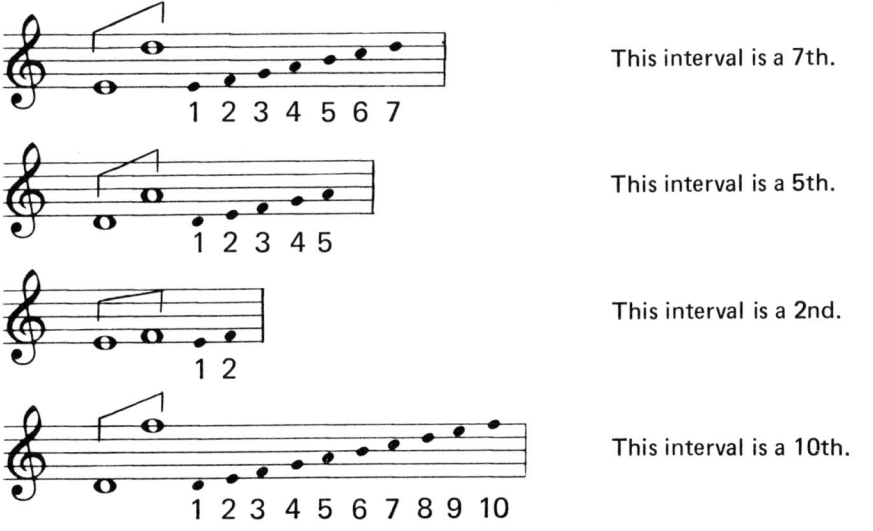

Notice that the number of staff steps **includes** both notes of the interval.

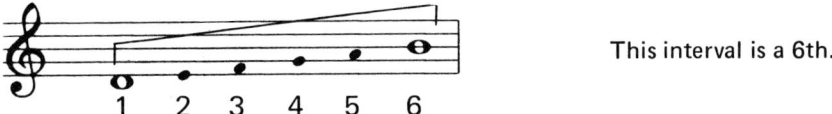

This interval is a 6th.

9

Write in the staff steps. Number them and name the interval. Do not rewrite the original pitches of the interval.

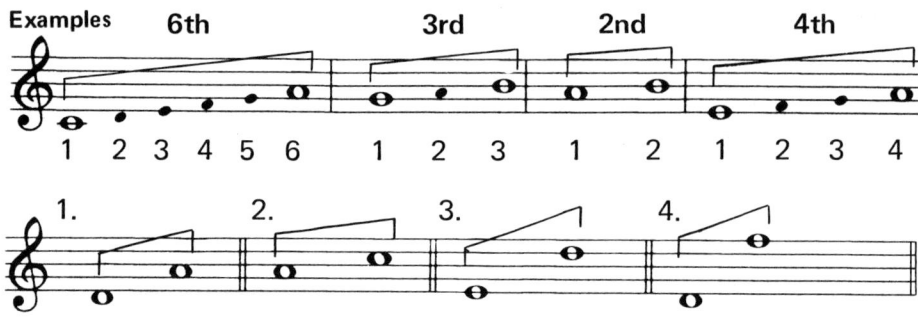

10

Identify these intervals by counting the staff steps to yourself. Do not write in the staff steps.

11
Above the given note, write the note which forms the correct interval.

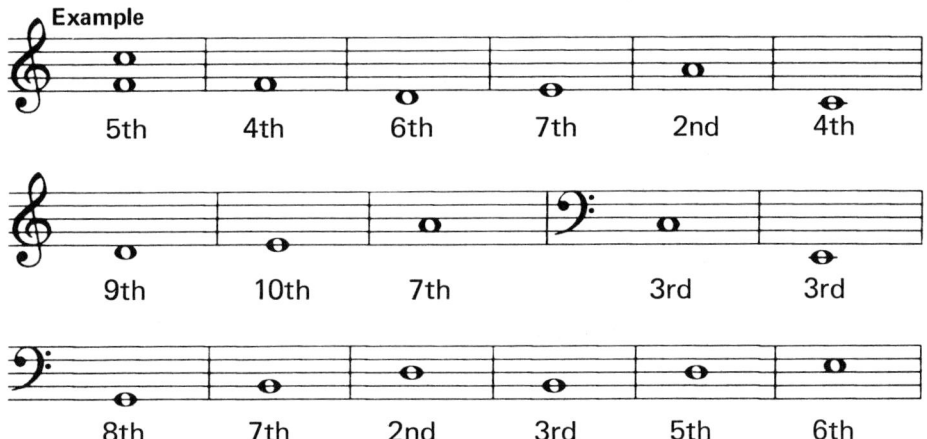

INVERSION

When the lower note of an interval becomes the higher note, or when the higher note becomes the lower note, the interval is *inverted*. For example:

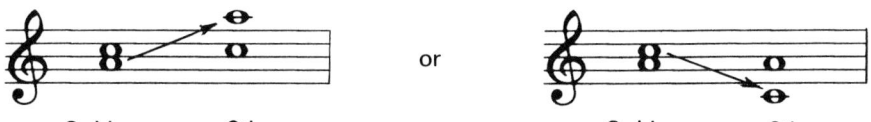

3rd becomes a 6th   3rd becomes a 6th

In the examples above, the 3rd is inverted. The *inversion* of a 3rd is a 6th. There is a numerical relationship between the original interval and its inversion: when an interval is inverted, its number plus the number of the inversion will always equal 9. Another way of stating this rule is: to find the number of an **inverted interval**, subtract the number of the **original interval** from 9. For example, what is the inversion of a 4th? Subtract 4 from 9: the inversion of a 4th is a 5th.

12
Invert each of the following intervals two ways. First, shift the lower note up an octave. Then, shift the higher note of the original interval down an octave. Name the inversions.

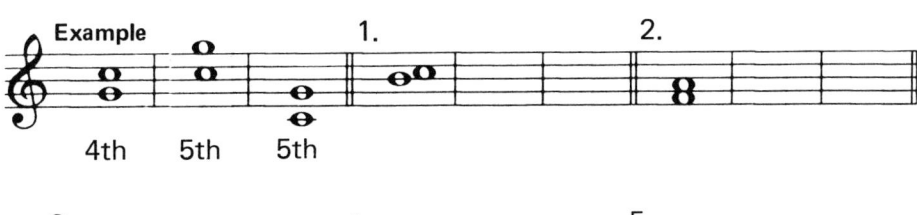

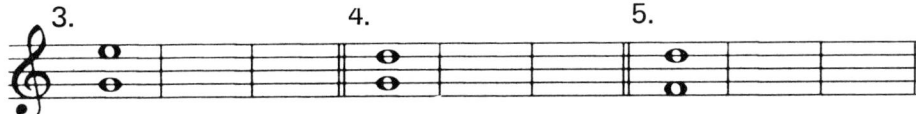

SUGGESTED ACTIVITIES

1. Explore some of the other kinds of scales listed in Appendix VI.
2. Explain why spelling a major scale with successive letter names is important.
3. Play and sing the major scales you have constructed.

TERMS AND CONCEPTS

Explain in your own words:

    scale

    diatonic scale

    construction of the major scale

    position of the half steps and whole steps between scale degrees

    "in the key of"

    tonal music

    tonic

    interval

    inversion

    number rule for inverted intervals

Contrast these terms:

    diatonic scale—chromatic scale

    whole step—half step

CHAPTER 5

KEY SIGNATURES

A melody retains its identity in any major key because the relationship between the scale degrees is constant. But you have found that in constructing major scales, the same musical pattern may look different because of the need for accidentals. The necessity for a system that organizes the use of accidentals is illustrated here:

1 Play and observe the beginning of *Frère Jacques* in these different major keys:

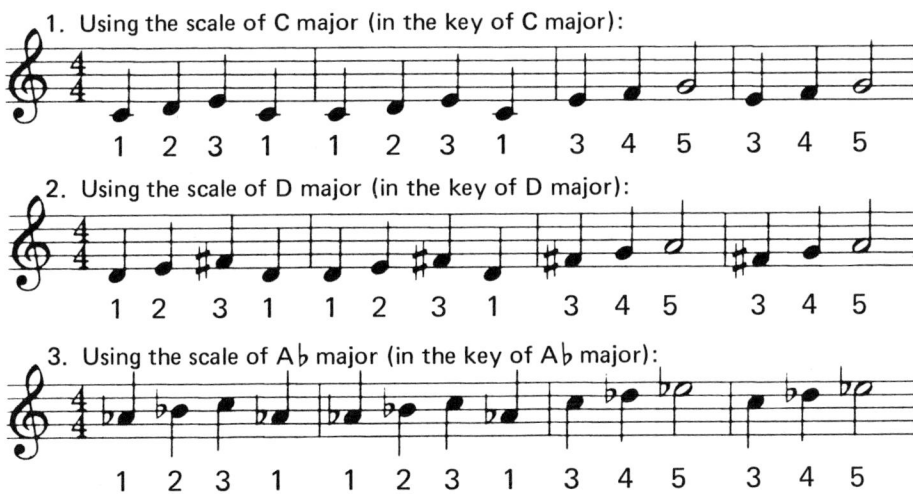

1. Using the scale of C major (in the key of C major):
2. Using the scale of D major (in the key of D major):
3. Using the scale of A♭ major (in the key of A♭ major):

We encounter two difficulties when we write this melody in different keys:
1. The need to keep writing the accidentals.
2. Music that sounds the same but looks different.*

---

*Some musicians find that the same music in different keys possesses different characteristics to the ear, but for our purposes here, we can assume that the basic scale relationships are so strong to the average listener that this minor qualification can be disregarded.

The system of *key signatures* evolved to solve these problems. Key signatures appear at the beginning of each staff line. They indicate which notes are to be regularly altered by sharps or flats without the accidentals being constantly repeated. Play the following excerpt, which is the key of D major, but does not use a key signature.

2 Play:

Key of D

In Chapter 4, you discovered that a D-major scale needs F♯ and C♯. Instead of writing each accidental as it occurs, we can use a key signature. Both accidentals are written at the beginning of the staff and **continually** alter all F's to F♯'s and all C's to C♯'s throughout the staff line. The above example can be written with a key signature in the following manner:

(**Play:** remember, you are playing **exactly** the same melody that is notated above.)

Key of D

This same procedure can be followed using flats.

3 Play:

Key of B♭

Play and compare:

Key of B♭

Now compare the following versions of *Frere Jacques* with the three corresponding versions shown on page 61 in **1**.

Key of C

Key of D

Key of A♭

4 How does the use of key signatures affect the visual representation of the melody?

_____

_____

To Summarize

The use of key signatures solves two problems:
1. There is no need to write in the accidentals continually.
2. The intervals are more easily identifiable within the context of the diatonic scale.

5 In each example circle the note altered by the key signature. A sharp or flat alters its own letter name in **any** octave.

6 In each example, write the actual note name resulting from the use of the key signature. Also, mark its position on the keyboard. Remember, the key signature affects **all** octaves.

Example

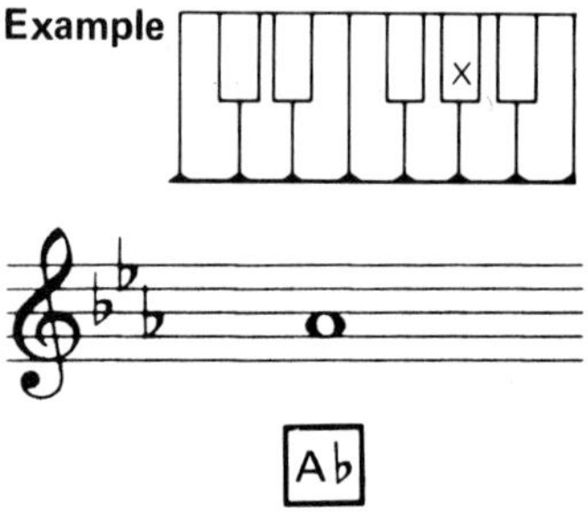

1.

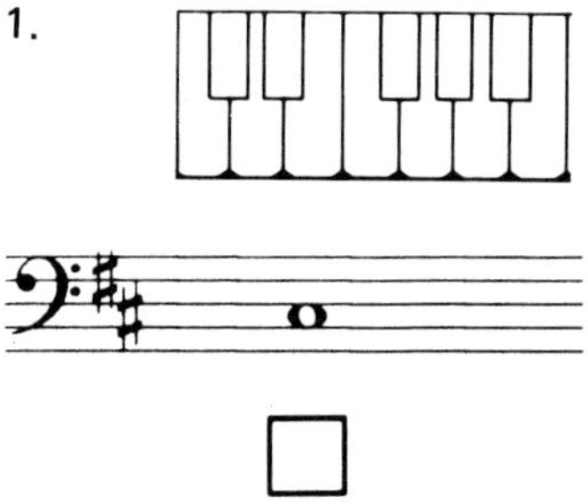

2.

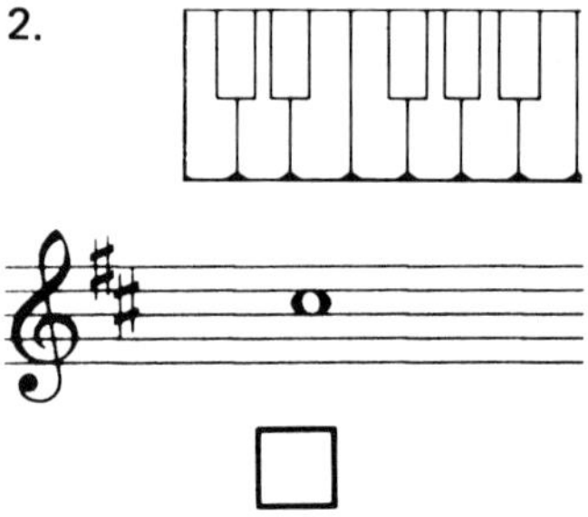

3.

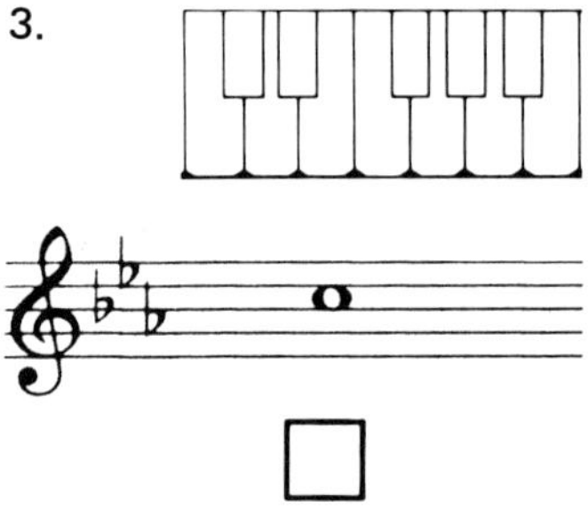

4.

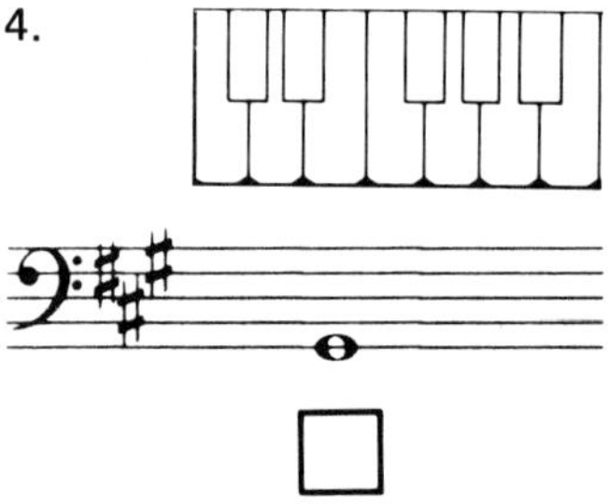

5.

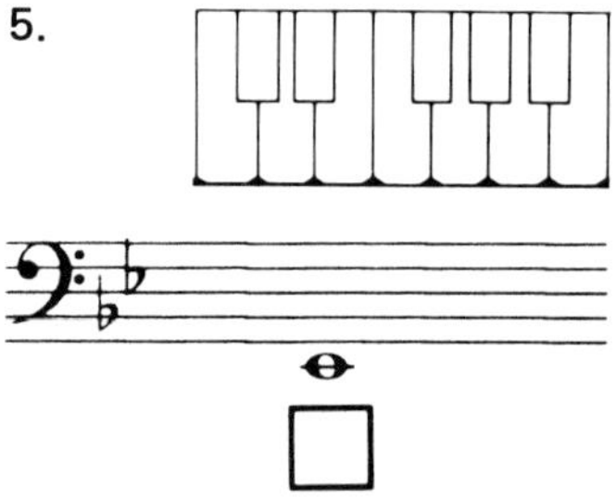

6.

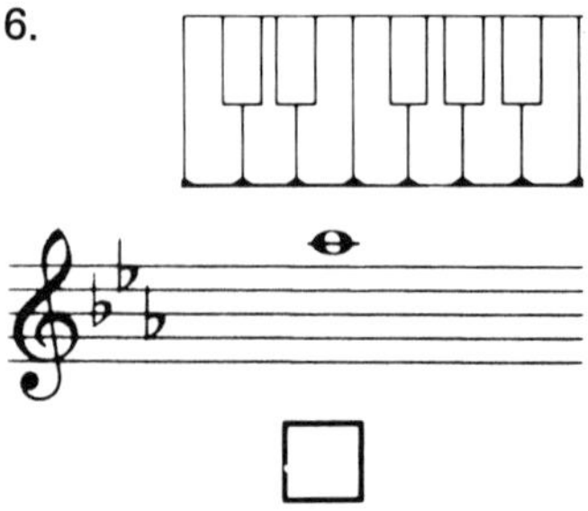

7.

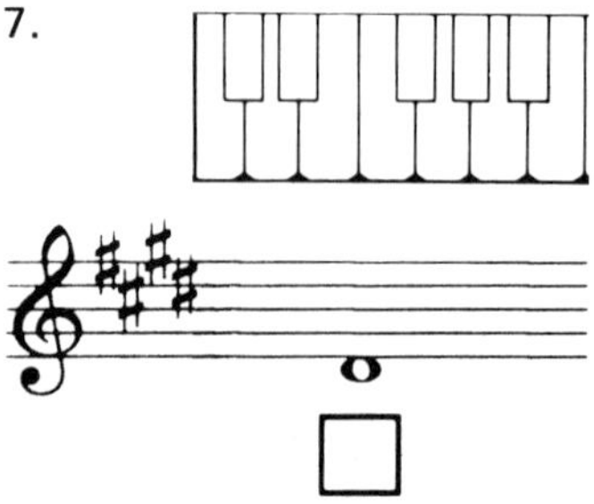

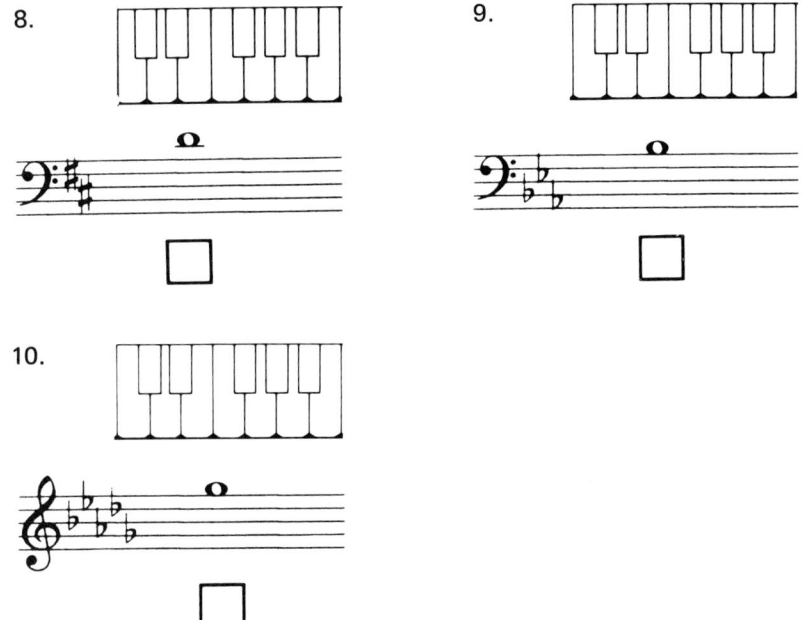

THE MAJOR-SCALE KEY SIGNATURES
Here are the fifteen major-scale key signatures:

THE CIRCLE OF 5ths

The key signatures are conveniently organized in a traditional order called the *circle of 5ths*.

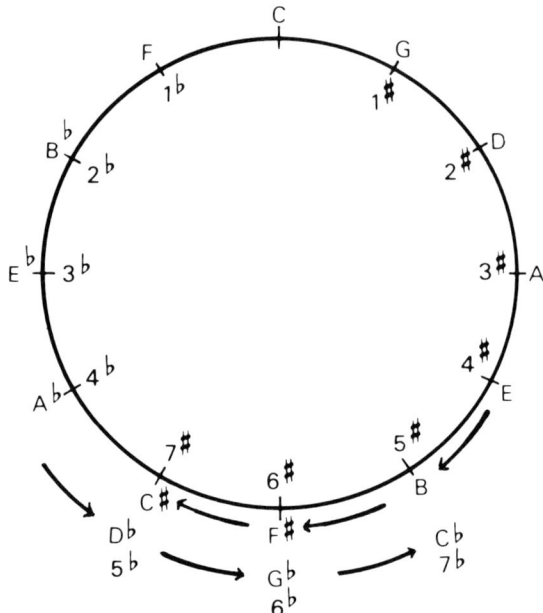

You will notice the following patterns to use as a memory aid:

Sharp Keys

1. The **names of the keys** are organized in ascending 5ths (add a sharp to the key names F and C):

   A B C D E F G A B C D E F G A B C D E F G A B C D E F♯ G A B C♯ D E F G

2. The **names** and **order** of sharps added to the key signature are also organized in ascending 5ths:

   A B C D E F♯ G A B C♯ D E F G♯ A B C D♯ E F G A♯ B C D E♯ F G A B♯ C D E F G

Flat Keys

1. The **names of the keys** are organized in ascending 4ths—the inversion of descending 5ths (add flats to the key names from B on):

   A B C D E F G A B♭ C D E♭ F G A♭ B C D♭ E F G♭ A B C♭ D E F G

2. The **names** and **order** of flats added to the key signature are also organized in ascending 4ths.

   A B♭ C D E♭ F G A♭ B C D♭ E F G♭ A B C♭ D E F♭ G A B C D E F G

This system has no special theoretical significance. It is a traditional memory aid only!

7 Write the indicated key signatures. Be careful to retain the exact left-to-right position of the sharps or flats.

| G major | D major | A major | E major |

| F major | B♭ major | E♭ major | A major |

| B major | F♯ major | C♯ major |

| D♭ major | G♭ major | C♭ major |

8 Complete the following exercises by writing the correct sharps or flats. For example, since number 1 (key of B♭) uses B♭ and E♭ in the key signature, they are written in the appropriate boxes. Number 2 is also filled in as an example.

Key of	F♯	C♯	G♯	D♯	A♯	E♯	B♯	B♭	E♭	A♭	D♭	G♭	C♭
1 B♭								B♭	E♭				
2 A	F♯	C♯	G♯										
3 A♭													
4 C													
5 D													
6 G													
7 E													
8 D♭													
9 E♭													
10 C♯													
11 F													
12 B♭													
13 G♭													
14 F♯													
15 B													
16 A													
17 B♭													

9 Answer (number 1 is completed as an example):

1. The key signature of D major uses __♯__ s. In order, they are __F♯, C♯__

2. The key signature of B♭ major uses _____. In order, they are _____.

3. C major uses _____. In order, they are _____.

4. A major uses _____. In order, they are _____.

5. E major uses _____. In order, they are _____.

6. The key signature that uses five ♯ s is _____. In order, they are _____.

7. The key signature that uses four ♭s is _____. In order, they are _____.

8. The key signature that uses one ♭ is _____. It is _____.

9. The key signature that uses one ♯ is _____. It is _____.

10. The key signature that uses seven ♯s is _____. In order, they are _____.

11. The key signature that uses seven ♭s is _____. In order, they are _____.

12. The key signature that uses six ♭s is _____. In order, they are _____.

13. The only key signature that has not been used in the above example is _____. It uses ♭s. In order, they are _____.

TRANSPOSITION

In *Frère Jacques* on page 61, we shifted a piece of music from one key to another. This practice is known as *transposition*. Thus we transposed *Frère Jacques* from the key of C to the keys of D and A♭ **without** the use of key signatures. Here we shall learn transposition **with** the use of key signatures. Transposition has many practical values in music. For example, you may find a certain song in the key of D major too high for your own voice. In order to sing it, you must transpose it to a lower key. Transposing also helps you to develop proficiency in understanding the use and interrelationships of different keys. While observing the process of transposition, keep intervals and scale degrees in mind.

10 Observe how to transpose *Frère Jacques* from F major to A major.

Step 1: Write the new key signature. Write the first note, making sure it is the same scale degree as the original.

Step 2: Rewrite the music with exactly the same rhythm and the same order of intervals. Check to be sure that the scale degrees correspond.

11 1. Transpose the first 4 measures of *Frère Jacques* to the keys indicated below. Follow the steps for transposition already shown. Play each version.

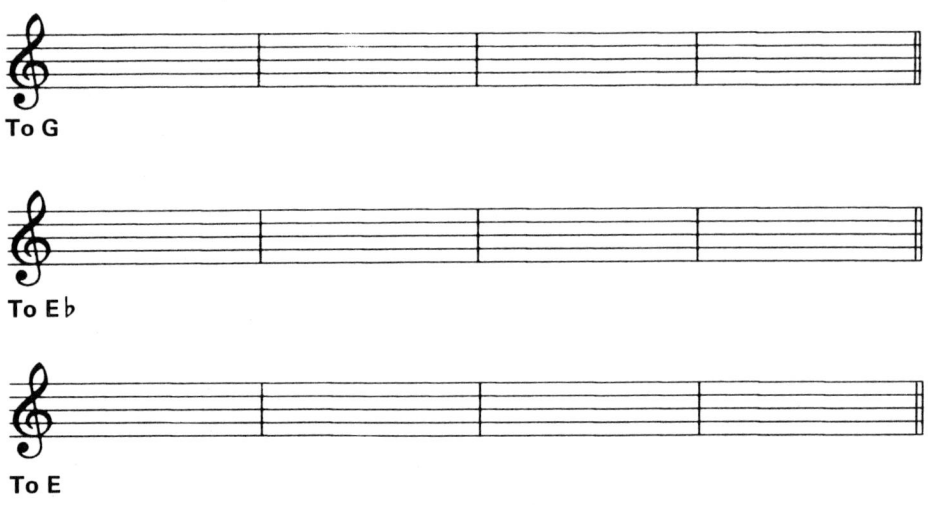

To G

To E♭

To E

2. Transpose the first 8 measures of the *Ode to Joy* (SB 50) to the keys indicated, and play each version.

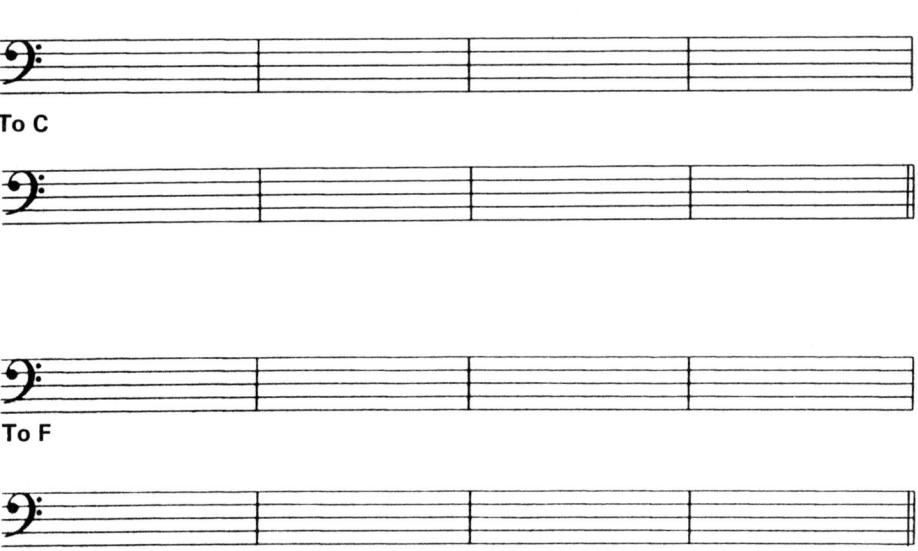

To C

To F

If you have done the examples above correctly, the only accidentals you had to write are those in the key signatures. However, if an accidental other than those in the key signature should appear in a piece that you are transposing, you must perform the same alterations in the new version. Remember, an accidental is a symbol that alters the pitch of a note. The accidental in the transposed melody may be a different symbol than the one in the original melody, but it must perform the same **function**. Observe this practice in the following example:

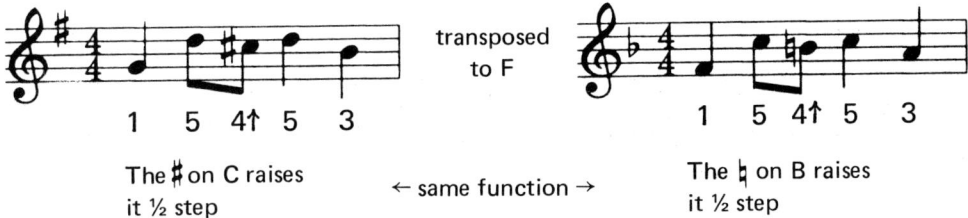

Thus we see that in transposing we may have to use different accidentals to perform the same function.

12 Transpose these examples. Indicate the function of the accidental (write "raise ½ step" or "lower ½ step").

13 Transpose to the key indicated. Play the original and the transposed version. Write the scale degree under the first note of each.

1. *Go Tell Aunt Rhody*

To D:

2. *Twinkle, Twinkle, Little Star*

To F:

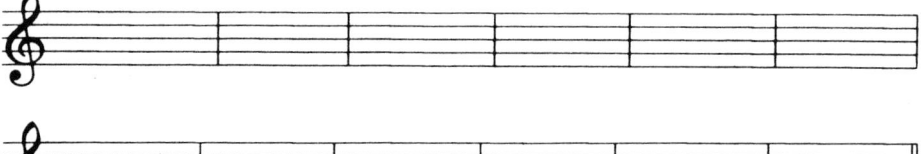

3. *Old Smoky*

ACCIDENTALS: TWO DEFINITIONS

1. An accidental is a symbol which alters the pitch of a note in a scale previously defined by a key signature. This is the more traditional definition of an accidental.
2. In a more modern usage, the term accidental refers to any chromatic alteration. This usage has special relevance to much contemporary music, where often no key signatures (or even keys) are used.

SINGING MAJOR-SCALE MELODIES

There are several different methods of singing the major scale degrees. One good way is to use numbers. Hand signals can be a definite aid in developing such singing skills, since they physically help your body discover scale-step relationships. The hand signal system appears in the Appendix on page 231. There are other sight singing methods which may be employed. The most important question is: What can you do to hear, feel, and sing music correctly?

14 Sing this major scale slowly with numbers.

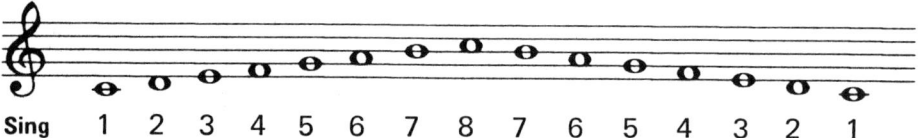

Sing   1   2   3   4   5   6   7   8   7   6   5   4   3   2   1

Repeat in different keys. Listen for the characteristic sound of each scale degree. Observe which ones feel more stable in contrast to those which seem to push toward another pitch.

SYLLABLES

Another popular method of singing the major scale is with syllables.

15 Sing up and down:

do   re   mi   fa   sol   la   ti   do   ti   la   sol   fa   mi   re   do

SINGING MELODIES

To gain experience in sight singing melodies with numbers and syllables, we will use some of the more familiar songs and rhymes.

16 Sing each of these songs with scale numbers or syllables. Start on C, then repeat in different keys. Sing it once with words if you need a reminder of the exact melody. The music is not printed here, so you can focus your attention on the sound of each scale step.

1. Sing:
do do   sol sol   la la sol   fa   fa mi mi   re   re   do
 1   1   5   5   6 6   5   4   4 3 3   2   2   1
Think: Twinkle, twinkle, little star, How I wonder what you are.

sol sol fa fa   mi mi   re   sol sol fa fa   mi mi   re
 5   5   4   4   3   3   2   5   5   4   4   3 3   2
Up above the world so high, Like a diamond in the sky,

do do   sol sol   la la sol   fa   fa mi mi   re   re   do
 1   1   5   5   6 6   5   4   4 3 3   2   2   1
Twinkle, twinkle, little star, How I wonder what you are.

2. Sing:
mi re   do re mi mi   mi   re re   re   mi sol sol
 3 2   1   2 3 3   3   2 2   2   3 5   5
Think: Mary had a little lamb, little lamb, little lamb,

mi re   do re mi mi   mi   mi   re   re   mi   re   do
 3 2   1   2 3 3   3   2   2   3   2   1
Mary had a little lamb, his fleece was white as snow.

3. Sing:
mi   mi   re   do do   re   re   fa   mi re do
 3   3   2   1 1   2   2   4   3 2 1
Think: Go tell Aunt Rhody, Go tell Aunt Rhody,

sol sol   fa   mi mi   mi   re   fa   mi   re   do
 5   5   4   3 3   3   2   4   3   2   1
Go tell Aunt Rhody, The old grey goose is dead.

OCTAVE RELATIONSHIPS
Scale degrees often occur above or below the span of an octave. They are notated by placing an apostrophe **above** the number to indicate a higher octave, or **below** the number to indicate a lower octave. Observe in the following example:

When discussing pitches below the tonic, refer to them as "low 5" or "low *sol*"; "low 6" or "low *la*", etc. In a like manner, pitches above the starting octave would be called "high 1" or "high *do*"; "high 2" or "high *re*," etc. Observe this method in the opening of *Taps:*

5, 5, 1   5, 1 3
sol, sol, do   sol, do mi

This melody starts on the fifth degree of the scale but below scale degree 1; thus, the notation of 5, or *sol*,.

17

Sing *I Know Where I'm Going* (SB 2, S 2, B 3) and *The Water Is Wide* (SB 5, S 3, B 1) along with the record. Use numbers or syllables. Before you sing, write the correct numbers or syllables below the notes in the *Scorebook*.

SUGGESTED ACTIVITIES

1. Improvise singing melodies with major scale numbers or syllables.

2. Sing the telephone numbers of all of your friends (the numbers are 1 through 0; 9 becomes 2' and 0 becomes 3').

3. The Octave Game: the distinct characteristic of scale degrees, no matter what octave they occur in, can be demonstrated by a singing game that often seems easier for children than for accomplished musicians, probably because children have fewer inhibitions. The Octave Game works like this: sing a familiar easy song but change octaves on each successive note. Here is an illustration using a part of *Frère Jacques*:

Original Version

1 2 3 1   1 2 3 1   3 4 5   3 4 5
Sing do re mi do   do re mi do   mi fa sol   mi fa sol

Octave Game Version I

1 2' 3 1'   1 2' 3 1'   3 4' 5   3' 4 5'
Sing do re' mi do'   do re' mi do'   mi fa' sol   mi' fa sol'

Octave Game Version II (start in the upper octave)

Sing: 1' 2 3' 1 1' 2 3' 1 3' 4 5' 3 4' 5
do' re mi' do do' re mi' do mi' fa sol' mi fa' sol

This game creates several interesting ways of using a familiar song to explore more complex musical practices: for example, the use of very large intervals, the characteristics of a melodic pitch in relationship to a key center regardless of its octave placement, and the musical result of using different octave placements of melodic pitches. Suggested melodies for the Octave Game are: *My Bonnie Lies Over the Ocean, Alouette, Mary Had a Little Lamb,* and *Twinkle, Twinkle, Little Star.*

4. Study all the major-scale key signatures on page 65.
5. Transpose any of the major-scale songs to various keys.
6. Transpose a major-scale song to another key and rewrite in the bass clef.
7. Sing the following songs from the *Scorebook* using numbers or syllables:

Barbrie Allen (SB 9)
Drink to Me Only With Thine Eyes (SB 7)
Shoo Fly (SB 11)
Down in the Valley (SB 12)
Hush, Little Baby (SB 17)

This Old Man (SB 18)
Silent Night (SB 31)
The First Noel (SB 32)
The Riddle Song (SB 6)
Brahms's *Lullaby* (SB 8)
Ode to Joy (SB 50)

TERMS AND CONCEPTS
Explain in your own words:
key signature
circle of 5ths
transposition
transposing accidentals (function)
methods for singing major-scale melodies

CHAPTER 6

INTERVALS

We have seen how intervals are defined by the number of staff steps between the notes of the interval. This is only an approximate measurement of an interval. Now we will discover a more precise measurement, because two intervals that contain the **same** number of staff steps may contain a **different** number of semitones—thus, they may be different in actual size. Observe this difference in the following examples:

I.
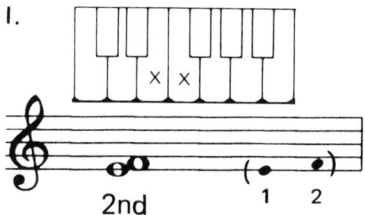

II.
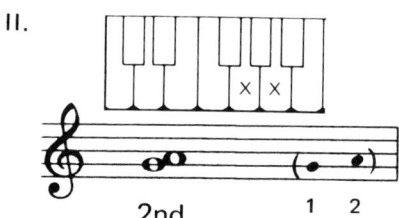

III.
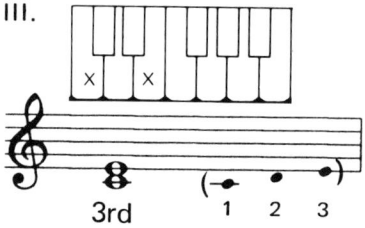

IV.
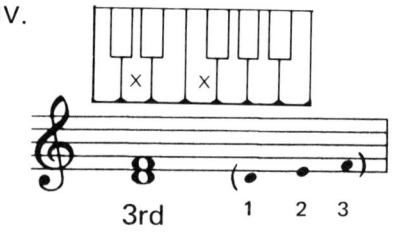

Count the number of half steps in the two 2nds. Interval I contains one half step, while interval II contains two half steps. Both intervals are 2nds, by the number of staff steps, but interval I is larger than interval II by one half step.

Count the number of half steps in the two 3rds. Interval III contains four half steps while interval IV contains 3 half steps. Both intervals are 3rds but interval IV is smaller than interval III by one half step.

1 Count the number of half steps in each pair of intervals. Write the number of half steps in each. Circle the larger interval. Also, name the interval by number of staff steps.

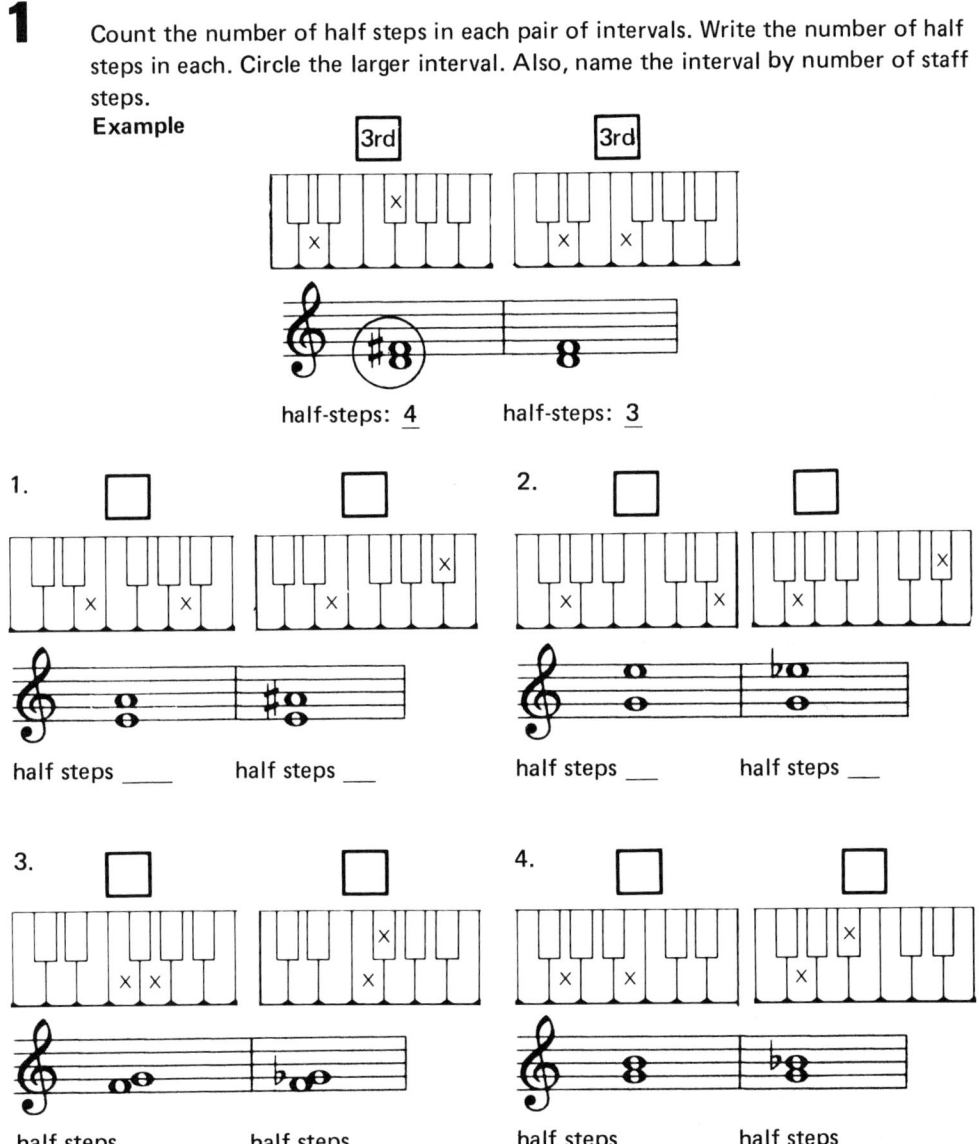

THE QUALITY OF AN INTERVAL

We have seen in the examples above the need to differentiate between two intervals having the same number of staff steps but a different number of semitones. This is done by *interval quality*. The terms which describe quality (and their abbreviations) are: major (M), minor (m), perfect (P), augmented (aug), and diminished (dim or ^{0}). The complete measurement of any interval requires the combination of quality plus staff-step number.

2 Compare with the example on page 78:

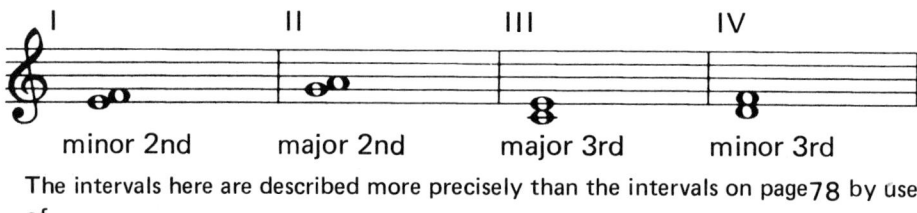

minor 2nd   major 2nd   major 3rd   minor 3rd

The intervals here are described more precisely than the intervals on page 78 by use of _____ .

WHICH TERM OF QUALITY APPLIES?

1. *Major* and *minor* are used to identify 2nds, 3rds, 6ths, and 7ths.
2. *Perfect*, *augmented*, and *diminished* are used to identify unisons (primes), 4ths, 5ths, and 8ves (octaves).

These are the basic applications of quality designation. Augmented and diminished can be applied to 2nds, 3rds, 6ths, and 7ths in complex intervals.

RELATIONSHIPS OF QUALITY DESIGNATIONS

1. Major is one half step larger than minor.
2. Augmented is one half step larger than perfect (and major, in complex intervals).
3. Diminished is one half step smaller than perfect (and minor, in complex intervals).

Each interval designation indicates an exact number of half steps between two notes. For example, all perfect 5ths contain seven half steps. However, this is not a practical way to learn intervals. Intervals are recognized by a combination of factors involving their relationship to other musical elements. One such method of identifying intervals is through their relationship to the major scale. We will study this shortly.

3 Answer the following questions:

1. Intervals containing the same number of staff steps but different numbers of semitones are differentiated by _____ .
2. 2nds, 3rds, 6ths, and 7ths are identified by the terms _____ .
3. Unisons, 4ths, 5ths, and 8ves are identified by the terms _____ .
4. Perfect is one half step larger than _____ .
5. Major is one half step larger than _____ .
6. Augmented is one half step larger than _____ .
7. All major 3rds contain (the same, different) _____ number of semitones.

RELATIONSHIPS OF INTERVALS TO THE MAJOR SCALE
Play:

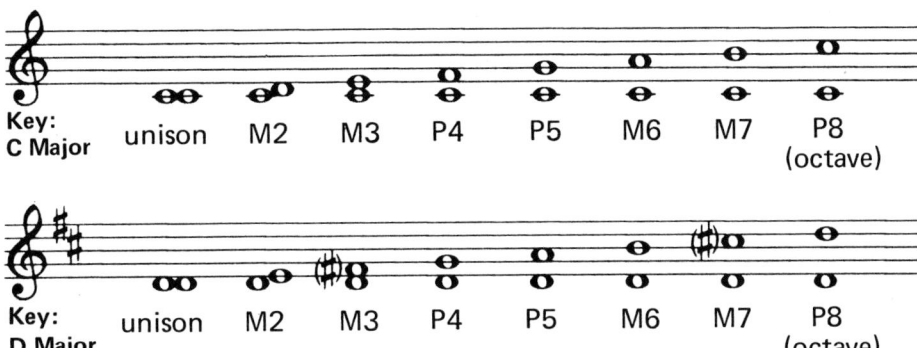

(Sharps in parentheses are included in the D-major scale key signature.)

No matter which major key is used, the interval size between the tonic and the various scale degrees remains constant. The intervals may not look the same: for example, compare the major 3rd (M3) in the C-major scale to the major 3rd (M3) in the D-major scale. Even though a sharp is used in the M3 above D, it contains the same number of semitones as the M3 above C.

MAJOR-SCALE INTERVAL RELATIONSHIPS

The intervals of the major scale, between tonic and each of the other scale degrees, follow these rules:

> 1. 2nds, 3rds, 6ths, and 7ths are always major.
> 2. Unisons, 4ths, 5ths, and 8ves are always perfect.
> 3. There are no minor intervals.

4 Answer the following questions:

1. The interval from the tonic to the 3rd of a major scale is a _____.
2. The interval from the tonic to the 7th of a major scale is a _____.
3. The interval from the tonic to the 4th of a major scale is a _____.
4. The interval from the tonic to the 2nd of a major scale is a _____.
5. A major 7th above D is (name the note) _____.
6. A major 7th above C is _____.
7. A major 2nd above D is _____.
8. A perfect 5th above D is _____.
9. A major 3rd above D is _____.
10. A major 6th above C is _____.
11. A perfect 4th above C is _____.
12. A perfect 4th above D is _____.
13. In a major scale, the intervals from the tonic up to each scale degree can be major or perfect but never _____.

ALTERING MAJOR-SCALE INTERVALS

The major-scale intervals can be altered to form smaller or larger intervals by adding accidentals. Sing the tonic first, then the higher pitch:

5 Name these 2nds, 3rds, and 5ths. The intervals within the major scale of the indicated key are all major and have no accidentals other than the sharps or flats found in the key signature. An interval which is a half step **smaller** than major is minor and uses an accidental. Sharps and flats in parentheses are in the major-scale key signature. Play each interval.

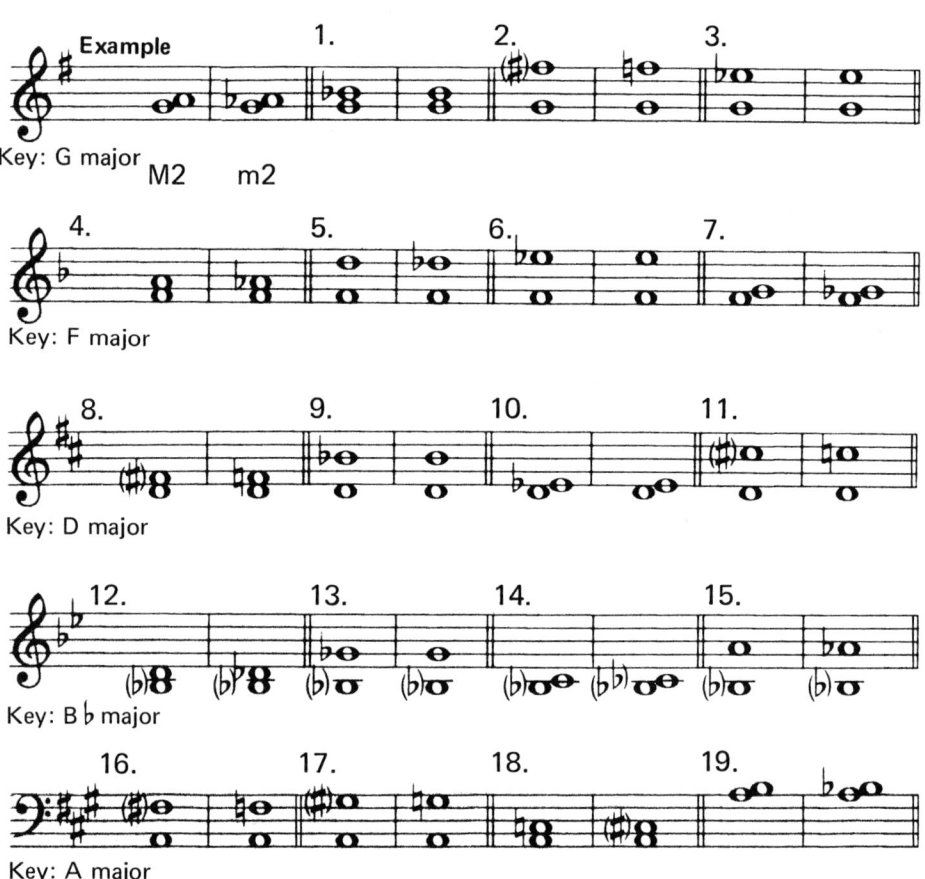

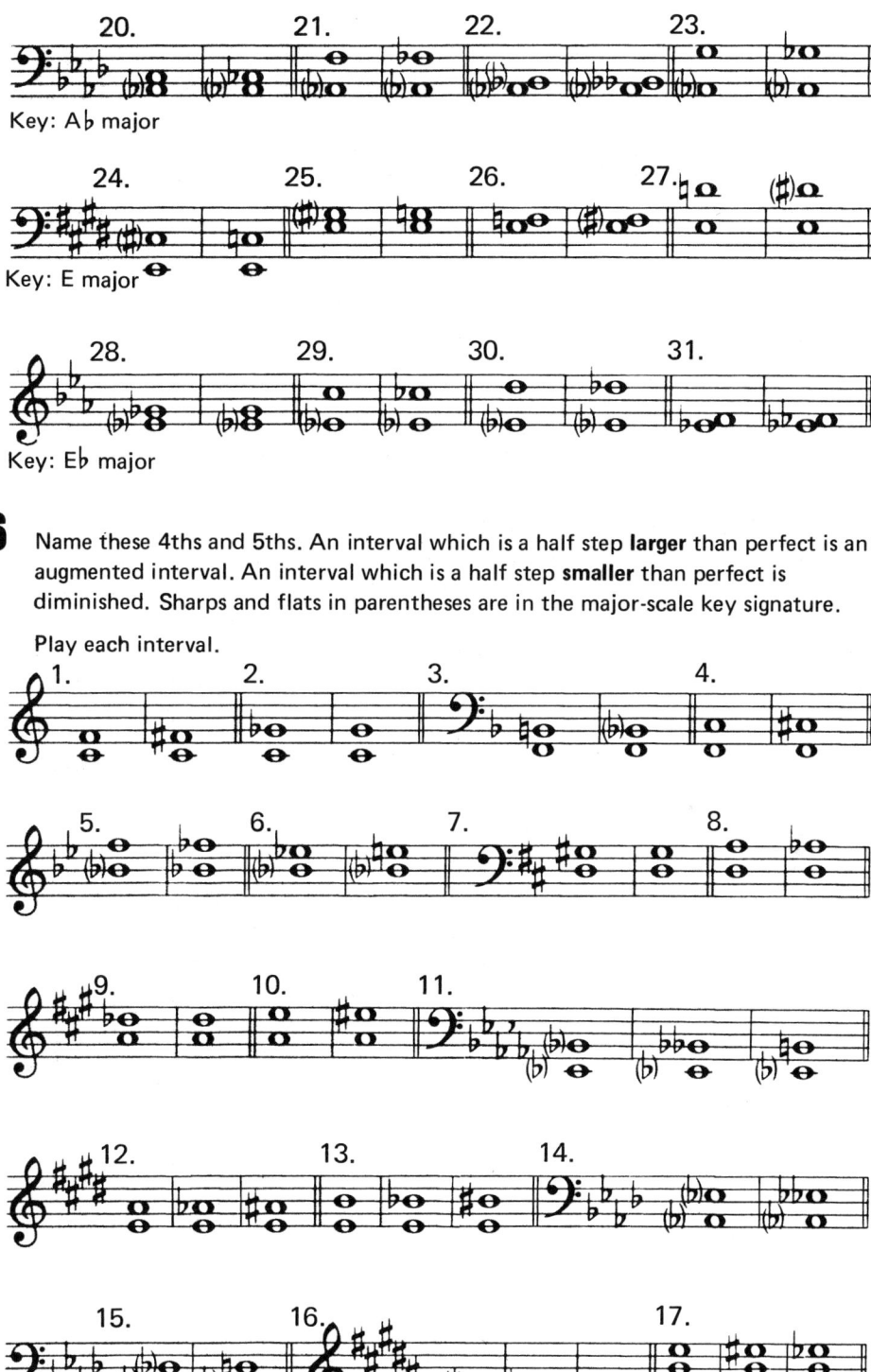

RULE FOR IDENTIFYING INTERVALS BY MAJOR-SCALE RELATIONSHIPS

When measuring an interval: if the upper note of a 2nd, 3rd, 6th, or 7th is in the major scale of the lower note, the interval is **major**. If the upper note of a 4th or 5th is in the major scale of the lower note, the interval is **perfect**.

7 Answer:
1. In order to measure an interval through use of major-scale relationships, one must know key signatures because _____
_____.

2. In major 2nds, 3rds, 6ths, and 7ths the (upper, lower) _____ note of the interval is in the major scale of the (upper, lower) _____ note.

CONSONANCE AND DISSONANCE

Intervals are often described as consonant or dissonant. The term dissonance is often associated with harsh and displeasing sounds, while consonant sounds are considered harmonious and "correct." A more accurate way to define consonance and dissonance is: *dissonant* sounds create an active and unstable feeling, while *consonant* sounds create the opposite, a relaxed and stable feeling. These descriptions are generalizations taken out of musical contexts. Within a piece of music, each sound may take on new meaning. When a dissonant interval or sound moves to a consonant interval or sound, the change from active to stable sounds is called a *resolution*. The dissonant sound is said to *resolve* to the consonant sound.

8 Play each pair of intervals. Mark those which seem dissonant with a "D." Mark the consonant intervals with a "C." If the second interval is a resolution of the first (dissonant moving to consonant), circle both intervals.

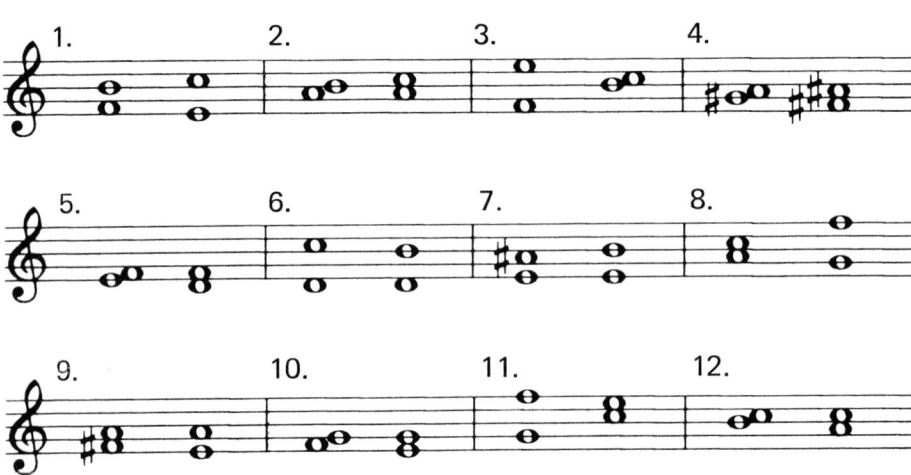

CONSONANT AND DISSONANT INTERVALS

Traditionally, intervals have been classified in this way:

Dissonant: major and minor 2nds and 7ths; augmented and diminished 4ths, 5ths, and octaves.

Consonant: major and minor 3rds and 6ths; perfect 5ths and octaves.

Perfect 4ths are a special case. When heard in relation to the bass (the lowest note), they are considered dissonant. Otherwise, they are considered consonant.

9 Examine *Study in C*, by Sor (SB 49). Look for any dissonances and their resolutions.

10 Circle the most dissonant interval of each group of three. Play:

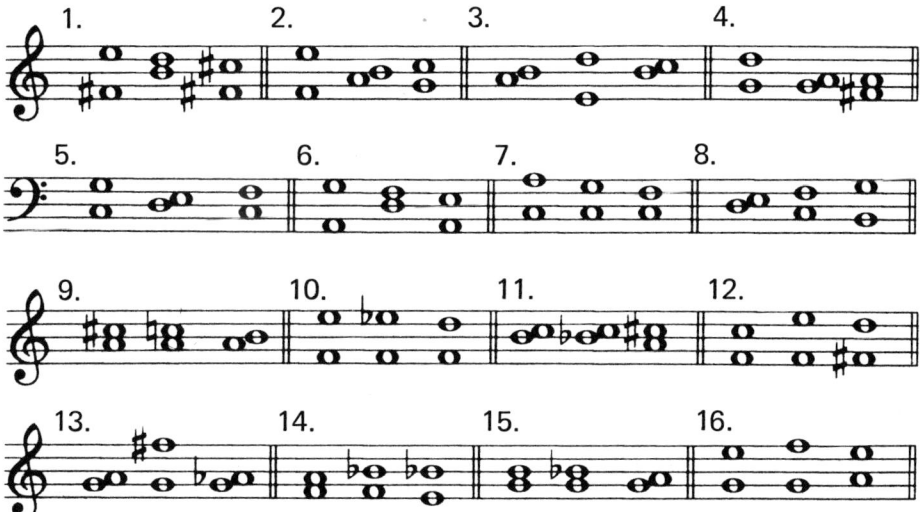

11 Examine the Mozart *Minuet* (SB 48) for dissonant intervals. Circle any dissonances in measures 4, 12, 16, 20, and 24. For example, in measure 4, circle F and E.

TERMS AND CONCEPTS

Explain in your own words:
- quality
- major-scale intervals
- altering major-scale intervals

Contrast these terms or concepts:
- major/minor (interval qualities)
- perfect/diminished
- perfect/augmented
- consonance/dissonance

CHAPTER 7

A SECOND LOOK AT INTERVALS
Because intervals are sometimes hard to understand, but are so vital to basic musicianship, we now take a second look at them to gain further skills and understanding. Mastery of intervals at an early stage in your study of music is essential.

INTERVALS WITHOUT KEY SIGNATURES
Examining intervals without key signatures can be an aid in recognizing them and understanding their notation.

1 Play each interval. Identify it as a half step (m2) or whole step (M2). Use the keyboard as a reference.

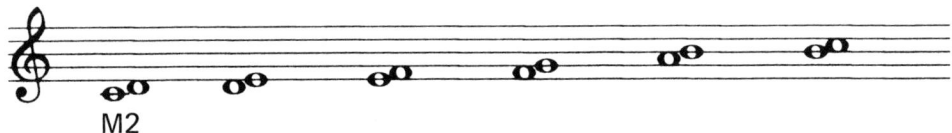
M2

You have found that on the white keys, the only half steps (m2's) are between E–F and between B–C. These two half steps are called the *natural diatonic semitones*. They are the **only** natural semitones on the staff since they do not require accidentals.

2 Answer:
1. On the white keys, the only semitones are between _____ – _____ and between _____ – _____.
2. The two semitones that do not require accidentals have a special name. They are called the _____.

3. Other terms for half steps are _____ and _____.

4. Other terms for whole steps are _____ and _____.

3 Compare these intervals by identifying the number and type of natural diatonic steps that each interval contains. Study the example carefully.

1.

2.

3.

4.

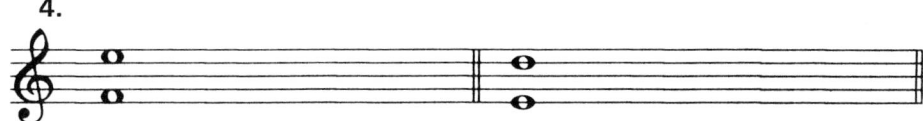

You have found that the size of an interval is affected by the kind of natural diatonic steps it contains. In 1, above, both intervals are 3rds; but the first (G–B) contains two whole steps, while the second (A–C) contains one whole step and one half step. Therefore, the second interval is smaller although both intervals **look** the same. Because there are only two natural diatonic semitones, it is easy to develop a rule for identifying natural intervals based on whether or not they contain the two natural diatonic semitones.

For an interval to contain a natural diatonic semitone, both notes of the semitone must lie **within** the notes of the interval. For example, does this interval contain a natural diatonic semitone?

The answer is yes. B–C lies within the interval:

Does this interval contain a natural diatonic semitone?

The answer is no. E–F lies **outside** the interval:

1. Write the word "within" or "outside" to indicate whether the interval contains a natural diatonic semitone:

within   outside   within   outside

2. These intervals contain one, two, or no natural diatonic semitones. For an interval to contain one natural diatonic semitone, both notes of the semitone must lie **within** the interval. The interval contains both natural diatonic semitones if all four pitches of the semitones lie **within** the interval. The interval contains

no natural diatonic semitones if both semitones lie **outside** the interval. Study the examples, then write "none," "one," or "two" below each interval.

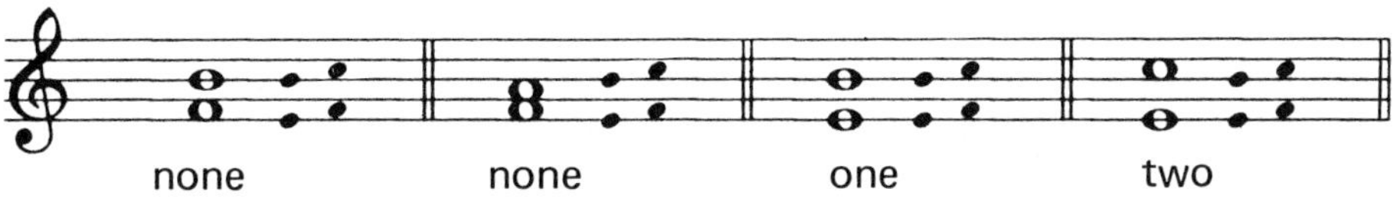

none   none   one   two

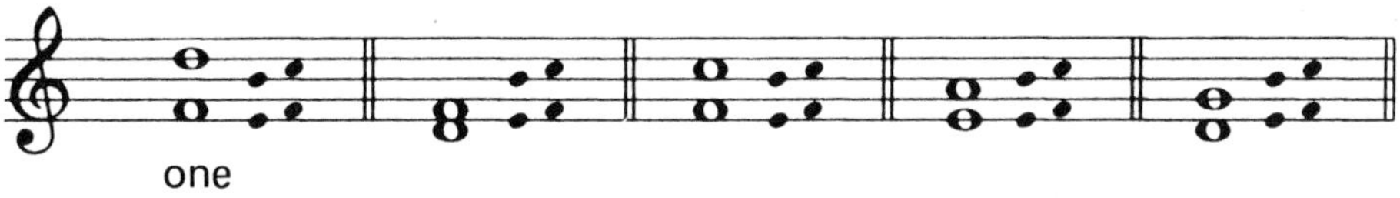

one

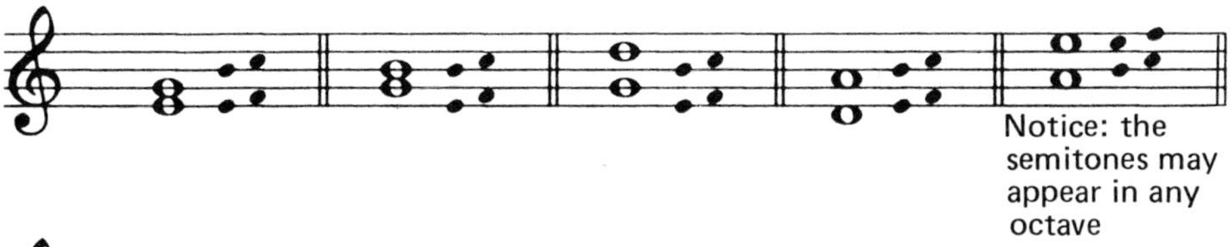

Notice: the semitones may appear in any octave

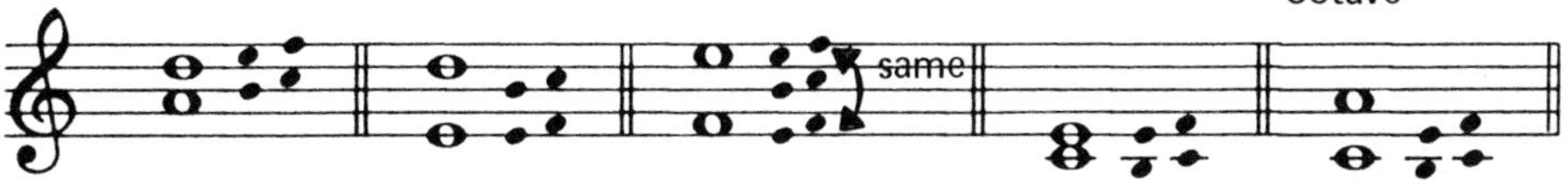

same

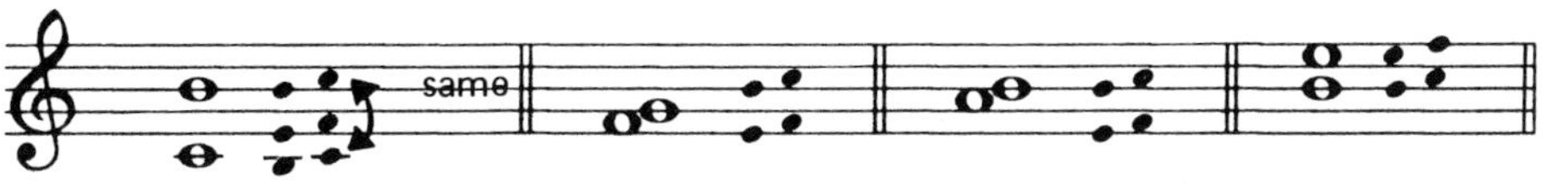

same

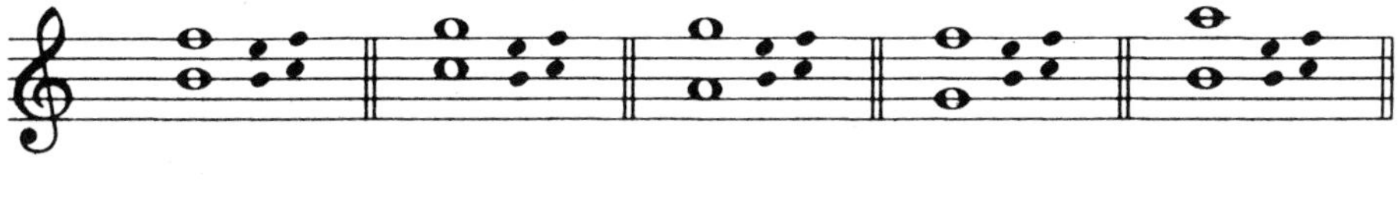

USE OF THE NATURAL DIATONIC SEMITONE

The following rules can be used to identify natural intervals:

> **Seconds.** If the 2nd is not a natural diatonic semitone, it is major. If the 2nd is a semitone, it is minor.

M2   M2   m2   M2   M2   M2   m2

Thirds. If the 3rd does not contain a natural diatonic semitone, it is major. If it does contain the semitone, it is minor.

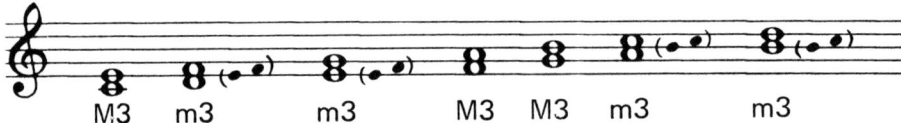

Fourths. If the 4th contains a natural diatonic semitone, it is perfect. If it does not contain the semitone, it is augmented.

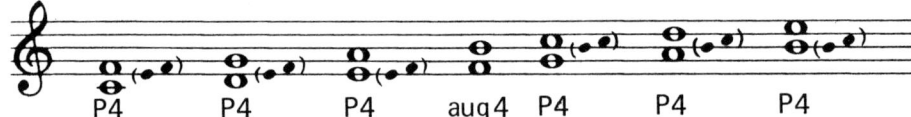

Notice that there is only one 4th which contains **no** natural diatonic semitones. That 4th is F–B. The rule can be restated thus: all natural diatonic 4ths are perfect **except** F–B, which is augmented.

Fifths. If the 5th contains one natural diatonic semitone, it is perfect. If it contains two natural diatonic semitones, it is diminished.

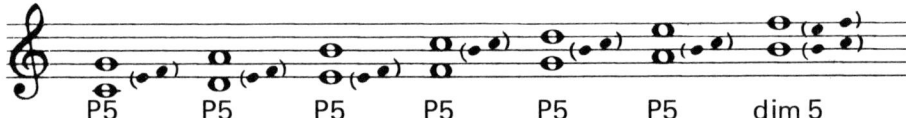

Notice that there is only one 5th which contains two natural diatonic semitones. That 5th is B–F. The rule can be restated thus: all natural diatonic 5ths are perfect **except** B–F, which is diminished. Notice also that B–F is the inversion of F–B.

Sixths. If the 6th contains one natural diatonic semitone, it is major. If it contains two natural diatonic semitones, it is minor.

Sevenths. If the 7th contains one natural diatonic semitone, it is major. If it contains two natural diatonic semitones, it is minor. (The same rule as for 6ths.)

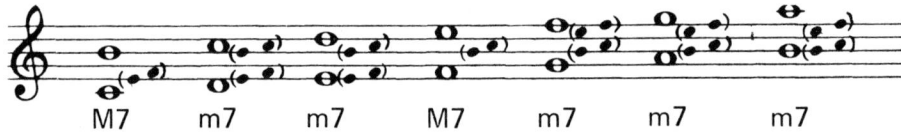

The rules above apply to all natural intervals; that is, all intervals without sharps or flats. All possible natural intervals (except for octave duplication) are shown above.

5

Using the rules and diagrams above as a reference, answer the following questions:

1. A natural 2nd is minor if _____
   _____.

2. D–E is a _____ 2nd.

3. If a natural 3rd does not contain one of the natural diatonic semitones, it is _____.

4. The interval A–C is a _____ 3rd.

5. There is only one natural augmented 4th. It is _____ – _____.

6. The interval D–G is a _____ 4th.

7. The interval B–F is a _____ 5th.

8. The only natural dim5 is F–B. It is diminished because it contains _____ natural diatonic semitones.

9. The interval D–A is a _____ 5th.

10. The interval F–D is a _____ 6th.

11. The interval E–C is a _____ 6th.

12. The interval A–F is a _____ 6th.

13. The interval C–B is a M7 because it contains _____ natural diatonic semitones.

14. The interval G–F is a _____ 7th.

15. The interval F–E is a _____ 7th.

6

Write in the natural diatonic semitones contained in each interval. If an interval does not contain a natural diatonic semitone, **do not** write anything on the staff. Name each interval according to the rules above.

Example

    a. Interval   b. Write in diatonic   c. Name the interval
                                         semitones it contains

                                                                                          M7

ADDING ACCIDENTALS

If you know the quality of the natural intervals, you can identify complex intervals by relating them to their basic natural spellings. Follow this line of reasoning **slowly** and **carefully**, as formulated in the examples below:

1. If you raise or lower **both** notes of an interval the same distance, the quality of the interval remains the same.

   raise both notes   lower both notes

   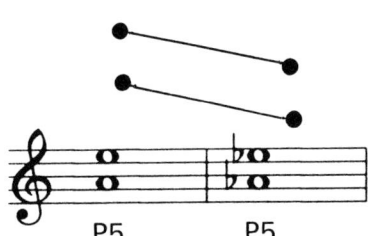

2. If you **raise** only the **higher** note of the interval, the interval **increases** in size.

   raise the higher note   raise the higher note

    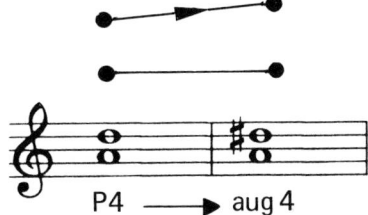

3. If you **raise** only the **lower** note of an interval, the interval **decreases** in size.

   raise the lower note   raise the lower note

4. If you **lower** only the **higher** note of an interval, the interval **decreases** in size.

   lower the higher note   lower the higher note

   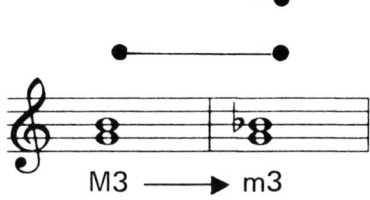 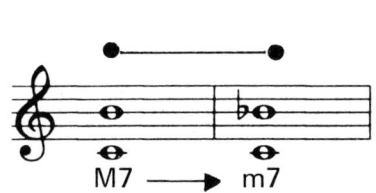

5. If you **lower** only the **lower** note of an interval, the interval **increases** in size.

7 Answer the following questions. Refer to the rules and diagrams above.

1. If you lower the higher note of an interval, it _____ in size.

2. If you lower the lower note of an interval, it _____ in size.

3. If you raise both notes of an interval the same distance, the quality of the interval _____.

4. If you lower both notes of an interval the same distance, the quality of the interval _____.

5. If you raise the lower note of an interval, the interval _____ in size.

6. If you raise the higher note of an interval, the interval _____ in size.

8 Review the following rules:

1. If a **major** interval is increased a half step in size, it becomes **augmented**. If it is decreased a half step in size, it becomes **minor**.
2. If a **minor** interval is increased a half step in size, it becomes **major**. If it is decreased a half step in size, it becomes **diminished**.
3. If a **perfect** interval is increased a half step in size, it becomes **augmented**. If it is decreased a half step in size, it becomes **diminished**.

9 Cover the accidentals in the following intervals with your finger. First, pretend each note is without accidentals, and think of the name of the interval. Then, lift your finger and name the interval by determining whether it has increased or decreased in size or remained the same. Refer to the previous exercises, if necessary.

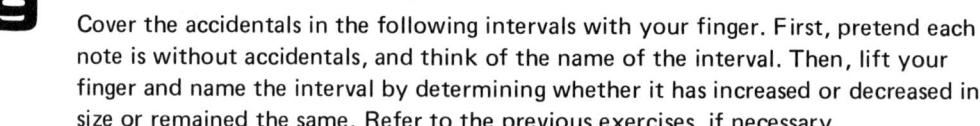

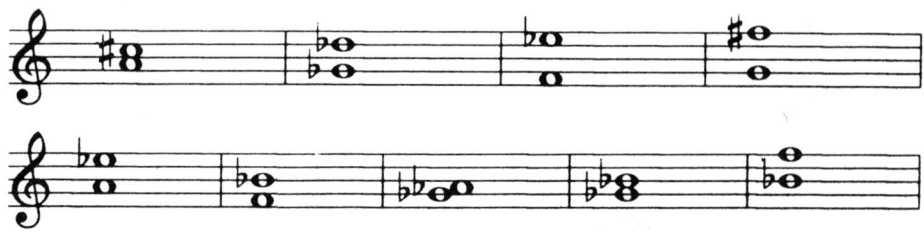

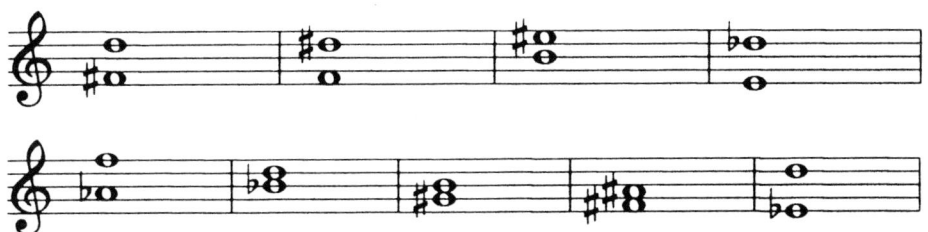

SINGING INTERVALS IN FAMILIAR SONGS

You should be able to sing intervals both up and down. This will help you recognize them by ear. Familiar songs can be an aid in singing and hearing intervals. If part of a song you know uses a specific interval, that part can be used to help you sing and hear that interval. For example: the song *Maria* from *West Side Story* begins with an aug 4; *My Bonnie Lies Over the Ocean*, with a M6; *Michael, Row the Boat Ashore*, with a M3. A list of songs, each with its opening interval, appears below. You and your teacher can add others to it, as necessary.

FAMILIAR SONGS AND PIECES FOR AID IN SINGING INTERVALS

m2 *Drink to Me Only with Thine Eyes*
    Ode to Joy
    Mame
    Something (in the Way She Moves)
    Let There Be Peace on Earth (Let It Begin with Me)

M2 *Frère Jacques*
    Mary Had a Little Lamb
    Yesterday
    People (Who Need People)

m3 *The Star Spangled Banner*
    America the Beautiful
    Lullaby, by Brahms
    Greensleeves
    This Old Man

M3 *Michael, Row the Boat Ashore*
    Fifth Symphony, by Beethoven (beginning)
    Shoo Fly
    Day by Day (from *Godspell*)

P4 *Down in the Valley*
    Taps
    Tonight (from *West Side Story*)

aug 4/dim 5 *Maria* (from *West Side Story*)

P5 *Scarborough Fair*
    Georgy Girl
    Moon River
    Twinkle, Twinkle, Little Star

m6 *Go Down, Moses*
    Love Story (Where Do I Begin)
    Waltz in C-Sharp Minor, by Chopin

M6 *Hush, Little Baby*
    My Way
    My Bonnie Lies Over the Ocean

m7 *Somewhere* (from *West Side Story*)
    Close to You (1st and 3rd pitches)

M7 *Bali Hai* (1st and 3rd pitches)
    Misty (the word "helpless")

8ve *Bali Hai*
     Somewhere Over the Rainbow

THE PENTATONIC SCALE

While singing the intervals of the major scale, you may have noticed that certain combinations are more difficult than others. These difficult melodic patterns often include scale degrees 4 and 7. For example, compare the relative difficulty of these patterns by singing them: 1-3-2 with 1-4-2, and 6-5-3 with 7-4-3. One scale that avoids these difficulties is a scale of five notes, called the *pentatonic scale*, whose structure corresponds to that of the major scale, **without** scale degrees 4 and 7.

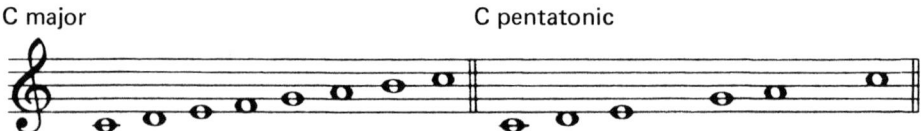

10 Starting on each pitch, write a major scale and its related pentatonic scale. Use a key signature for the major scale, but include accidentals in parentheses. Do not use a key signature for the pentatonic scale.

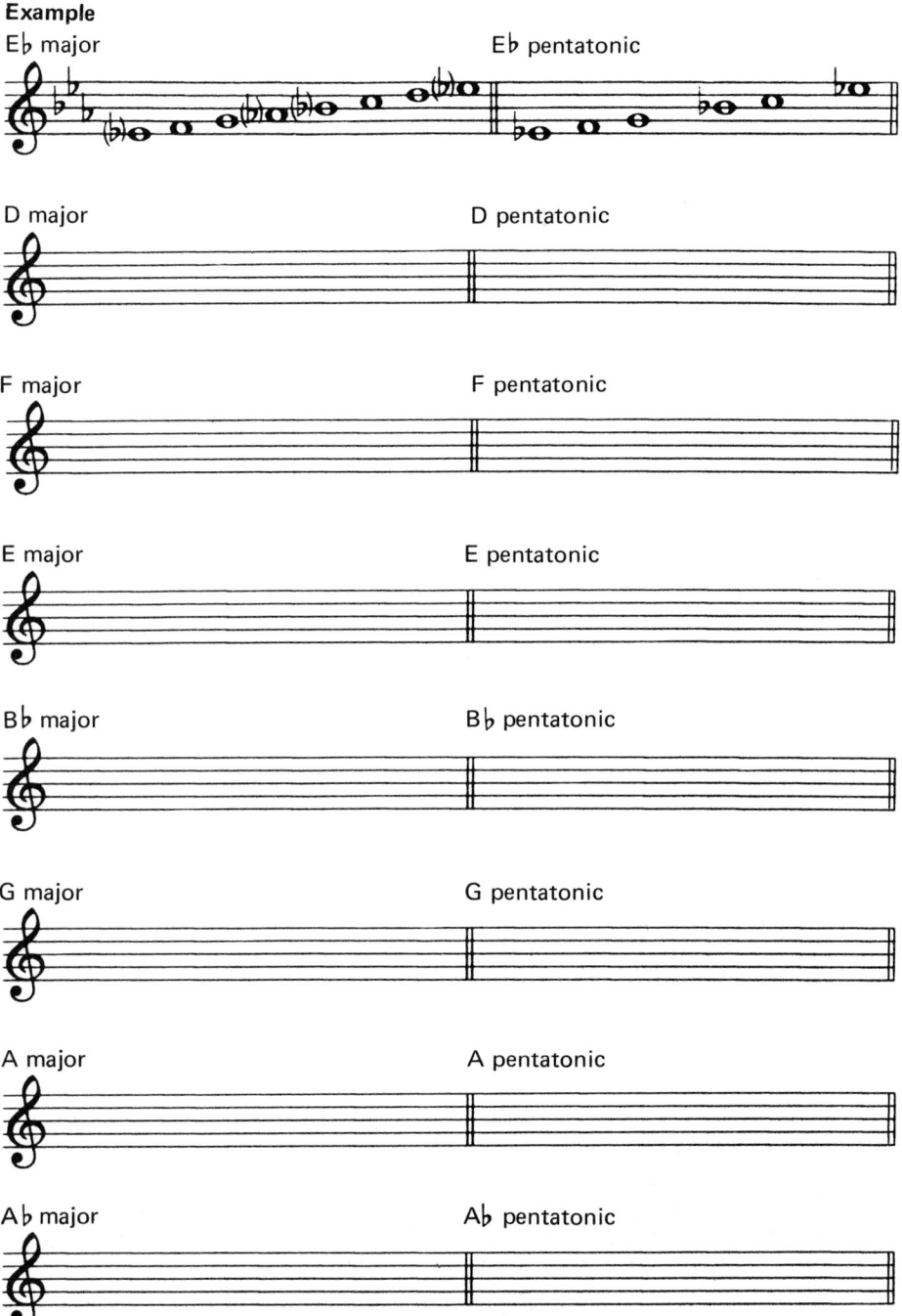

SINGING THE PENTATONIC SCALE

Sing the pentatonic scale with the corresponding numbers or syllables from the major scale.

11 Sing these songs, which use the pentatonic scale. First write syllables or numbers below the notes.

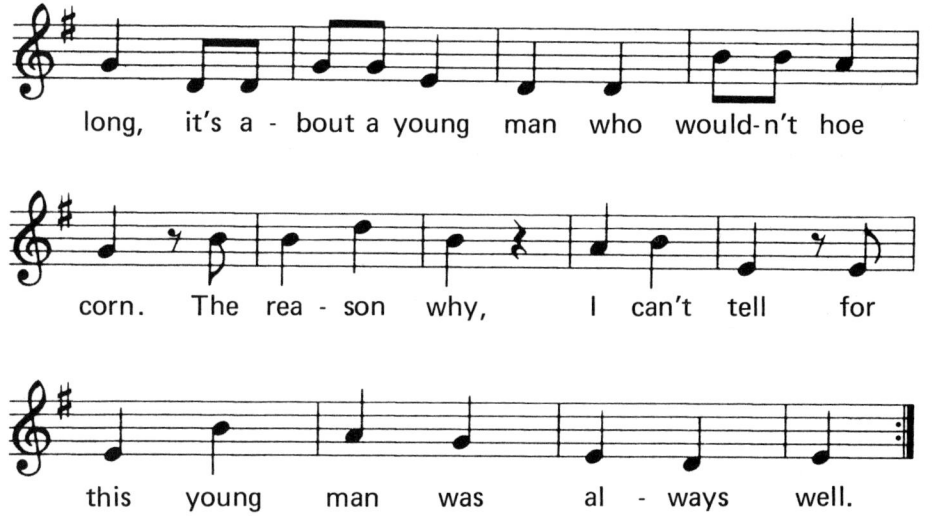

COMPOSING MELODIES

Your knowledge of singing both major and pentatonic melodies can help you start to compose. Follow these steps, starting with a simple rhythm, then adding pitches. As you gain more facility, the steps may be eliminated as rhythm and pitch become a simultaneous flow.

Compose a simple rhythm:

Sing and write scale degrees:

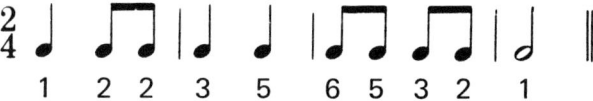

1 2 2 3 5 6 5 3 2 1

Notate rhythm and pitch:

12 Compose melodies, using the major and pentatonic scales. Use key signatures.

SUGGESTED ACTIVITIES

1. Sing these major-scale patterns:
   1-2-3 2-3-4 3-4-5 4-5-6 5-6-7 6-7-1 7-1-2 1
   1-3-2 2-4-3 3-5-4 4-6-5 5-7-6 6-1-7 7-2-1
   1-5-3-4-2 2-6-4-5-3 3-7-5-6-4 4-1-6-7-5 1
   1-3-4-2 2-4-5-3 3-5-6-4 4-6-7-5 1

2. Sing *The Riddle Song* (SB 6).

3. Sing the intervals in **6** (p. 91) using the scale degrees of C major.

4. Choose a poem and compose a melody for the words. First write a rhythm that fits the meter of the poem. Then add pitch, using scale degrees from the major or pentatonic scale. Notate in the key of D.

TERMS AND CONCEPTS

Explain in your own words:

   natural diatonic semitone

   rules for identifying natural intervals

   adding accidentals to natural intervals

Contrast these terms or concepts:

   natural diatonic semitone/diatonic semitone (Chapter 3)

   raise the lower note of an interval/raise the higher note of an interval

   lower the lower note of an interval/lower the higher note of an interval

   major scale/pentatonic scale

CHAPTER 8

MINOR SCALES

Play *The Wraggle Taggle Gypsies, O!* (SB 16) and *The Welcome Song* (SB 39), in order to hear the sound of the minor scale, which is widely used in Western music. Its basic form is the *natural minor scale*; its design can be observed on the white keys from A to A. Notice between which scale degrees the half steps occur.

1 Play the A natural minor scale.

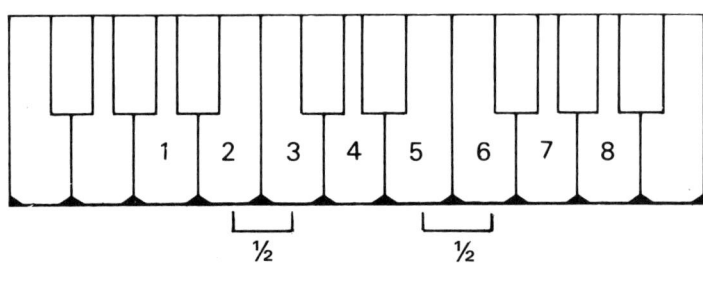

In the natural minor scale, there are half steps between 2–3 and between 5–6; the others are all whole steps. Compare this half step–whole step pattern with that of the major scale:

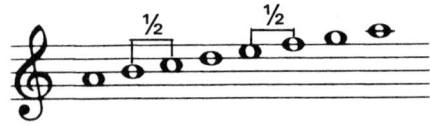

	1	2	3	4	5	6	7	8
Major scale	1	2	3	4	5	6	7	8
			½				½	
Natural minor scale	1	2	3	4	5	6	7	8
		½			½			

We can see that the major scale and the natural minor scale are both made up of eight scale degrees. Each scale has two half steps and five whole steps. It is the placement of the two half steps that identifies the scale.

 Write these natural minor scales on the keyboard and staff, being careful to maintain the correct half step–whole step relationship. Review the process for forming major scales, if necessary. Bracket the half steps. Scales 1 through 3 use flats, 4 through 7 use sharps.

Example: G natural minor

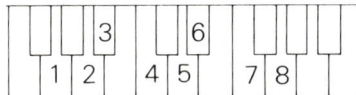

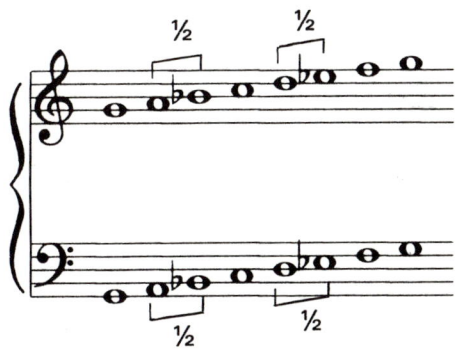

1. D natural minor

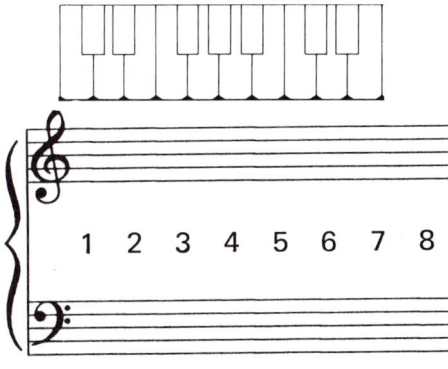

2. C natural minor

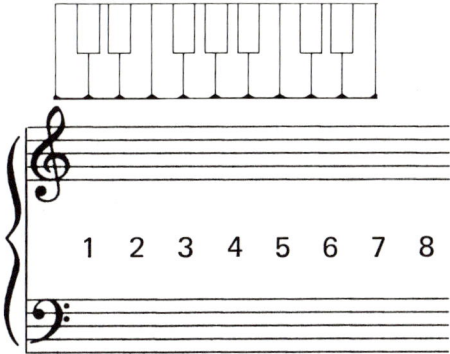

3. F natural minor

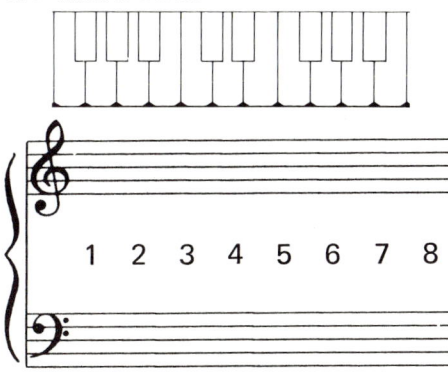

4. E minor

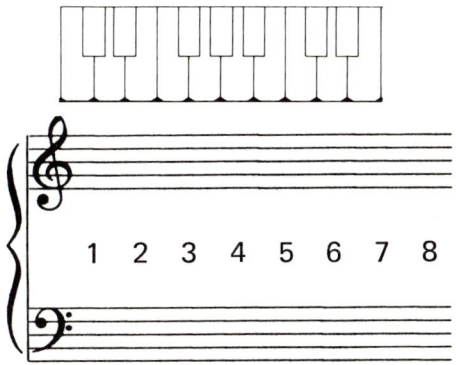

5. B minor

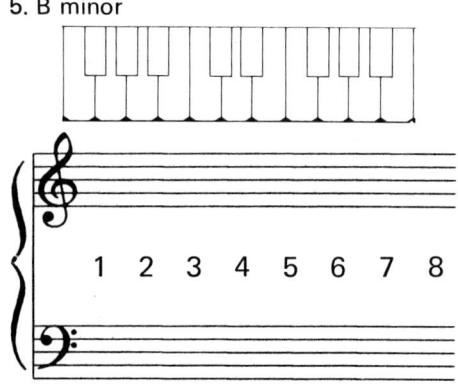

6. F# minor

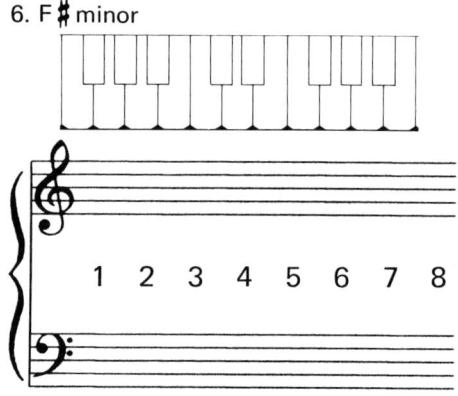

7. C# minor

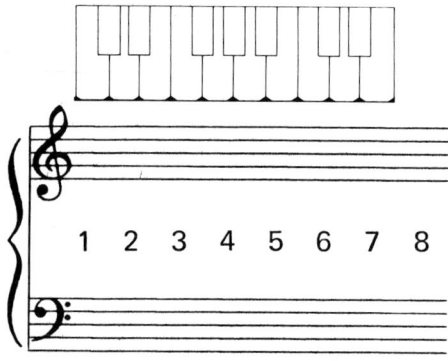

Other minor scales appear in Appendix III.

MINOR-SCALE KEY SIGNATURES
The pitches of the natural minor scale are contained within the major scale. Start a scale on the major scale's sixth degree. The result is a natural minor scale:

C-major scale

A natural minor

The two scales overlap. They contain exactly the same pitches and have exactly the same key signatures (in the case of C major and A minor, no sharps or flats). Because they are so closely related, A minor is called the *relative minor* key of C major. C major is called the *relative major* key of A minor.

3 Answer:

1. The natural minor scale is made up of the pitches of a major scale, starting on the major scale's _____ degree.

2. Because the two scales are made up of the same pitches, they have the same _____.

3. A minor is called the _____ key of C major.

4. C major is called the _____ key of A minor.

FINDING THE RELATIVE MINOR SCALES

To find the relative minor scale of a specific major scale: start on the tonic of the major scale and go down the interval of a third (within the scale). This note is the tonic of the relative minor scale. Observe the process in this example.

Example: Find the relative minor of G major.

G-major scale

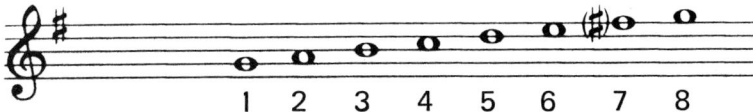

Go down a third from G (3 scale degrees).

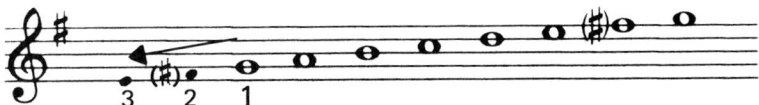

Build a scale on E using the same key signature and pitches as G major.

E natural minor

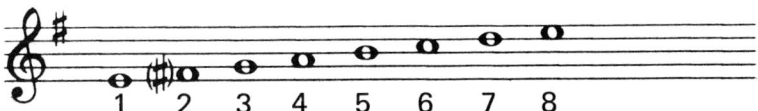

4 Name the relative minor of these major keys. Write out those relative minor scales, complete with key signature.

Example: F

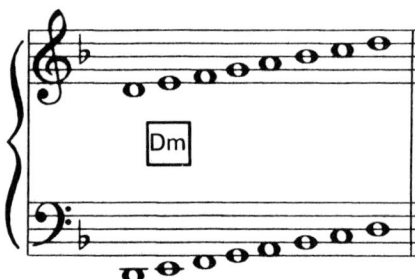

1. D   2. B♭

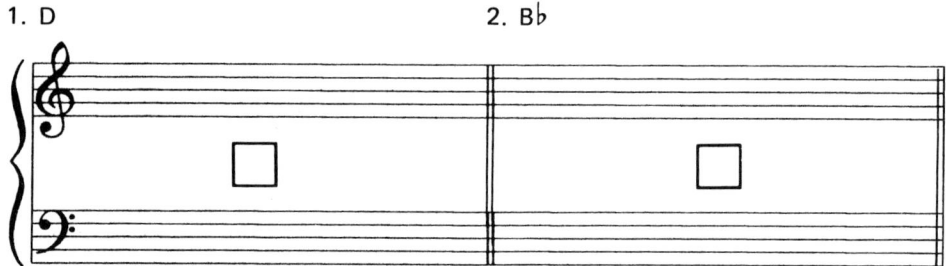

3. A   4. E♭

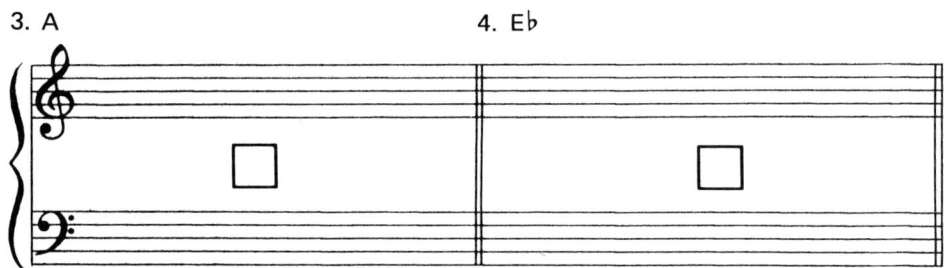

5. E   6. A♭

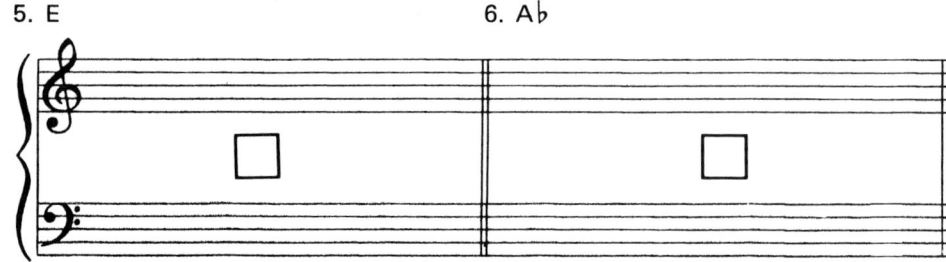

FINDING THE RELATIVE MAJOR SCALE

To find the tonic of the relative major scale, reverse the process: go up a third from the tonic of the natural minor scale.

D natural minor

F major (relative major of D minor)

5 Fill in the key signatures of these minor scales. Write the tonic and the name of the relative major key.

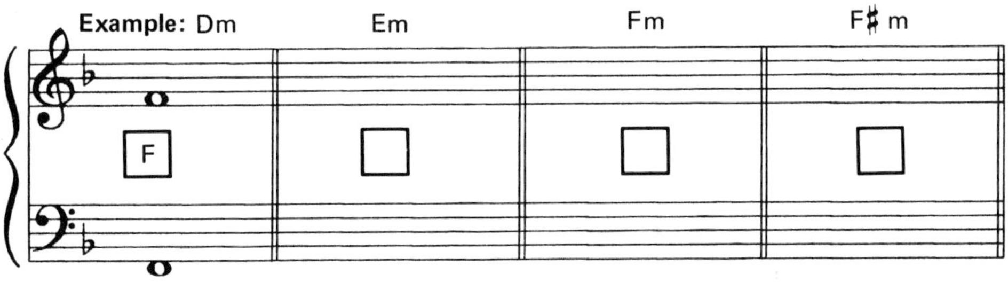

Example: Dm   Em   Fm   F♯m

F

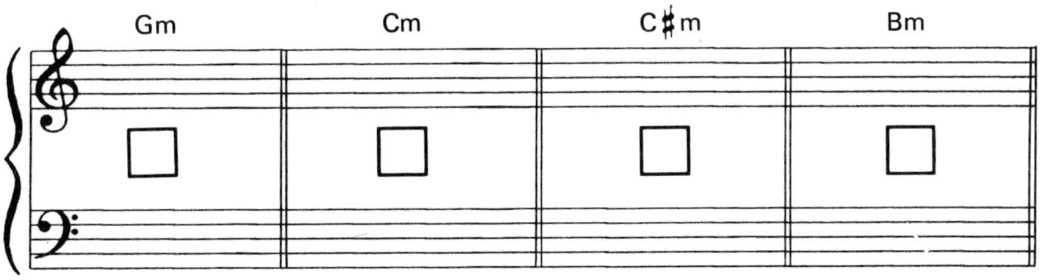

Gm   Cm   C♯m   Bm

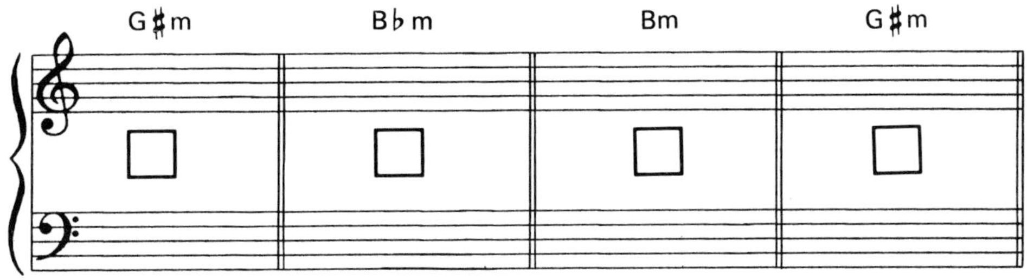

G♯m   B♭m   Bm   G♯m

6 Review the major-scale key signatures, then identify each of these key signatures, first as a major key, then as a minor key.

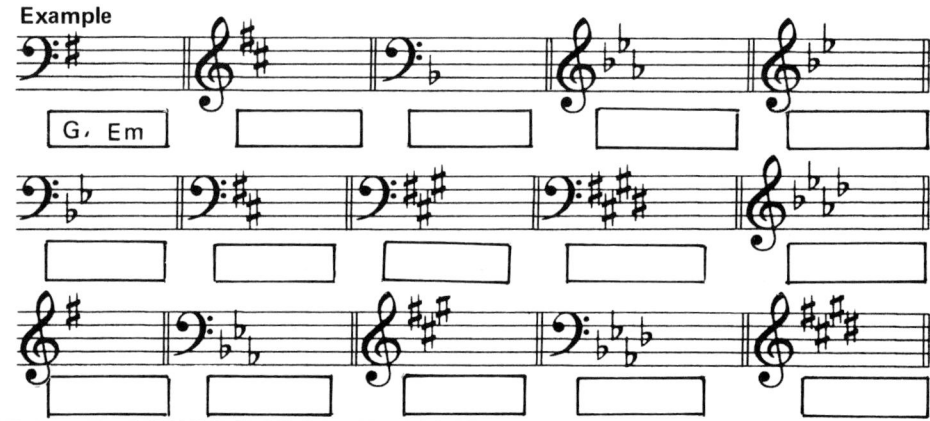

PARALLEL MINOR/PARALLEL MAJOR

Parallel major and minor scales and keys begin on the **same** note but have **different pitches and key signatures**. Remember that relative major and minor scales start on **different** notes but have the **same pitches and key signature**. The parallel minor key of C major is C minor; the parallel minor key of B♭ major is B♭ minor, etc.

7 Play

Since parallel major and minor scales have the same tonic, they are closely related in a tonal sense. A piece may shift into its parallel major or minor scale with ease, since the basic **tonality** (the key of the tonic) remains the same. Observe the change from G minor to G major in this excerpt:

Slavonic Dance, **Op. 46, No. 8**   Dvořák

SINGING THE NATURAL MINOR SCALE

The natural minor scale can be sung in two ways: with numbers and with syllables. For a further discussion of other ways to sing the minor scale, refer to Appendix V.

8 Sing the following scale with numbers or syllables:

9 Sing *The Trees They Do Grow High* (SB 1). Instead of singing the words, sing numbers, after first lightly penciling them in above each note.

10 Write in the corresponding numbers or syllables and then sing.

OTHER MINOR-SCALE FORMS

Other forms of the minor scale have evolved through musical practices. One such practice was to raise the seventh degree of the natural minor scale a half step, thus creating a stronger *leading-tone* effect of 7 moving to 1. The leading tone describes the characteristic of the seventh degree of a scale when it is a half step below the tonic. In this half-step relationship, the seventh degree tends to **lead into the tonic**. This leading-tone characteristic is much stronger when the seventh degree is a half step rather than a whole step from the tonic. This can be observed in the following examples:

Fugue in C Minor (excerpt)

J. S. Bach

This musical practice of raising the seventh degree of the natural minor scale results in the *harmonic minor scale*.

11 Play:

Harmonic Minor Scale

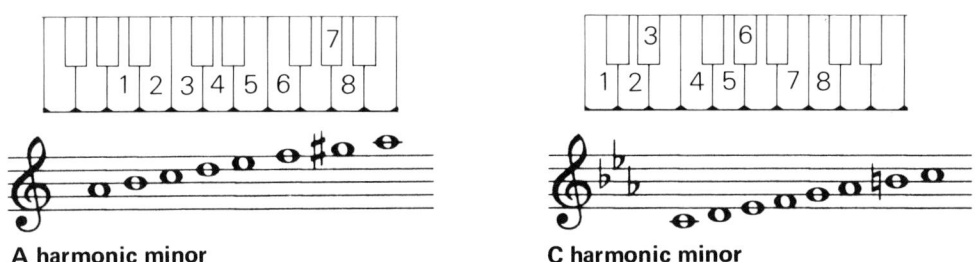

A harmonic minor   C harmonic minor

THE AUGMENTED 2nd

In the scales above, you will observe that between scale degrees 6 and 7 there is a 2nd containing three semitones. This 2nd, which is one half step larger than major, is called an *augmented 2nd*. The augmented 2nd is a unique feature of the harmonic minor scale.

12
Change each of these natural minor scales to a harmonic minor form. Notice that in the scales above, a sharp was needed for A harmonic minor, while a natural was needed for C harmonic minor. Both accidentals perform the same function: raising the seventh degree one half step.

13 Write these harmonic minor scales on the keyboard and, using key signatures, on the staff. If necessary, review natural minor scales and key signatures.

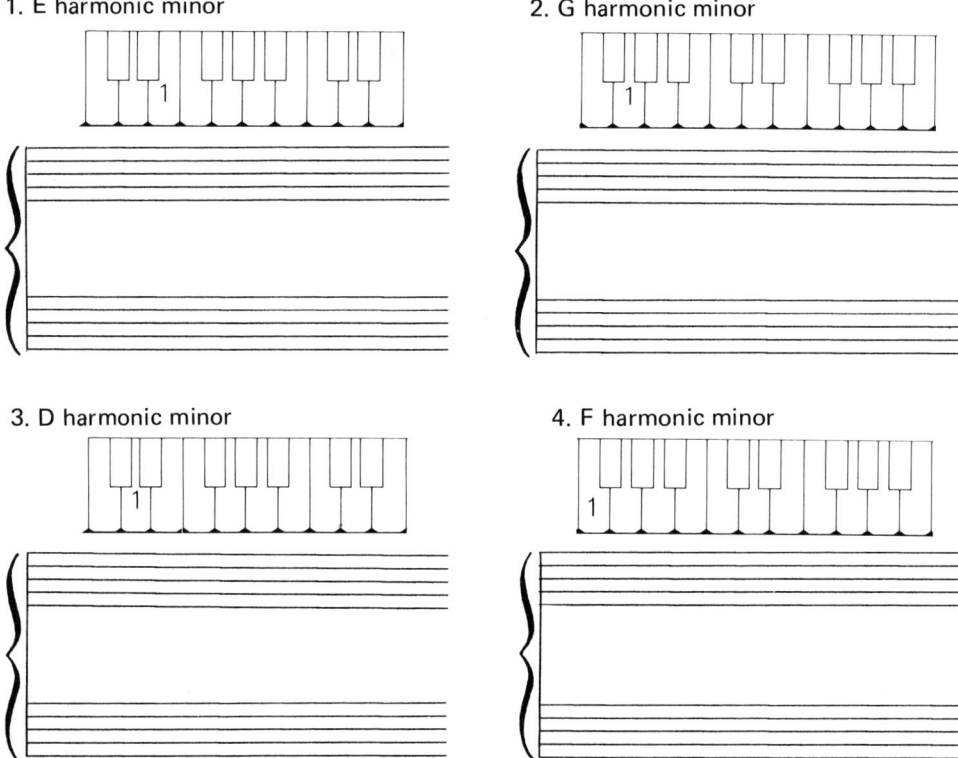

1. E harmonic minor
2. G harmonic minor
3. D harmonic minor
4. F harmonic minor

Other harmonic minor forms are in Appendix III.

THE MELODIC MINOR SCALE

This form of the minor scale is different from the other forms in that it ascends one way and descends another. Again, comparing the new scale to the natural minor, the *melodic minor* uses a raised 6th and 7th degree going up; going down, the 6th and 7th degrees are lowered a half step, restoring them to their natural form. Like the other scales, the melodic minor form evolved from musical practice. Composers sometimes heard in their melodies that the rising 6th and 7th degrees of the scale seemed to push towards the tonic. Descending, the natural form fell towards the 5th degree. This is a generalization, and not a rule. These characteristics of the melodic minor scale may be observed in the following excerpt.

On the keyboard and staff, the melodic minor scale looks like this:

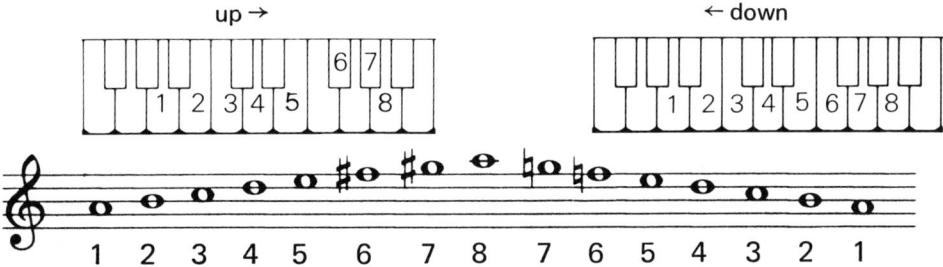

14 Write these melodic minor scales. First write in the key signature.

1. C melodic minor

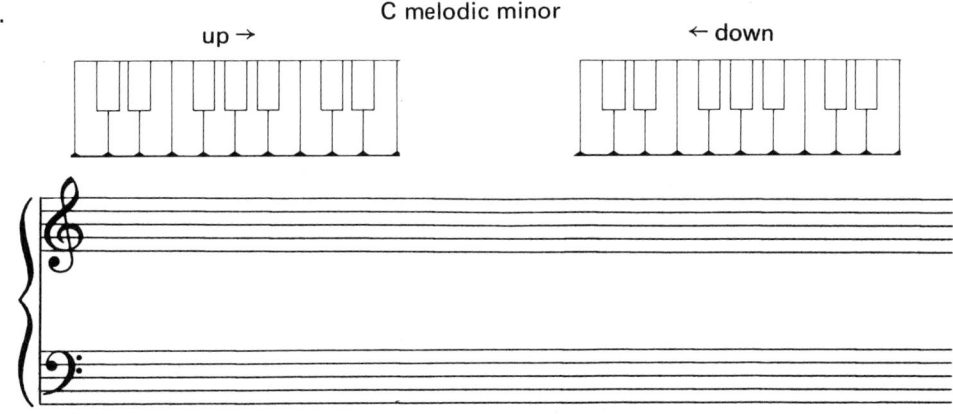

2. D melodic minor

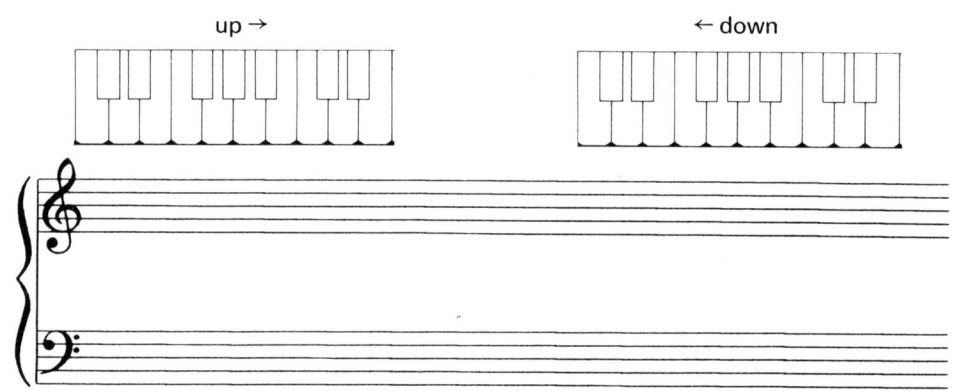

3. B melodic minor

15 Sing with numbers:

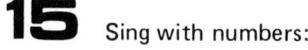

Natural

Harmonic

Melodic

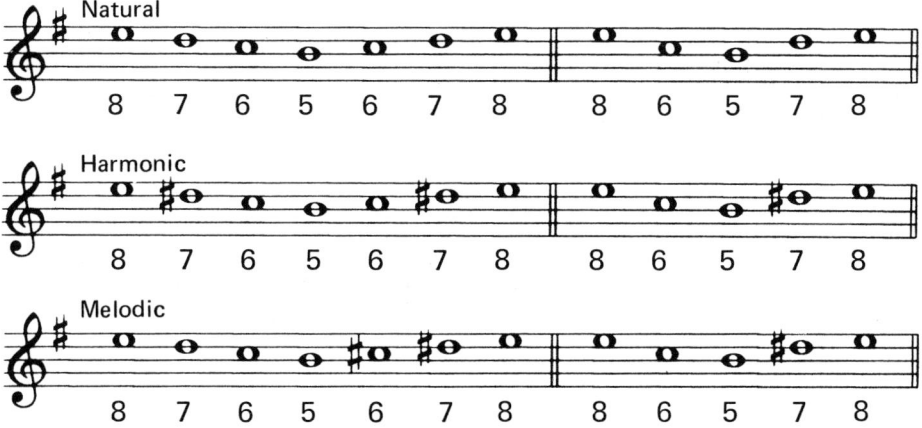

MODES

The major and minor scales studied thus far have been the basic scales of Western music from approximately the seventeenth century to the beginning of the twentieth. Before that time, the major and minor scales were only two of a larger group of diatonic scales called *modes*. The modes were scales upon which Church music and, by extension, most Western music since the time of Christ was based. *Modal music* gave way to music utilizing major and minor scales, but came back into use at the end of the nineteenth century. Like the major and minor scales, the modes are diatonic, made up of eight scale degrees, including two half steps and five whole steps. The models for the modes can be found by exclusive use of the white notes of the keyboard, but, like the major and minor scales, they can be transposed through the use of sharps and flats.

16

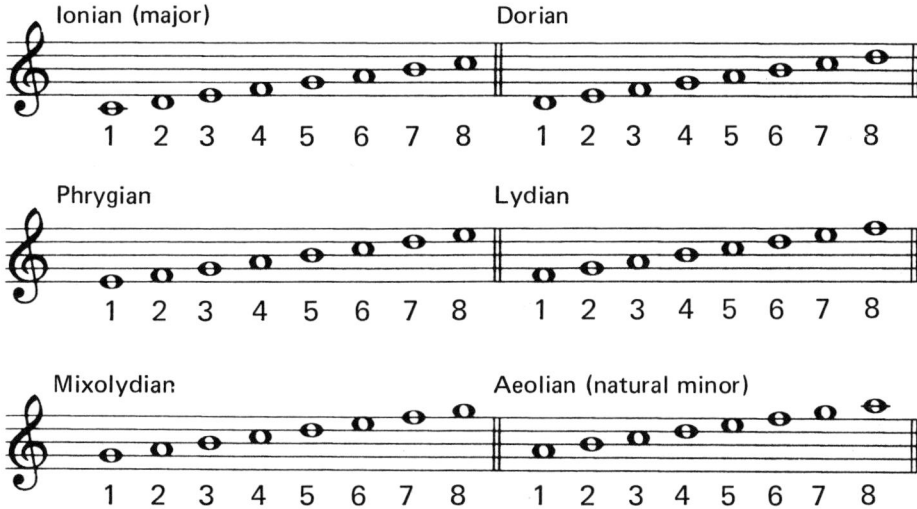

Play these modal examples:

1. Dorian — Hymn tune

2. Phrygian — Hymn tune

3. Lydian — English folk song

4. Mixolydian — Gregorian chant

Ve - ni Cre - a - tor— Spi - ri - tus, Men - tes tu - o - rum vi - si - ta: Im - ple— su - per - na— gra - ti - a, Quae— tu cre - a - sti——— pec - to - ra.

MODE MIXTURE

Many songs are a mixture of various scales and modes. *Greensleeves* (SB 3, S 5, B 1), for example, is a combination of the natural minor, the melodic minor, and the Dorian mode, all utilizing A as the tonic. This mixture of scales and modes gives us another insight into tonality. In the following example, although various modes are present, the rhythm and choice of scale degrees focus on one pitch as a tonic.

17 Play and sing:

Remember, O Thou Man

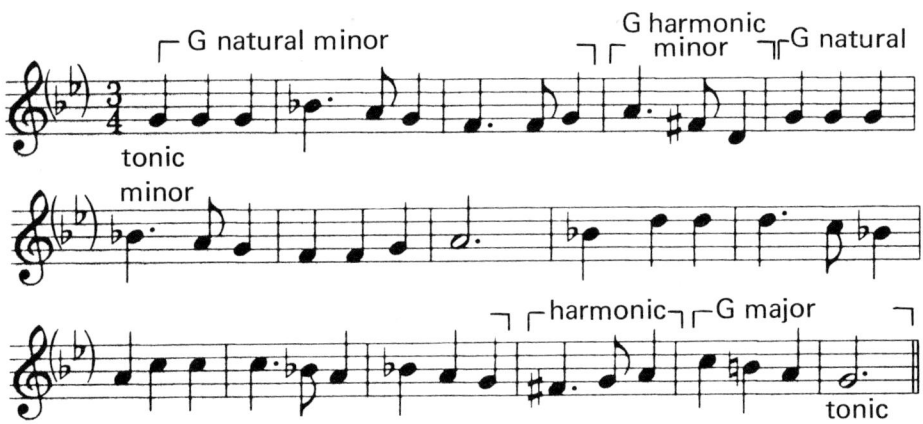

In the example above, we hear G as the tonic because:
1. G begins and ends the piece.
2. In the first two phrases, G is repeated many times.
3. All the pitches of the melody are scale patterns from one of several scales and modes which start on G.

To illustrate mode mixture further, we will sing familiar songs in different scales and modes. Notice that the tonic is still strong, although the mode or scale has been changed.

18 Play and sing:

Frère Jacques

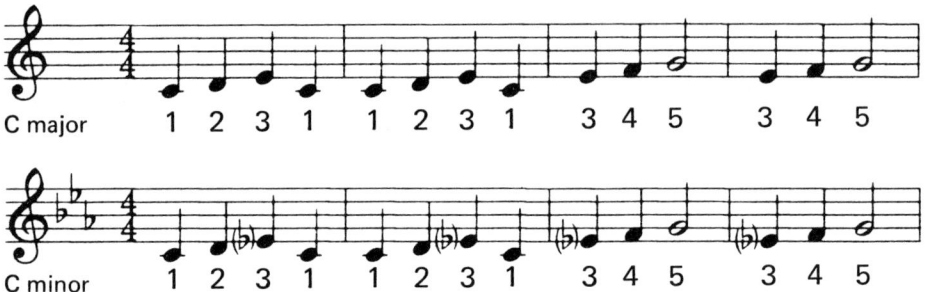

Twinkle, Twinkle, Little Star

19 Listen to *Adieu, Sweet Amarillis* (SB 41, S1, B3). This piece has a mixture of modes (or scales). In what measure is there a change of mode (scale)? _____. In which scale or mode does the piece begin? _____. In what scale or mode does the piece end? _____.

SUGGESTED ACTIVITIES

1. Play the traditional Finnish melody (SB 29). Write the word "harmonic" above measures that have a raised 7th (leading tone). Write the word "natural" above measures in which the 7th has been restored to the natural form. Can you give a musical reason for the use of both the natural and raised 7th in the melody? _____

_____

_____

_____

2. Compose a melody in one of the minor scales.
3. Sing these natural minor songs and pieces: *Dona, Dona* (SB 13), *Black, Black, Black* (SB 14), *Wayfaring Stranger* (SB 15), *The Wraggle Taggle Gypsies, O!* (SB 16).
4. Sing these minor songs and pieces that use the harmonic minor scale: *Jeune Fillette* (SB 26), *Que ne suis-je la Fougère* (SB 28), *Minuet for Lute* (SB 46), *Minuet,* by Purcell (SB 47).
5. Listen to the use of the melodic minor scale throughout the *Fugue in C Minor* (SB 51, S1, B2).
6. Compose a melody in one of the modes.
7. Transpose the modes to other pitches.

TERMS AND CONCEPTS

Explain in your own words:

    natural minor scale
    relative minor
    relative-minor key signature
    relative major
    relative-major key signature
    singing the natural minor scale
    modes

Contrast these terms or concepts:

    major scale/minor scale
    natural minor/harmonic minor
    natural minor/melodic minor
    augmented 2nd/M2
    natural minor/Dorian mode
    major scale/Mixolydian mode
    major scale/Lydian mode
    minor scale/Phrygian mode
    relative minor/parallel minor

CHAPTER 9

PART SINGING

Singing together two or more melodies (or parts, as they are commonly referred to) is called singing in *harmony.* When you *harmonize* a melody, you create another melody which can be sung along with the original one. Singing in harmony has been a natural tradition in our folk-music heritage. Parts were improvised (made up) by people for whom part singing was only a musical pastime, just as listening to records is today. A beautiful example of this type of spontaneous harmonization is *The Young Convert* (SB 42), from a New England hymnal printed in 1805. The parts were obviously not composed by a trained musician since they include certain practices traditionally forbidden to the professional composer. This hymn harmonization was the result of trial and error or "singing by ear," until a trained musician wrote down the parts as he heard them sung.

Each part is written on a separate music staff. This is the customary way of notating music in parts. Another way of indicating separate parts is by the use of stems. In the following two-part version of *The First Noel*, the higher part has stems going up and the lower part has stems going down. When the stems are attached to the same note, both parts sing the same pitch—that is, they sing *in unison.* This version begins with both parts in unison. Then the parts separate, forming intervals of 3rds and 6ths.

1 Sing in two parts. Circle all unisons and write a 6 under all 6ths.

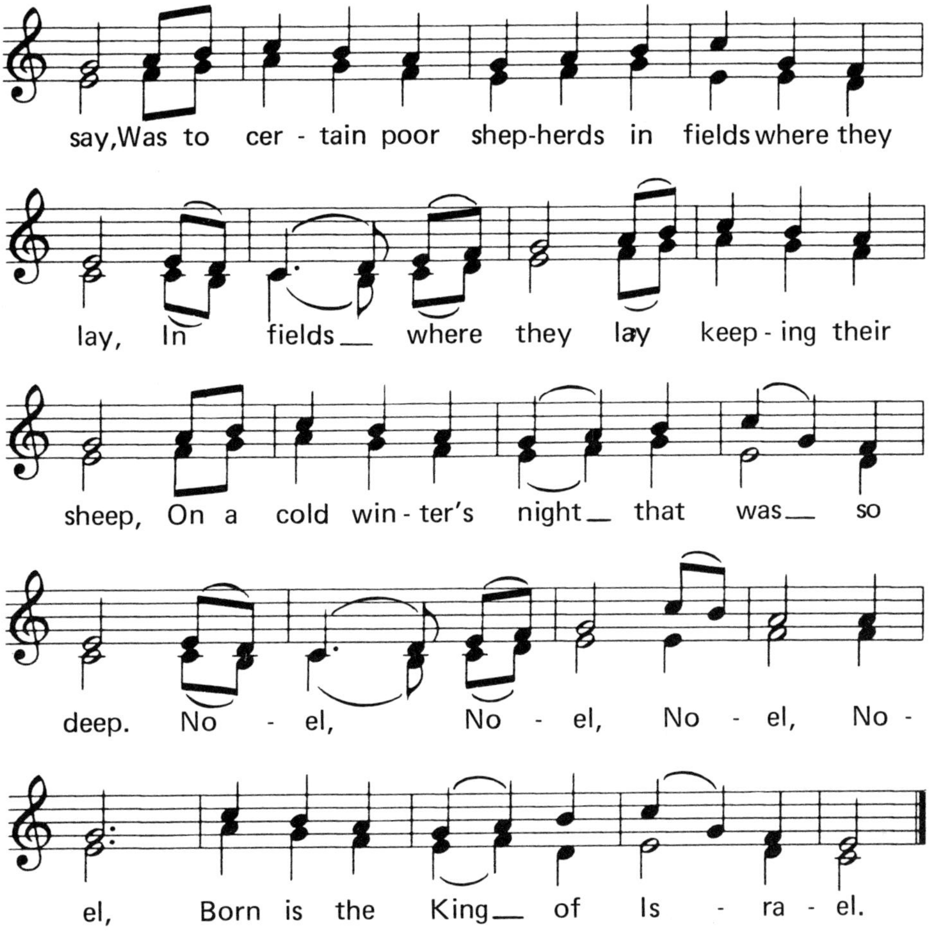

HARMONY WITH 3rds AND 6ths

2 Write a harmony for the word "Alleluia" in the following song. For the first "Alleluia," write the harmony a 3rd below the melody; for the second "Alleluia," write the harmony a 3rd above the melody.

Michael, Row the Boat Ashore

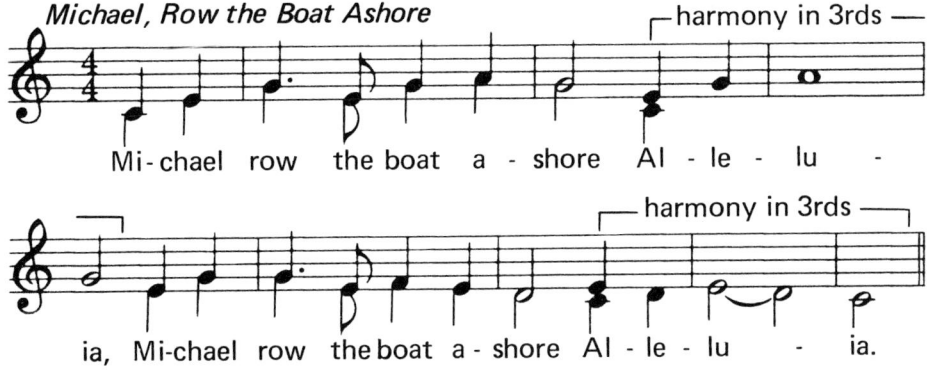

3 Write a harmony for each of these melodies using 3rds or 6ths.

CANONS AND ROUNDS

Another popular form of part singing in our musical heritage is the *canon*, or *round*. A canon is a piece in which two or more parts perform the same melody at different times. A round is the popular name for a canon which is constructed so that it can continue indefinitely as each part repeats itself. The concept of *canonic writing* can be observed in the round *Frère Jacques*. This round has four possible parts. In the example below, the numbers indicate the place where each part begins.

4 Sing in parts:

Frère Jacques

COUNTERPOINT

Canons are conceived as melody against melody. Expressed another way—line against line—we have the definition of *counterpoint*. The canon is only one example of the use of counterpoint in music. We will discuss counterpoint in more detail in the chapter on texture.

CHORDS

We have seen that the combination of two pitches forms an interval. The simultaneous sounding of three or more notes forms a *chord*. Example of chords:

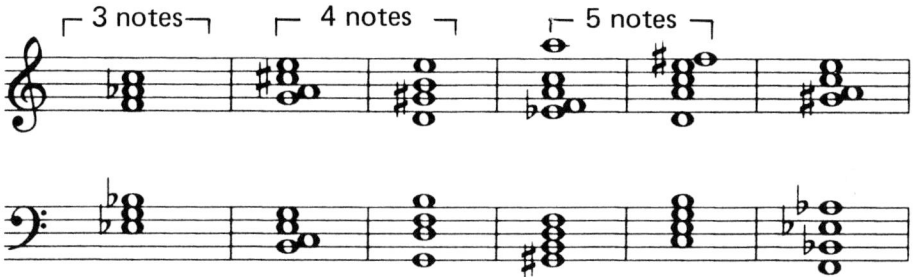

TRIADS

A *triad* is a specific type of chord. It is a three-note chord built in 3rds. Triads are the basic chord structures of our traditional system of harmony. The lowest note of a triad is called the *root*, the middle note is the *3rd*, and the highest is the *5th*. This terminology is based on the interval relationship with the root.

Observe these triads. The lowest note (the root) gives the triad its letter name.

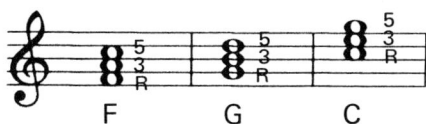

5 Build triads on each of the specified notes. Notice that if the root of a triad is a space, all the notes will be consecutive spaces. If the root is a line, all the notes will be on the lines. Label each triad with R, 3, and 5 (representing the root, 3rd, and 5th). Name the root. Use no sharps or flats.

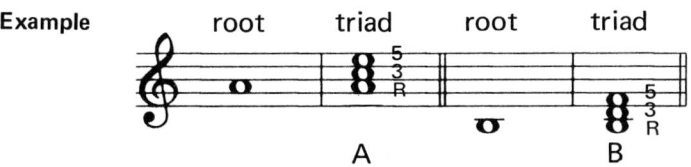

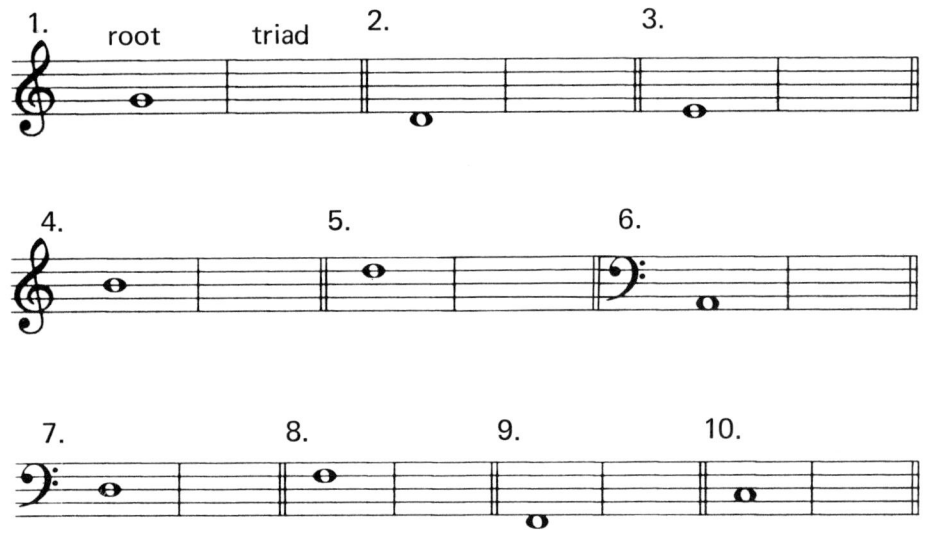

QUALITY OF TRIADS

Like intervals, triads differ in quality. The quality depends on the intervals that make up the triad. Two basic triads are the *major triad* (those containing a M3 and P5 from the root), and the *minor triad* (those containing a m3 and a P5 from the root).

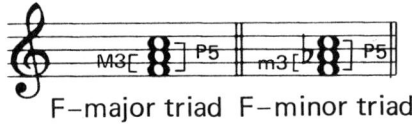

F–major triad   F–minor triad

SINGING THE TRIADS

The major and minor triads can be easily sung. Sing the first five notes of either scale. Then sing the 1st, 3rd, and 5th degree of that same scale.

6 Sing with numbers.

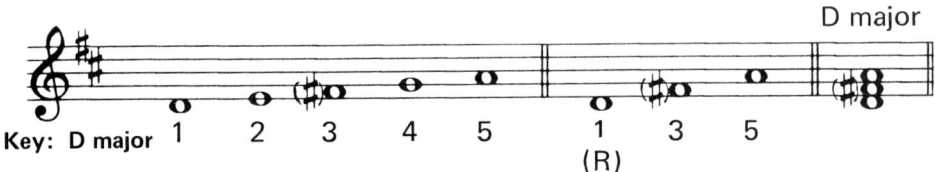

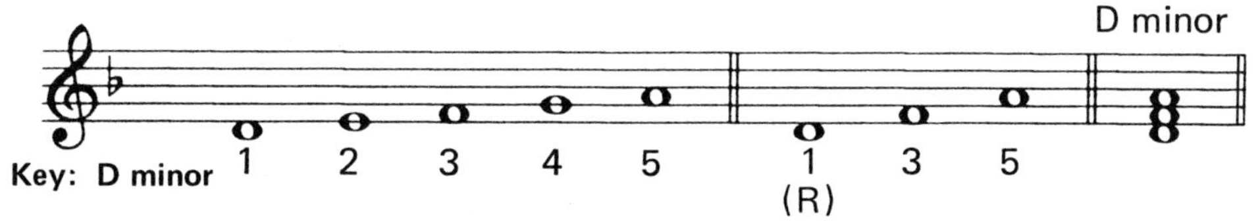

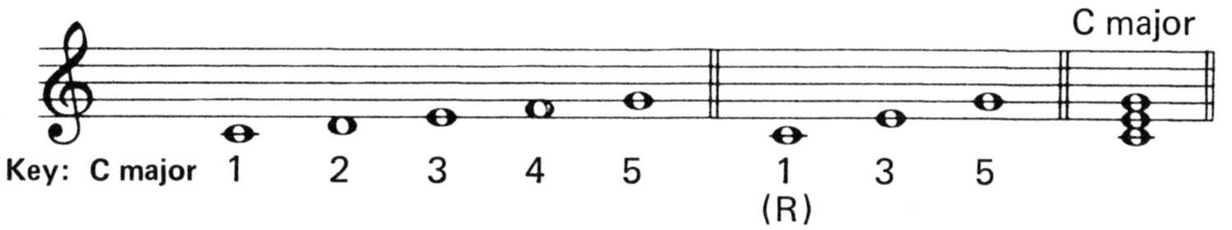

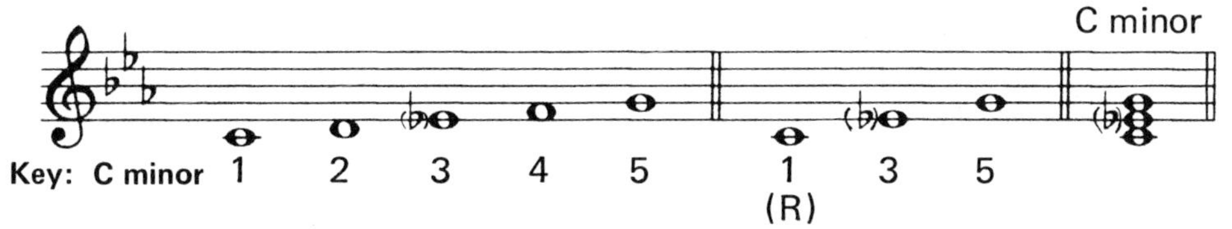

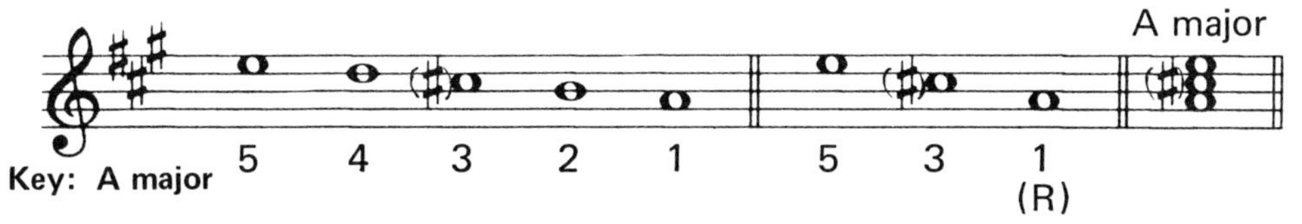

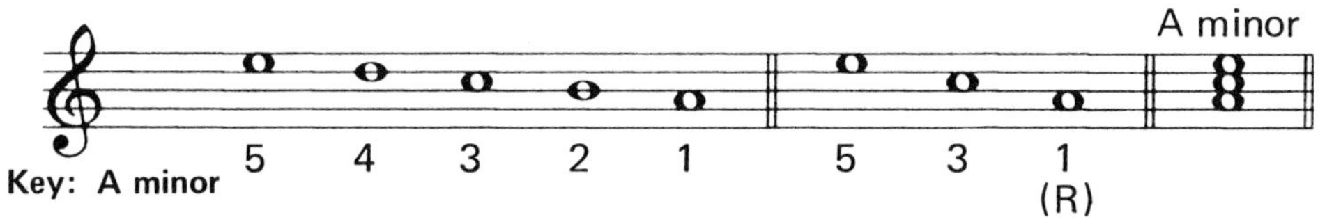

Notice that the only difference between major and minor triads is the location of the 3rd: the major triad has a major 3rd, the minor triad has a minor 3rd. Both major and minor triads have a P5 as the interval between root and 5th. Examine the major and minor triads on D with the keyboard diagram. Play them. Notice the location of the 3rd in each.

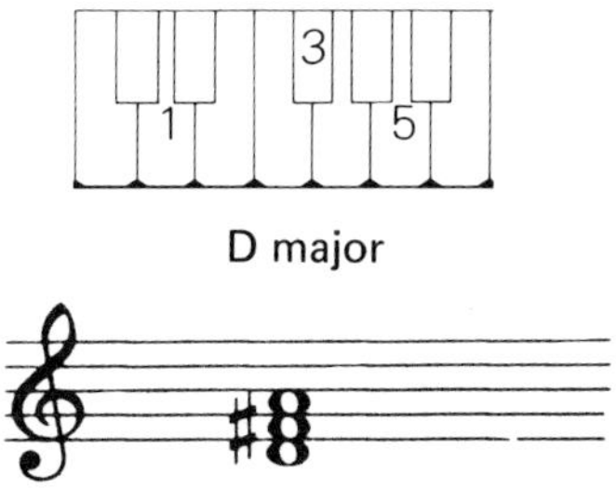

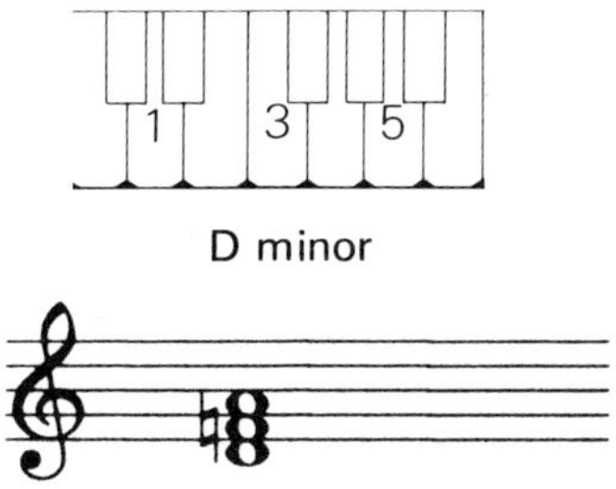

7 Change each of these major triads to a minor triad by **lowering** the 3rd one half step. This alteration can only be accomplished by adding an accidental to the 3rd of the chord or by changing the accidental already there. The letter-name spelling must remain the same (consecutive lines or consecutive spaces). Indicate the change on the keyboard diagram. Remember: to lower a natural note (white key), use a flat; to lower a sharp note, use a natural sign.

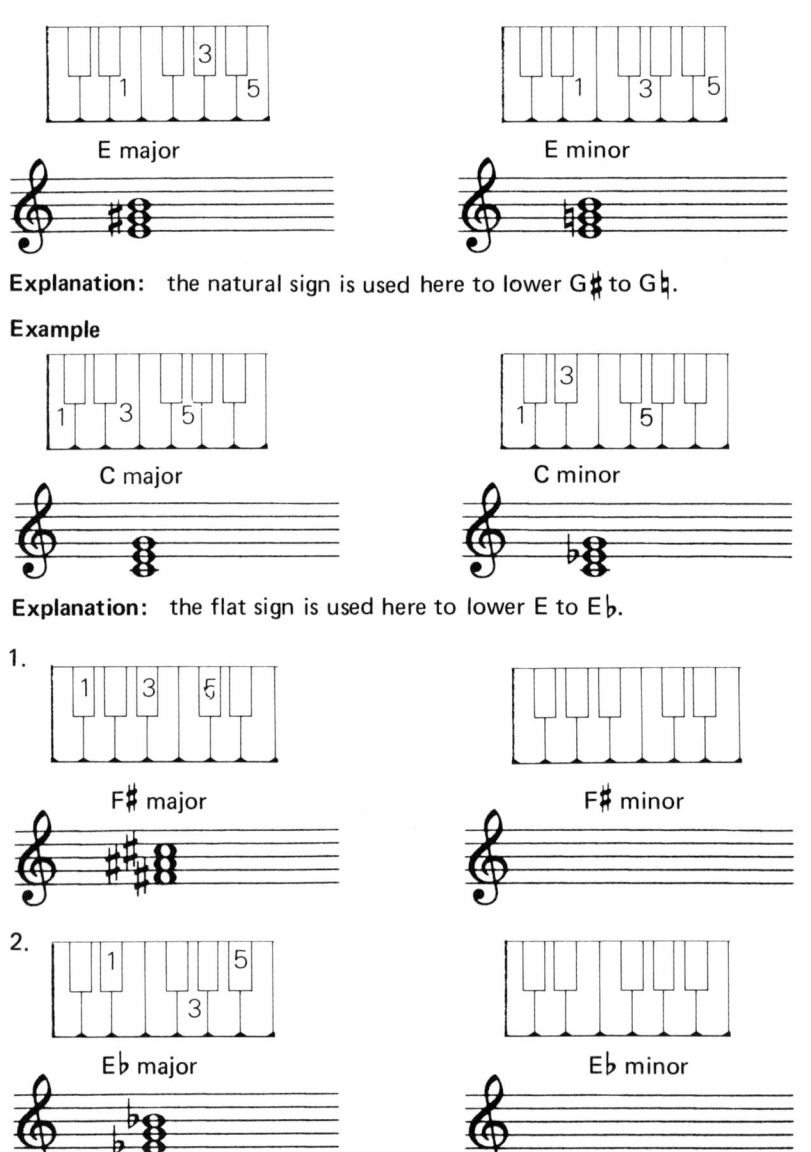

3.

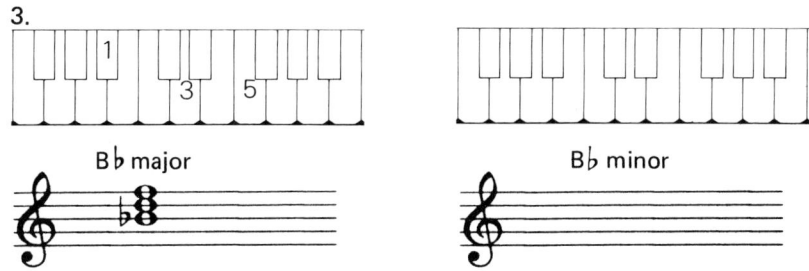

8

Change each of these minor triads to a major triad by **raising** the third one half step. To raise a natural note, use a sharp. To raise a flat note, use a natural sign.

Example

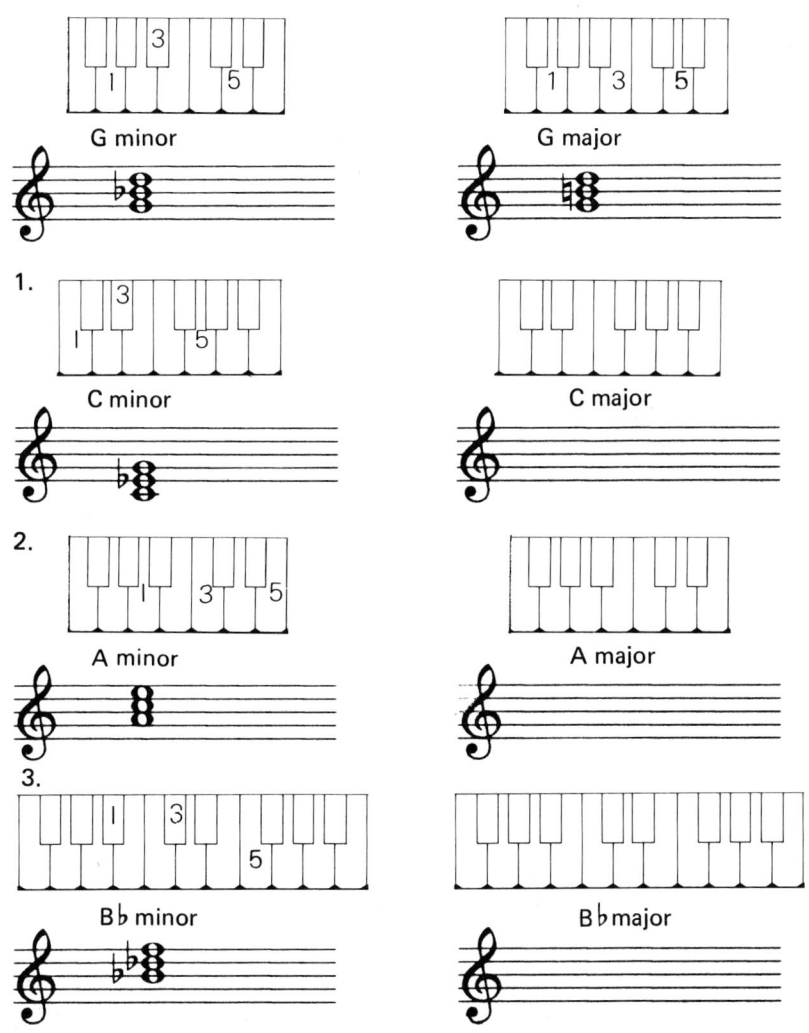

DIFFICULT TRIAD SPELLINGS

The spelling of some triads can become complicated when double sharps, double flats, and natural notes are involved. No matter how complex the accidentals, the letter-name spelling always remains the same. Thus, any triad built on a G♮, G♯, or G♭ will have the same letter-name spelling: G–B–D. The same holds true for the triads C–E–G, D–F–A, E–G–B, F–A–C, A–C–E, and B–D–F. It will be helpful to know these basic letter-name spellings when notating triads. Observe the spelling of the following triads:

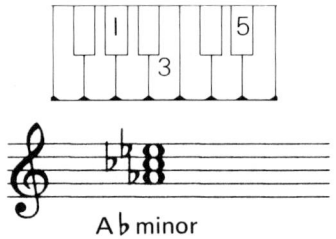

A♭ minor

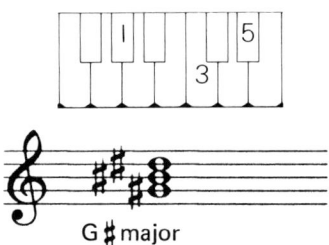

G♯ major

Notice that since the basic letter-name spelling is A–C–E, the 3rd must be spelled C♭, **not** B♮.

Notice that since the basic letter-name spelling is G–B–D, the 3rd must be spelled B♯, **not** C.

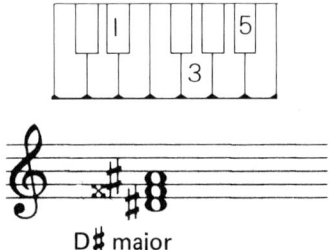

D♯ major

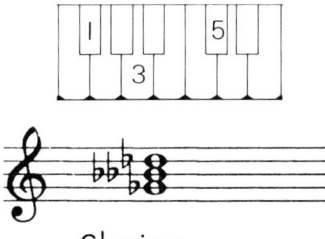

G♭ minor

Since the basic letter-name spelling is D–F–A, the 3rd must be spelled F double sharp (F𝄪), **not** G.

Since the basic letter-name spelling is G–B–D, the 3rd must be spelled B double flat (B♭♭), **not** A.

ENHARMONIC SPELLINGS: THE REASONS

Triads can often be spelled more simply by using their enharmonic equivalents. For example, E♭ major is easier to spell than D♯ major. But as we go on to study triads in relationship to keys, we shall discover that D♯ has a different musical meaning than E♭. Spelling the triad with D♯ as the root may be necessary to represent the music correctly. Another reason for using correct triadic spelling involving complex accidentals is to preserve the appearance of the 3rds and 5ths of the triad. Compare these enharmonically spelled triads. The incorrect and correct versions will sound the same if you play them on the piano, but observe the visual clarity of the correct spelling.

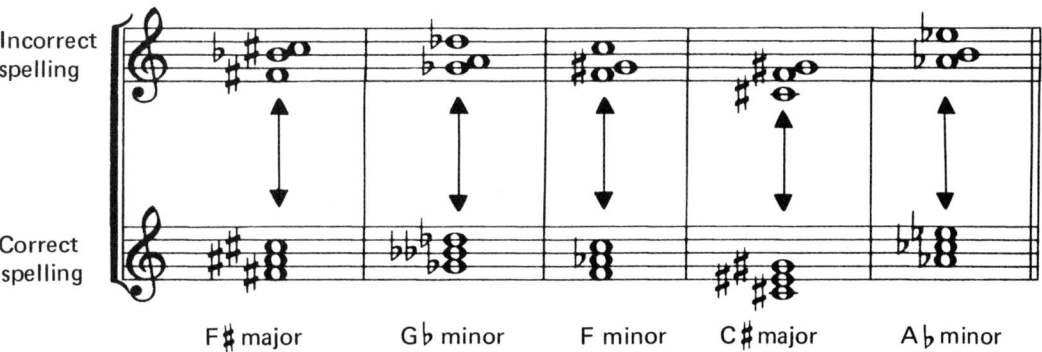

Ask yourself: Which version **looks** like a triad?

DIMINISHED AND AUGMENTED TRIADS

Two other triad qualities, in addition to major and minor, are diminished and augmented. The *diminished* triad (dim or °) is built with a m3 and a dim 5 above the root.

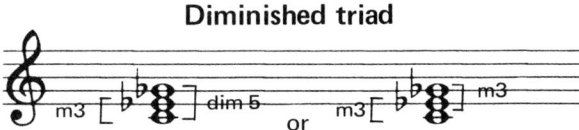

The *augmented* triad (aug) is built with a M3 and an aug 5 above the root.

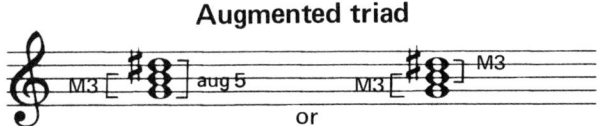

9 Write the triad whose root is given for each of the examples below.

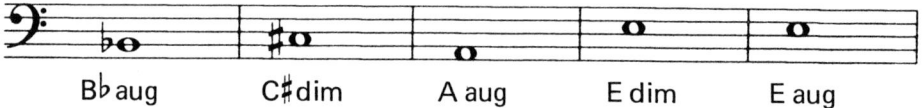

SUGGESTED ACTIVITIES

1. Sing pieces in parts from the *Scorebook,* depending upon the availability of voices.
2. Explain the need for correct spelling of triads.
3. Compose a canon or round.
4. Write the correct triad.

5. Write the correct triad.

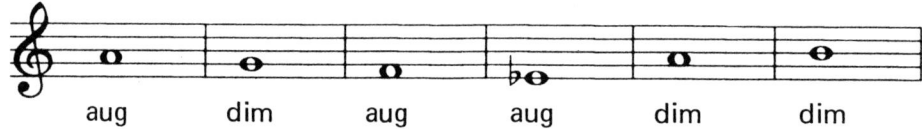

TERMS AND CONCEPTS

Explain in your own words:

      part singing

      canon

      chord

      triad

      triad quality

      correct spelling of triads

Contrast these terms or concepts:

      major triad/minor triad

      major triad/augmented triad

      minor triad/diminished triad

CHAPTER 10

WORKING WITH TRIADS

The only way to learn triads thoroughly is to work with them. In this chapter, your objectives are:

1. to learn two specific groups of triads, note perfect;
2. to understand the process by which all the other triads can be formed;
3. to hear triads as building blocks in traditional harmony; and
4. to hear the triadic background of many melodies.

For the moment, we will limit ourselves to two groups of triads that are simple and easy to remember.

We will start using a more abbreviated way of naming those triads: C major becomes C; C minor becomes Cm; D major, E♭ major, and A major become D, E♭, and A, while their minor versions become Dm, E♭m, and Am.

1   Rewrite each of these triads using their abbreviations.

A♭ major _____

D♭ minor _____

G major _____

G minor _____

B major _____

B minor _____

F major _____

F minor _____

Much of the work in this chapter is done without key signatures for two reasons: first, you learn the correct spelling of a triad more quickly if you always have to write in any required accidental; and second, you will use combinations of triads in modes other than major and minor. Think of triads as new words in a new language. In that light, the following work can be thought of as practice in conversation.

LEARNING THE TRIADS

2 Learn these two groups of triads in both clefs. Sing and play each triad. What is the pattern of accidentals in Group I? There is a different pattern in Group II. What is it?

Group I: Major and Minor Triads on G, C, and F

Group II: Major and Minor Triads on E, A, and D

You can see that the major triads of Group I have no accidentals; to form the minor triad you add a flat to the 3rd. In Group II, the major triads have a sharp on the 3rd of the chord, while the minor triads have no accidentals.

3 Name, play, and sing each triad. Do not write their names.

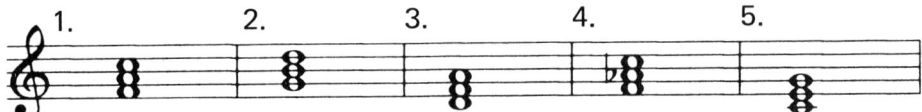

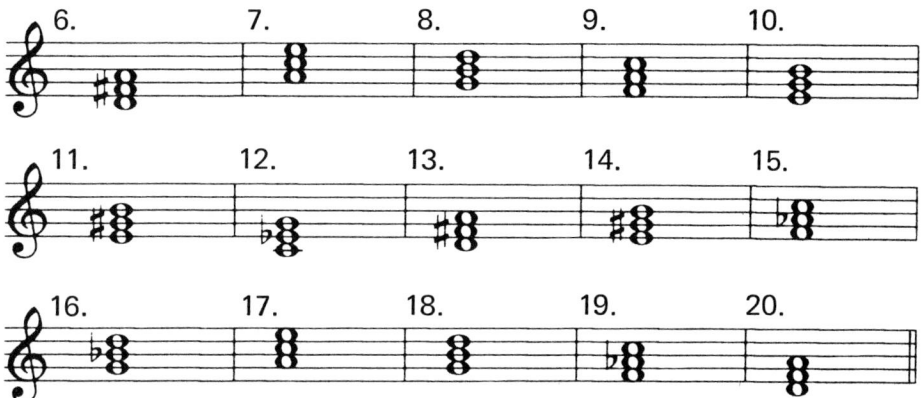

4 Write and name each of the triads above in the bass clef.

5 Describe the pattern of Group I and Group II triads.

Group I
_____
_____

Group II

 What interval separates the roots of Group I triads; of Group II triads?

VOICING

We have been studying triads in their simplest form. When they are used in actual musical compositions, the root, 3rd, or 5th may appear in different octaves and in different combinations. Such positioning of the pitches of a triad is called *voicing*. The following example shows different voicings of the Gm triad. If a pitch appears more than once, we say it is *doubled*. No matter how complicated these different chords may seem, they all use only the root, 3rd, and 5th of the Gm triad.

Basic triad

Different voicings

The following shows several voicings of a Gm triad set for four-part chorus (soprano, alto, tenor, and bass). With four parts and only three notes to work with, doubling becomes necessary.

Voicings with doublings

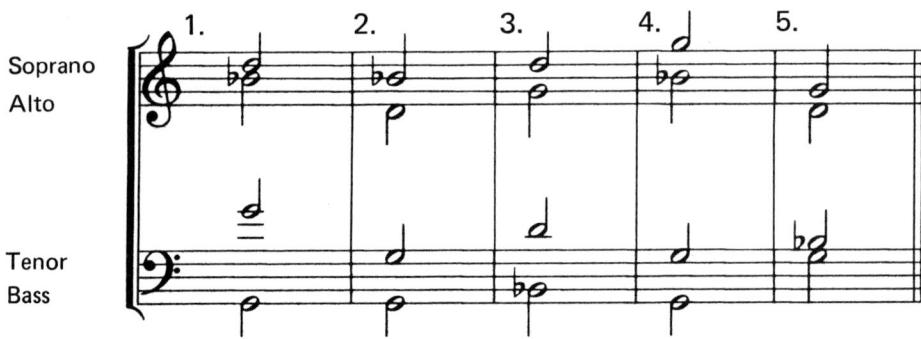

The example below left shows some of the countless possibilities of voicing a triad. Even though the Gm triad is the same, each voicing has its own characteristic sound. You can hear this by singing each one or playing it on the keyboard. Sometimes, one of the pitches of the chord is left out, as in the fifth voicing shown, which has no 5th, but three roots and one 3rd.

7 Rewrite the triad in its simplest form. Name the triad, then label each note as root (R), third (3), or fifth (5).

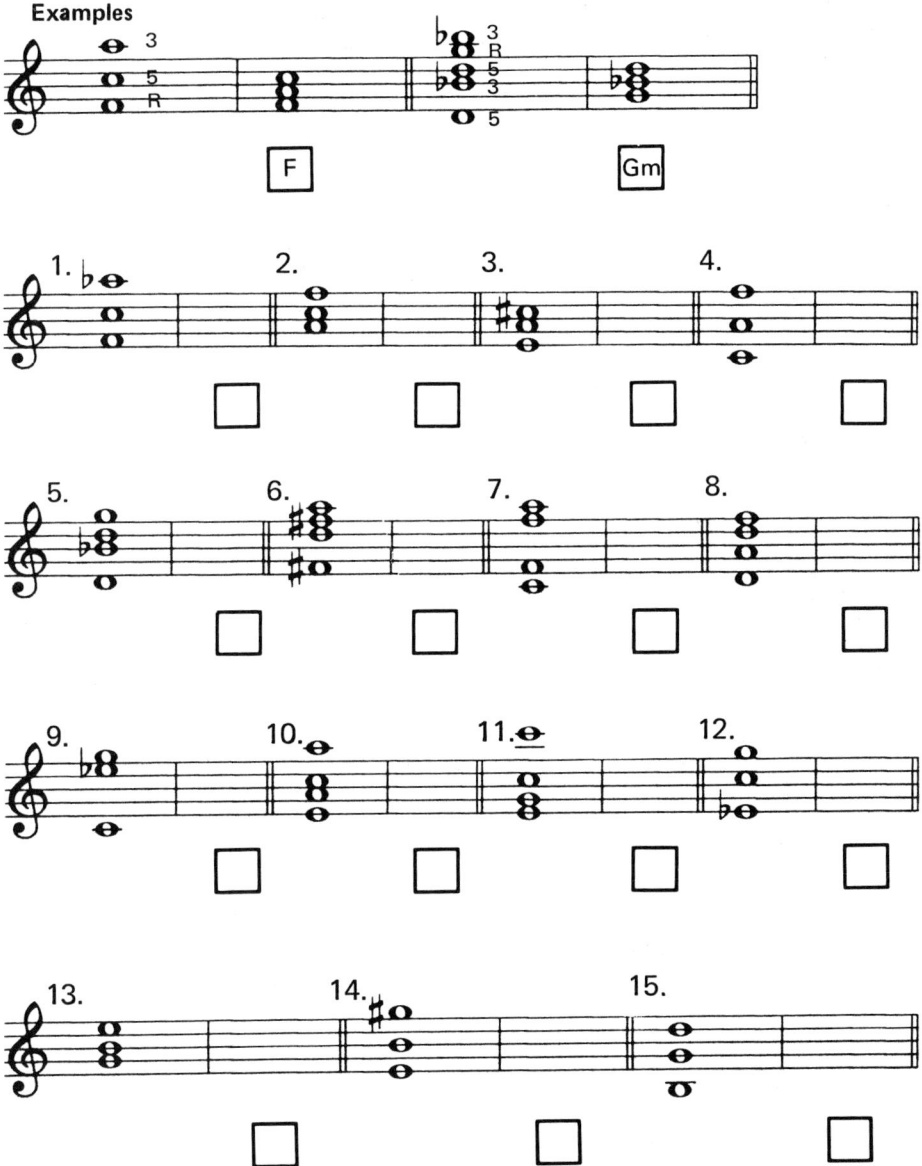

8 Name the chords and label each note as R, 3, or 5 in the following excerpt by Lassus:

INVERSIONS

When the lowest note of a triad voicing is the root, the triad is said to be in *root position*. When the lowest note of a triad voicing is **not** the root, the triad is said to be *inverted*. When the 3rd is the lowest note, the triad is in the *first inversion*; when the 5th is the lowest note, it is in the *second inversion*.

Inversions of a triad

root position   first inversion   second inversion

9 Write out the first and second inversions of these triads. Use the diagram above as a model. Name each triad.

1.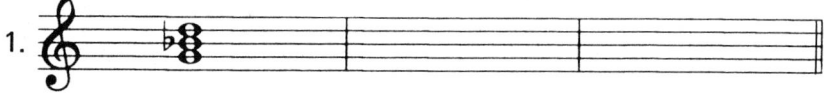

2.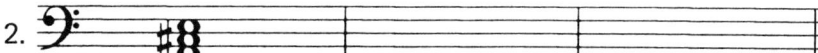

3.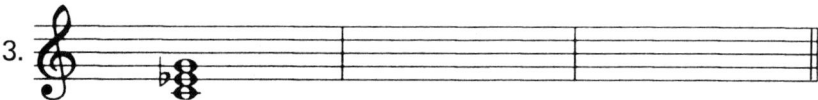

HARMONIC BACKGROUND OF A MELODY

The intervals of some parts of a melody often outline a triad. This melodic indication of a triad is one of the elements that form the *harmonic background*. The *harmonic background* is a chord pattern which fits the melody. The chord names are often written above the melody, especially in folk and popular music. Observe the triads that are outlined in these melodies:

10

Write in the triads that the melody outlines in the Mozart *Minuet* (SB 48). Name only those triads which have a box under them.

This triad outline is only one factor in determining the harmonic background. Other factors involved will be discussed in Chapter 11. For now, we shall work with triads as the basis for writing melodies of the kind we call *chord melodies*. The succession of triads (or chords) in a musical composition is called the *harmonic progression*, often shortened to just *progression*. Thus, in discussing the harmony of the first phrase of *Black, Black, Black,* one might say, "The progression of the first phrase is Dm to Am."

COMPOSING A CHORD MELODY

In each measure, use one of the three tones of the given triad. Follow the rhythm shown. These exercises do not use key signatures, but the key is indicated. Every accidental must be written!

Example: write a chord melody to this progression and rhythm.

Illustrations

11

Compose chord melodies to these progressions. Play and sing the melodies as you compose them.

If more than one chord appears in a measure, use the pitches of the first chord until the next chord starts. For example:

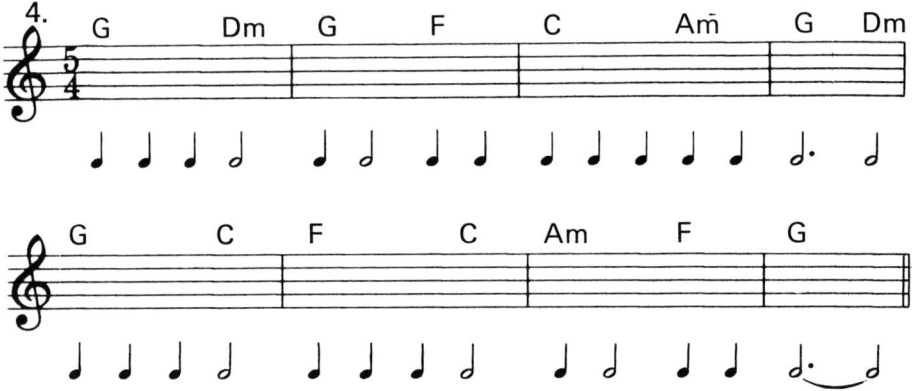

Make up your own rhythm.

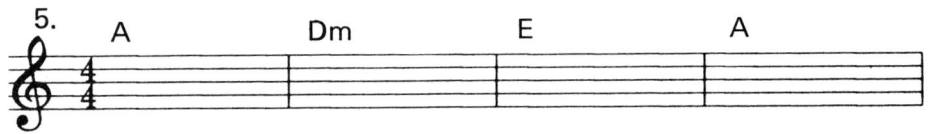

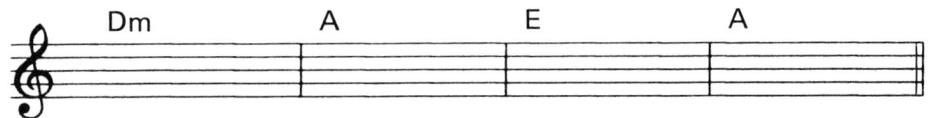

Rewrite Number 4, using the key signature of A major. You will need accidentals only in measures 2 and 5. Review key signatures if necessary.

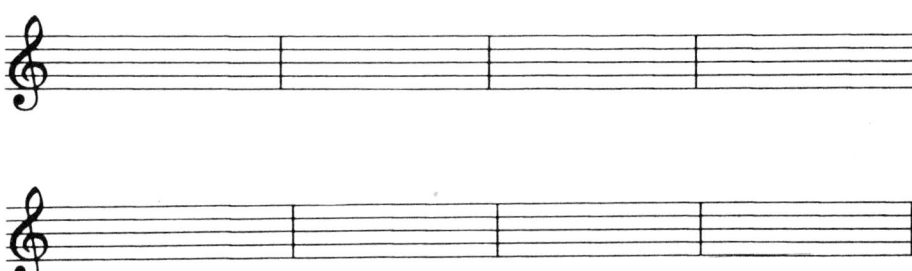

NONHARMONIC TONES

While chord melodies may exist for parts of a tune, other parts of the melody may use notes that are not from the chord background. Tones which do not fit into the chords of the harmonic background are called *nonharmonic tones*. Observe in this example how chord tones are followed by scale passages. Some of the notes of the scale passages fit the harmony, others do not. Those that do not are the nonharmonic tones.

12 Mark the nonharmonic tones with an X:

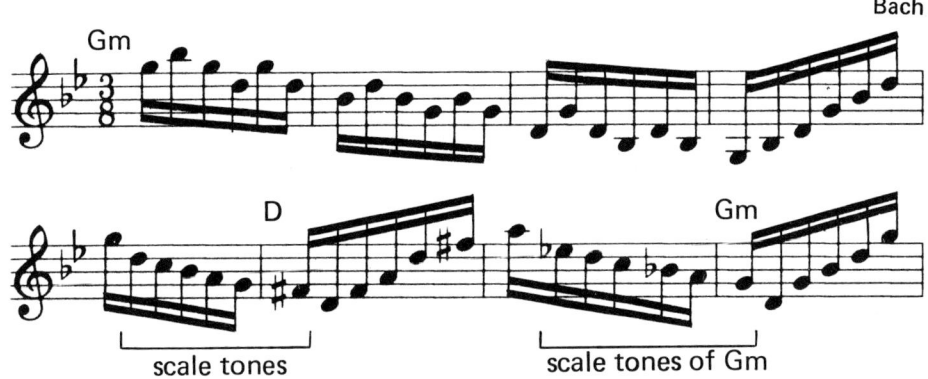

In the example above, the nonharmonic tones are called *passing tones*, since they pass from one chord tone to the next chord tone. Another type of nonharmonic tone is the *neighbor note* (or *neighbor tone*), which moves stepwise from a chord tone and returns to it immediately. Neighbor tones are marked "n."

In the example above, the neighbor tone is **below** the chord tone; therefore, it is called a *lower neighbor*. A neighbor tone a step **above** the chord tone is called an *upper neighbor*.

13 Mark the upper neighbors with ⌒ and the lower neighbors with ℓ :

Nonharmonic tones often create dissonances (see page 84) with the harmonic background. In unaccompanied melodies, they create implied dissonances. Since a melody by itself can imply a harmonic background, the tones which do not fit this background are heard as implied nonharmonic tones. The degree of this dissonance and whether or not it is resolved may be an important factor in the interplay between the melody and the harmonic background. In contemporary music, a great deal of dissonance is often created by nonharmonic tones.

Observe the dissonances created by the use of one of the "blues" scales above a standard progression in G major (the "blues" scale patterns appear in Appendix VI.

14 Circle the nonharmonic tones in these melodies in the *Scorebook*:

Black, Black, Black (SB 14)

Wayfaring Stranger (SB 15)

I Know Where I'm Going (SB 2)

This Old Man (SB 18)

AN AID FOR SPELLING OTHER TRIADS

The triads of Group I and Group II comprise all the major and minor triads on every one of the white keys except B. These triads can be used as one way to find the correct spelling of other triads:

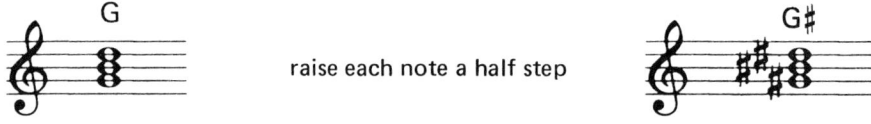

In the example above, since each note has been raised a half step, the same interval relationship is maintained. The G triad becomes the G♯ triad. The same process applied to the minor triad on G:

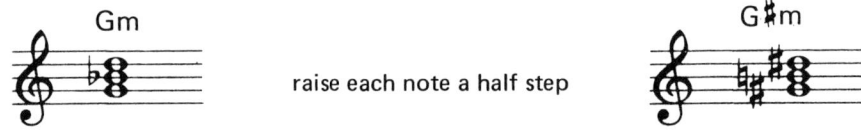

In the example above, notice that in order to raise B♭ a half step you must use a natural. Whether to use a sharp, flat, or natural is determined by function. This will often involve a combination of various accidentals. However, sharps and flats will **never** appear together in the correct spelling of a major or minor triad. Observe how these triads are derived from the Group I and II triads.

15 Play.

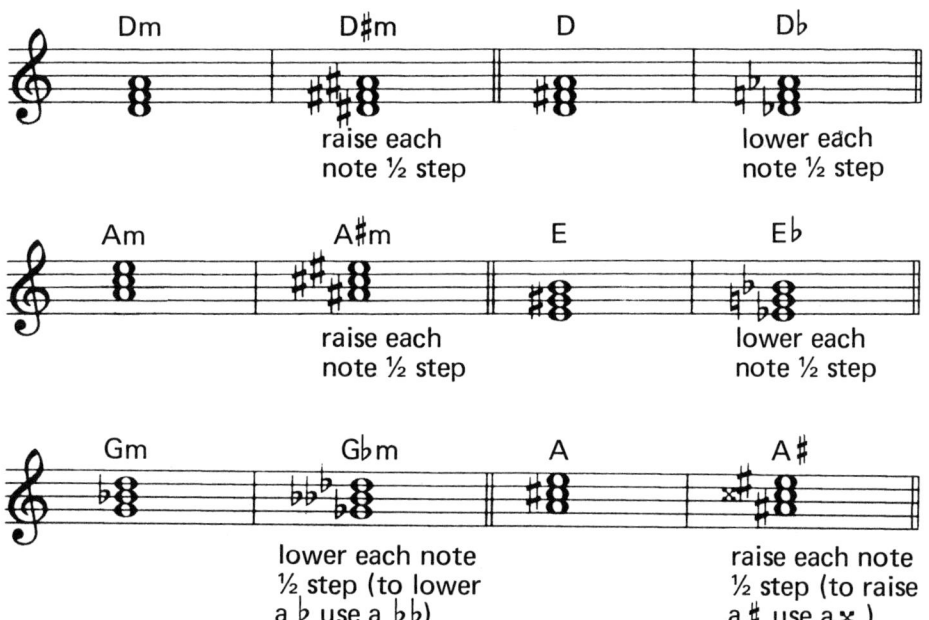

16 Review the use of accidentals, if necessary.
Answer the following questions:

1. If you raise all the notes of a triad a half step, the new triad will have (the same, a different) _____ quality.

2. To raise a flat a half step, you add a _____.

3. To lower a sharp a half step, you add a _____.

4. To lower a flat a half step, you add a _____.

5. To raise a sharp a half step, you add a _____.

GROUP III: TRIADS ON B AND B♭

There is one exception to the rule of spelling perfect 5ths: those built on B or B♭ (see page 90). Since triads built on B or B♭ use these perfect 5ths, learn them as a special group:

Group III: Triads on B and B♭

17 Name all triads and nonharmonic tones in *Adieu, Sweet Amarillis* (SB 41, S1, B3), except for those places marked "X." Notice the harmonic analysis of the first measure. Do all the tones of a triad need to be present to indicate a harmonic background? _____ .

THE USE OF PROGRESSIONS IN SCORES

In popular music, a chord progression can serve as the basic outline upon which the performer improvises. While the improvisation is based on the progressions, the exact choice of rhythm, chord tones, and nonharmonic tones will be up to the performer. In addition, many popular scores (or *charts,* as they are often called) include the notation of basic motives and rhythms. Observe this type of score notation by listening to and following *How Strange* (SB 53, S7, B1).

SUGGESTED ACTIVITIES

1. Name the triad around which *Ho There, Brother* (SB 30) is based. _____
2. Learn all the triads in Appendix IV.
3. Create progressions of triads from Groups I and II and write chord melodies for them.
4. Sing your chord melodies using the words "root," "3rd," or "5th."
5. How can your knowledge of triads help you know P5's, M3's and m3's? _____

   _____

   _____

6. How can your knowledge of major and minor scales help you know triads?

   _____

   _____

7. Use some of the progressions in Appendix VII as the basis for chord melodies or compositions.
8. In the following example, name all chords except those marked "X".

TERMS AND CONCEPTS

Explain in your own words:

    different voicings of triads

    doubling

    inversion

    root position

    first inversion

    second inversion

    harmonic background

    progression

    nonharmonic tone

    passing tone

Contrast these terms or concepts:

    upper neighbor/lower neighbor

    chord tone/nonharmonic tone

    Group I triads/Group II triads

CHAPTER 11

THE HARMONIC SYSTEM

In our study of harmony so far, we have been concerned with the aspects of root and quality of triads. We shall now examine the harmonic system within which the triads are organized in relationship to each other and to a key. This is done by building triads on each scale degree, using only tones from the scale. Observe the resulting quality of each triad when this procedure is followed in C major.

Play:

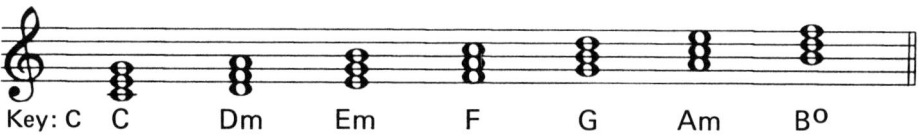

Each one of these triads is now given a Roman numeral designation which represents its **position within the key**. The triads that are major are designated with large Roman numerals (I, IV, V); the minor triads are designated by small Roman numerals (ii, iii, vi); and the one triad that is diminished is designated by a small Roman numeral followed by a diminished symbol ° (vii°).

Here is identification procedure repeated in the keys of B♭ and D. Play:

Root and quality:

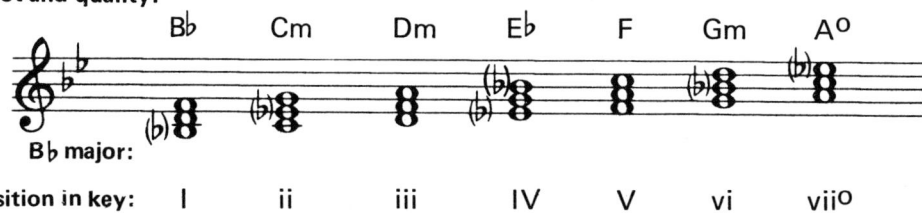

Position in key: I   ii   iii   IV   V   vi   vii°

Root and quality: D Em F#m G A Bm C#°

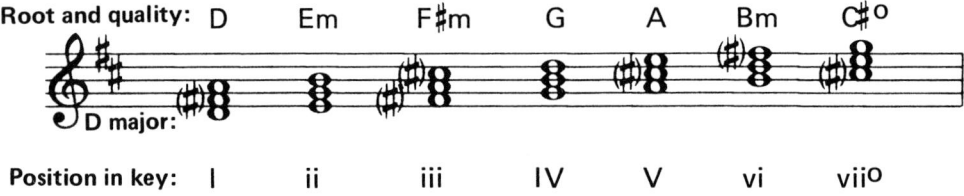

D major:

Position in key: I ii iii IV V vi vii°

1 Repeat this procedure in E♭ and F. Write the key signatures first. Place parentheses around any accidentals from the key signature when they appear in a chord. Name the root and quality as above.

Root and quality:

E♭ major:

Position in key: I ii iii IV V vi vii°

Root and quality:

F major:

Position in key: I ii iii IV V vi vii°

The quality of each Roman numeral chord will be the same in every major key, as long as you use scale tones only to build the triad. The reason is that you are transposing relationships unchanged from one key to another.

MAJOR-SCALE TRIAD QUALITY

I chord is major.

ii chord is minor.

iii chord is minor.

IV chord is major.

V chord is major.

vi chord is minor.

vii° chord is diminished.

2. Answer the following questions.

If only scale tones have used to build the chord:

1. The ii chord in the key of B♭ major is _____.

2. The iii chord in the key of D major is _____.

3. The IV chord in the key of C major is _____.

4. The IV chord in the key of B♭ major is _____.

5. The V chord in the key of C major is _____.

6. The vi chord in the key of B♭ major is _____.

7. The vii° chord in any major key is always _____.

8. The V chord in a major key is always _____.

9. The iii chord in a major key is always _____.

10. The IV chord in a major key is always _____.

PRACTICAL USE OF THE HARMONIC SYSTEM

This system of naming chords within a key serves a very important function in understanding harmonic movement, or, as we have called it, "the progression." This can be illustrated in a practical way by imagining a guitar player trying to transpose a song from one key to another. The printed song looks like this:

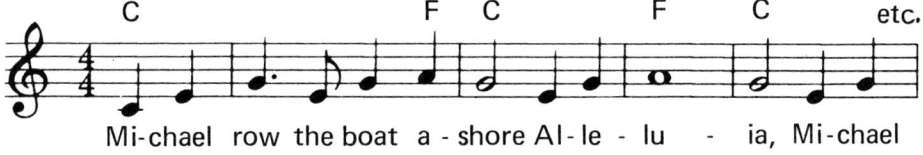

The guitar player wants to play the song in a higher key—let's say, G major. What chords will sound right in the new key? The chord letter names are no help, for they will be different in a different key. The guitarist must think of the chords as Roman numeral chords first, in the original key.

The song can now be played in any key in which the guitarist knows the I–IV progression. For example:

This system becomes even more essential when you are transposing a more complex progression. For example:

Progression	I	vi	iii	IV	V	I
Chords in key of C	C	Am	Em	F	G	C
Chords in key of D	D	Bm	F♯m	G	A	D
Chords in key of B♭	B♭	Gm	Dm	E♭	F	B♭

Many untrained musicians pick up this system through trial, error, and ear. But how much more time could be spent making music if a little more time were spent studying theory! A beautiful harmonic progression is like a perfect law of science and should be described in a system that indicates its general meaning, not merely one application.

For present purposes, limit yourself to the use of a few basic progressions. Allow sufficient time to absorb these relationships. You can refer to Appendix VII, which lists basic chords in all keys to explore this system further.

 Write the key signatures and scales. Then write the I, IV, and V triads. Add sharps and flats in parentheses as they would appear in the chord if no key signature were present. Name each chord.

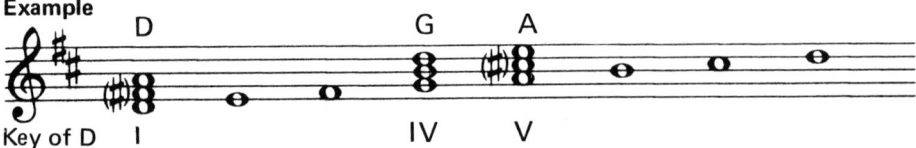

1.

Key of F

2.

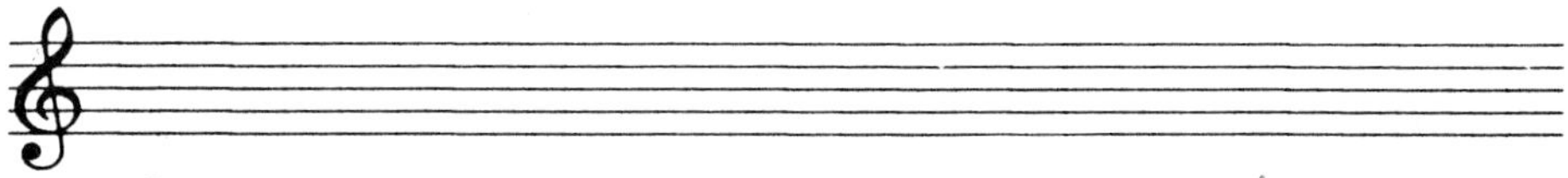

Key of G

3.

Key of E

4.

Key of E♭

5.

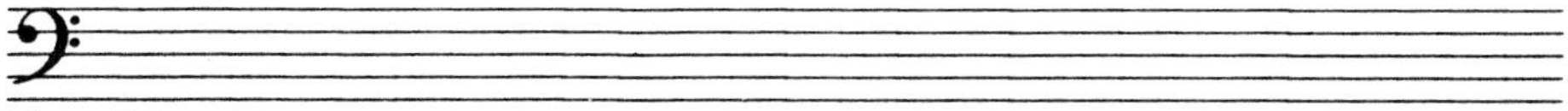

Key of A

6.

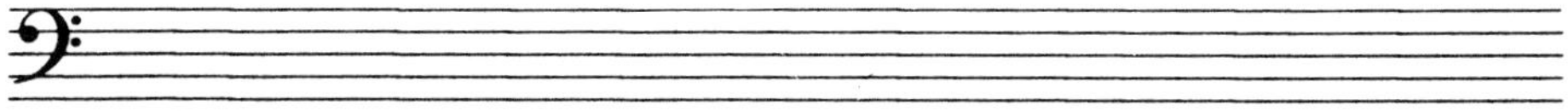

Key of B♭

SEVENTH CHORDS

A *seventh chord* is a **four-note chord** built in 3rds. It is formed by adding a 3rd above the 5th of a triad. The term seventh chord derives its name from the interval between the root and the highest note, which is a 7th.

Play:

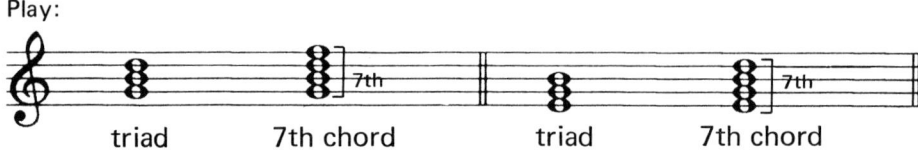

Like the triad, it is either on lines or in spaces.

 Write seventh chords above each note (no accidentals).

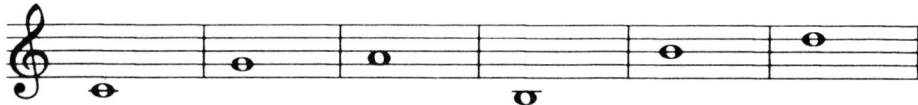

Like triads, seventh chords can have different qualities, illustrated here by the different kinds of seventh chords all built on D.

For our purposes, we shall explore only one quality—the *dominant seventh chord* (V^7 *chord*). For other seventh chords, see Appendix IV.

THE V⁷ CHORD

The V⁷ chord is widely used in traditional harmony. It is constructed on the fifth scale degree of a major key. For example, here is the V⁷ chord in the key of C:

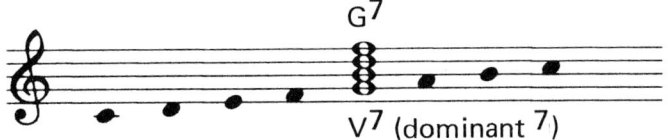

The exact intervallic make-up of the V⁷ chord is a major triad plus a m3. Play these V⁷ chords:

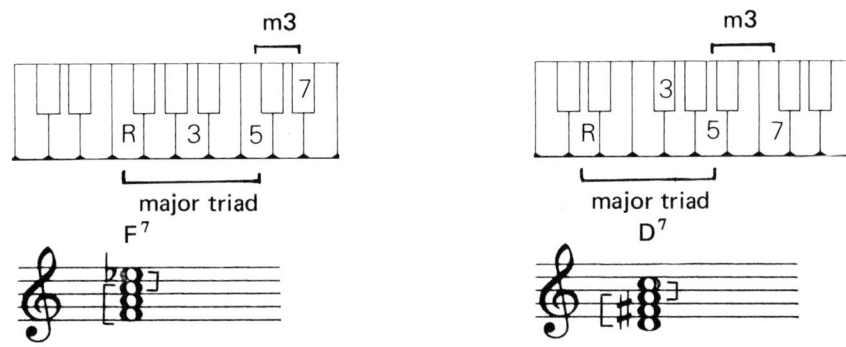

5 Write out the indicated V⁷ chord on the staff and keyboard as in the example above. Play each chord

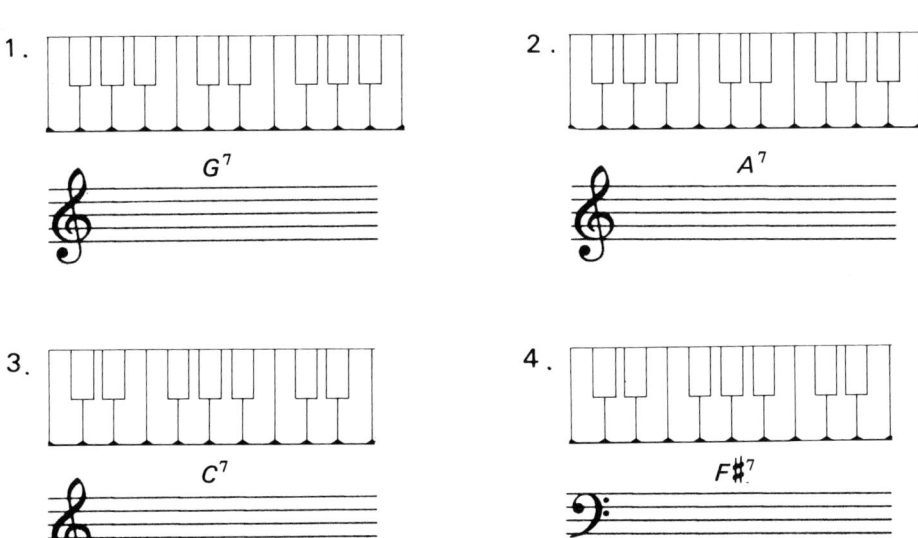

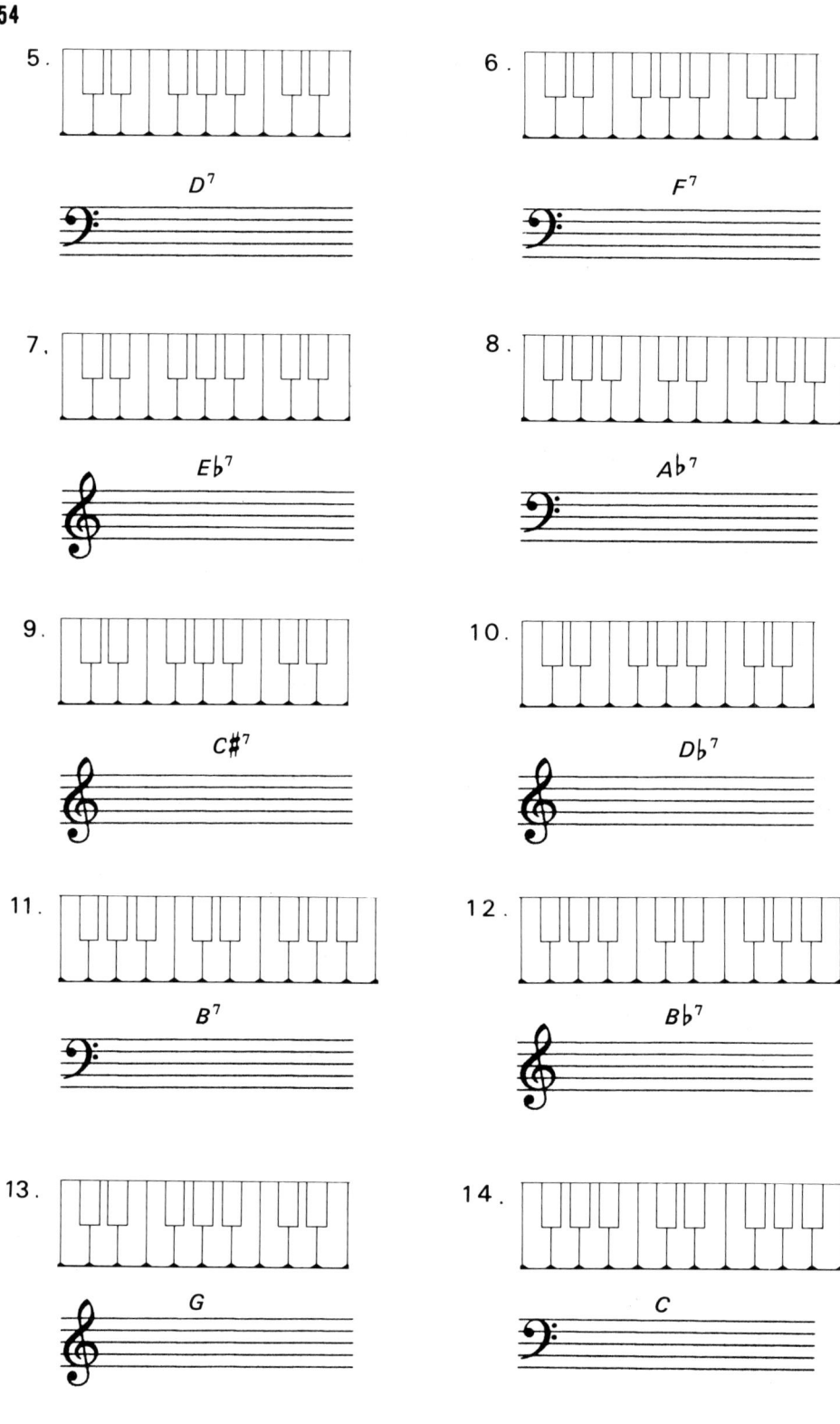

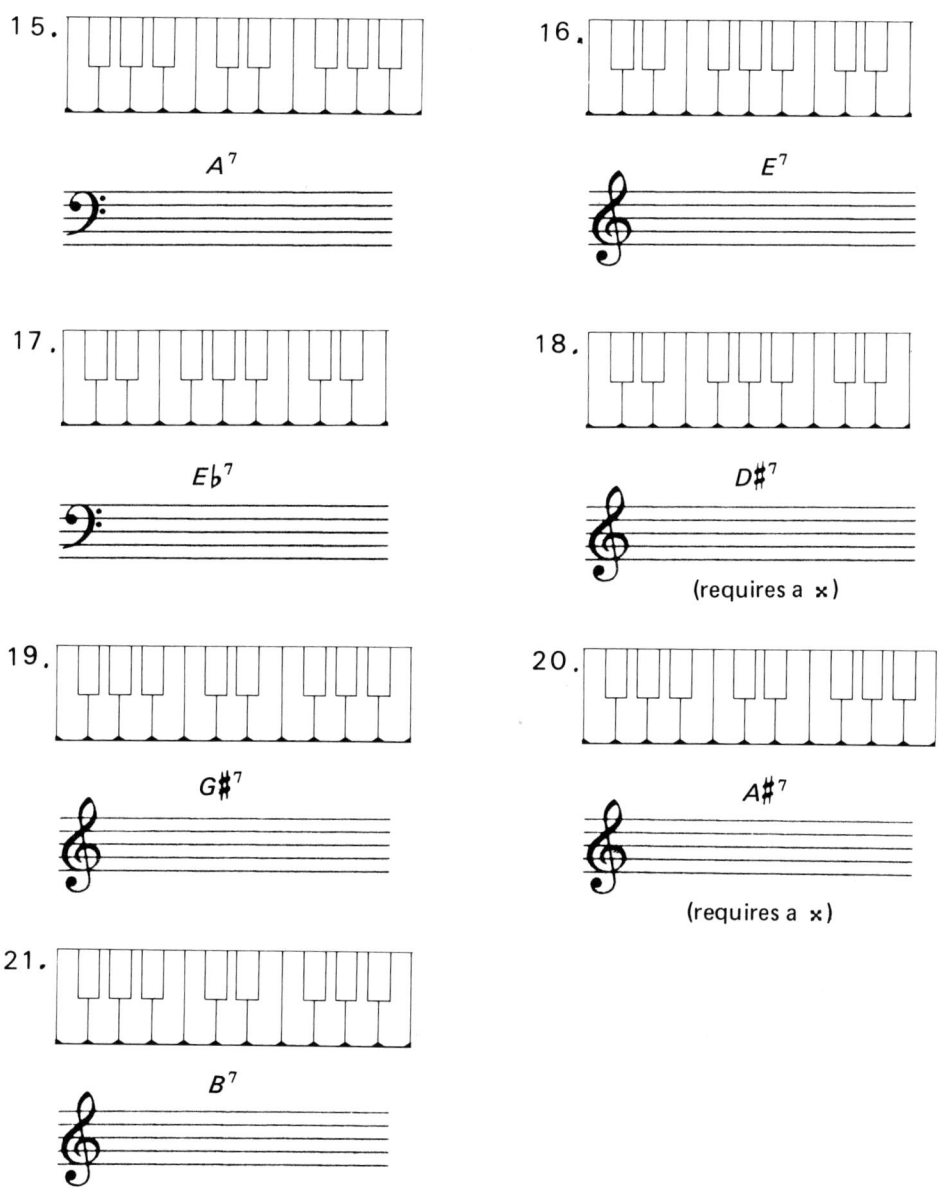

6 Build a V⁷ chord on the fifth degree of each of these major keys. Write any sharps or flats in the chord in parentheses. Name each chord.

THE SOUND OF THE V⁷ CHORD

The dominant seventh chord can be heard melodically in the folk song *Down in the Valley*, on the words "hang your head over."

Coordinating the words with the chord members of the V^7 chord, we have:

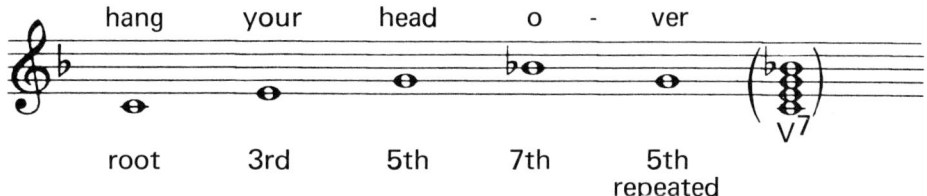

7 Sing these V^7 chords up and down with letter names, including accidentals. Name all chords.

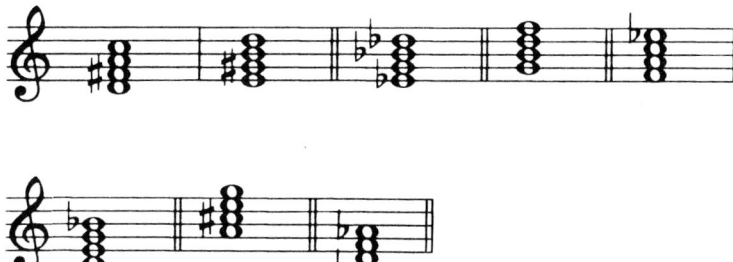

MINOR-SCALE TRIADS—POSITION IN KEY

The "position in key" concept applied to the natural minor scale results in the following triad qualities. Play:

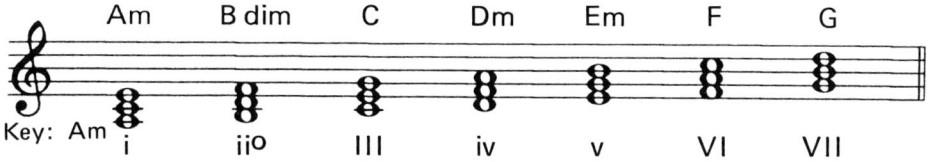

Often the melodic patterns of the harmonic minor scale cause the 7th degree of the scale to be raised, thereby making the leading tone available. The v chord (minor) of the natural minor then becomes a major triad (V). With the addition of a m3 above the 5th of a V chord, a V^7 chord is formed.

Alteration of the natural minor to form V and V^7

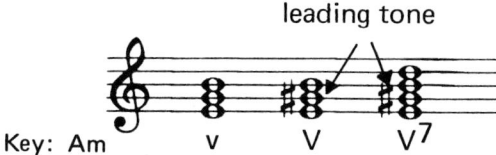

8 Write the V and V⁷ chords in the following minor keys. Remember to raise the 3rd of the chord, which is the 7th degree of the minor scale, to produce a leading tone. Without this alteration, the V and V⁷ chords will lack the leading tone. Write the key signature first.

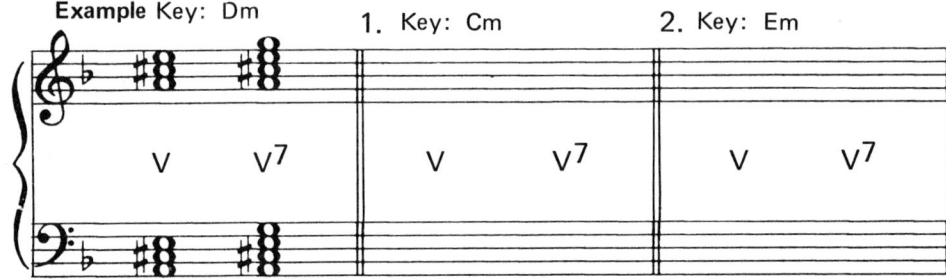

Example Key: Dm   1. Key: Cm   2. Key: Em

V   V⁷   V   V⁷   V   V⁷

9 Write the V⁷ chord in the following major or minor keys. Notate the chord on the keyboard diagram. Name the chord. Write the **key signature** first.

Example

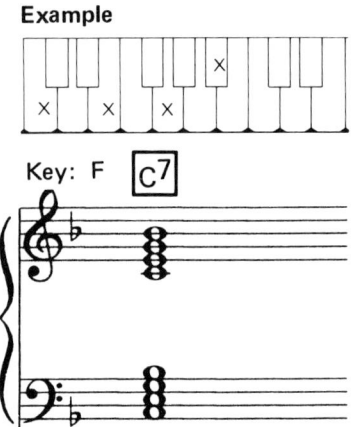

Key: F [C⁷]

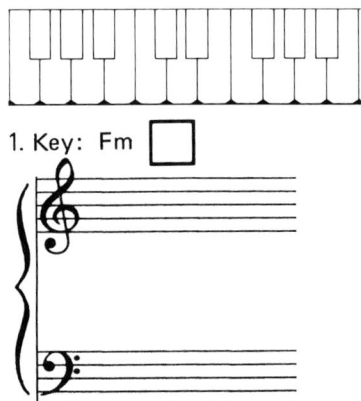

1. Key: Fm ☐

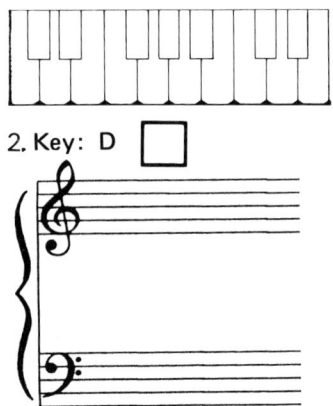

2. Key: D ☐

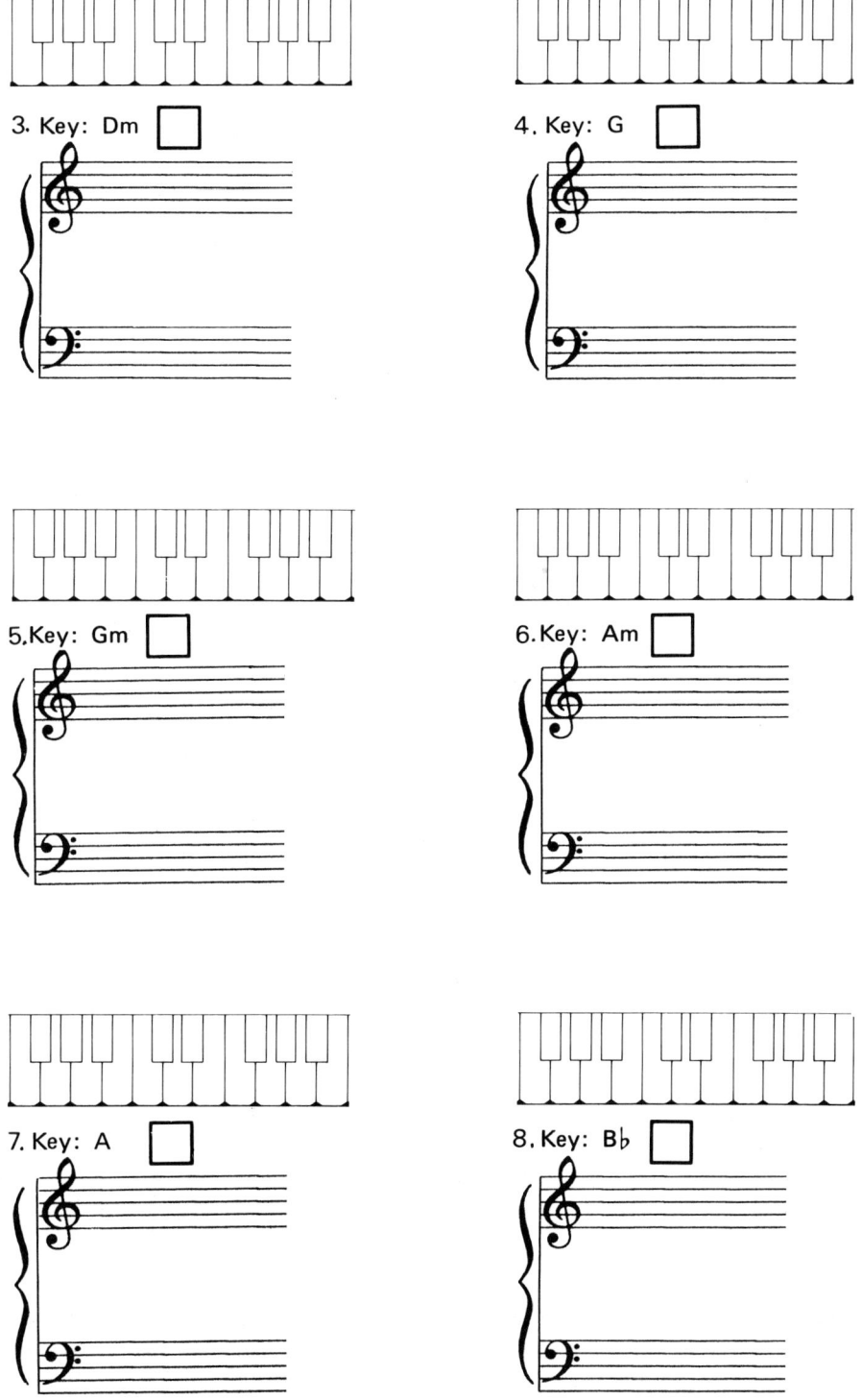

160

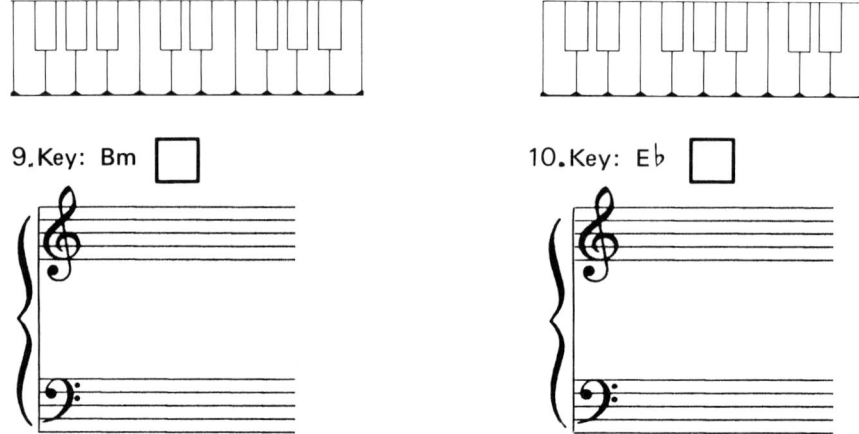

9. Key: Bm ☐   10. Key: E♭ ☐

TONALITY

Harmonic progressions play an important role in establishing key centers. In our discussions of scales, we observed how recognizable scale patterns can cause a pitch to be heard as the tonic. In the same way, recognizable harmonic progressions can cause the listener to hear one pitch as the tonic. Different progressions have varying effects on tonality. Traditionally, the strongest harmonic progression for establishing a key center is V–I or V^7–I. This can be observed in the following examples. Play:

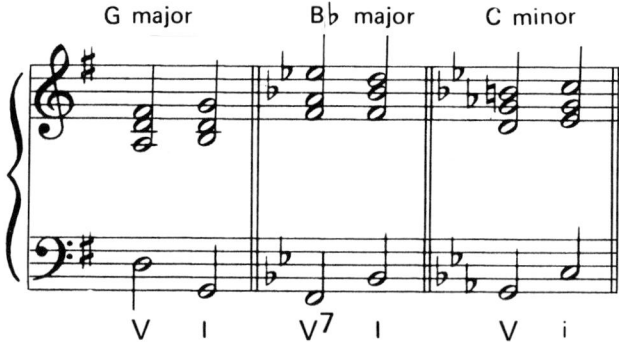

This progression has such a strong tonal effect that it is often used to create a new key center by the introduction of a new V–I relationship. A change of key center is called *modulation*. Observe this through the use of a new V–I relationship in the following exercise.

10 Listen to *Adieu, Sweet Amarillis* (SB 41, S 1, B 3). In the score, indicate the point where you hear a modulation to the key of B♭. This happens in measure _____. The V of the new key is _____.

11 Play or sing the following example, using chords, if possible:

French Folk Song — Traditional

In this folk song, the key of D minor is established by a simple progression moving to V. In the third line, the song modulates through E^7 which is the V^7 chord in the new key, A minor. Notice that the modulation requires those accidentals that would occur in the new key.

HARMONIZATION: METHODS FOR HARMONIZING A MELODY

1. Knowledge of the key and the chords in that key are an indispensable starting point.

2. Many traditional songs can be harmonized using I, IV, and V in a major key, or i, iv, and v (V) in a minor key.

3. Important pitches (those that last a long time, those on the beat, beginning and ending pitches, and repeated notes) may be chord tones. (This is not a rule, but a generalization: the opposite may also be true.) As a starting point, try different combinations of chords that fit the important tones of the melody.

4. If you have found places where the I, IV, or V chord seems to fit, sing through the song playing those chords but leaving all others out. Repeat this procedure, experimenting gradually with different chords in the blank spots.

5. If you think a song modulates to a new key, make sure you use the basic chords of the new key at the point of modulation.

In the final analysis, your ears will be the judge. These methods are only a starting point for your discovery of harmony.

SUGGESTED ACTIVITIES

1. Choose a harmonic background for this melody, using I, IV, and V^7.

This Old Man

Key: D major

2. Choose a harmonic background for *Que ne suis-je la Fougère* (SB 28), using i and V^7.

3. Transpose the melody of *Down in the Valley* (SB 12) to D major. Then, choose a harmonization using I and V^7.

4. Identify the progressions of these songs using Roman numerals to indicate position and key: *Barbrie Allen* (SB 9), *Shoo Fly* (SB 11), *Down in the Valley* (SB 12), *Dona, Dona* (SB 13).

5. Write in Roman numerals for the *Wraggle-Taggle Gypsies, O!* (SB 16); notice the use of the minor v chord.

6. Write in Roman numerals for *Greensleeves* (SB 3); notice the use of both the minor v and major V.

7. Rewrite the progression of *Barbrie Allen* in G and E♭, using both chord names and Roman numerals.

8. Rewrite the progression of *Dona, Dona* in the key of Cm using both chord names and Roman numerals. Is there any possible change of key center? (Look for a repeated **new** V^7–I relationship.)

TERMS AND CONCEPTS
Explain in your own words:

    quality of a triad

    position in key of a triad

    Roman numeral designation

    I, IV, V major triads

    ii, iii, vi minor triads

    vii^0 diminished triad

    value of position in key for transposition and musical understanding

    seventh chords

    V^7 chord

    the harmonic minor practice of raising the 7th effecting the V and V^7

    V–I, V^7–I

    key center

    modulation

    harmonization

Contrast:

    quality/position in key

CHAPTER 12

ACCOMPANIMENTS TO SONGS

1 Listen to *The Water Is Wide* (S3,B1) and *I Know Where I'm Going* (S2, B3). In these songs, the harmonic background is provided by guitar and piano chords. Chord backgrounds that accompany melodies can be played on many different instruments. Among the most popular in our folk culture are the guitar (and its relatives, the ukelele and banjo), the autoharp, and the piano.

GUITAR AND AUTOHARP ACCOMPANIMENTS
On both of these instruments, the chord is fingered directly: on the strings of the guitar or by pressing a button on the autoharp (see Appendix VIII for guitar and autoharp chording). Once the correct chord is fingered, the instrument is strummed in a rhythmic pattern that fits the meter of the song.

PIANO ACCOMPANIMENTS
The piano has the potential for much more variety in types of chord backgrounds than the guitar or autoharp. Harmonic backgrounds on the keyboard are a part of our classical tradition as well as our folk heritage. Here are two examples of classical harmonic backgrounds on the keyboard.

Trio No. 2, excerpt

Franz Joseph Haydn

The broken chord pattern in the right hand of the piano part is called an *arpeggio*.

Stabat Mater, excerpt

G. B. Pergolesi

In this example, the chords are divided between both hands, and the accompaniment uses the repeated rhythm of eighth notes.

VOICING

In most traditional keyboard accompaniments, the chords are arranged according to the concept of good *voice leading*. This means that every note of the chord is considered a separate line or voice and its motion from one chord to another follows a coherent pattern. Here is an illustration of how the voicing of a chord progression can form several accompaniment patterns. Play:

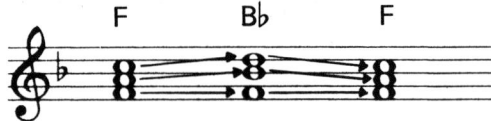

The following accompaniment patterns are derived from the model. Play:

Notice that in every case, the voices move to the same pitches even though the rhythm may change. The top line C always goes to D and returns to C. The middle voice A moves to B♭ and returns to A. The lowest voice F stays on F, since F is common to both chords. When a voice remains on the same pitch as the harmony changes, it is called a *common tone*, since the pitch is common to both chords. In the above voicing, F is a common tone.

2 Identify the common tones in these exercises by drawing horizontal lines between them. Name all chords.

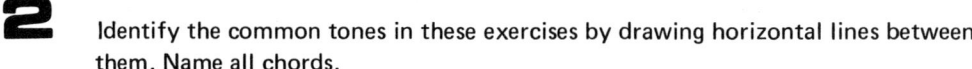

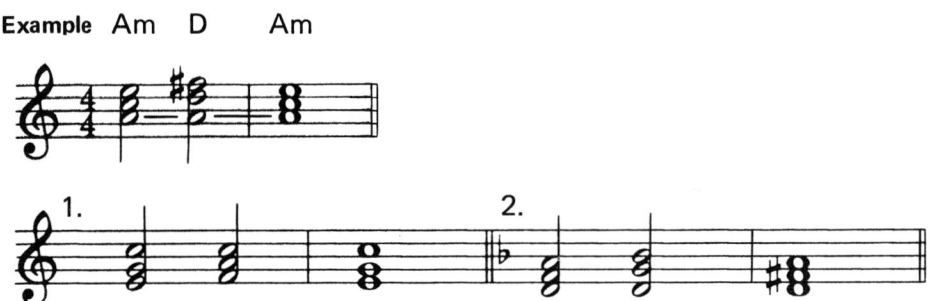

A popular voicing for keyboard accompaniments using the I, IV, and V⁷ chords is illustrated below. Notice that the V⁷ chord is in the first inversion and is incomplete (no 5th). Play:

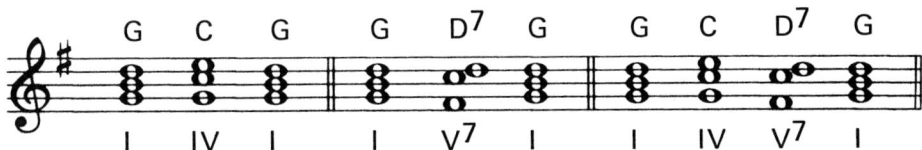

3 Transpose the voicing in the illustration above to D, F, and E♭ (write key signatures first). Name the chords.

In a minor key, the same voicing would appear as illustrated below. The 3rd of the chord is raised so that the quality of the chord is a dominant 7th.

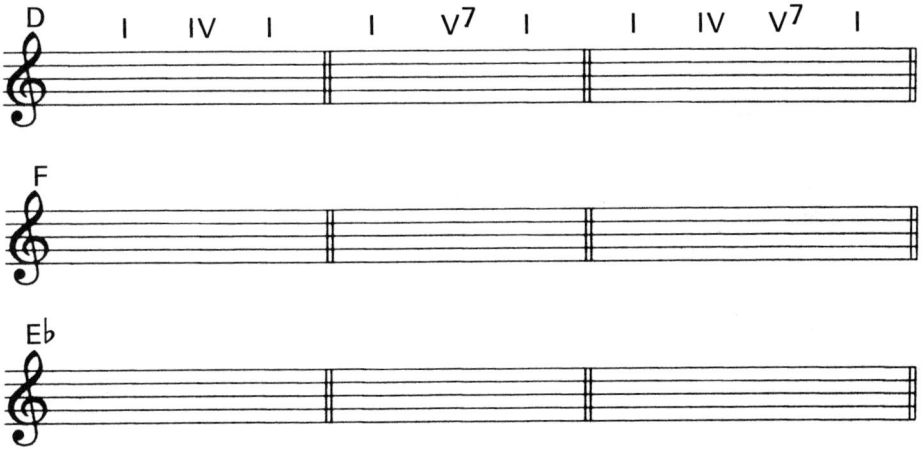

Now, by adding the **root** of the chord in the left hand, you can complete the harmony.

Here are some patterns derived from the models found above. Observe that in the V^7 chord, the fifth of the chord is omitted and the root doubled.

4 Continue these accompaniment patterns using the voicings shown above.

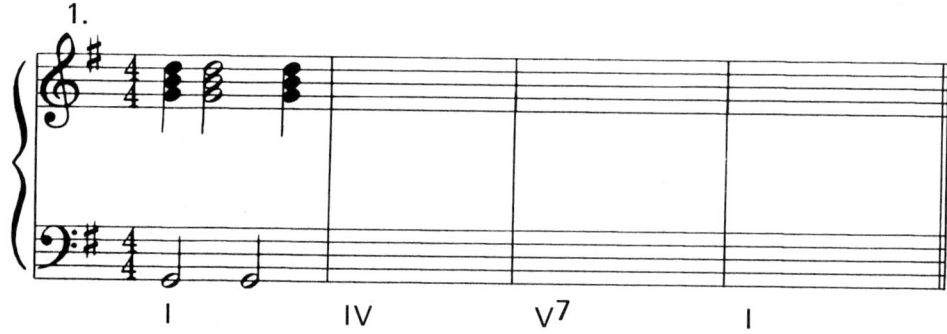

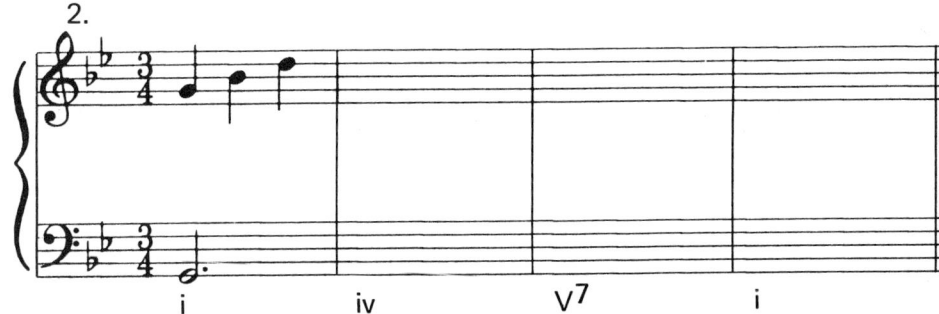

Here are other voicings of the I, IV, and V^7 chords. Compare them with the previous models. Observe which voice is the common tone.

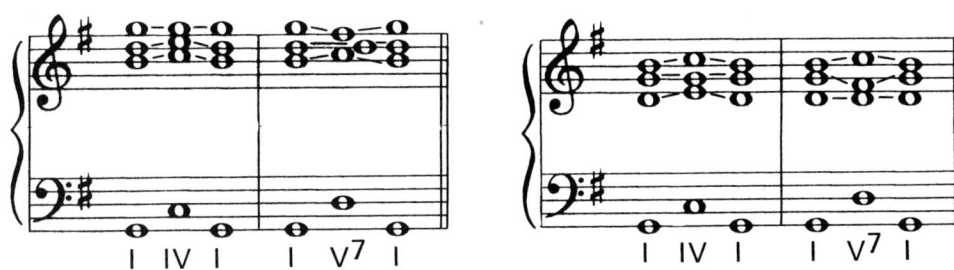

5 Here are some more traditional types of accompaniments using the I, IV, and V^7. Again, the 5th of the V^7 is not used in order to create smoother voice leading. Name the keys and chords.

6 Finish this piano accompaniment using the same rhythmic pattern in each measure.

7 Finish this piano accompaniment using the same rhythmic pattern in each measure. Compare with **6**: **7** is in the _____ minor key of **6**.

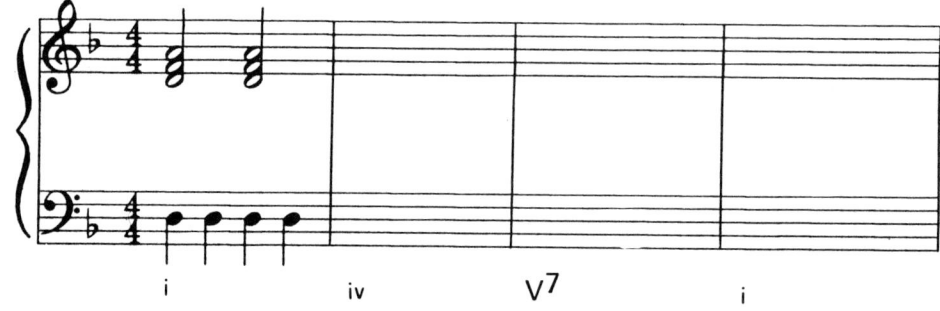

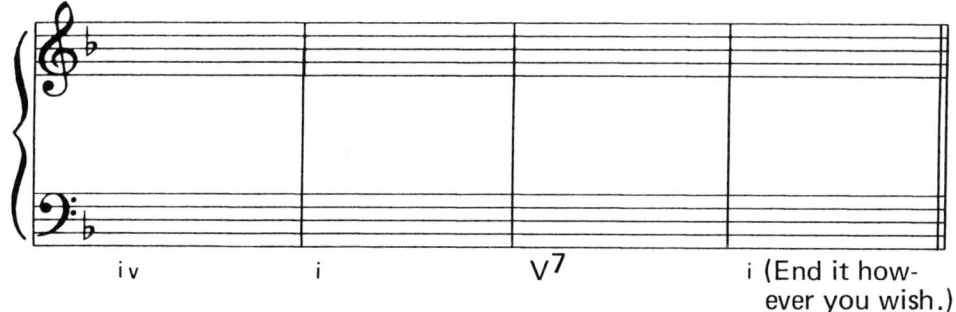

iv   i   V⁷   i (End it however you wish.)

8 Using the same progression, write out an accompaniment in Dm continuing with the motive shown in the first measure.

9 Finish this accompaniment for *Silent Night*. Which note in the first measure is a nonharmonic tone? _____.

I   V⁷   I

MODERN ACCOMPANIMENTS

In our brief study of voicing and chord progressions, we have been observing traditional voice-leading concepts. This tradition did not include a certain type of voice leading known as *parallelism*, frequently associated with twentieth-century music. When the harmony changes and the voicing remains the same, the voice leading shows parallelism.

In current popular accompaniments, parallelism is combined with traditional voice-leading concepts, as seen in these examples:

SUGGESTED ACTIVITIES

1. Choose from these songs and write accompaniments for them, using traditional voicings with the I, IV, and V^7 chords.

    The Riddle Song (SB 6)

    Shoo Fly (SB 11)

    Down in the Valley (SB 12)

    Hush, Little Baby (SB 17)

    This Old Man (SB 18)

    Alouette (SB 20)

2. These songs require chords other than I, IV, and V, so you will have to determine your own voicings.

   Dona, Dona (SB 13)

   The First Noel (SB 32)

3. Compose your own melody and a keyboard accompaniment. The melody could be for a solo instrument like flute or violin.

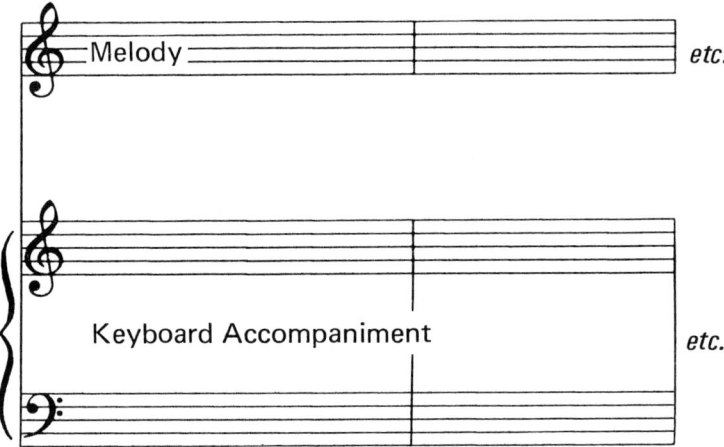

4. Listen to the following keyboard pieces, following the music in the *Rhythm Reader*:

   Study I (p 41)

   Study II (p.47)

5. Write an accompaniment to a current popular song, using one of the styles of the pieces in number 4.

6. Observe how the piano motive is based on the three-part chord above each measure. Finish the second phrase, keeping the same motive.

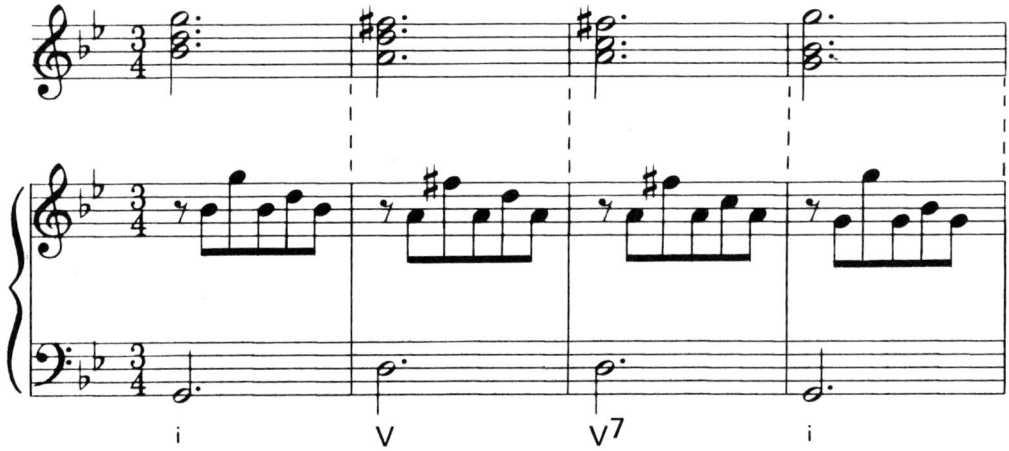

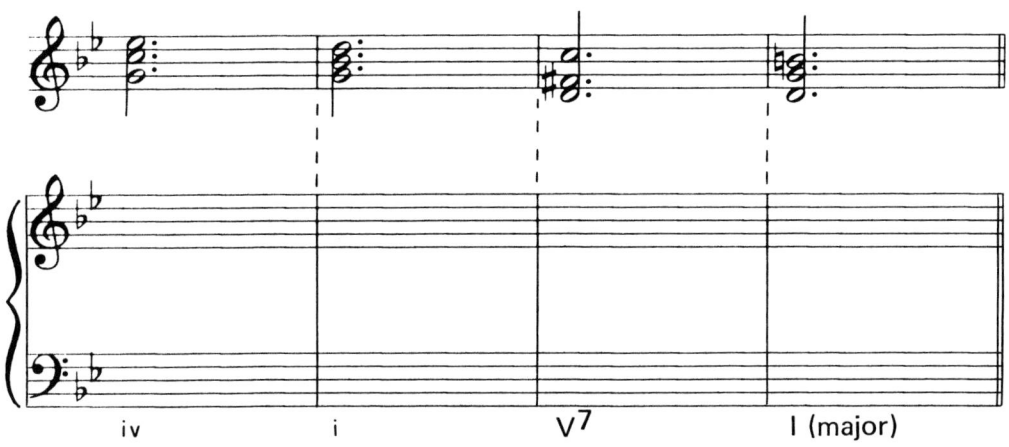

TERMS AND CONCEPTS
Explain in your own words:

        harmonic background

        arpeggio

        voicing

        voice leading

        common tone

        parallelism

CHAPTER 13

FORM: PHRASE DESIGN

1 1. Read the lyric of *One Grain of Sand* aloud:

One grain of sand, one grand of sand in all the world;
One grain of sand, one little boy, one little girl.

One drop of rain, one drop of rain on all the land;
One drop of rain, one little hand all in my hand.

One little star, one little star up in the blue;
One little star, one little me, one little you.

One grain of sand, one grain of sand in all the world;
One grain of sand, one little boy, one little girl.

—Appalachian Lullaby

2. Now listen to *One Grain of Sand* (S 4, B 1). Follow the words.

There is a specific design to the music and lyrics of this song. In music, as in poetry, drama, painting, and other arts, this design or structure is known as *form*. Let us examine some of the elements of the form of this song:

1. The song is divided into verses. In each verse, although the words change, the music is essentially the same.
2. Although the words change in successive verses, each verse has the same poetic design.
3. The form of each verse, both words and music, consists of units called *phrases*. Each phrase expresses a **complete** musical thought concluding in a point of rest

called a *cadence*. The phrase and cadence design of *One Grain of Sand* can be diagramed like this (the brackets indicate the beginning and end of each phrase; the word [and pitch] where each cadence occurs is underlined):

```
                                                     cadence
            ┌─────────────────────────────────────────────┐
Phrase I:   One grain of sand, one grain of sand in all the world

                                              cadence
            ┌───────────────────────────────────────┐
Phrase II:  One grain of sand, one little boy, one little girl
```

 Listen again. Follow the words. Listen for phrase and cadence. This is only part of the study of form. We will examine other aspects in this and later chapters; the main concept to recognize now is that form is *design* and *structure*, or—in the words of one student—"how it's put together."

WORDS AND MUSIC

In *One Grain of Sand*, the form of the music is inseparable from the form of the words. There is a very definite relationship between spoken language and music. Spoken language can often be helpful in understanding musical concepts, so we will turn to the spoken word in order to examine the characteristics of phrase and cadence and the close relationship between language and music.

Spoken language is organized into groups of words called sentences. Spoken sentences are organized and comprehended by the listener in two basic ways: intellectually, when a complete idea is expressed; and aurally, when the voice inflection of the speaker falls and there is a slight pause before the next sentence. The necessity of this sound organization through inflection and ideas in spoken language can best be understood by listening to the sound of your own voice.

 Speak the following words in two ways:

1. Without any emphasis or pauses, like a computer or robot, in an absolute monotone.

   The increasing noise of the city has made the silence of the country a beautiful sound perhaps it is time to consider finding a new home

2. In a normal manner. Under words where your voice inflection falls and you tend to pause, notice the arrow pointed down. After each complete idea (sentence), a vertical line has been drawn.

   The increasing noise of the city has made the silence of the country a beautiful sound / perhaps it is time to consider finding a new home /

Thus, when you speak normally, pauses, emphasis, and inflection help convey the message to the listener, which is not the case when you speak in a monotone.

When you compare the organization of spoken language to the organization of music, the **sentence** equals the **phrase**, and the **pause** and **drop in inflection** are synonymous with the **cadence**.

Analysis in musical terms

Phrase I:

The increasing noise of the city has made the silence of the country a beautiful sound
                                                                                                  cadence

Phrase II:

Perhaps it is time to consider finding a new home
                                  cadence

The two phrases above are *asymmetrical* (uneven) in their design: the first phrase is longer than the second. More balanced phrase construction can be found in traditional poetry where length, rhythm, accents, and rhymes are more *symmetrical* (even).

4   Speak aloud:

    Tell all the Truth but tell it slant—Success in Circuit lies
    Too bright for our infirm Delight the Truth's superb surprise

                                                                   ——Emily Dickinson

Observe the following analysis for accents, syllables, and cadence. Emphasized words or syllables are underlined.

5   Speak again, even more rhythmically:

    Phrase I:

    Tell all the Truth but tell it slant—Success in Circuit lies
                                                          cadence

    Phrase II:

    Too bright for our infirm Delight the Truth's superb surprise
                                                            cadence

Unlike our first example, these lines of poetry have a regular, rhythmic pulse. This adds a new element in defining phrases and their relationship to each other. In poetry and music, a rhythmic pulse creates a forward motion which naturally results in a cadence. This rhythmic drive towards a cadence can be felt by speaking the first line but leaving out the last word:

    Tell all the Truth but tell it slant—Success in Circuit . . .

Here we feel the drive of a rhythmic pulse to reach a point of rest, the cadence. This rhythmic pulse combined with the force of a rhyme scheme creates a symmetrical balance between the two phrases. The first phrase does not seem complete without the second. Thus, these two phrases are completely balanced in length, rhythm, and rhyme (each line contains fourteen syllables). In music, this relationship between two phrases, dependent on each other for balance, is called a *period*. The first phrase is called the *antecedent* and the second phrase is called the *consequent*. What unites these two phrases into a period is the need for the antecedent phrase to be balanced by the consequent phrase. One determinant of this relationship is the type of cadence at the end of each phrase. Here we will discuss two main types of cadences: the semicadence and the full cadence.

TWO TYPES OF CADENCES

1. *Semicadence (half cadence)*: Although this cadence is a point of rest at the end of a phrase, it seems incomplete. It creates a desire for more rhythmic motion to balance the first phrase.

2. *Full cadence:* The full cadence is a point of rest at the end of a phrase that seems complete. It needs no more rhythmic motion to balance it.

CADENTIAL DESIGN OF *ONE GRAIN OF SAND*

In this *cadential design* (scheme of the cadences), we find that phrase I ends in a semicadence, and phrase II ends in a full cadence. The semicadence at the end of phrase I is on the pitch of B—the 7th degree of the C♯-minor scale. The full cadence at the end of phrase II ends on C♯—the **tonic** and **key center** of C♯ minor.

One Grain of Sand—**period**

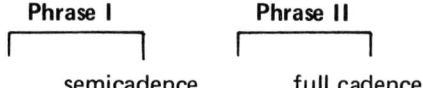

The two phrases depend upon each other for balance. The first is the antecedent phrase; the second, the consequent phrase. Therefore, the form of each verse is a period.

 Play *The Trees They Do Grow High* (SB 1). Each four-measure phrase naturally results in a cadence through the steady rhythmic flow (in the same manner as the poetry excerpt). Here we find a form called the *double period*, which is made up of two periods separated by a semicadence.

The Trees They Do Grow High—**double period**

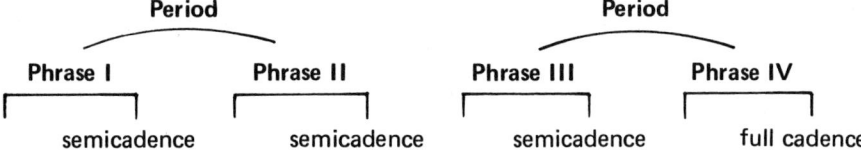

7 Answer:

1. On which degrees of the A-minor scale do the semicadences of *The Trees They Do Grow High* occur? _____

2. On what scale degree does the full cadence occur? _____

THE HARMONIC ASPECTS OF THE CADENCE

In addition to the choice of scale degree, the harmonic progression (V^7–I) ending a phrase can further define the type of cadence. We will examine traditional examples of cadences classified by harmonic progressions. Each of these progressions occurs at the end of a phrase. They are presented in C major; the V chords could also be V^7 chords.

PERFECT AUTHENTIC CADENCE

The *perfect authentic cadence* is a full cadence with the highest voice ending on the tonic. This cadence is the most final in its effect.

IMPERFECT AUTHENTIC CADENCE

The *imperfect authentic cadence* is a full cadence with the highest voice ending on a note other than the tonic. This cadence is less final than the perfect authentic cadence, but not as incomplete as the semicadence.

SEMICADENCE

The semicadence, I (or another chord) to V, is the most incomplete cadence and creates the feeling of need for more motion. Cadences on other chords, such as II or III, may also be considered semicadences.

PLAGAL CADENCE

The plagal cadence, IV to I, is often used at the end of hymns and is referred to as the "Amen cadence."

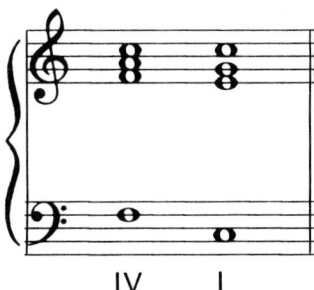

DECEPTIVE CADENCE

The deceptive cadence, V to vi, is so named because you expect it to go to the I chord, but it "deceives" you and moves to an unexpected chord, vi.

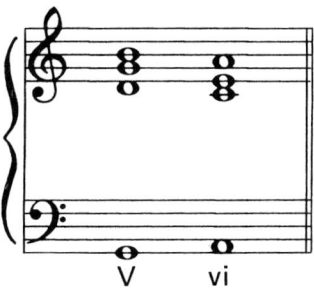

1. Listen to *Greensleeves* (S 5 , B 1). Follow these diagrams, rather than the music. Be sure to listen to the cadences.

Phrase I	Phrase II	Phrase III	Phrase IV
semicadence	perfect authentic cadence	semicadence	perfect authentic cadence

2. Listen to *The Water Is Wide* (S 3 , B 1). Listen to the cadences.

Phrase I	Phrase II	Phrase III	Phrase IV
imperfect authentic cadence	semicadence	imperfect authentic cadence	plagal cadence

3. Listen to *I Know Where I'm Going* (S 2 , B 3). This song is unusual because it ends on a semicadence, which seems to leave the song "hanging."

Phrase I	Phrase II
semicadence	semicadence

 Listen to *Adieu, Sweet Amarillis* (SB 41, S 1 , B 3) and follow the score. Identify the cadences in these measures:

10–11 _____

16–17 _____

38–39 _____

51–52 _____

61–62 _____

Listen to Chopin's *Waltz in C-Sharp Minor* (SB 52, S 2 , B 1) and follow the score. Name the obvious cadences in the score.

THE DESIGN OF PHRASE FORMS

10 1. Play *Au Clair de la Lune*:

Notice that the piece is made up of four phrases. Phrases I, II, and IV are all the same; phrase III is different. This design is indicated in the following way: phrase I is labeled **a**. Because phrase II is an exact repeat of phrase I, it is also labeled **a**. Phrase III is new music, so we give it a new letter—**b**. Phrase IV is labeled **a**, because it is another repeat of the first phrase:

>   Phrase I   a
>   Phrase II   a
>   Phrase III   b
>   Phrase IV   a

Add the appropriate letter at the beginning of each phrase in the music above.

2. Listen to *Greensleeves* (SB 3, S 5, B 1). Notice that the second phrase is a modified repeat of the first. It is therefore labeled **a′**. The third phrase is new. The fourth phrase is a modified repeat of the third. This phrase design can be written in the following way:

Greensleeves: Phrase Design

>   Phrase I   a
>   Phrase II   a′ (almost the same as I)
>   Phrase III   b   (new music)
>   Phrase IV   b′ (almost the same as III)

Phrase design: **a a′ b b′**

3. Now play *The Trees They Do Grow High* (SB 1) and observe the phrase design.

The Trees They Do Grow High: **Phrase Design**

>   Phrase I   a
>   Phrase II   a'
>   Phrase III   a
>   Phrase IV   b

Phrase design: **a a' a b**

PARALLEL AND CONTRASTING PERIODS

When two phrases start the same, they are called *parallel*; when they start differently, they are called *contrasting*. We can describe a parallel period as "**aa**" and a contrasting period as "**ab**".

11
1. In *Drink to Me Only with Thine Eyes* (SB 7), mark the phrases with a bracket (as on page 179) and the cadences with the words "semicadence" or "authentic cadence." What is the form? _____

2. Mark the phrases and cadences of *This Old Man* (SB 18). What is the form? _____

THE THREE-PHRASE PERIOD

A piece made up of three phrases in which the third phrase completes the beginning phrases is called a *three-phrase period*. An example of this form is the Christmas carol *Silent Night* (SB 31).

12 Sing *Silent Night* and follow this diagram of the phrase design.

Silent Night: **Phrase Design**

>   Phrase I   Phrase II   Phrase III
>   ⌈a   ⌉   ⌈b   ⌉   ⌈c   ⌉

COMPOSING PERIODS

13 Add pitch and rhythm to any two of the following shapes to create the first phrase of a period. Compose the second phrase using your own shape as the structure. The shapes are only guidelines to get you going. Do not follow them too closely. Your ears should be the final judge of what notes to use.

Example

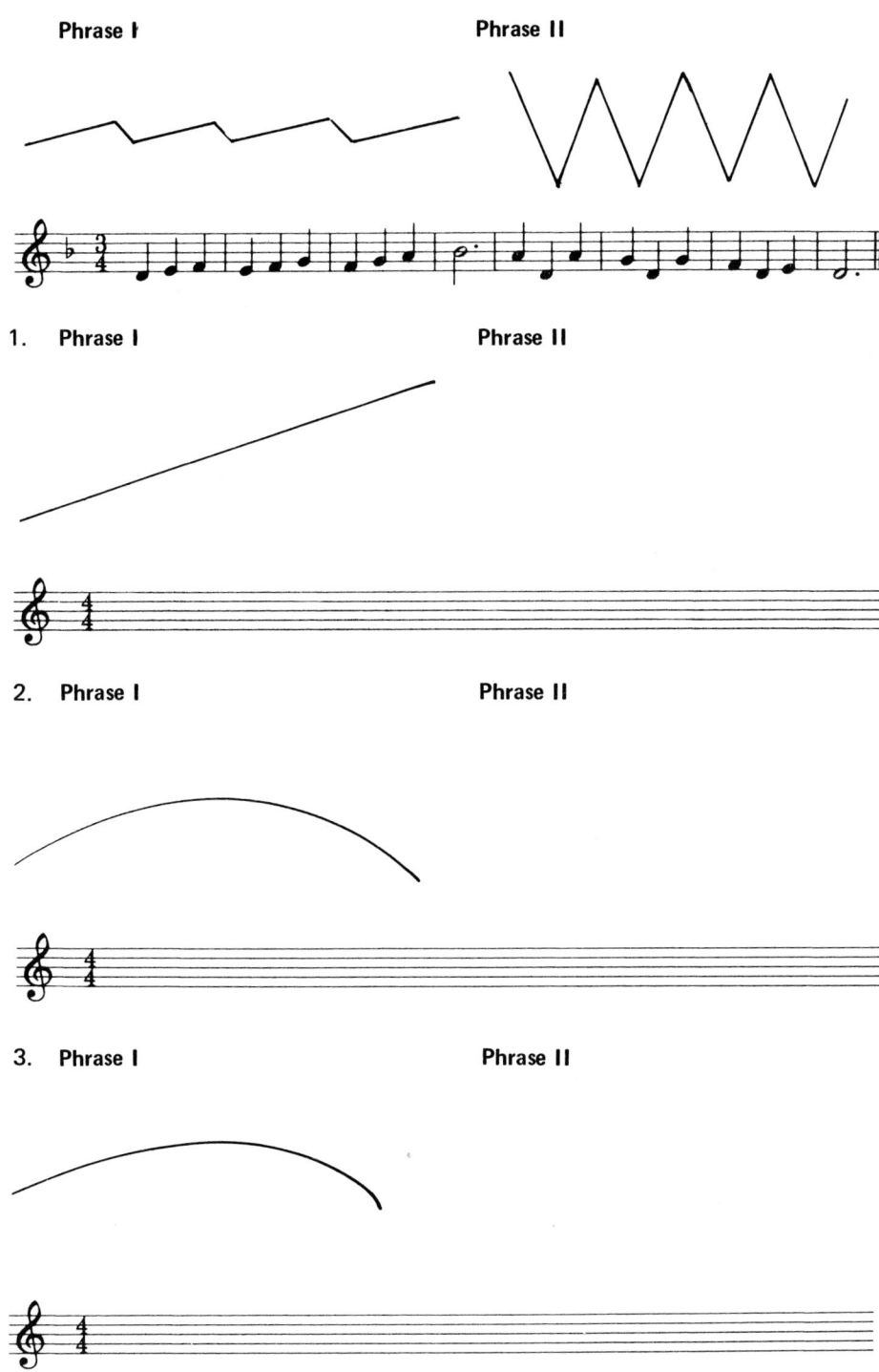

4. Phrase I   Phrase II

14 Compose a parallel period. Choose your own key and design.

15 Compose a double period in the key of Em.

SUGGESTED ACTIVITIES

1. Listen to *Short-Legged Soul Brother*, by Philip Markowitz (S 4, B 2). As you hear the beginning of a phrase, start drawing a bracket in the space below. **Continue** the bracket until you hear the end of the phrase or the beginning of a new one. Draw a bracket for each phrase in the piece. Listen a second time, adding to your phrase diagram a $\wedge$ at any point that you hear a definite cadence.

2. Mark the phrases and cadences in *Drink to Me Only with Thine Eyes* (SB 7). Name each cadence.
3. Mark the phrases and cadences in *Down in the Valley* (SB 12). Name each cadence.
4. Mark the cadences in *Jeune Fillette* (SB 26). Label each phrase with a small letter to indicate parallel or contrasting material. You will need **a**, **b**, and **c**.
5. Mark the phrases and cadences in *Que ne suis-je la Fougère* (SB 28). Name each cadence as a full cadence or semicadence.
6. Mark phrases, cadences, and phrase relationships of *The Riddle Song* (SB 6), Brahms's *Lullaby* (SB 8), and *Wayfaring Stranger* (SB 15).
7. Identify as a parallel period or contrasting period: *Believe Me, If All Those Endearing Young Charms* (through measure 8; SB 10), *Shoo Fly* (through measure 8; SB 11), *I Know Where I'm Going* (SB 2), *The Wraggle Taggle Gypsies, O!* (SB 16).
8. Name the cadence that ends *The Welcome Song* (SB 39).

TERMS AND CONCEPTS

Explain in your own words:
>form
>phrase design
>cadence

Contrast these terms and concepts:
>symmetrical phrase design/asymmetrical phrase design
>semicadence/full cadence
>perfect authentic cadence/imperfect authentic cadence
>period/double period
>parallel period/contrasting period

CHAPTER 14

THE MOTIVE
In a musical composition, a melodic idea that continually returns is called a *motive*. It can be thought of as a unifying element which holds a piece together by its repetition. Here we shall examine it from a traditional point of view as the subdivision of the phrase.

This is the first phrase of the Christmas carol *We Three Kings*.

One phrase is made up of two smaller units. In this case, they are exactly the same. The smaller unit is the motive. It is the building block of the phrase.

Now examine the first phrase of this excerpt from *Symphony No. 7*, by Beethoven:

In this example, we see that the phrase is built on a recurring rhythmic motive.

1 Study the Mozart *Minuet* (SB 48). What is the rhythmic motive? _____.

One way to build the phrase is to repeat the motive, starting on a different pitch. This is called a *sequence*.

2 Play. Observe the sequence of the motive.

Skip to My Lou

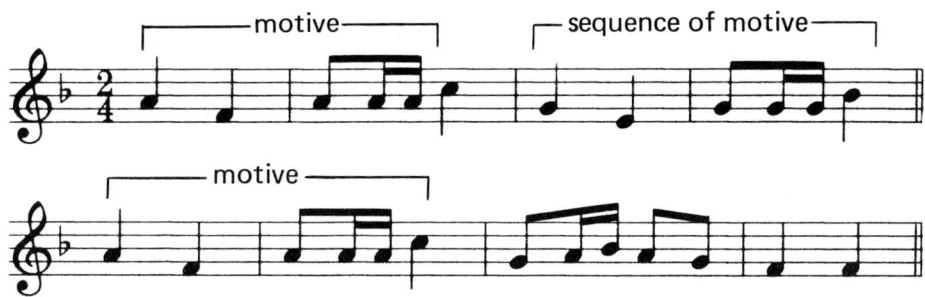

3 Play and mark the sequences of the indicated motive. Show your choice by the use of brackets.

Sonata for Cello and Piano, Opus 5, No. 2 (excerpt) — Beethoven

Gm

CHARACTERISTICS OF THE MOTIVE
We can now make some observations about the characteristics of a motive: 1) **Rhythmic identity**: a motive can be a repeated rhythmic pattern, even though the pitches may change (e.g., Beethoven's *Symphony No. 7*); 2) **Rhythmic and pitch identity**: a motive can have both a rhythmic pattern and a pitch design that are repeated (e.g., *We Three Kings, Skip to My Lou*, Beethoven's *Cello Sonata* Op. 5, No. 2).

IDENTIFYING THE MOTIVE
How do you identify a motive in a musical composition? Look and listen for a musical unit that can be recognized by repetition, of either pitch or rhythm, or of both. It can be as long as a few measures or as short as a few beats.

4 Identify the motive in these excerpts:

Study in A (excerpt) — Fernando Sor

Stabat Mater (excerpt) — Pergolesi

5 In the *Scorebook*, bracket the motives of the following pieces. Remember, the motive may appear only a few times, and not throughout the entire melody.

The Riddle Song (SB 6)
Alouette (SB 20)
This Old Man (SB 18)
I Know Where I'm Going (SB 2)
Hush, Little Baby (SB 17)

MOTIVIC DEVELOPMENT

Below are the technical terms to describe the development of a motive, with their applications to a particular motive.

Motive

Rhythmic Identity
(rhythm only)

Pitch Identity
(pitch design only)

Repetition

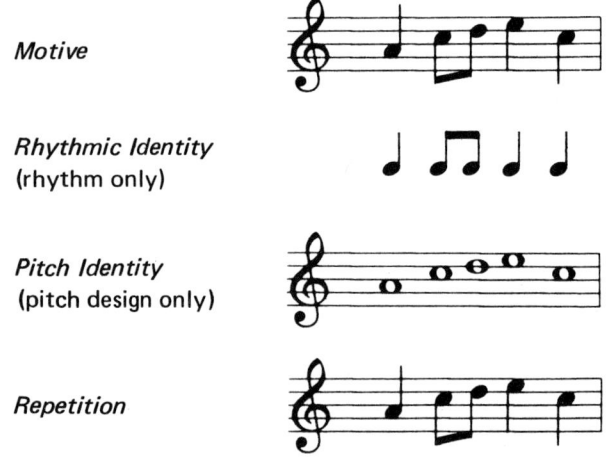

Sequence
(repetition starting
on another pitch)

Inversion
(changing the direction
of each melodic interval;
if the original goes up
a 3rd, the inversion goes
down a 3rd, etc.)

Augmentation
(making the rhythmic
values longer)

Diminution
(making the rhythmic
values shorter)

These are strict examples of the development of a motive. There are many times when the intervallic or rhythmic repetitions are not exact, but we still hear the basic process of motivic development at work. For example, even if an inversion is not quite literal, it is still heard as an inversion.

The analysis of motives and their development has been based on the occurrence of motivic patterns in all types of music, from anonymous folk songs to symphonies by great composers. This supports the thesis that motivic repetition and development are natural musical practices, not simply technical acts. A beautiful example of both musical and technical development of the motive is the following melody by Brahms:

Symphony No. 3, second movement

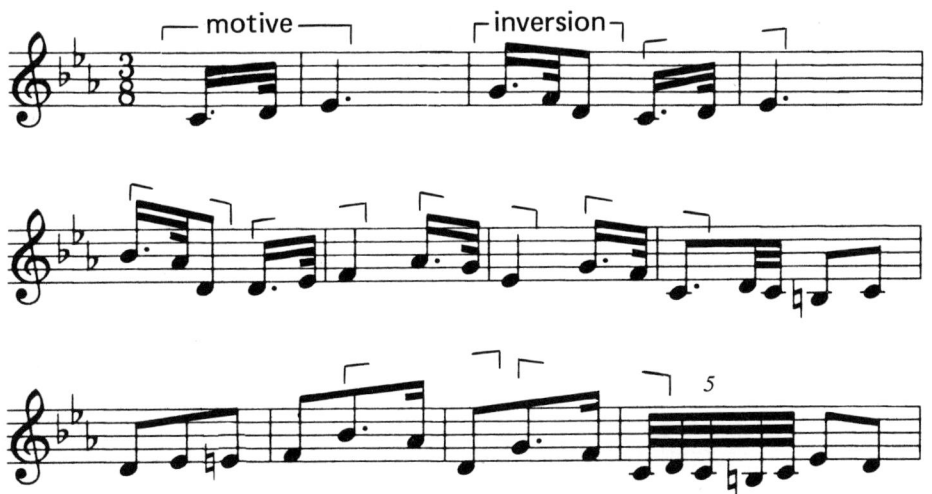

6 Answer the following questions about the melody above:
1. What rhythmic development takes place in measure 2? _____
2. Are the inversions of the original motive exact? _____
3. Are there any exact repetitions of the original motive? _____

7 Exercises with motives: the written notes indicate either the starting point for motivic repetition or a cadence. Sing and play, supplying the notes necessary to complete each sequence.

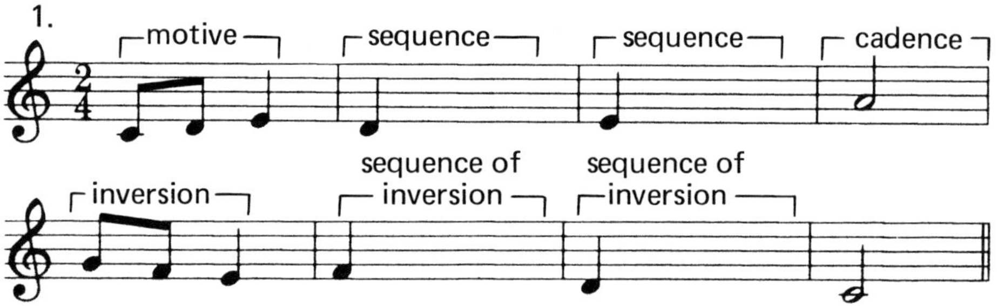

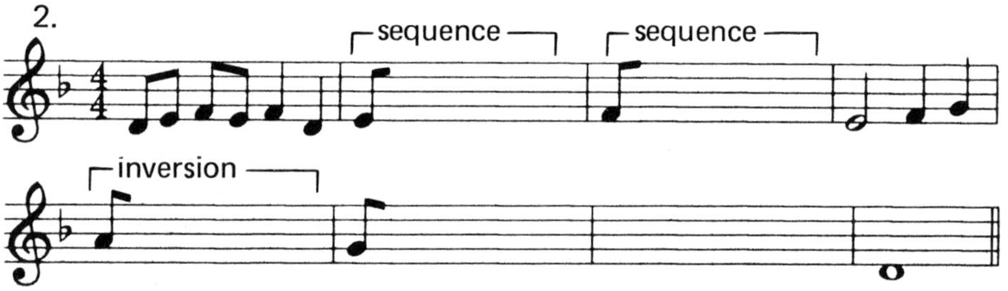

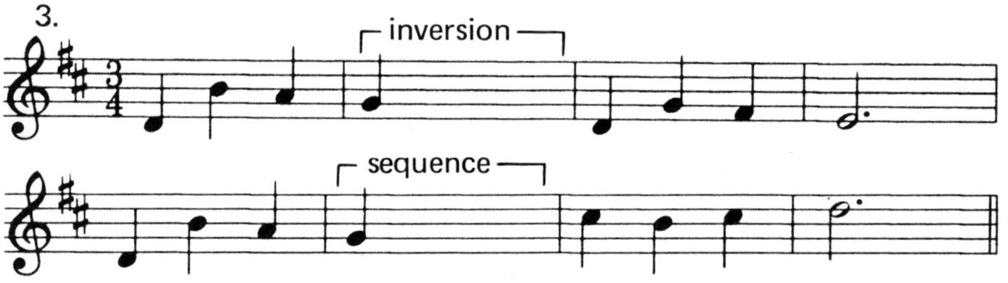

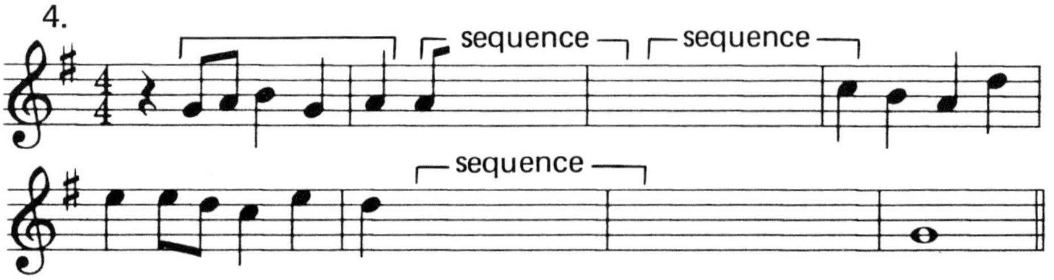

5. Write the rhythmic identity of this motive.

6. Write the pitch identity of this motive (in o notes).

7. Identify the motive. Name the process that takes place in the second line.

Line I

Bach
etc.

Line II (later on in the piece)

etc.

POPULAR USE OF THE MOTIVE

In many rock and jazz pieces, a single motive forms whole sections through repetition. The process of development often takes place through improvisation. When the motive is repeated continuously in the bass, the result is called an *ostinato*; the motive may be called an *ostinato motive*. (The terms "ostinato" and "ostinato motive" are applicable to classical music as well as popular music.)

8 Listen to *Nature Trail*, by Ted Moore (S 3 , B 2). The first part of this piece is built on the following ostinato motive:

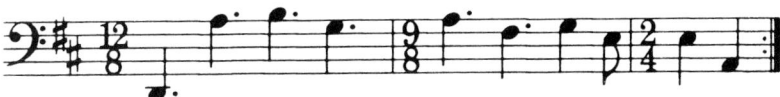

The piece has a second section using the following ostinato motive, which is not repeated literally.

Answer the following questions:

1. In the first section of the piece, does the electric piano play the ostinato motive or a motive of its own? _____

2. At the end of the first section of the piece, what motive does the electric piano play? _____

3. The third section of the piece is formed by a return to _____

4. The end of the piece is based on which motive? _____

9 Listen to the electronic piece *Fuego*, by Neil Waltzer (S 2 , B 2). There are three sections in this piece, represented by the boxes below. Write the word *ostinato* in the box or boxes corresponding to the section(s) where an ostinato motive occurs.

10 Listen to the beginning of the *Waltz in C-Sharp Minor*, by Chopin (SB 52, S 2 , B 1) Notice that the motive has two different parts. These parts are indicated below:

A large motive often consists of smaller parts. The motive may be repeated intact or the parts may be repeated separately. Repetition of part of the motive is called *fragmentation*.

11 Listen to *How Strange* (SB 53, S 7 , B 1). This piece is also built on a motive containing two distinct parts. On first listening, follow the score. On second listening, follow this diagram for the beginning of the piece.

improvisation by all instruments till end of section :||

Answer the following questions based on *How Strange*:

1. The word that describes the repetition of the motive in the measure 9 is
_____ .

2. Is the motive present in measure 17? _____

3. In the last part of the piece (the coda), what happens to the motive that has not happened before? _____

_____

_____

12 Listen to *Reasons* (S 6, B 1). Listen particularly to the introduction, which will present the various motives and parts of motives to you. After a few careful listenings, answer the following questions:

1. When the guitar enters, what motives or parts of motives is the synthesizer playing? _____

2. When the tambourine appears, a new section starts. Which instrument improvises a new motive of its own? _____

3. In the last section (the coda), what motive or parts of a motive does the synthesizer play? _____

4. In the coda, what is the piano playing? _____

13 Listen to *Short-Legged Soul Brother*, by Philip Markowitz (S 4, B 2). How many important motives do you hear? _____ List them by number: motive I, motive II, etc. After each motive, state the instrument that first plays it.

_____

_____

_____

_____

SUGGESTED ACTIVITIES

1. Develop any one (or more) of these motives in the exact way indicated in the discussion of motivic development, pages 190-191. First copy the motive, then using pages 190 and 191 as guides, write the rhythmic identity, pitch identity, repetition, sequence, inversion, augmentation, and diminution of the motive.

2. Repeat this process with motives of your own invention in your own manuscript book.

3. Write a melody that uses melodic development. Don't try to use all the procedures for motivic development. Let your ears guide you.

4. Find motives in music that you listen to often, or in music that you sing or play. You may be surprised to find motives in familiar music.

5. Contrast the meaning of the term "motive" as it applies to music, with its meaning as applied to a personal action (a topic for discussion, writing, or thinking).

6. Follow the use of the motive throughout *Remember, O Thou Man* (SB 44). How do the words affect the motive structure?

7. Compose an ostinato piece.

8. Compose motives which are suggested by these designs. You don't have to be too literal in your reaction to the design. If some designs don't move you, leave them out. If you find one you like, extend the motive into one or two phrases.

Examples

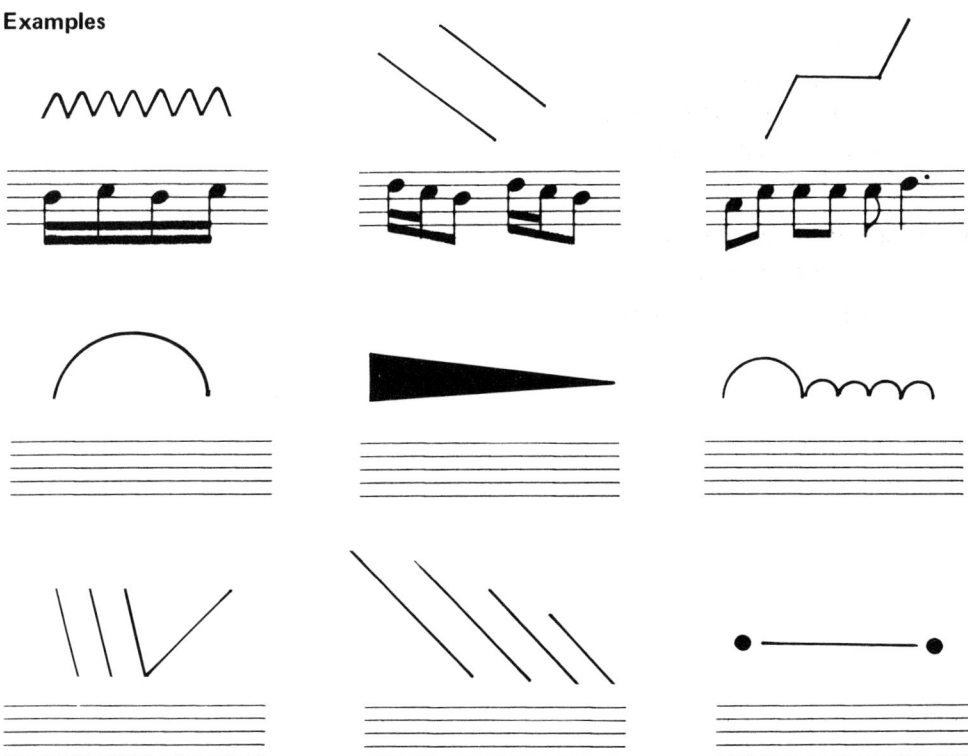

9. Create your own designs, then the motives.

TERMS AND CONCEPTS
Explain in your own words:

    motive
    repetition
    rhythmic identity of a motive
    pitch identity of a motive
    motivic development
    ostinato

Contrast these terms and concepts:
    sequence/inversion
    augmentation/diminution

CHAPTER 15

MELODY

When you try to remember "how a song goes," just what is it that you are trying to remember? First, you might try to recall the words, which act as a stimulant for remembering the two important elements of the melody: rhythm and pitch. For rhythm and pitch work together to create melody.

Most melodies that we hear are accompanied by other instruments, but a good melody really doesn't need any help. A solo voice, flute, or other melodic instrument can satisfy the listener if the music has a good melody. And just what is a good melody? A difficult question. Good melodies are a combination of inspiration and technique. Since inspiration is somewhat difficult to analyze, let us examine some of the more tangible technical characteristics of melody.

MELODIC SHAPE

One aspect of melodic design is its *shape* or *contour*. This characteristic can be represented graphically by outlining the pitch direction of the melody.

1 Listen to *The Water Is Wide* (S 3 , B 1) and observe how this pitch outline indicates the shape of each phrase.

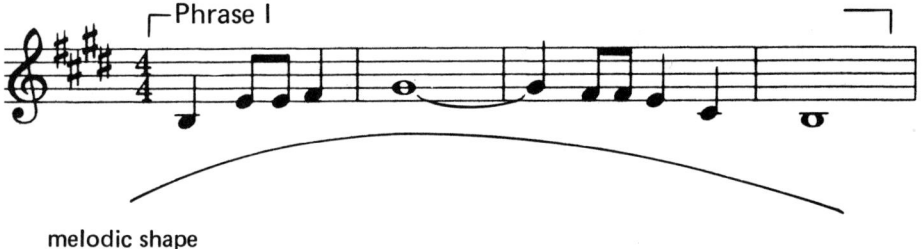

melodic shape

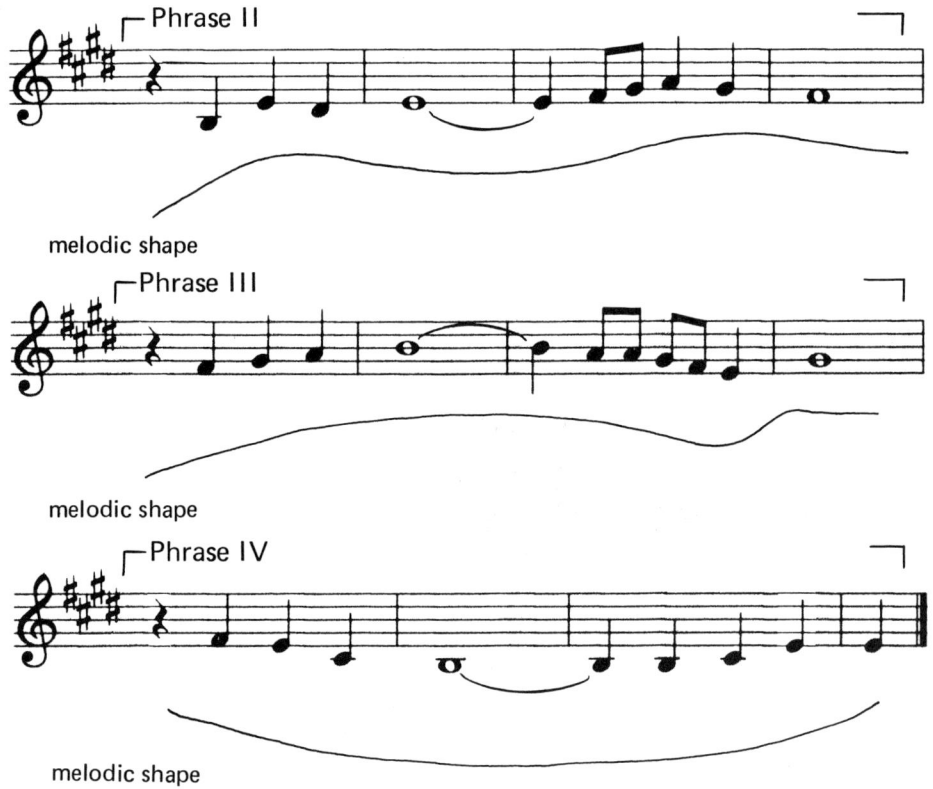

melodic shape

Phrase I of the melody follows a simple design, rising to peak at the middle of the phrase and falling back at the end. Phrases II and III are more complex shapes, with more curves toward the ends of the phrases. This relative complexity creates an active feeling, pushing toward the last phrase. The concluding shape is, once again, a more simple design, a reflection of the first. Also notice that the highest pitch of phrase II (A) is a step above the highest pitch of phrase I (G♯). Phrase III rises another step to B, the highest pitch of the song. In reaction to the rising shape of the first three phrases, the final one falls to B and then rises to a cadence on the tonic E.

2 Carefully play and sing the following melodies. Observe the shapes.

1.

4. *Symphony in D Minor,* second movement

Franck

MELODIC GOAL

Sometimes a phrase may peak at a high or low pitch. This is called the *melodic goal*. It's not just the highest or lowest note, but rather that pitch towards which the phrase is directed by melodic shape and rhythmic design.

4 Circle the melodic goal in each of these excerpts. Play each; name the key.

MELODIC GOALS IN IMPROVISATIONS

Climaxing at a melodic goal is a device often used by soloists in contemporary improvisation. A guitarist, pianist, or other soloist often plans his solo to drive rhythmically toward one or many peaks. This is part of his concept of shaping a good solo.

5 Listen to the middle section of *How Strange* (S 7 , B 1), which is a guitar solo. On first listening, just find the melodic goal. On the second listening, follow the score (SB 53) and find the measure where it occurs. Which measure? _____

6 Listen to *I Know Where I'm Going* (S 2 , B 3), *One Grain of Sand* (S 4 , B 1), and *The Water Is Wide* (S 3 , B 1) for melodic goals. On a second listening of each song, use the scores (SB 2, SB 4, and SB 5). In these songs, you are looking for the high point of the entire song. In which phrase does the melodic goal occur in *One Grain of Sand*— _____ ; *I Know Where I'm Going*— _____ ; and *The Water Is Wide*— _____ ?

In many melodic designs, you will find that the goal comes somewhere after the middle of the phrase or song. Very often, it comes about three quarters of the way through the phrase or piece. This gives the musical line a chance to flow toward the melodic goal, and then subside. Possible locations of the melodic goal are shown here.

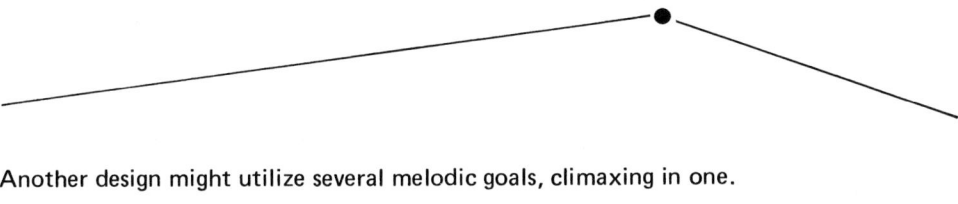

Another design might utilize several melodic goals, climaxing in one.

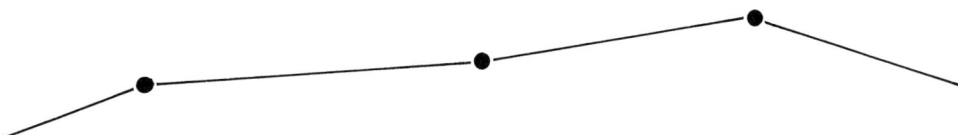

Another interesting design might be this:

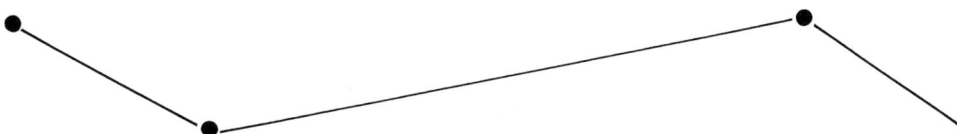

Every melody is different, so the melodic goal may come at almost any point. There also are beautiful melodies that have no distinct melodic goals.

MOTIVIC DEVELOPMENT

As we have seen in Chapter 14, a melody can be designed by developing its motive. Just as a phrase can flow towards a melodic goal, its musical flow can result from motivic development. Observe this process in this example:

Notice that nothing is written above the last two measures. To end the melody, motivic development stops and a new concluding thought is added.

7 Another way to develop a motive is to add notes.
Study for motivic development:

The motive is stated in the first measure. It is developed in the second measure by the addition of one note, E. The addition of still another note, G♭, in the third measure helps propel the melody to its goal in the fourth measure.

8  Play:

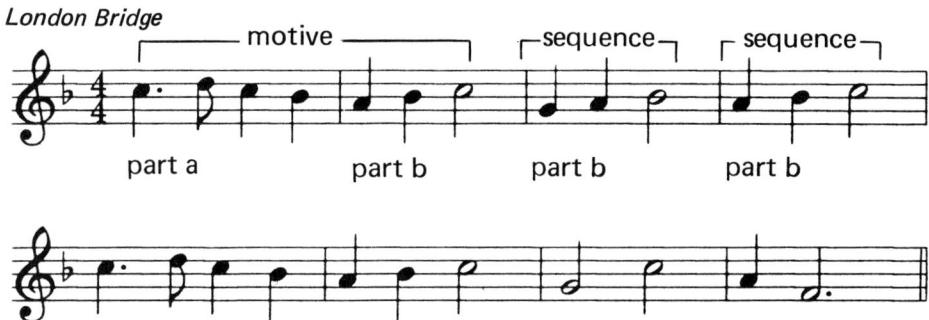

In the overall design, **part** of the motive is repeated by sequence, again illustrating why a motive may have to be considered in parts.

9 Examine the motivic development in these excerpts. Things to look for: repetition, use of parts of the motive, sequence, inversion (review pages 190–191). If you recognize that a motive is being developed but can't tell how, just write "development" ("dev.").

Play:

1. Haydn

2. Schubert

10 Listen to *Adieu, Sweet Amarillis* and follow the score (SB 41, S 1 , B 3). Bracket the main motives throughout the piece. In your manuscript book, write the melodic shapes of all four parts for the first 6 measures.

SUGGESTED ACTIVITIES

1. Analyze for basic motive, development, and melodic characteristics:

2. Analyze for motive and melodic goal. Draw the shape.

Shape

Shape

3. Listen to Chopin's *Waltz in C-Sharp Minor* (SB 52, S 2, B 1). Circle the melodic goal of each section in the *Scorebook*. Each section is 32 measures long, and may have one or two melodic goals.

4. Listen to the last section of *Nature Trail*, by Ted Moore (S 3, B 2). Observe the shape of the **bass line**. There is a high melodic goal followed by a push toward a low melodic goal. Can you hear them?

5. Listen to the second guitar solo in *Reasons* (S 6, B 2) for melodic goal. Does it occur at the beginning, the middle, or the end of the solo? _____

6. Listen to *Short-Legged Soul Brother*, by Philip Markowitz (S 4, B 2). Draw below a **free** impression of the shape of the phrases as you hear them.

7. Analyze *Sarabanda* (SB 45) for all melodic characteristics.
8. Analyze *Study in C* (SB 49) for sequences and melodic goal.
9. Compose a melody which shows the techniques of melodic development.
10. Compose a four-phrase melody in which there is a definite design to the melodic shape. If you wish, draw the shape first. In the third phrase, reach a melodic peak.
11. Analyze the Bach *Fugue* (SB 51) for sequence, melodic goals, and basic motive.

TERMS AND CONCEPTS
Explain in your own words:
    melody
    melodic shape (contour)
    melodic goal
    melodic goal in improvisation
    motivic development
    development by sequence

CHAPTER 16

TEXTURE

Consider the meaning of the word *texture*. If you were a painter, you might use different thicknesses of pigment, deep, clashing colors, and broad strokes; or on the other hand, even application of pigment, soft colors, and very fine lines. Also consider the texture of different types of fabric, produced by varying combinations and methods of weaving. For example, how does velvet look and feel compared to cotton? In all these examples, a specific texture is determined by the choice and combination of different elements, and the way they are combined. Most important, different textures produce different affects.

As in painting, texture plays an important role in forming musical structures and producing different reactions in the listener. Texture takes many different forms in music. One such form is the combination of voices. Again, we shall use language and rhythm as a starting point.

1
1. In a group, speak this line in unison with a steady rhythm. One leader counts off 1, 2; the group starts speaking on 3 and accents the word "heard." Repeat the line.

2. Now divide into two groups, but separate the groups in different parts of the room to create space between the sources of sound. The voices still speak in unison with the same steady rhythm.

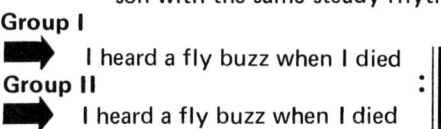

3. Now choose one person to improvise a little solo on the word "buzz" in any rhythm he chooses.

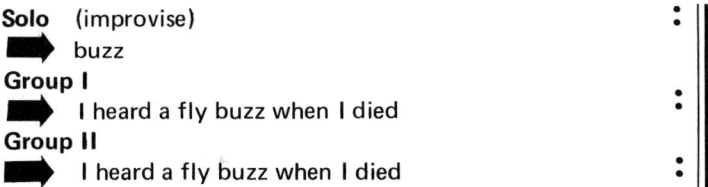

Solo (improvise)
➡ buzz

Group I
➡ I heard a fly buzz when I died

Group II
➡ I heard a fly buzz when I died

4. Now add another soloist who will repeat the words "I died, I died, I died" in a high, choppy voice. Have Group II say each word slowly and in low-pitched voices, following one member acting as conductor.

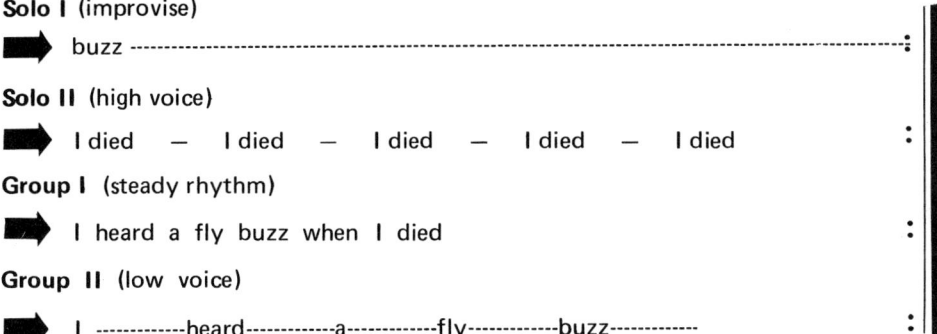

Solo I (improvise)
➡ buzz --

Solo II (high voice)
➡ I died — I died — I died — I died — I died

Group I (steady rhythm)
➡ I heard a fly buzz when I died

Group II (low voice)
➡ I ------------heard------------a------------fly------------buzz------------

Which of the "pieces" above creates the most tension or feeling of motion? Which is the least tense, and thus more stable (although still forward-moving)? In general, the more complex and diverse the various elements are, the more active and forward-moving the result. When the individual lines are similar, the texture becomes less active and more stable.

ELEMENTS THAT AFFECT TEXTURE

Many factors can affect texture. Some that we have just explored are:

1. pitch—high or low;

2. rhythm—use or non-use of a steady pulse;

3. directional source of sound (think of why a stereo recording is more interesting than a mono recording);

4. style of delivery—smooth, broken up, etc.;

5. isolation and emphasis of different parts of the motive—in musical terms, this is called *fragmentation*;

6. contrast between parts.

The possibilities for creating different textures are endless. This is one of the most fascinating elements of composition. Remember that different combinations of lines, the number of lines, and their relationships to each other produce different musical affects.

2 These designs represent the shapes of three musical lines heard together. Describe the affects of each texture below.

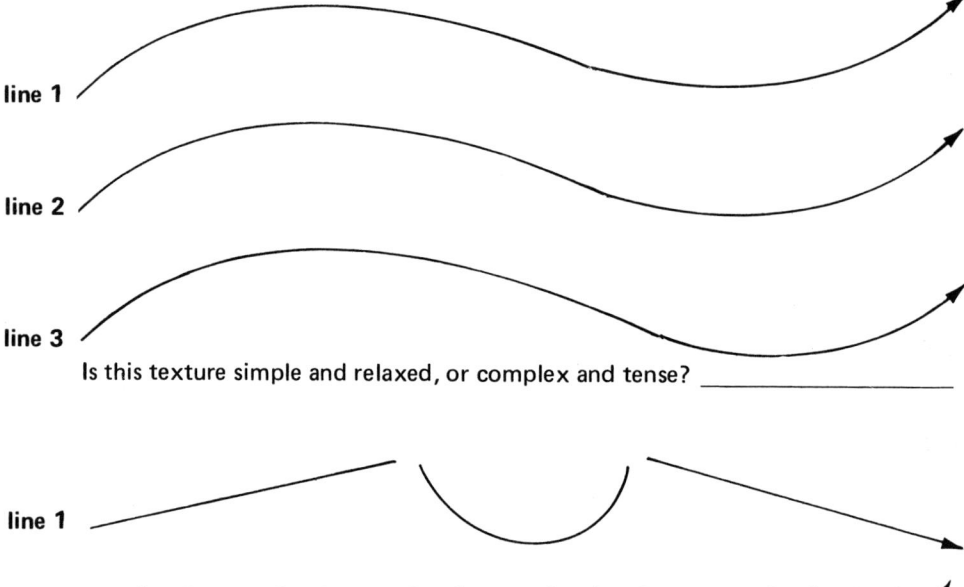

Is this texture simple and relaxed, or complex and tense? _____

line 1
line 2
line 3

Is this texture relaxed or tense? _____

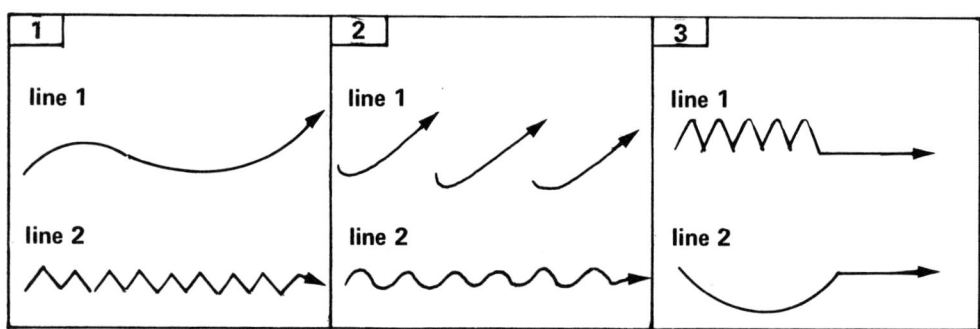

Which design shows change in the course of the phrase from activity to stability: design 1, 2, or 3? _____.

3 Listen to the fourth movement of *Antiphonies*, by Leo Kraft (S 1, B 1). There are two instruments in this piece: piano and synthesizer (the instrument that makes electronic sounds). As you listen, draw a visual representation of each. Your drawing should be simply your reaction to the various sounds and their pitch directions.

Electronic
Sounds
(synthesizer)

Piano

Do you feel that the synthesizer and piano are doing the same thing or different things?
_____

In what ways are they similar or different? _____
_____
_____
_____
_____

4 Listen to *Rhythm Improvisation*, by Jim Saporito and Ted Moore (S 5, B 2). Describe, in your own words, the texture of each of the sounds that make up the three sections. Your descriptions need not be technical; simply state your feelings about the sound textures in whatever word or words describe the sound to you. Write your description of each section in the corresponding box.

Textures of *Rhythm Improvisation*

5

Listen to *Fuego*, by Neil Waltzer (S 2 , B 2). The form is ternary (ABA). Which section is the most active and forward-moving? Which section is more simple in design and less forward-moving? Write the word "complex" or "simple" in the appropriate box to indicate the texture.

A	B	C

How many motives are there in Part A? _____

Is there a motive in Part B which is also in Part A? _____

VOICE COMBINATIONS: MUSICAL TERMS

The musical terms that describe the number and style of the combinations of lines are:

1. monophonic—one-voice texture;
2. homophonic—one main melody accompanied by secondary voices, often providing harmony;
3. polyphonic—many voices of equal importance.

6

Listen to these pieces as examples of monophonic, homophonic, and polyphonic textures. Follow each in the *Scorebook*.

monophonic: *One Grain of Sand* (SB 4, S 4 , B 1).

homophonic: Chopin, *Waltz in C-Sharp Minor* (SB 52, S 2 , B 1).

polyphonic: Bach, *Fugue in C minor* (SB 51, S 1 , B 2).

Answer the following questions:

1. Why is *One Grain of Sand* a monophonic texture?

   _____

2. The *Waltz in C-Sharp Minor* is a homophonic texture because of the relationship between the left hand and right hand. Describe this relationship:

   _____

   _____

   _____

3. The *Fugue in C Minor* is a polyphonic texture because of the relationships among the various lines. Describe these relationships: _____

HARMONY AND COUNTERPOINT

When a voice or instrument performs a melody, that melody is called a musical *line*. If more than one musical line is performed at the same time, two elements result: harmony and counterpoint.

> *Harmony* is the system which organizes the chords created by the various musical lines.
>
> *Counterpoint* is the combination of lines in relation to each other.

The basic concept of these elements, harmony and counterpoint, can be represented by the following designs. The dots indicate individual pitches and the direction of the resulting musical line (melody):

Musical line (melody—a succession of pitches)

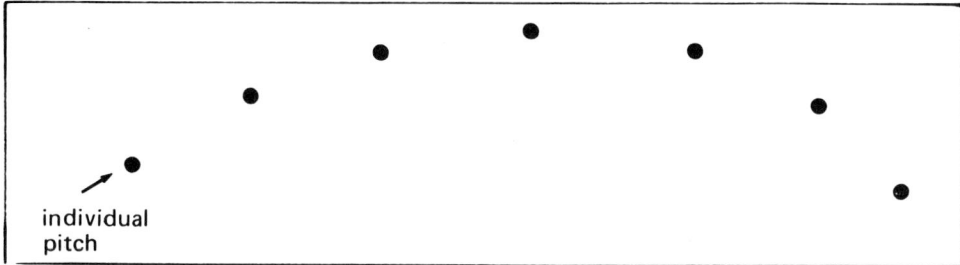

Combination of 3 lines (melodies)

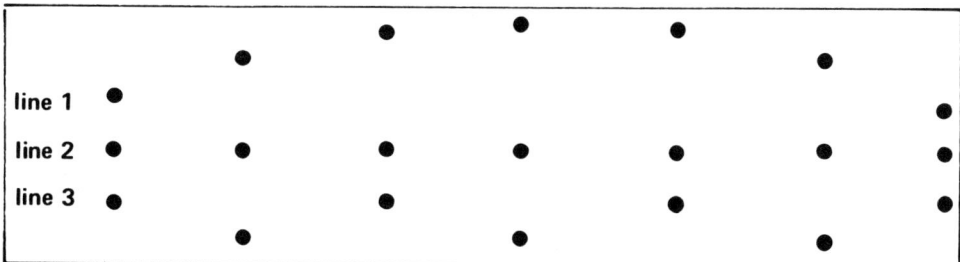

Harmony—relationship of vertical structures

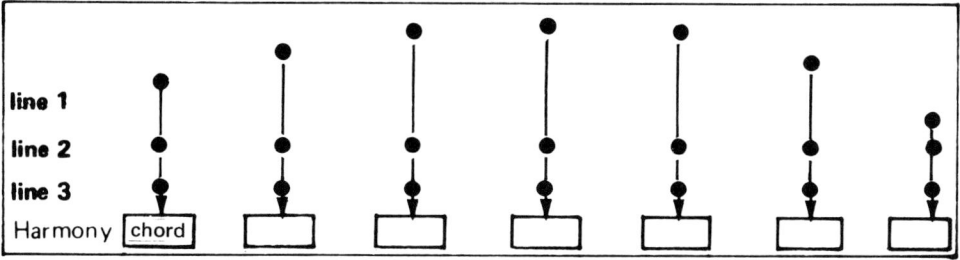

Counterpoint— horizontal relationships

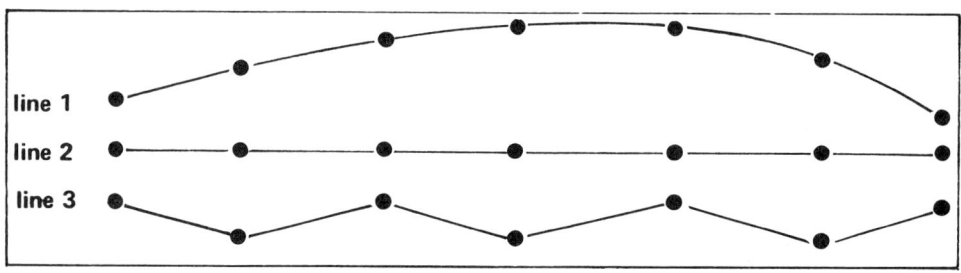

Actually, harmony and counterpoint are closely related and exist as **integrated** elements that produce musical textures. Counterpoint, for example, is greatly affected by the succession of intervals and chords. The interaction of these two forces might be represented in the following diagram:

Harmony and Counterpoint—interaction of two forces

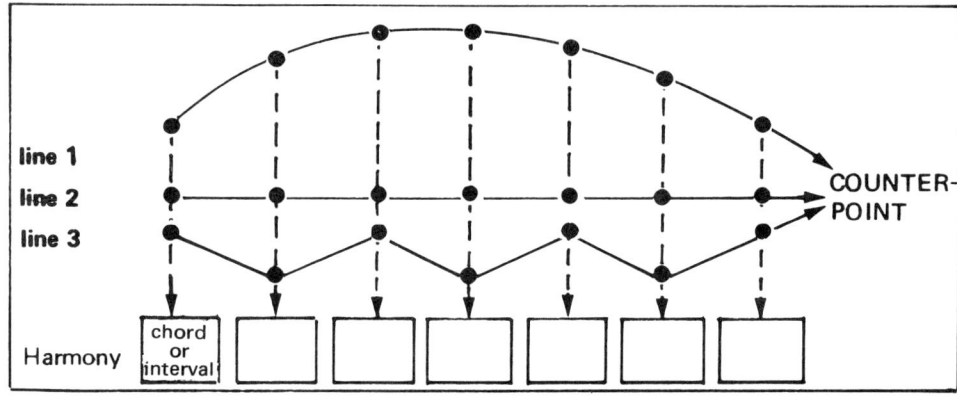

How do these forces interact? Let us first consider counterpoint. In the diagram above, a complex three-part texture is indicated. It is very *contrapuntal* because each line has melodic independence. The complexity of the counterpoint creates a forward-moving feeling. Now consider the harmony: if the chords (or intervals) are dissonant and complex in their relationship to each other, this will reinforce the forward movement of the music. But what if the harmony is consonant and stable? Let us look at this interaction in a real piece of music.

7 Listen to *Adieu, Sweet Amarillis*, by John Wilbye (SB 41, S 1 , B 3). Follow the music in the score. Pay special attention to the first phrase.

Adieu, Sweet Amarillis (excerpt)

The counterpoint is formed by *imitation*, one voice answering another at different times. The soprano motive is imitated by the alto motive, while the tenor motive is imitated by the bass. In terms of counterpoint, it seems quite complex—two different motives simultaneously treated by the process of imitation in a four-voice texture. But what of the harmony? It is very simple and stable, alternating between i and V in an even *harmonic rhythm* (rhythm of harmonic change). The result: a relaxed, stable section in which the harmony allows the voices to weave in and out gently with the words "Adieu, sweet Amarillis."

8 Listen to the *Fugue in C Minor*, by Bach (SB 51, S1, B2). The fugue is one of the most contrapuntal of all musical styles. The motive (in a fugue, it is called the *subject*) is introduced in the first 2 measures. It is then restated by every voice throughout much of the piece. Mark the entry of every subject. Are there any similarities between a fugue and a canon? _____

_____

_____

INSTRUMENTATION

The combination of instruments has a definite affect on the texture.

9 Listen to *How Strange* (S 7, B 1), *Reasons* (S 6, B 2), and *Nature Trail*, by Ted Moore (S 3, B 2). In each, a motive is presented in one instrument, and then other instruments join the music with counterpoint and duplication of the motive. What is the effect of adding instruments? _____

_____

Which instruments have the greatest affect on the rhythmic texture?

_____

10 How is the texture of *Remember, O Thou Man* (SB 44) different from that of *Adieu, Sweet Amarillis* (SB 41)? _____

_____

FORM AND TEXTURE

11 Listen to *How Strange* (S 7, B 1) and follow it in the score (SB 53). How is the texture affected in measure 17 (where the instruments abandon the motive and improvise freely over the chord progression)? _____

_____

At that same point, the drum beat changes and a new rhythm instrument appears. What is that instrument? _____
What is the effect of the new beat? _____

_____

In the middle of the piece, there is a drastic change in the rhythmic texture. Describe it. _____

_____

12 Listen to *Short-Legged Soul Brother*, by Philip Markowitz (S 4, B 2). Notice how changes in the rhythmic texture are used to create new sections, although the motive may stay the same. Does the electronic piano solo sound like a new section? _____ What is the bass doing during this solo? _____ What was it doing just before the solo? _____

After the electronic piano solo, the bass and piano join together in the same rhythm. What kind of texture is this: monophonic, homophonic, or polyphonic? _____ _____

What is the texture of the piece in general; monophonic, homophonic, or polyphonic? _____

13 Listen to *How Strange* (S 7, B 1) and follow this diagram, not the score.

A		A	B	A	Coda
					A
a	b	a b		a b	a
repetition of motive	improvisation tambourine added	repeat	guitar solo change in texture	triangle is added to rhythm	repetition of motive

Observe the following aspects of the form:

1. Part **A** is made up of smaller parts **a** and **b**.

2. **A** is repeated.

3. The guitar solo opens a new section, **B**, made up of one part, so there is no need to break it up.

4. **A** returns.

5. **A** starts again, but doesn't go into the improvisation section (**b**). Instead, it acts as a *coda* (the section which ends a piece).

6. In naming musical forms, sections that are repeated can be combined. Therefore, **AABA** coda becomes **ABA** coda. The form is ternary (three-part).

7. Within the first **A** there was a smaller form **ab**, a binary design (two-part). Thus we have a smaller form within a larger form; this is known as *compound form*.

ELEMENTS OF FORM

In identifying the sections of a piece, the following elements may be explored:

1. Texture—are there different textures?

2. Harmony—are there different key centers or progressions?

3. Motives—are there different motives?

4. Repetition—are there repetitions of melodies or chord progressions?

5. Cadences—what types of cadences define phrases or sections?

Designs using these elements: these are general outlines of possible designs.

Binary:

A	B
Motive I	Motive I or II
Key:G (or possible change of key)	Key:G (or possible change of key)

Ternary:

A	B	A
Motive I	Motive II	Motive I
	change of key	
Key: Dm		Key: Dm

Rondo form:

A	B	A	C	A
Motive I	Motive II	Motive I	Motive III	Motive I
	change of key		change of key	
Key: G		Key: G		Key: G

TERMS USED IN DESCRIBING FORM

1. Binary—two parts.

2. Ternary—three parts.

3. Coda—a section which ends a piece. It can be based on motives from the piece or it can be made up of new motives.

ROUNDED BINARY FORM

In this design, a binary form is the basic structure, often clarified by repeat signs.

$$\|: A :\|: B :\|$$

However, sometimes at the end of the **B** section, the motives and key of **A** will return, hinting at an **ABA** structure. A typical rounded binary design looks like this:

A	B	
Motive I	Motive II	Motive I
Key: Gm	Key: B	Key: Gm
(A)	(B)	(A)

14

1. Study the *Minuet for Lute* (SB 46). This is an example of a piece in rounded binary form. Mark the return of the original motive.

2. Listen to the *Minuet*, by Mozart (SB 48). This piece illustrates the harmonic design of the rounded binary form.

15 Listen to the *Waltz in C-Sharp Minor* (SB 52, S 2, B 1). Analyze for form. Write the form in letter names: _____
What theoretical term describes the relationship of the keys of the contrasting section and the original sections? _____
What section is a contrast harmonically? _____

SUGGESTED ACTIVITIES

1. Analyze for form: *Sarabanda* (SB 45); *Fugue*, by Bach (SB 51); *Minuet*, by Purcell (SB 47); *Dona, Dona* (SB 13); *Alouette* (SB 20); *Jeune Fillette* (SB 26); and *The First Noel* (SB 32).
2. Analyze *Reasons* (S 6 , B 2) in the same way that *How Strange* was analyzed in a box diagram. There are many similarities. Use as many boxes as you need. The first part is completed for you as an example.

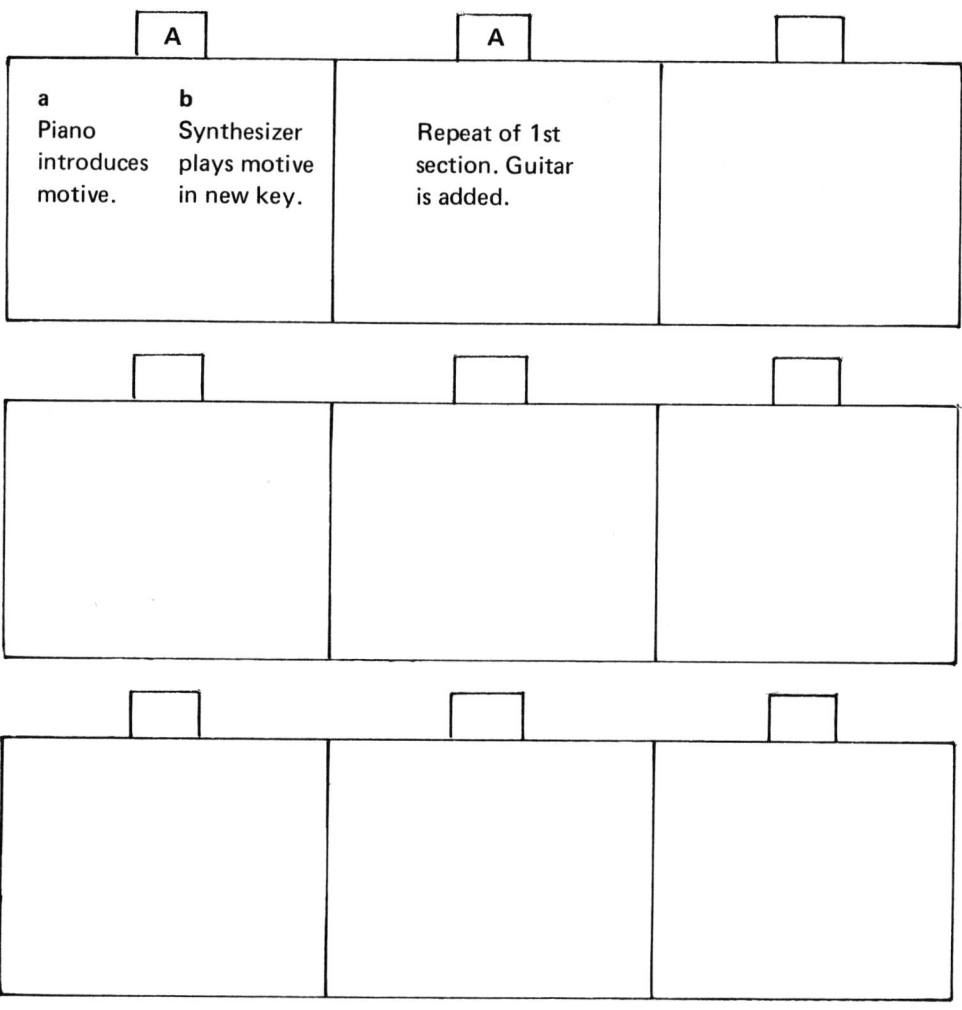

3. Listen again to the fourth movement of *Antiphonies* by Leo Kraft (S 1, B 1). In relationship to the other pieces we have studied, the form of this piece is unique. Describe it. _____

   _____ _____

4. Listen to *Nature Trail*, by Ted Moore (S 3, B 2). Name the form. _____

   _____

5. Listen to *Adieu, Sweet Amarillis* (SB 41, S 1, B 3). Analyze for form. The final section is in the key of _____.
   How do the words affect the form? _____

   _____

   _____

   _____

6. Listen to *Rhythm Improvisation* (S 5, B 2). Name the form. _____

TERMS AND CONCEPTS

Explain in your own words:

    texture
    melodic shape
    complexity and simplicity of musical texture
    monophonic
    homophonic
    polyphonic
    harmony
    counterpoint
    relationship between harmony and counterpoint
    imitation
    instrumentation
    harmonic rhythm
    coda
    prelude and postlude
    binary
    ternary
    rondo
    rounded binary
    compound form

APPENDICES

APPENDIX I

TABLE OF NOTE AND REST VALUES

The value of each of the following symbols is based on the quarter-note unit of one beat.

Name	Symbol	Value (in ♩s)
whole note	𝅝	4
whole rest	𝄻	4
half note	𝅗𝅥	2
half rest	𝄼	2
dotted half note	𝅗𝅥.	3
dotted half rest	𝄼.	3
quarter note	♩	1
quarter rest	𝄽	1
eighth note	♪	$\frac{1}{2}$
eighth rest	𝄾	$\frac{1}{2}$
sixteenth note	𝅘𝅥𝅯	$\frac{1}{4}$
sixteenth rest	𝄿	$\frac{1}{4}$
thirty-second note	𝅘𝅥𝅰	$\frac{1}{8}$
thirty-second rest	𝅀	$\frac{1}{8}$
sixty-fourth note	𝅘𝅥𝅱	$\frac{1}{16}$
sixty-fourth rest	𝅁	$\frac{1}{16}$

The relationship of note values to each other

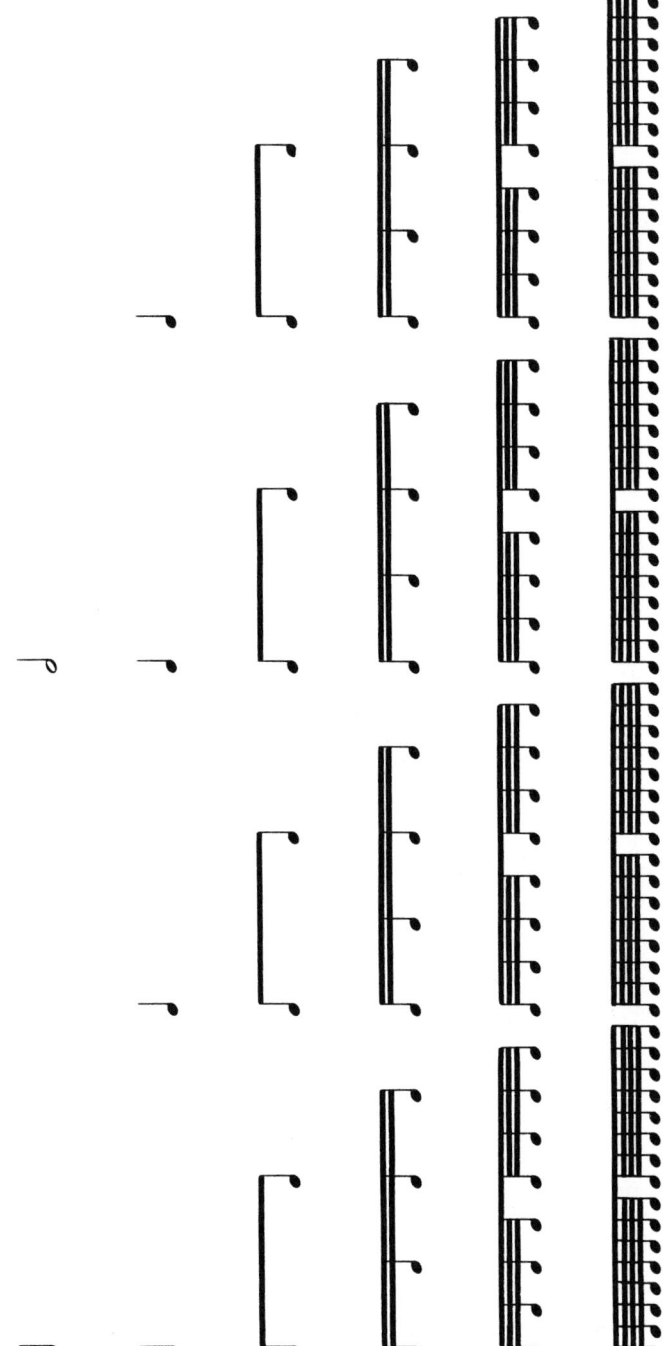

APPENDIX II
CHECKLIST OF NOTATION SYMBOLS

𝄞   treble clef (G clef): defines the second staff line from the bottom as G.

𝄢   bass clef (F clef): defines the second staff line from the top as F.

C   common time: represents $\frac{4}{4}$ meter.

¢   *alla breve*: represents $\frac{2}{2}$ meter.

⌢   slur: a curved line written above two or more notes to indicate that they are grouped together and played smoothly.

>   accent: indicates emphasis of a note.

—   stress: indicates slight emphasis or sustaining of a note.

<   *crescendo*: indicates a gradual increase in volume.

>   *decrescendo* (*diminuendo*): indicates a gradual decrease in volume.

♪   grace note: a small note whose time value is not strictly counted; it is played very quickly just before the beat or on the beat of the note immediately following it.

8- - - - - -   *all' ottava*: notes written beneath this symbol are played one octave higher than written.

℘   pedal: a signal to the pianist to depress the pedal of the piano.

✻   pedal release: a signal to the pianist to release the pedal.

tr, ⁓   trill: a musical ornament consisting of rapid alternation between the written note and the note above it.

𝄐   *fermata*: indicates that the note beneath it should be held longer than its normal duration.

𝄆   𝄇   repeat signs: the music enclosed within these signs is to be performed twice.

ff   *fortissimo*: very loud

f   *forte*: loud

mf   *mezzoforte*: moderately loud

mp   *mezzopiano*: moderately soft

p   *piano*: soft

pp   *pianissimo*: very soft

rit.   *ritardando*: gradually becoming slower

APPENDIX III
MAJOR AND MINOR SCALES AND KEY SIGNATURES

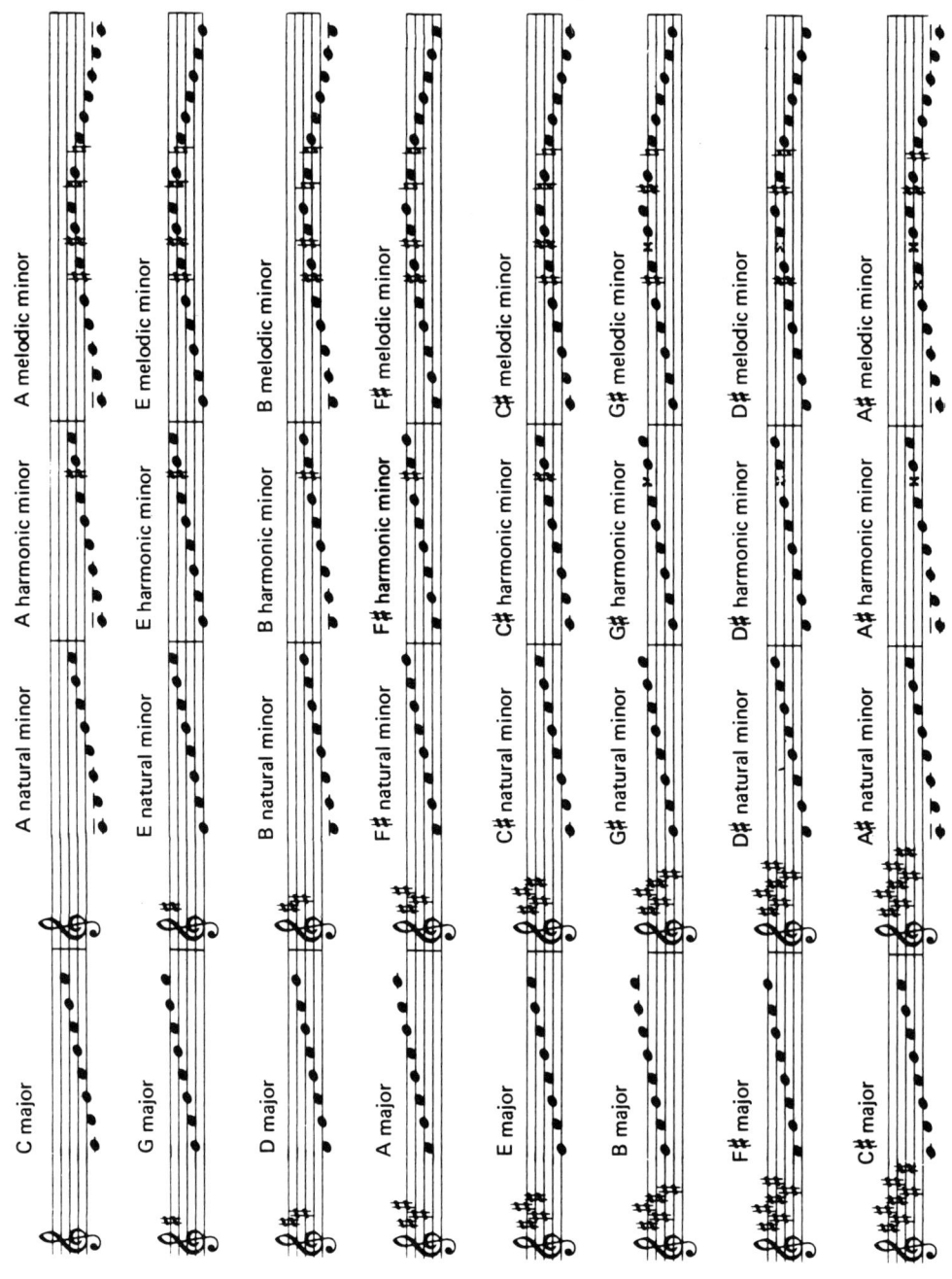

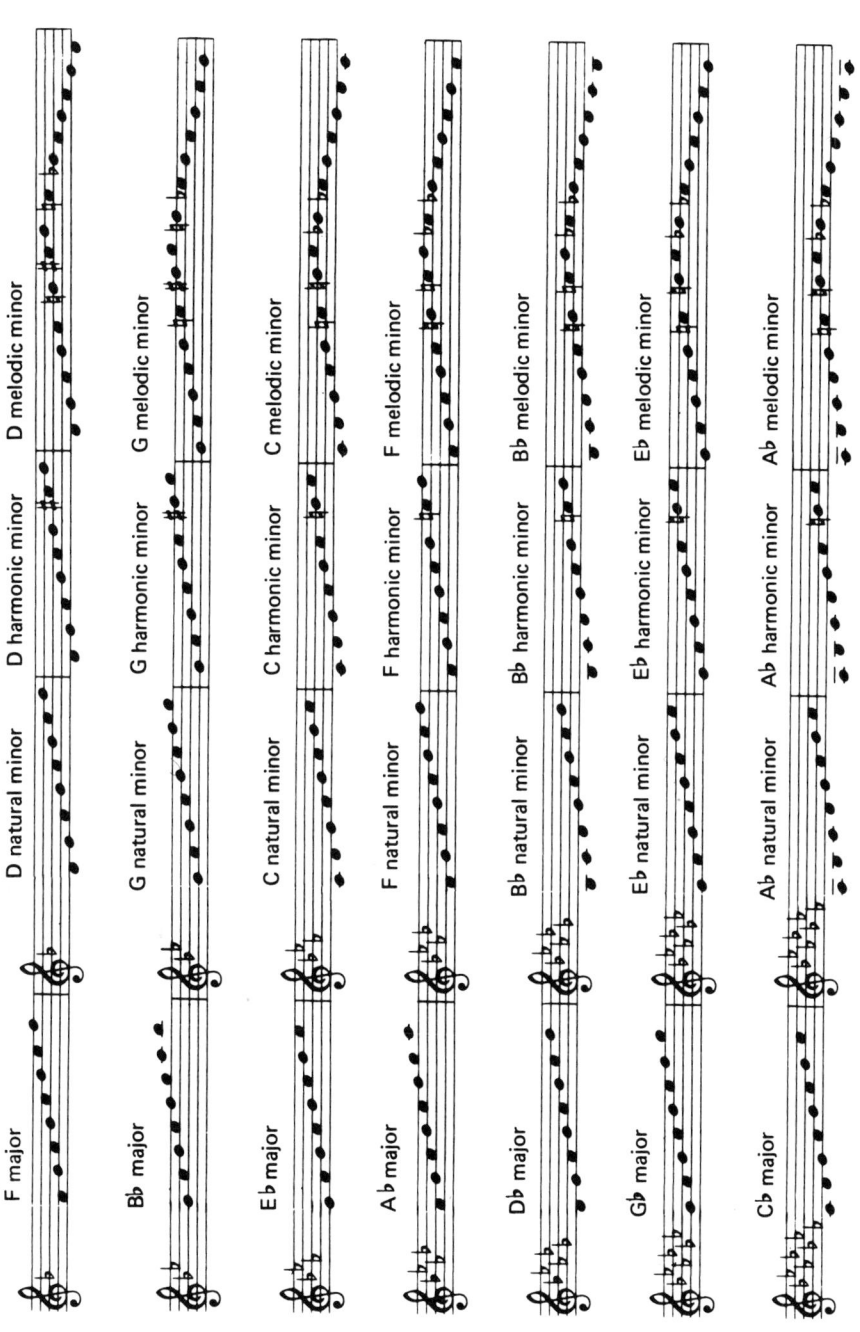

APPENDIX IV

TRIADS AND CHORDS

The following are the most commonly used triads and 7th chords. Although this listing is by no means comprehensive, it includes those chords you will most often encounter.

APPENDIX V
METHODS OF SIGHT SINGING

Fixed do: in the fixed *do* system, **each pitch** has only one syllable name. These are:

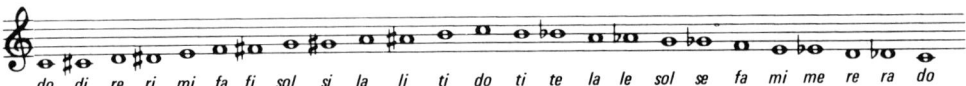

Movable do: in the movable *do* system, syllables apply to **scale degrees**. Therefore, in the key of C major, C is *do* and G is *sol*. In the key of F♯ major, F♯ is *do* and C♯ is *sol*, etc. Note the following variation of syllable names in the major scale and its relative minor:

		do	re	mi	fa	sol	la	ti	do
C Major	scale degree:	1	2	3	4	5	6	7	8

		la	ti	do	re	mi	fa	sol	la
A Minor	scale degree:	1	2	3	4	5	6	7	8

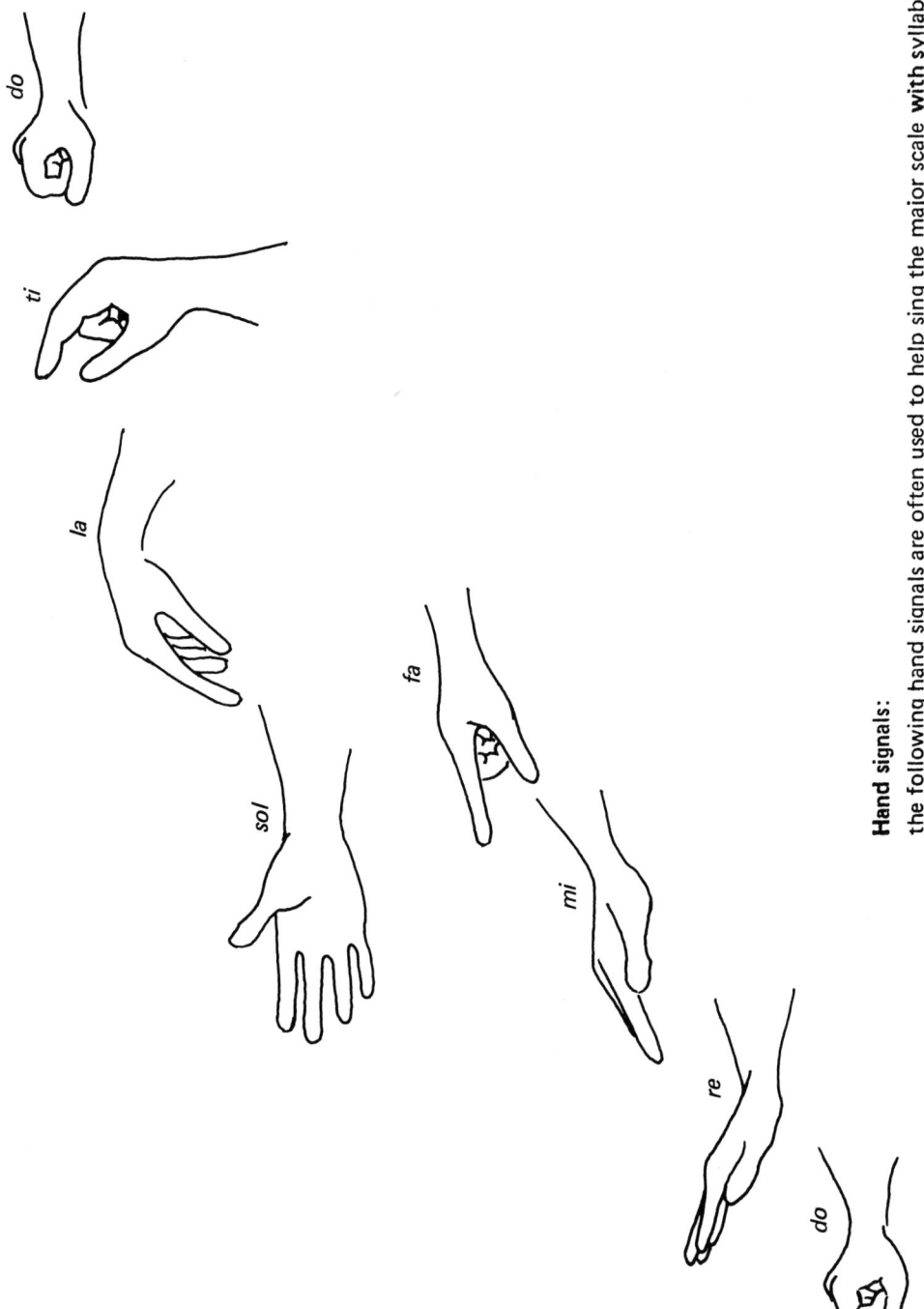

Hand signals:
the following hand signals are often used to help sing the major scale **with** syllables.

APPENDIX VI
ROCK AND BLUES SCALE PATTERNS

Below are three scales often used in contemporary popular music. Scale 1 is a rock or blues scale. Scale 2 is often used for folk and folk-rock music. Scale 3 is an all-purpose scale pattern: unlike the first two scales, the tones should not be used sequentially (one after the other); instead, choose tones carefully from Scale 3 according to the harmonic background.

The scales are presented on C, D, and A only; transpose them to other keys when necessary.

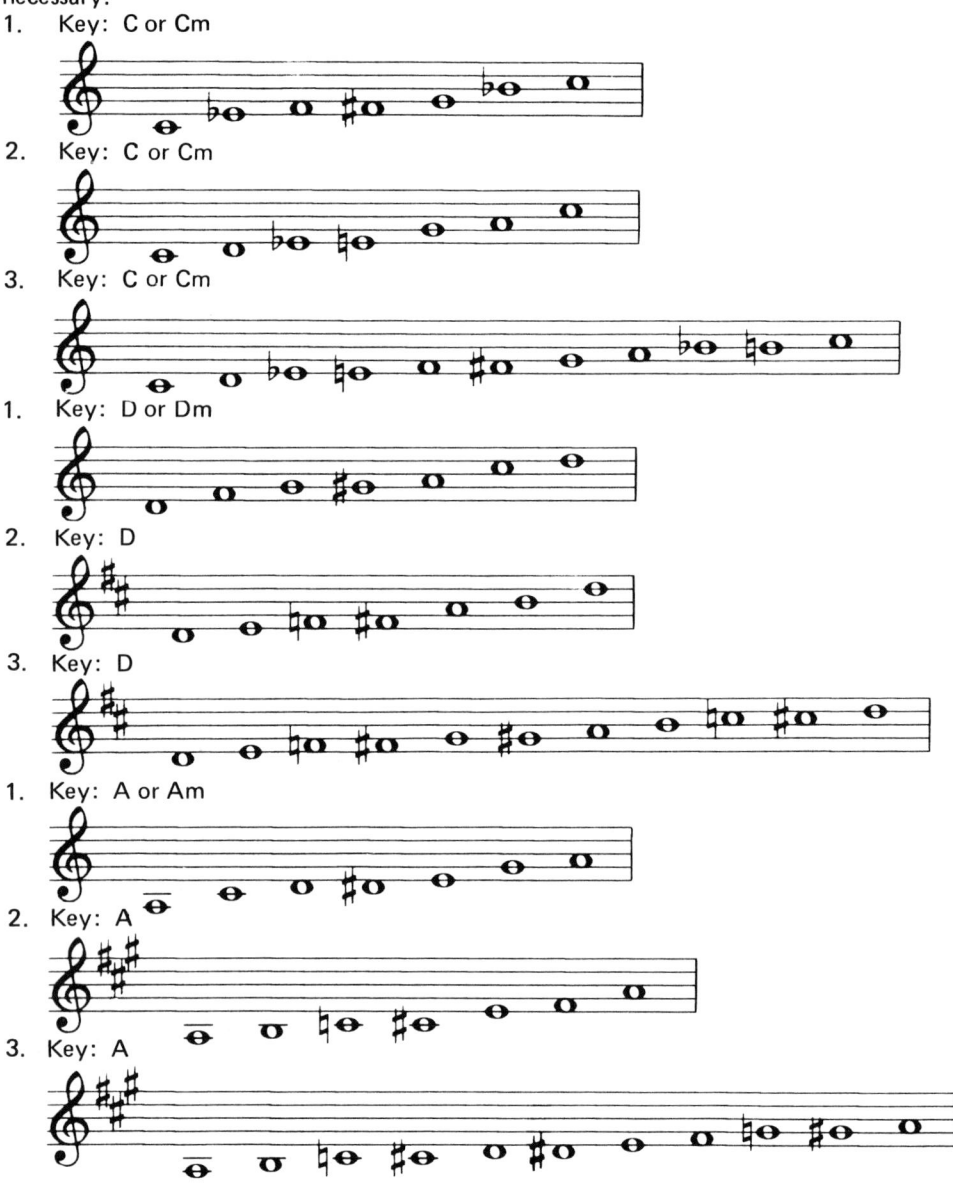

APPENDIX VII
PROGRESSIONS FOR IMPROVISATION AND COMPOSITION

The harmonic ideas given below are designed to help you create your own compositions. You may use these progressions to write chord melodies, as points of departure for original pieces, or as bases for improvisation. If you find that a part of one of the progressions appeals to you, you may use that part and complete it in your own way. Before you begin working with each progression, play it through and listen to it carefully. The brackets indicate possible phrase groupings.

1. Key: C

   C Gm F C Gm F B♭ C

2. Key: D

   D F♯m G A Em Bm D A D

3. Key: D

   D G F♯m Bm D A C G Bm Em A D

4. Key: F

   F Gm^7 A^7 Dm Gm^7 F C F

5. Key: G

   G B^7 Em G^7 C Bm A^7 Am^7 D^7 Bm Em B^7 Em G D^7 G

6. Key: Cm

   Cm Fm Cm B♭ E♭ Fm C G^7 C

7. Key: Dm

   Dm G Dm G B♭ F Am D (major)

8. Key: Am

   Am C Dm F Am C Dm E^7 Am C Dm F Am E^7 Am

9. Key: Bm

   Bm F♯m Em F♯ Bm E F♯m Bm

10. Key: A

    A A^7 D^7 F^7 B^7 E^7 A^7

11. Key: C

    C B♭ F Gm^7 C Gm B♭ C

12. Key: E

    E^7 G♯^{7} C♯m E^7 A E F♯^{7} B^7 E^7

APPENDIX VIII

THE GUITAR AND THE AUTOHARP

Both the guitar and the autoharp are used to accompany songs. Chords are fingered with the left hand, while the right hand strums the strings in the rhythm of the song.

THE AUTOHARP

On the autoharp, the chords are formed by pressing the appropriate button.

Chord buttons on the autoharp

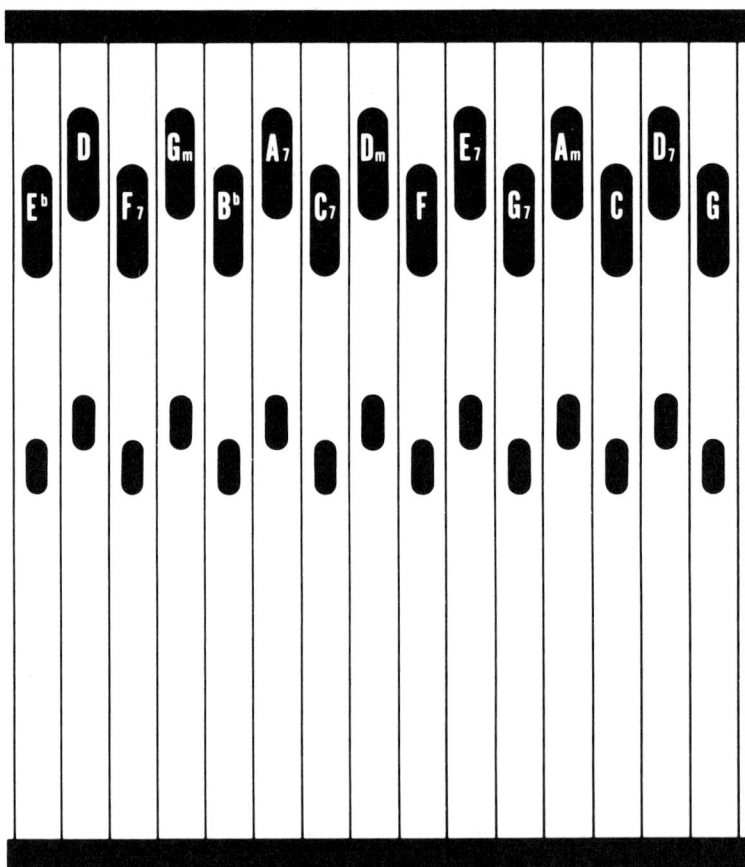

THE GUITAR

The guitar has six strings, tuned in the following way:

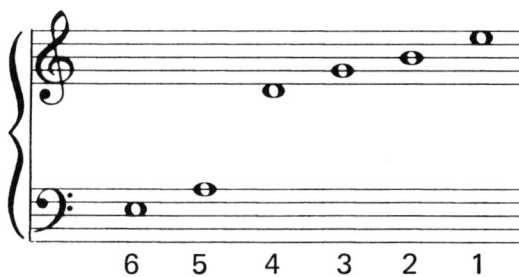

Chords are formed by placing the fingers of the left hand in the frets. The frets are numbered from 1 up, starting with the fret farthest from the body of the guitar. The strings are numbered from 1 to 6 (highest to lowest):

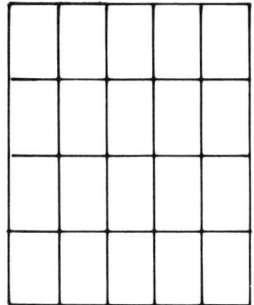

Diagrams are used to indicate the position of the fingers to form chords. The left hand fingers are numbered 1 to 4 (index to pinky). The thumb is never used to form chords.

A number above a string identifies which finger is used in the indicated fret:

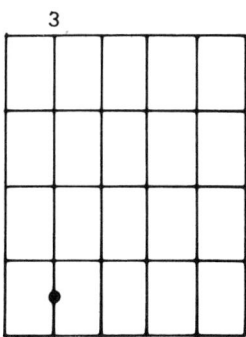

This diagram indicates that the third finger is to play in the fourth fret of the fifth string.

"X" over a string indicates that the string is not played. "0" indicates that the string is to be played, although it is not fingered. "(0)" indicates that playing the string is optional.

236

Below are the guitar fingerings for some frequently used chords.

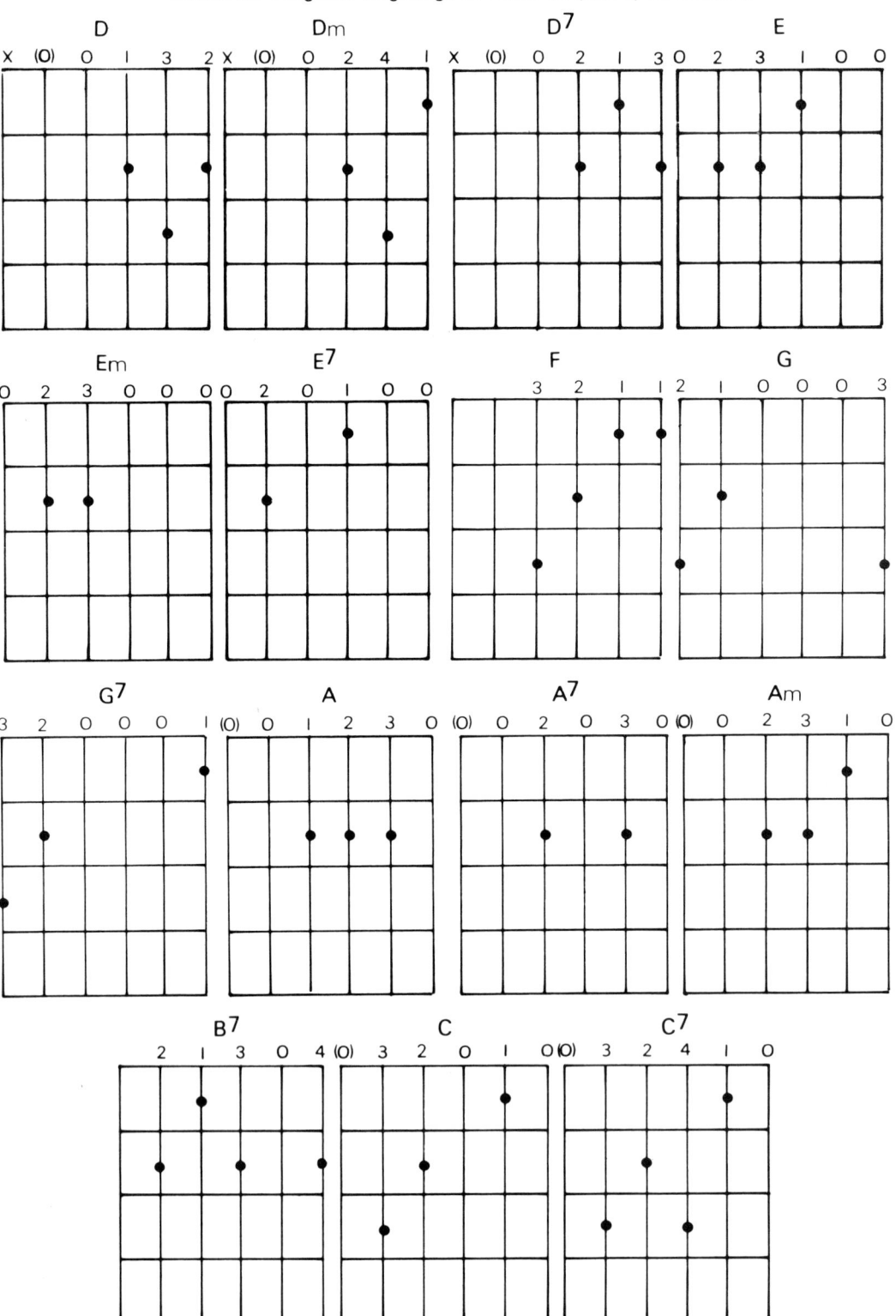

APPENDIX IX

RECORDER FINGERING

In the following fingerings for the soprano recorder,

- ○ indicates an open hole;
- ● indicates a closed hole;
- ◐ indicates a hole half-closed with the thumb.

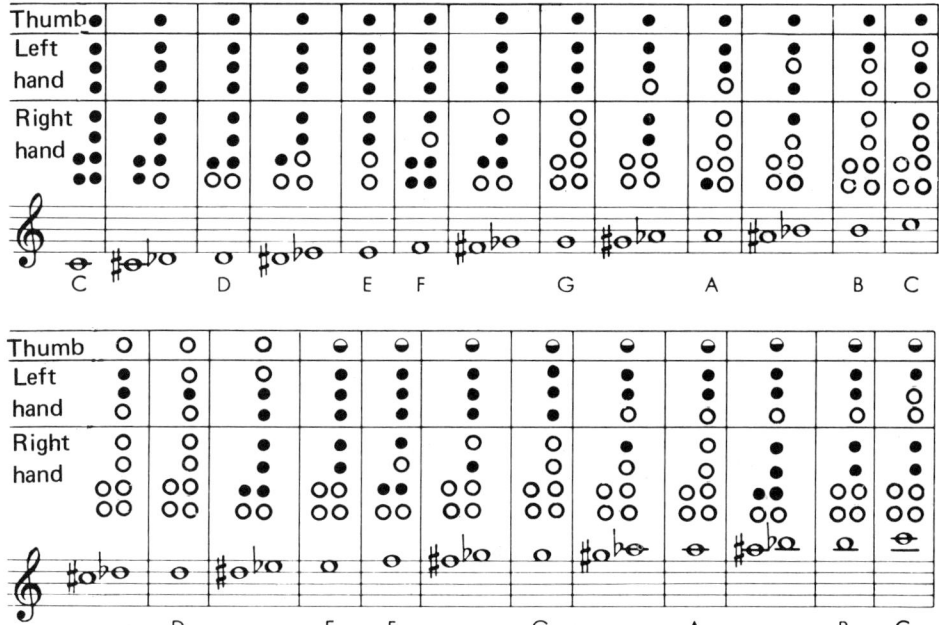

APPENDIX X

HOW TO READ A LEAD SHEET

Popular music is often notated on *lead sheets*, a type of musical shorthand in which only the melody, harmony, and lyric (if any) are indicated. The performer uses the information provided in the lead sheet as the basis for his improvisation. What follows is a key to the abbreviations and symbols in current use.

The chord names are abbreviated (all illustrations given on C):

C = C major

Cm = C minor

C⁷ = C dominant seventh

Cm⁷ = C minor seventh

CM⁷, CMaj⁷, C∆⁷ = C major seventh

Csus⁴ = C suspended fourth

Examples

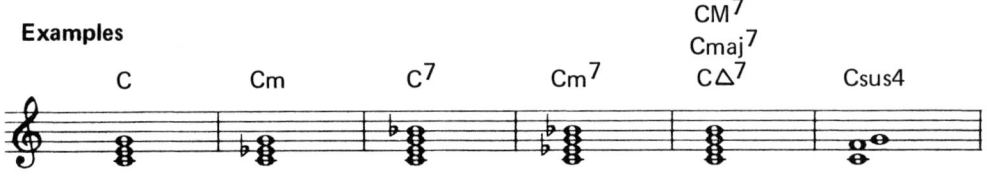

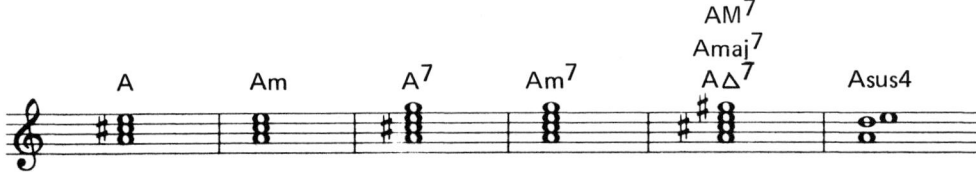

The root of the chord is always used as the bass note **unless** another note is indicated together with the chord name. C/G, for example, indicates a C major chord played over the bass note G.

Notes may be added to a chord:

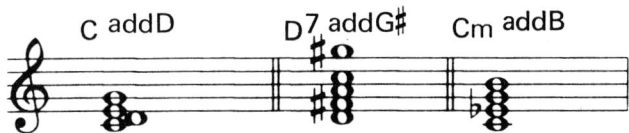

The harmonic rhythm (those points in time at which chord changes take place) is indicated by the position of the chord designation in relation to the melody or measure. If no chord name appears over a measure, the chord from the previous measure is continued.

It is up to the performer to choose rhythm, register (choice of octave), and melodic patterns (sometimes called "licks"). A specific rhythm or melodic pattern may be indicated in the lead sheet in small notes (the same size as cue notes).

240

Examples

3. Melody and accompaniment from a single-line lead sheet.

There are countless possibilities in the realization of a lead sheet. It is interesting to hear how two musicians will interpret the same musical outline. Each one brings to the music his own style and sound. In popular music, the performer is often a composer as well.

Playing from a lead sheet is a special skill sometimes disparaged as being of a lower order than reading music. But in some ways, the opposite is the case. In order to create interesting music from the barest of outlines, the performer must be totally aware of the underlying structure of the piece, he must have complete control over his technique, and he must have a good deal of talent.

APPENDIX XI
GLOSSARY OF TERMS

Words appearing in **bold face** in the definitions are themselves defined in the glossary.

accidentals: symbols used to raise or lower the **pitch** of a given **note**.
alla breve (₵): a **tempo** mark indicating fast double time. The half note is the basic pulse.
anacrusis: see *upbeat*.
arpeggio: the **notes** of a **chord** played separately rather than together.
asymmetrical phrase design: characterizing a piece whose **phrases** are of unequal lengths.
augmentation: the presentation of a **motive** in **notes** of longer duration than those originally assigned to it.
augmentation dot: a dot written after the **notehead** which extends the duration of the **note** by half its own value.
authentic cadence: see *full cadence*.

barline: a vertical line which separates music into **measures.**
bass clef (𝄢, also called the *F clef*): a symbol written on the **staff** to identify the second line from the top as F. Used primarily for the notation of music lying below middle C.
beam: a heavy, horizontal line used to join together a group of **notes** smaller than the quarter note.
beat: the basic rhythmic pulse of music.
binary form: characterizing a piece of music in two parts.

cadence: a point of rest usually at the end of a **phrase** or a piece.
canon (popular name: *round*): a **polyphonic** piece in which each part performs the same material, beginning at different times.
chord: three or more different **pitches** sounding at the same time.
chord tone: a **pitch** that does not fit into the **harmonic background.**
chromatic scale: a **scale** made up entirely of successive **half steps.**
chromatic semitone: a **half step** consisting of two **notes** with the same letter name.
circle of fifths: the graphic representation of all the **keys** with their **sharps** and **flats.**
coda: a section at the end of a piece or movement which is designed to bring it to an end.
common time (𝄴): four-quarter time.
common tone: a **pitch** that remains constant while the **harmony** changes.
compound form: characterizing a piece of music in which small **forms** are contained within the larger structure.
compound meter: a **meter** whose basic pulse regularly subdivides into three beats.
consonance: musical sound considered to be stable and nonactive; a term commonly used to describe the agreeable effect of certain **intervals** (**octave, third,** etc.).
contrasting period: a **period** in which the two **phrases** start differently from one another.
counterpoint: music consisting of two or more independent lines that sound simultaneously.

da capo (*D.C.*): literally, "from the head." A term which directs the performer to go back to the beginning of the piece. The end is marked *fine*.

dal segno (D.S.): literally, "from the sign." A term which directs the performer to go back to a point in the piece marked with a sign §.

degree: see *scale degree.*

diatonic scales: a group of seven-note **scales** containing five **whole steps** and two **half steps** in various fixed relationships and notated with consecutive letter names.

diatonic semitone: a **half step** notated with two different letter names.

diminution: the presentation of a **motive** in **notes** of shorter duration than those originally assigned to it.

dissonance: musical sound considered to be unstable and active. The term is commonly used to describe the jarring or disagreeable effect of certain **intervals** (second, seventh, etc.).

Dorian mode: a medieval Church **mode** which may be recreated by playing D to D on the white **keys** of the piano.

double bar: two vertical lines indicating the end of a section or piece.

double flat (♭♭): a symbol which lowers the **pitch** of a **note** a **whole step.**

double period: two **periods,** separated by a **semicadence,** which serve to balance each other.

double sharp (×): a symbol which raises the **pitch** of a **note** a **whole step.**

doubling: the practice of giving the same **chord tone** to more than one part.

enharmonic: characterizing **pitches** that sound the same but are notated differently.

F clef: see *bass clef.*

fermata: a pause, indicated by the sign.

fifth: 1. the distance in **pitch** between **diatonic scale degrees** 1 and 5;
2. the uppermost member of a **root-position triad.**

first inversion: the rearranging of a **chord** so that its **third** is in the lowest part.

flag: a curved line drawn on the **note stem** to identify **notes** smaller than a quarter note.

flat (♭): a symbol which lowers the **pitch** of a **note** a **half step.**

form: the underlying design and structure of a composition.

full cadence (or *authentic cadence*): a **harmonic progression** from V to I which suggests conclusion.

G clef: see *treble clef.*

grand staff (also called *great staff* or *piano staff*): the **staffs** of the **treble clef** and the **bass clef** joined with a bracket or brace. The grand staff is used for the notation of music in both high and low registers.

half cadence: see *semicadence.*

half step (also called *semitone* or *m2*): the smallest written **interval** in Western music.

harmonic minor scale: the **scale** resulting from the alteration of the **natural minor** by raising the seventh **degree** a **half step.**

harmonic progression: a group of **chords** upon which a **melody** or a piece is based; sometimes called *harmonic background.*

harmonic rhythm: the rhythmic pattern provided by changes of **harmony.**

harmonization: the practice of adding suitable **chords** to a **melody.**

harmony: the vertical structure resulting when two or more lines are sounded simultaneously.

homophonic: characterizing music in which one main voice is supported by **harmony.**

imitation: the repetition of the same melodic materials in different voices.
imperfect authentic cadence: a **full cadence (authendic cadence)** in which the highest voice concludes on a **note** other than the **tonic.**
instrumentation (or *orchestration*): the choice of instruments in a composition.
interval: the distance in **pitch** between two **notes.**
inversion: 1. a **chord** whose lowest **note** is not the **root**;
    2. an **interval** whose higher and lower **notes** have been interchanged;
    3. the development of a **motive**, melodic fragment, or **melody** whose ascending or descending direction has been reversed.

key: 1. the term used to describe the main **note** or **tonal** center of a piece;
    2. in keyboard, woodwind, and brass instruments, the lever depressed by the player's fingers.
key center: the main **key** around which a piece or section is based.
key signature: the group of **sharps** or **flats** written at the beginning of each **staff** line to indicate the required alterations of basic letter names which form the **scale** and **key** of the piece.

ledger lines: lines written above or below the **staff** to extend its range. They are used for notation of **pitches** that are too high or low to be written on the **staff.**
lower neighbor: a **nonharmonic tone** that results when a part moves stepwise down and then returns to a **chord tone.**
Lydian mode: a medieval Church **mode** which may be recreated by playing F to F on the white **keys** of the piano.

major scale: the **diatonic scale** most frequently used in Western music.
measure: a group of **beats** enclosed within **barlines,** with the first **beat** usually accented.
melodic goal: the definite high or low point in a musical line.
melodic minor scale: the **scale** which results when the **natural minor scale** is altered by raising the sixth and seventh **degrees** a **half step** in the ascending form and lowering them to the original in the descending form.
melodic shape: the direction and contour of a **melody.**
melody: a succession of **pitches** with **rhythm.**
meter: a pattern of fixed **beats**; also, the number and value of those **beats** in a **measure.**
minor scale: related to the **major scale,** and widely used in Western music. The minor scale has three forms: **natural, harmonic,** and **melodic.**
Mixolydian mode: a medieval Church **mode** which may be recreated by playing G to G on the white **keys** of the piano.
modal music: music based on the medieval Church **scales** rather than on the **major** and **minor scales.**
mode: a term generally referring to the **diatonic scales** of the medieval Church which may be formed on the white **keys** of the piano.
modulation: the shift to a new **key center** within a piece.
monophonic: characterizing music consisting of **melody** only.
motive (or *subject*): a short melodic idea whose rhythm and **pitch** design serve as the basis for a **melody** or piece.

motivic development: the compositional technique of exploring the different characteristics and potentialities of a **motive**.

natural diatonic semitones: E to F and B to C, the only **semitones** that do not require **sharps** or **flats**.
natural minor scale: the basic, unaltered **diatonic** form of the **minor scale**.
natural sign (♮): a sign which cancels the effect of a previous **sharp** or **flat**.
nonharmonic tone: a **pitch** that does not fit into the **harmonic background**.
note: the written symbol of a musical **pitch**.
notehead: the rounded part of the **note** written on a line or space which indicates **pitch**.

octave: 1. the **interval** separating two **pitches** of the same name;
  2. the eighth **note** of a **diatonic scale**.
orchestration: see *instrumentation*.
ostinato: a repeated figure, usually found in the lowest part, over which a piece may be built.

parallelism: the movement of two or more voices in the same direction and at the same intervallic distance from each other.
parallel keys: **major** and **minor keys** whose **scales** begin on the same **pitch** but have different **key signatures**.
parallel period: a **period** in which both **phrases** start the same.
passing tone: a **nonharmonic tone** that results when a part moves stepwise from one **chord tone** to another.
pentatonic scale: an easily sung five-**note scale** upon which many of the world's folk songs are based.
perfect authentic cadence: a **full cadence (authentic cadence)** in which the highest voice rests on the **tonic**.
period: a two-**phrase** melodic unit in which the second **phrase** completes the musical thought started by the first.
phrase: a unit of **melody** comparable to a sentence in prose.
phrase design: the relationship of **phrases** within a composition.
Phrygian mode: a medieval Church **mode** which may be recreated by playing E to E on the white **keys** of the piano.
piano staff: see *grand staff*.
pitch: the highness or lowness of musical tones.
polyphonic: characterizing music consisting of two or more equally important musical lines.

quality: the measurement by which we distinguish 1) **intervals** of the same number; and 2) **chords** with the same **root**.

relative major: the term used to identify the **major key** and **scale** having the same **key signature** as its related **minor key** and **scale**. The relative major begins on the third **degree** of its **relative minor scale**.
relative minor: the term used to identify the **minor key** and **scale** having the same **key signature** as its related **major key** and **scale**. The relative minor begins on the sixth **degree** of its **relative major scale**.

repeat sign (𝄆 𝄇): symbols used to indicate that the music between them should be played again.

repetition: the reiteration of a musical idea.

rest: a symbol which indicates the absence of sound for a fixed duration.

rhythm: the organization of music in respect to time.

rondo: a form of instrumental music with a recurring section (usually the first).

root: the **note** used as a fundament upon which a **chord** is built.

root position: the arrangement of a **chord** so that the **root** is in the lowest voice.

round: see *canon*.

rounded binary: characterizing a two-part musical **form** with features of a three-part design.

scale: a group of **pitches** arranged in ascending or descending order upon which **melodies** and compositions are based.

scale degreees: the individual components of a **scale**.

second inversion: the rearranging of a **chord** so that its **fifth** is in the lowest part.

semicadence (half cadence): a point of rest on a chord other than I which seems incomplete and creates a desire for additional music.

semitone: see *half step*.

sequence: the repetition of a musical pattern on a different **pitch**.

seventh chord: a four-note **chord** built in **thirds**.

sharp (♯): a symbol which raises the **pitch** of a **note** a **half step**.

simple meter: a **meter** whose basic pulse regularly subdivides into two **beats**.

slur: a curved line connecting a group of **notes** to indicate that they are to be played smoothly.

staff: the five lines upon which **notes** are written to indicate their **pitch**.

stem: a vertical line drawn to the head of all **notes** smaller than the whole note.

subject: see *motive*.

symmetrical phrase design: characterizing a piece whose **phrases** are of equal length.

syncopation: accents off the **beat**.

tempo: the rate of speed of the basic pulse.

ternary: characterizing a piece of music in three parts.

texture: the result of the combination of different musical elements (i.e., **harmony, melody, instrumentation**).

third: the **interval** comprised by two **notes** written on adjacent lines or spaces of the **staff**.

treble clef (𝄞): the symbol that indicates that the second line from the bottom of the staff is G. Used primarily to notate music lying above Middle C.

triad: a three-**note chord** built in **thirds**.

triplet: a group of three **notes** which are performed in the time usually alotted to two **notes**.

upbeat (anacrusis): the **note** or **notes** that occur at the beginning of a piece on a **beat** other than the first.

upper neighbor: a **nonharmonic tone** that is produced when a part moves stepwise up and then returns to a **chord tone**.

voice leading: the principles governing the movement of separate voices in **contrapuntal** music.

whole step (also called *whole tone* or *M2*): an interval consisting of two **half steps.**

RHYTHM READER

RHYTHM READER

THE MUSIC KIT
TOM MANOFF

W·W·NORTON & COMPANY·INC·NEW YORK

RHYTHM READER DESIGNED BY ELSA ANN DANENBERG

Copyright © 1976 by Tom Manoff. All rights reserved.

Published simultaneously in Canada by George J. McLeod Limited, Toronto.

Printed in the United States of America.

First Edition

ISBN 0 393 09179 1

1 2 3 4 5 6 7 8 9 0

Library of Congress Cataloging in Publication Data

Manoff, Tom.
   The music kit.

     CONTENTS: [1] Workbook.—[2] Rhythm reader.—[3] Scorebook.
    1. Music—Theory, Elementary.   I. Title.
    MT7.M267   781   76-1006
    ISBN 0-393-09179-1

CONTENTS

CHAPTER 1.   1

    Rhythm • The Quarter Note and the Eighth Note • Beaming Eighth Notes • Speaking Rhythms • Double Bar • Repeat Signs • Fermata Sign • Terms, Symbols, and Concepts

CHAPTER 2.   6

    Rests • Meter • Strong and Weak Beats • Meter Signs and Time Signatures • Rhythms with and without Meter • Counting Pulses in the Measure • Terms, Symbols, and Concepts

CHAPTER 3.   12

    Eighth Rest • Note Values • Speaking the Eighth Rest • Using Both Hands—Coordination • Terms, Symbols, and Concepts

CHAPTER 4.   18

    Notes Control Space • 1st and 2nd Endings • Other Types of Repeats • Terms, Symbols, and Concepts

CHAPTER 5.   25

    Notes Longer than the Quarter Note • Speaking the Longer Notes • Counting Nonmetered Rhythms with Numbers • Counting Rhythms in Meter • Rests Longer than the Quarter Rest • Conducting • Terms, Symbols, and Concepts

CHAPTER 6.   32

Note Symbols • Beams • Combinations of Notes with Beams • The Values of Notes in Relationship to Each Other • The Tie • The Dotted Note • Anacrusis • Terms, Symbols, and Concepts

CHAPTER 7.   40

Subdivision of the Basic Pulse • Terms, Symbols, and Concepts

CHAPTER 8.   45

Subdivision of the Quarter Note into Sixteenths • Subdividing into Sixteenths, in Meter • Terms, Symbols, and Concepts

CHAPTER 9.   51

Triplets • Counting Triplets by Subdivision • The Triplet Rest • Terms, Symbols, and Concepts

CHAPTER 10.   57

Compound Meter • Another Way of Counting • Terms, Symbols, and Concepts

CHAPTER 11.   62

Syncopated and Nonsyncopated Rhythms • Visualizing Where the Beat Falls • Terms, Symbols, and Concepts

CHAPTER 12.   66

Alternating Hands: Developing Coordination

CHAPTER 13.   70

Different Values of the Basic Pulse • 𝄴 and 𝄵 • Terms, Symbols and Concepts

CHAPTER 14.   74

Clear Notation • Beams • Rests • Aligning Two Parts • Terms, Symbols, and Concepts

CHAPTER 15.   78

Testing Your Rhythmic Skills

RHYTHM READER

CHAPTER 1

RHYTHM

Rhythm is action in time. Whether it be a drum beat, the steady ticking of a clock, or your own heartbeat, all are specific actions that occur in a space of time. Rhythmic notation is the system used to indicate the number of actions, the time each action takes, and the relationship of these actions to a *beat.* This basic beat, or pulse, is what we feel when we step in time to a marching band or tap our feet to a rock or jazz tune. The speed of the beat is described by the term *tempo.* A polka or rock dance has a fast tempo; a funeral march has a slow tempo. The rhythms we **hear** are represented by symbols we **see**, called *notes.*

THE QUARTER NOTE AND THE EIGHTH NOTE

The first notes we learn are the quarter note (♩ or ♩) and the eighth note (♪ or ♪). Quarter notes are twice as long in duration as eighth notes; conversely, it requires two eighth notes to equal the duration of one quarter note.

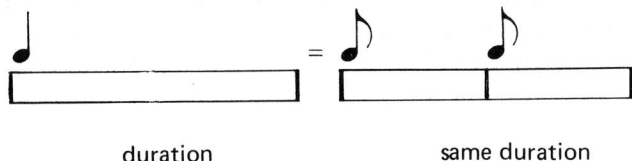

duration   same duration

The several parts of the eighth note are the *notehead, stem* and *flag:*

2

BEAMING EIGHTH NOTES
Eighth notes can be beamed together for easier reading.

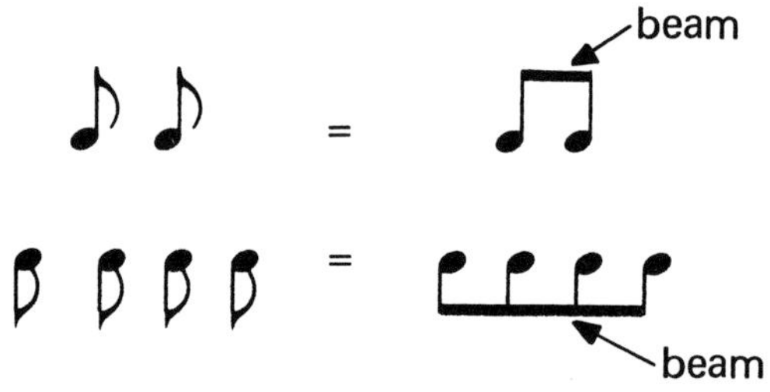

♪ ♪ = ♫ ←beam

♪ ♪ ♪ ♪ = ♬♬ ←beam

1 Rewrite these eighth notes, using beams:

Example:

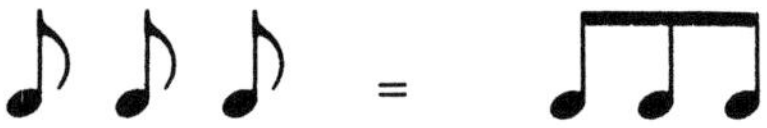

♪ ♪ ♪ = ♬

1.  ♪ ♪ ♪ ♪ =

2.  ♪ ♪ ♫ =

3.  ♪ ♪ ♪ ♪ =

SPEAKING RHYTHMS
To get you started reading and comprehending rhythm quickly, we use a method for speaking simple rhythms. Quarter notes (♩ or ♩) will be spoken "ta." Eighth notes (♪, ♪, ♫, or ♫) will be spoken "tee."

2 Speak in an even, steady manner, and at a moderate tempo:

♩ ♩ ♩ ♩ ♩ ♩ ♩ ♩
ta ta ta ta ta ta ta ta

Speak in an even, steady manner:

tee tee tee tee tee tee tee tee tee tee tee tee

3 1. Listen to *Rhythm 1* (S 7 , B 5) a few times, then speak the rhythm with the recording. Before each exercise, you will hear a count to establish the tempo. In this case, the count is "one, two, three, four."

Rhythm 1

2. Repeat *Rhythm 1,* speaking and following this version, which is the same rhythm as the one just above, but notated differently.

DOUBLE BAR
A *double bar* (‖ or ‖) indicates the end, as in the example directly above.

REPEAT SIGNS
A group of notes is repeated when it is enclosed by *repeat signs,* ‖: :‖ . Therefore:

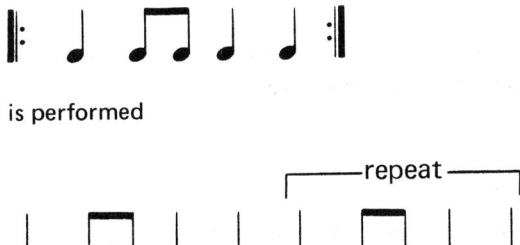

is performed

4 Rewrite each of these rhythms, writing out the repeat:
Example:

In performing a line of music, go back to the beginning without any lapse of the beat when you reach a repeat sign.

5 Speak these rhythms with the recordings. Remember the repeat signs.

1. *Rhythm 2* (S 7, B 5)

2. *Rhythm 3* (S 7, B 5). You will hear "one, two, three" before the rhythm.

6 Repeat *Rhythms 2* and *3* with the recording. This time, speak and **clap**.

7 Repeat *Rhythms 2* and *3* with the recording. These versions are the same rhythms as in **5**, but notated differently. Speak and clap:

1. *Rhythm 2*

2. Rhythm 3

8 Do these on your own. Speak first, then speak and tap with one hand on a table or desk.

9 Tap and imagine you are speaking these rhythms. Don't speak!

FERMATA SIGN
The *fermata* symbol, (𝄐) when placed above a note, indicates that the note is to be held for a longer duration than its indicated value. The duration is left to the discretion of the performer. The fermata is also called a hold.

TERMS, SYMBOLS, AND CONCEPTS:
Explain in your own words:
    rhythm
    basic pulse
    duration
    tempo
    the relationship between  and
    beaming eighth notes

CHAPTER 2

RESTS

Just as there are symbols which represent musical sounds for specific time durations, there are symbols which represent the absence of musical sound, or silence. These symbols are called *rests*. A *quarter rest* (𝄽) has the same time value as a quarter note. In the following rhythms, speak the quarter rest as "rest."

1   Speak with the recording. Do not clap.

1. *Rhythm 4* (S 7, B 5)

speak: ta ta rest ta ta rest ta ta

2. *Rhythm 5* (S 8, B 1)

3. *Rhythm 6* (S 8, B 1)

4. *Rhythm 7* (S 8, B 1)

no repeats

2 Repeat *Rhythms 4* through *7*. Speak and tap with the recording. Do not **tap** the rests, just say "**rest,**" as on the recording.

3 Repeat these new versions of *Rhythms 6* and *7*. Speak and tap with the recording.

1. *Rhythm 6*

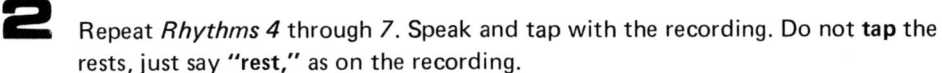

2. *Rhythm 7*

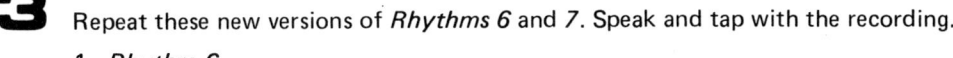

METER
We naturally hear rhythm in groups of two or three. Think, for example, how often you hear a "tic" followed by a "toc." In music notation, this organization into groups of beats is called *meter*. The most common groupings are two, three, and four beats. Each group is called a *measure* and is indicated by a vertical line, called a *barline*.

A rhythm without meter

A rhythm with meter (groups of 2 ♩'s)

Another rhythm with meter (groups of 3 ♩'s)

STRONG AND WEAK BEATS
Recognizing measure divisions by ear is the result of hearing strong or accented beats followed by weak or unaccented beats. In the following examples, the strong beat is indicated by an accent sign (>).

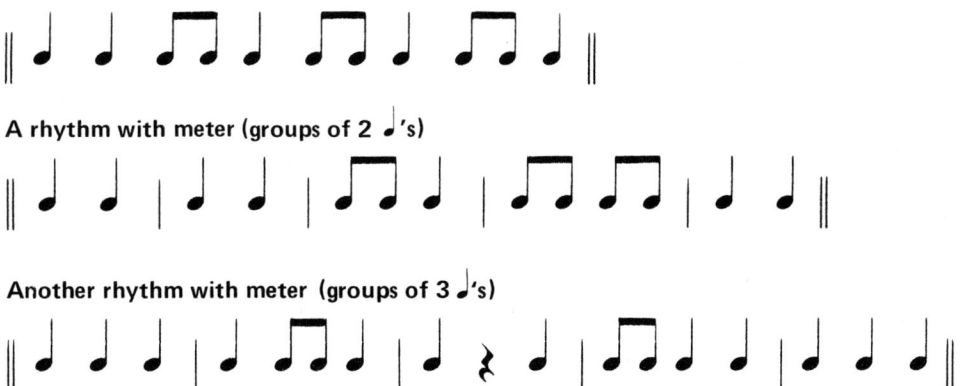

8

4 Speak these rhythms, accenting the "ta" or "tee" where indicated. Write the meter— as it is spoken—in the empty box.

METER SIGNS AND TIME SIGNATURES

The meter of a piece is indicated by a *meter sign*, or *time signature*, consisting of an upper number and a lower number. The upper number indicates how many beats there are in each measure; the lower number indicates the kind of note which receives one beat.

The time signature above is translated as "four quarters" or "four-quarter time."

5 Write the meaning of the numbers in these time signatures, as illuatrated above.

RHYTHMS WITH AND WITHOUT METER

An understanding of written rhythms with and without meter is helpful in becoming a good rhythm reader. Both types will be studied throughout this course. For example, plainchant (early Christian church music) is written without meter; most other music, especially dance music, is in a definite meter.

COUNTING PULSES IN THE MEASURE
Now we will count the number of beats or basic pulses per measure. For example:

6 Count each of these meters with the *Basic Pulse: Moderate Tempo* (S 7, B 3). Each spoken number must coincide with the steady pulse in the recording.

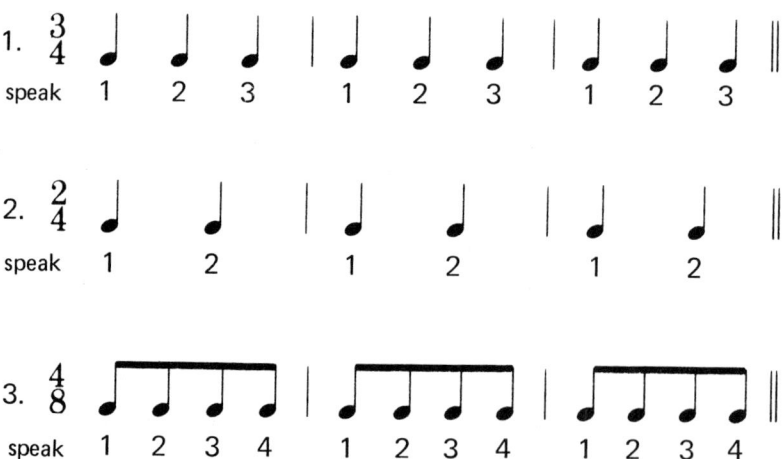

Notice in the example above that the eighth notes in (3) are spoken as slowly as the quarter notes in (1) and (2). This is a result of the choice of **tempo**. The tempo determines the duration of each specific type of note. Once this tempo has been established, the relationship of the eighth note to the quarter note will remain constant within that piece, unless a change of tempo is indicated.

7 Play each of these exercises on the piano or any other keyboard instrument (see Chapter 2 in the *Workbook*). First speak each rhythm, then play it.

TERMS, SYMBOLS, AND CONCEPTS
Explain in your own words:

meter
strong and weak beats
meter signs/time signatures
measure
barline
rhythm with and without meter
counting the basic pulse

CHAPTER 3

EIGHTH REST

A silence equal in duration to the eighth note (♪) is the *eighth rest* (↱). We now know four **rhythmic symbols**:

quarter note: ♩

quarter rest: 𝄽

eighth note: ♪

eighth rest: ↱

NOTE VALUES

If the quarter note is the basic pulse, it is given a value of one beat. The other rhythmic symbols can be measured against this quarter-note beat.

♩ = 1 beat

𝄽 = 1 beat

♪ = 1/2 beat

↱ = 1/2 beat

1 Add up the total number of beats of each rhythm.
Example

♩ 𝄽   ᾿ ᾿ ♫ ♩   ♪ } = 5½ beats
1 + 1 + ½ + ½ + ½ + ½ + 1 + ½

1. 𝄽 𝄽 𝄽 𝄽 ♫   =

2. ᾿ ᾿ ᾿ ᾿ ᾿ ᾿ ᾿ 𝄽   =

3. ♩ ♪ ♩ ♪ ᾿ ♪ ♩   =

4. ♫ ᾿ ♪ ♩ 𝄽 𝄽 ♪   =

5. ♩ 𝄽 𝄽 ♪ ᾿ ᾿ ♪   =

6. ♩ 𝄽 𝄽 𝄽 ♪ ♪ ᾿ ♩   =

7. ♪ ♩ ᾿ ᾿ ♩ ♩ ᾿ ᾿ ♩ ᾿ ♩ =

SPEAKING THE EIGHTH REST
When speaking rhythms, say the syllable "m" for the eighth rest. When clapping or tapping a rhythm, speak each rest but don't clap or tap it. Say "rest" for the quarter rest.

2 Speak these rhythms with the recording. Do not clap. The count for *Rhythm 11* is "one, two"; the count for *Rhythm 12* is "one, two, three."

1. *Rhythm 8* (S 8, B 2)

2. *Rhythm 9* (S 8, B 2)

3 Repeat *Rhythms 8–12*, speaking and clapping. This time, don't clap the rests, but speak them.

USING BOTH HANDS — COORDINATION

4 Speak and tap on a table or desk.

1. Use the right hand:

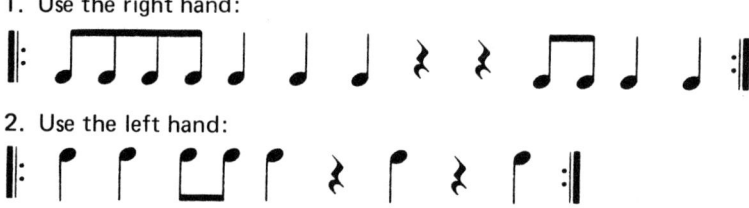

2. Use the left hand:

5 Now tap with both hands at once. Tap eighth notes with the right hand against quarters with the left. Do it twice, first speaking the eighths, then speaking the quarters.

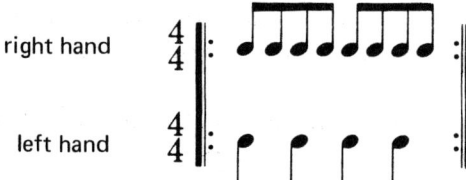

Repeat with the parts reversed.

6 Tap these rhythms with the *Basic Pulse: Moderate Tempo* (S 7, B 3). The pulse on the recording equals the quarter note. First start the left hand **alone**. When you have established the basic pulse (the beat on the recording, and the quarter notes you beat with your left hand), **add** the right hand. Speak the right hand part **only**. Some practice may be required for the accomplishment of these exercises.

7 To develop your coordination further, walk in even steps and think of each step as a quarter-note pulse.

Walk:

Clap and speak these rhythms while you walk.

Repeat several times.

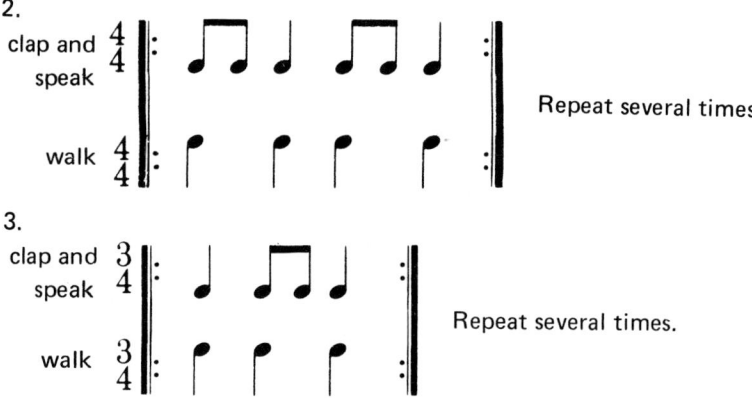

Repeat exercises (1) through (3), tapping your foot instead of walking.

8 If a group is available, form a circle. Let everyone speak and clap this rhythm **in unison** (everyone speaks and claps together).

Now at a moderate tempo, let everyone repeat the rhythm continually, but let the clapping go around the circle. Each person claps one note only in turn. Repeat the "game" with these rhythms:

9 Play these exercises. Speak the rhythm first, then play and only imagine you are speaking.

1.

2.

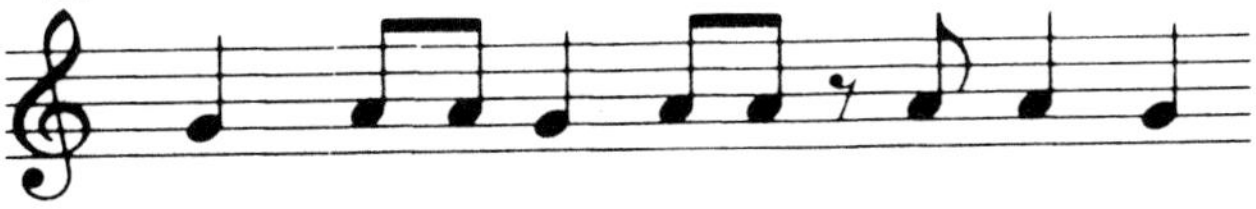

3.

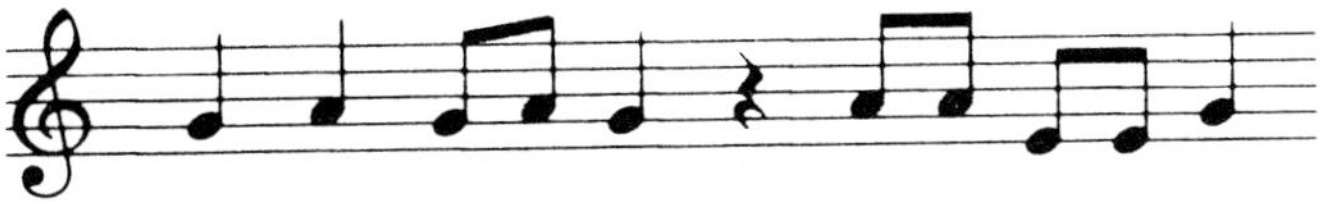

4.

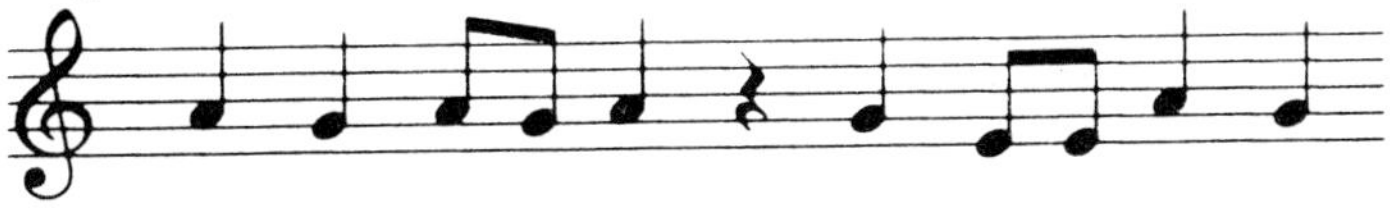

5.

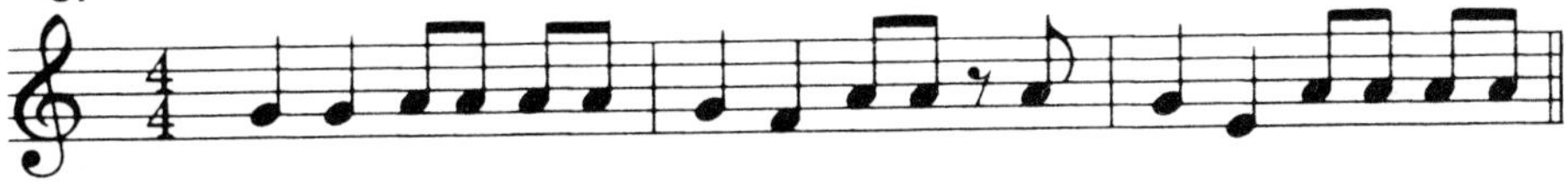

6.

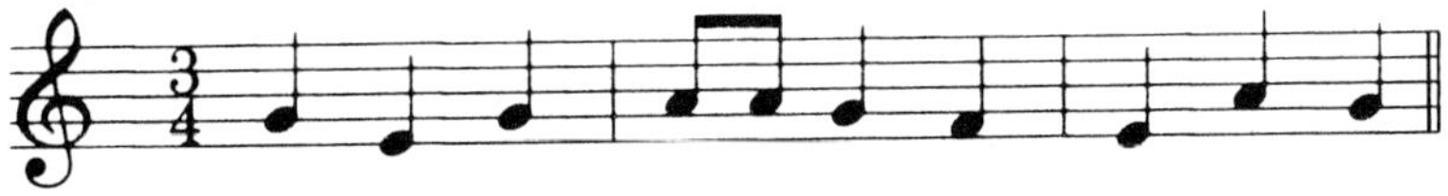

7.

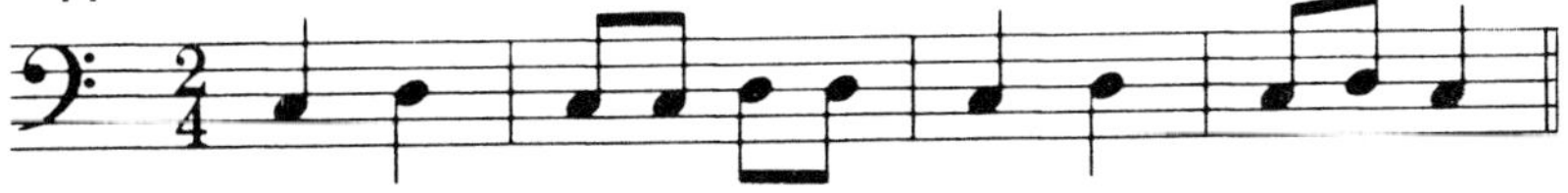

TERMS, SYMBOLS, AND CONCEPTS

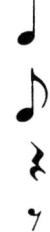

CHAPTER 4

NOTES CONTROL SPACE

The written note controls a space on the page in the same way that the sound it represents controls a period of time. Longer notes and rests control more space than shorter notes and rests. Observe how these notes and rests are written on the rhythm spacer below, which shows their relationship to a quarter-note pulse. The shaded part represents the amount of space that the note controls.

Rhythm Spacer

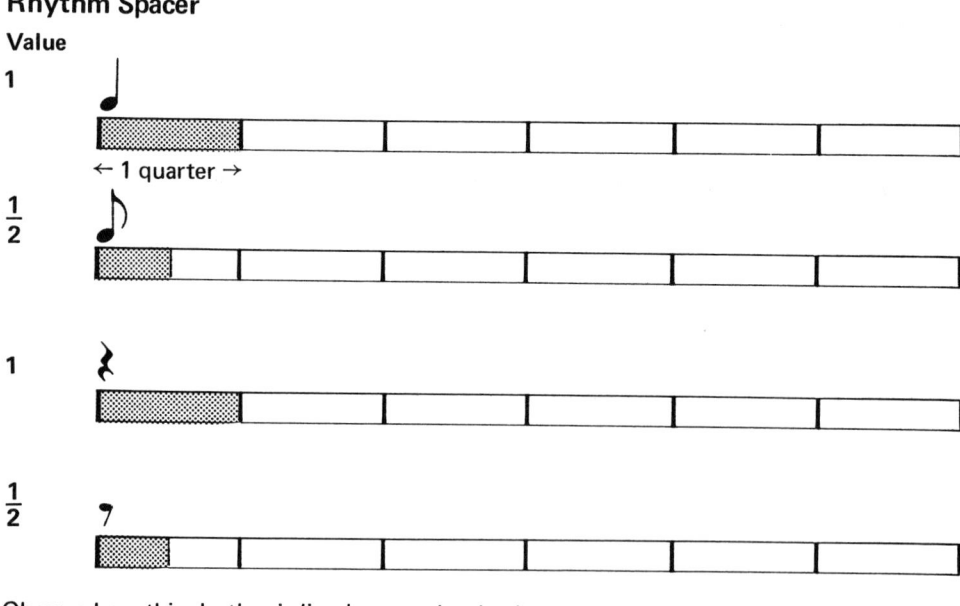

Observe how this rhythm is lined up on the rhythm spacer.

2 Tap these rhythms with the *Basic Pulse: Moderate Tempo* (S 7 , B 3). Tap each part separately with the recorded pulse. The pulse equals the quarter note. When you are secure with each hand alone, tap them together. Do not speak.

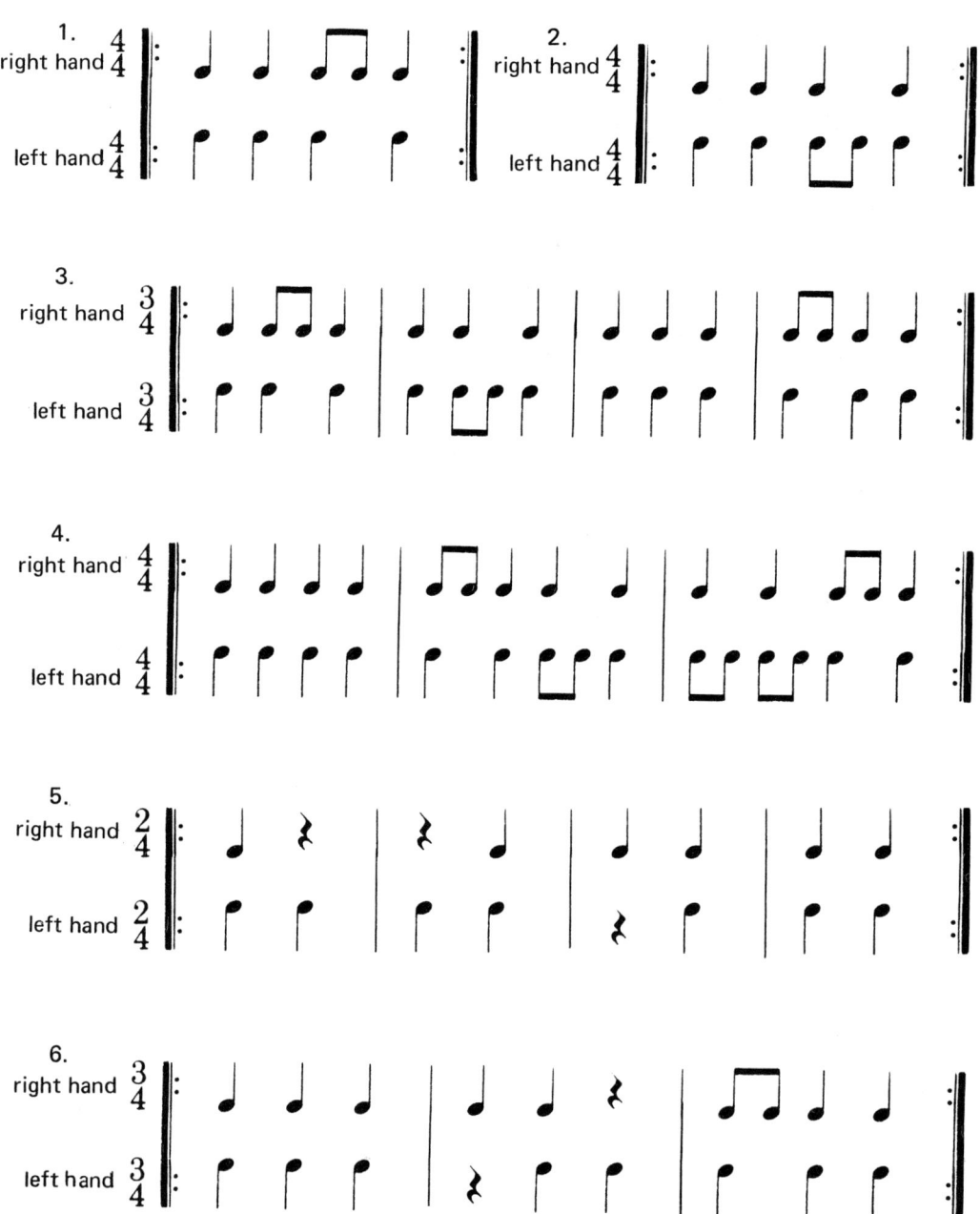

3 Tap and speak *Rhythms 1–12* (S 7, B 5 and S 8, B 1–3). Tap with your right hand when the stems go up; use your left hand for notes whose stems go down.

1ST AND 2ND ENDINGS

When an exercise or piece of music utilizes repeat signs, you may find two endings. If so, when you repeat, skip the measure or measures marked *1st ending* and go directly to the measure or measures marked *2nd ending*.

Example:

This is performed:

4 Tap:

OTHER TYPES OF REPEATS

D.C. al fine (*Da Capo al fine*: literally, "from the beginning to the end"). If you find this abbreviation at the end of a piece, go back to the beginning and repeat, stopping at the place marked *fine*.

D.S. (*Dal Segno*: literally, "to the sign"). If you find the letters *D.S.* at the end of a piece, go back to the sign (𝄋), not necessarily to the beginning, and repeat to the end.

5 Play these exercises. Speak the rhythm first, then play. Imagine you are speaking the rhythm when you play. When you play, do not speak!

TERMS, SYMBOLS, AND CONCEPTS

Explain in your own words:

    notes control space
    rhythm spacer
    1st and 2nd endings
    D.C. al fine
    D.S.

CHAPTER 5

NOTES LONGER THAN THE QUARTER NOTE

Most of the rhythms we have talked about have the quarter note as the basic pulse. We now use the quarter note to measure longer notes.

whole note	𝅝	=	♩ ♩ ♩ ♩
dotted half note	𝅗𝅥.	=	♩ ♩ ♩
half note	𝅗𝅥	=	♩ ♩

SPEAKING THE LONGER NOTES

When you reach a note longer than the quarter note, speak "ta— a— a" for as many quarters as the note equals.

1   Speak *Rhythm 13* with the recording (S 8, B 3). You will hear the count "one, two, three, four."

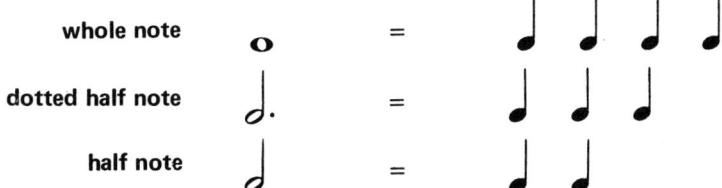

Speak *Rhythm 14* with the recording (S 8, B 4). You will hear the count "one, two, three, four."

2 Repeat *Rhythms 13* and *14*, speaking and clapping.

COUNTING NONMETERED RHYTHMS WITH NUMBERS
When counting nonmetered rhythms with numbers, give each note its value in quarter notes.

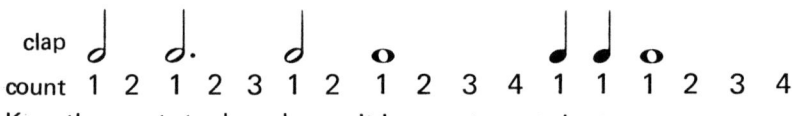

Keep the count steady and even; it is a quarter-note beat.

3 Clap and count with *Basic Pulse: Fast Tempo* (S 7 , B 2).

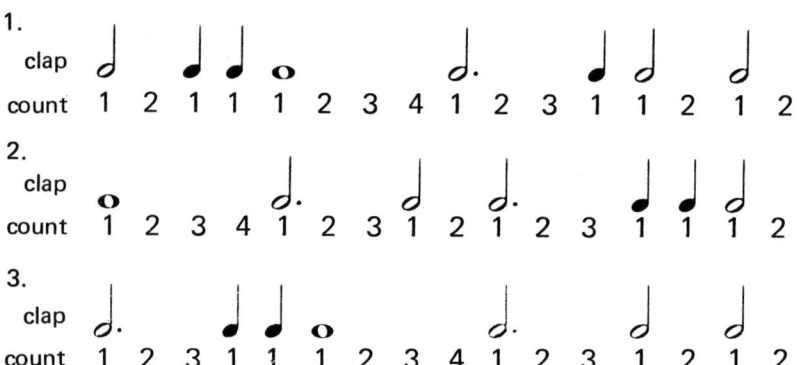

COUNTING RHYTHMS IN METER
When counting in a specific meter, you are counting the number of beats per measure. The value of each note fits into that metrical grouping.

4 Speak *Rhythms 13* and *14* with the recording. Observe the count of the beats per measure.

Rhythm 13 (S 8 , B 3)

Rhythm 14 (S 8, B 4)

5 Repeat *Rhythms 13* and *14*, clapping the rhythm and counting the beats in the measure (1 2 3 4).

6 Clap these rhythms, counting the beats in the measure with *Basic Pulse: Moderate Tempo* (S 7, B 3). The pulse equals the quarter note.

1.
clap $\frac{2}{4}$ ‖: ♩ ♫ | ♫ ♩ | ♫ ♫ | 𝅗𝅥 :‖
count   1 2   1 2   1 2   1 2

2.
clap $\frac{3}{4}$ ‖: ♩ ♩ ♩ | ♩. | ♩ 𝅗𝅥 | ♩ ♩ ♩ :‖
count   1 2 3   1 2 3   1 2 3   1 2 3

3.
clap $\frac{4}{4}$ ‖: 𝅗𝅥 𝅗𝅥 | ♩ ♩ ♫ ♩ :‖
count   1 2 3 4   1 2 3 4

4.
clap $\frac{4}{4}$ ‖: 𝅗𝅥 ♫ ♩ | ♩ ♩ 𝅗𝅥 | ♩. | ♫ ♩ | ♩ ♩ ♩ ♩ :‖
count   1 2 3 4   1 2 3 4   1 2 3 4   1 2 3 4

5.
clap $\frac{5}{4}$ ‖: ♩. 𝅗𝅥 | ♩ ♩ ♩ 𝅗𝅥 :‖
count   1 2 3 4 5   1 2 3 4 5

7 Clap and count these rhythms with the *Basic Pulse: Moderate Tempo* (S 7, B 3). When a rest appears, don't clap, but keep counting.

clap $\frac{3}{4}$ ‖: ♩ ♩ 𝄽 | ♩ 𝄽 ♩ | ♩ 𝅗𝅥 | 𝄽 𝅗𝅥 :‖
count   1 2 3   1 2 3   1 2 3   1 2 3

clap $\frac{4}{4}$ ‖: 𝄽 ♩ ♩ ♩ | 𝄽 ♩ 𝅗𝅥 | 𝄽 ♩ 𝄽 ♩ | ♩ 𝅗𝅥 𝄽 :‖
count   1 2 3 4   1 2 3 4   1 2 3 4   1 2 3 4

8 Tap both hands with *Basic Pulse: Moderate Tempo* (S 7, B 3). The pulse equals the quarter note.

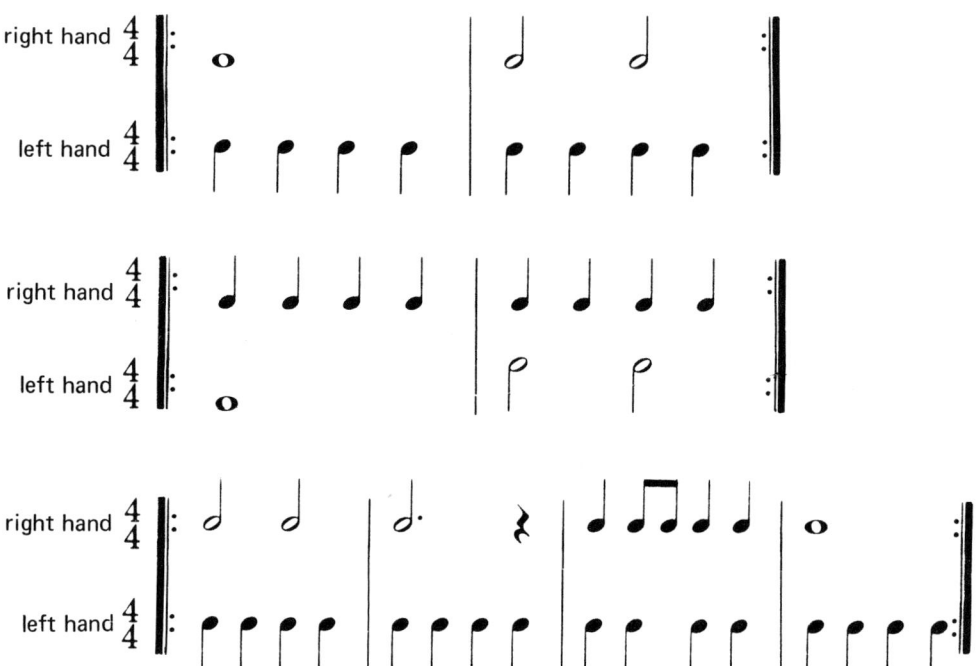

RESTS LONGER THAN THE QUARTER REST

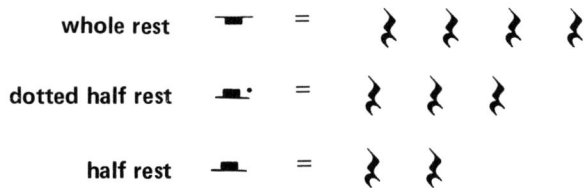

9 Tap and count with *Basic Pulse: Fast Tempo* (S 7, B 2). Do not speak or tap the rests. The pulse equals the quarter note.

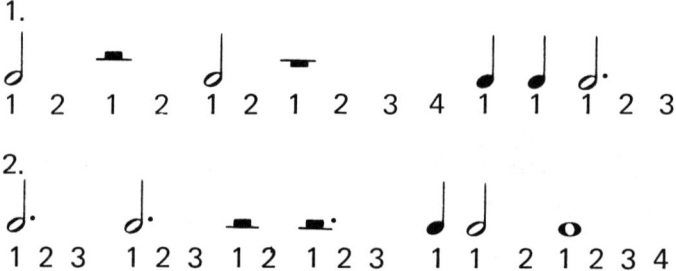

3.

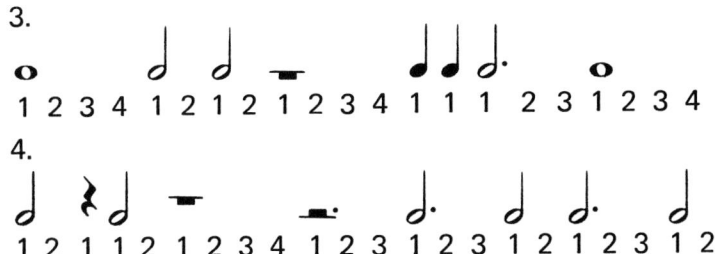

1 2 3 4   1 2   1 2   1 2 3 4   1 1 1   2 3   1 2 3 4

4.

1 2   1 1 2   1 2 3 4   1 2 3   1 2 3   1 2   1 2 3   1 2

CONDUCTING
Learn the basic conducting patterns. In this way, you translate each meter into physical action. The patterns are illustrated below. The lines indicate the motion of the arm led by the hand. The motion should be free and flowing. As you develop the basic movements, count the meter.

10 Practice these basic conducting patterns:

2 basic pulses

($\frac{2}{2}$ or $\frac{2}{4}$)

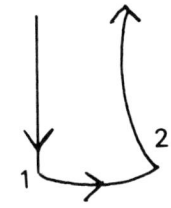

3 basic pulses

($\frac{3}{2}$ or $\frac{3}{4}$ or $\frac{3}{8}$)

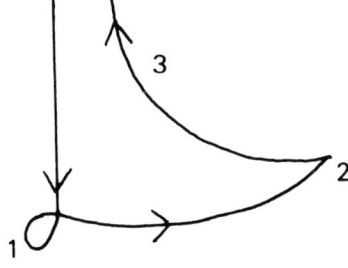

4 basic pulses

($\frac{4}{2}$ or $\frac{4}{4}$ or $\frac{4}{8}$)

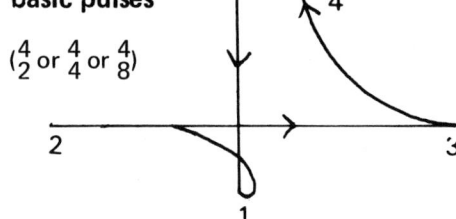

11 Play these exercises:

12 Tap out the rhythms of the following songs from the *Scorebook*.

The Wraggle Taggle Gypsies, O! (SB 16)
This Old Man (SB 18)
Philis, Plus Avare que Tendre (SB 27)
Que ne suis-je la Fougère (SB 28)
Oh How Lovely is the Evening (SB 35)
Shalom Chaverim (SB 38)
Sarabanda (SB 45)

TERMS, SYMBOLS, AND CONCEPTS
Explain in your own words:

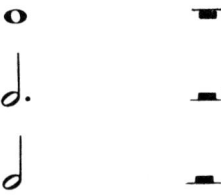

speaking notes longer than the quarter
counting nonmetered rhythm
counting metered rhythm
conducting patterns (2, 3, and 4 beats)

CHAPTER 6

NOTE SYMBOLS

We start our discussion of the note system with the whole note, which may be divided into smaller notes. The symbol for each note and its equivalent rest is presented here. The duration of each note or rest in this list is half the duration of the note or rest above it.

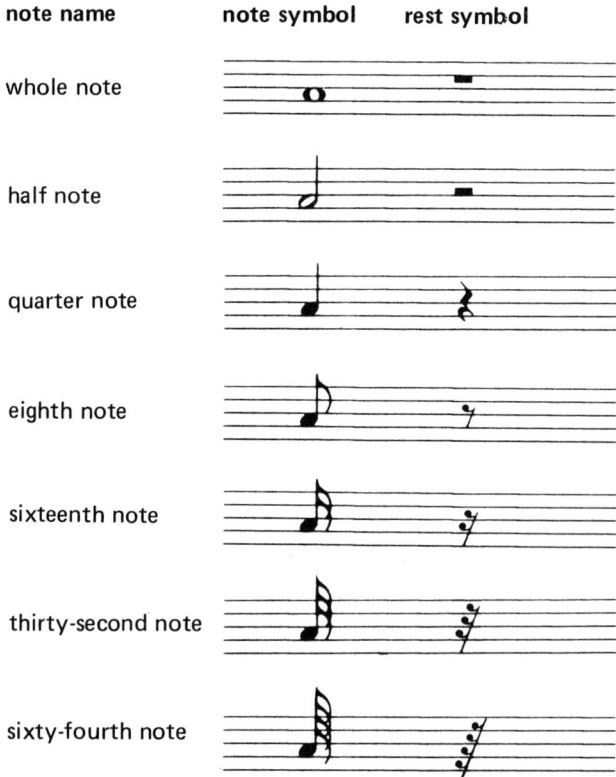

BEAMS

Notes smaller than the quarter note are written with *flags* (♪ ♫ ♬). When a group of flagged notes are written together, unifying *beams* are used.

Notice that the number of flags is replaced by the same number of beams.

COMBINATIONS OF NOTES WITH BEAMS

Notes of different time values can be joined together with beams.

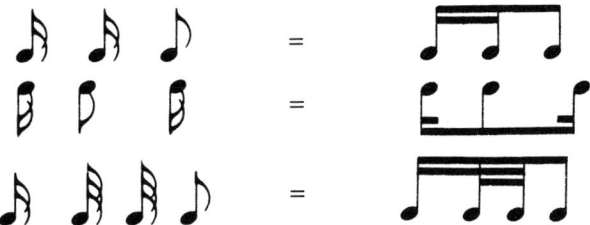

The beam may be on the left or right side of the note stem. It is the **number** of beams that touch the stem which determines the value of the note.

1 Rewrite these rhythms with flags:

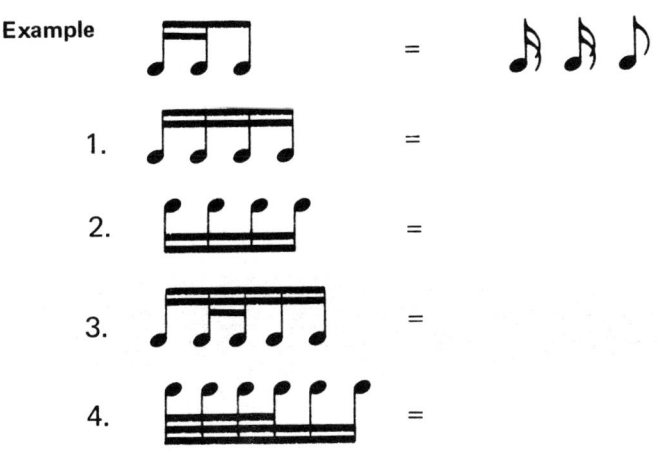

THE VALUES OF NOTES IN RELATIONSHIP TO EACH OTHER
The quarter note is often used as the basic unit for measuring the values of other notes. Below, each note is expressed in quarter notes.

1. Notes larger than the quarter note:

   𝐨 = ♩ ♩ ♩ ♩

   ♩. = ♩ ♩ ♩

   ♩ = ♩ ♩

2. Notes smaller than the quarter note are often beamed in groups equal to one quarter note in duration:

2 Write the number of smaller-value notes which equal the indicated larger-value note.

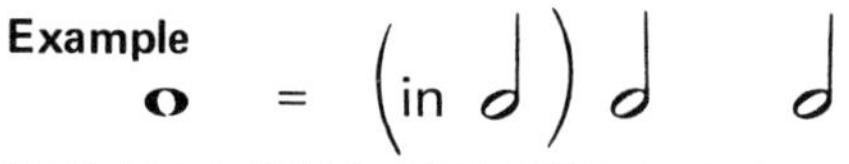

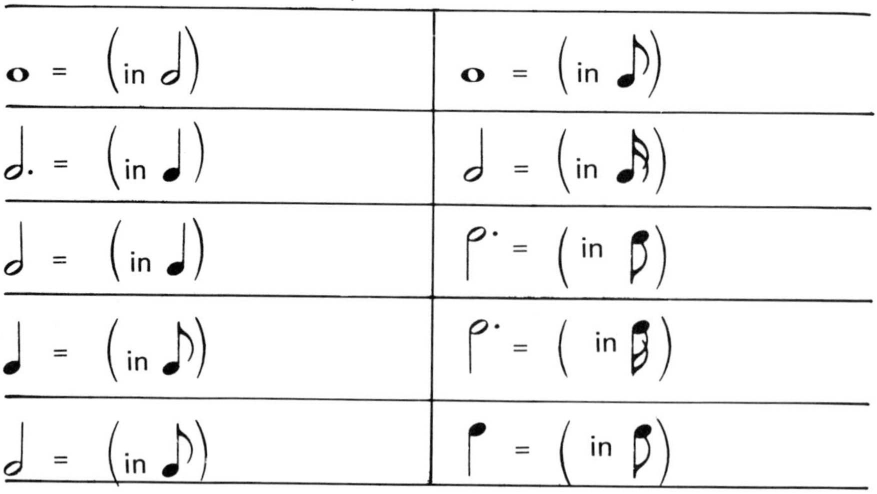

Example
𝐨 = (in ♩) ♩ ♩

𝐨 = (in ♩)	𝐨 = (in ♪)
♩. = (in ♩)	♩ = (in ♪)
♩ = (in ♩)	𝄽. = (in 𝄾)
♩ = (in ♪)	𝄽. = (in 𝄾)
♩ = (in ♪)	𝄽 = (in 𝄾)

THE TIE

Two notes of the same pitch may be connected with a curved line joining one notehead to the other. This line is called a *tie*. The first note is then prolonged by the value of the second.

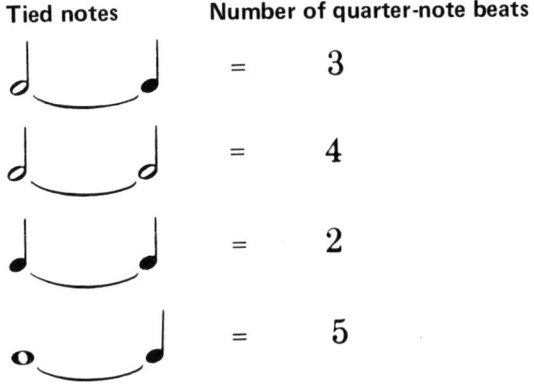

Do not confuse the tie with a similar curved line called the *slur*, which indicates that two or more **different** pitches are to be played smoothly (see *Workbook*, Appendix II). The tie always unites two notes of the **same** pitch.

THE DOTTED NOTE

A dot after a note is called an *augmentation dot*. This lengthens the note by half its own value. Note that prolonging a note with an augmentation dot is an alternative to using a tie to accomplish the same purpose.

The augmentation dot is **always** found in a space, even when the note it augments is on a line. For example:

3 With the **quarter note** valued at **one**, give the value of each of these notes or groups of notes.

Examples

𝅗𝅥. = 3   (𝅗𝅥 + ♩)
            2   1

♩. = 1½   (♩ + ♪)
            1   ½

♩. ♩. = 3 (♩. + ♩.)
            1½ 1½

𝅝. =	𝅘𝅥. 𝅘𝅥 =
𝅘𝅥 𝅘𝅥 =	𝅘𝅥 ♪ =
𝅘𝅥 ♪ =	𝅘𝅥. 𝅘𝅥. =
♩. ♩. =	♪ ♪ =
♪ ♩ ♪ =	𝅝. 𝅗𝅥 =

4 Write **one** note that equals each of these rhythmic groupings.

Example

♩ ♪ = ♩.   ♪ ♫ =

o ♩ =   o ♩ =

♩ ♩ (tied half notes) =   ♩ ♩ ♩ =

♩ ♩ =   ♪ ♩ ♪ =

♪ ♪ =   ♩. ♩ =

5 Name each symbol and give its value in quarter-note beats.

6 Total the value of quarter-note beats in each rhythmic group.

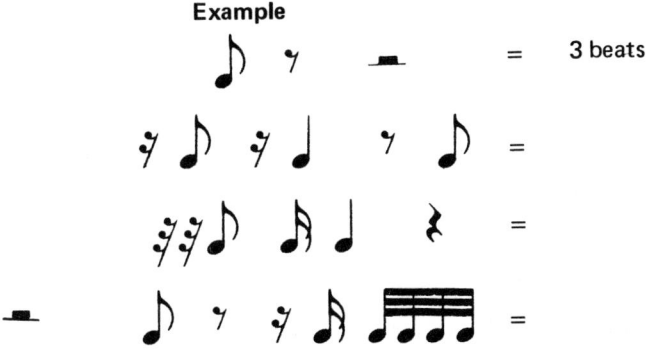

ANACRUSIS

Sometimes a piece or a rhythm will begin on the last part of the measure. This is called the *anacrusis*, or *upbeat*. The value of the anacrusis is subtracted from the final measure. Observe this practice in these two examples:

7 List the songs from the first twenty in the *Scorebook* that contain an anacrusis.

8 Play the following exercises:

TERMS, SYMBOLS, AND CONCEPTS
Explain in your own words:

beams

flag

stem

tie

augmentation dot

slur

anacrusis or upbeat

CHAPTER 7

SUBDIVISION OF THE BASIC PULSE

One way to aid understanding certain rhythms is to **subdivide** the basic pulse. This helps to locate the exact place where notes occur when they fall between beats. There are many ways of subdividing, and working with all of them will expand your understanding of rhythmic notation.

Common count of 4/4

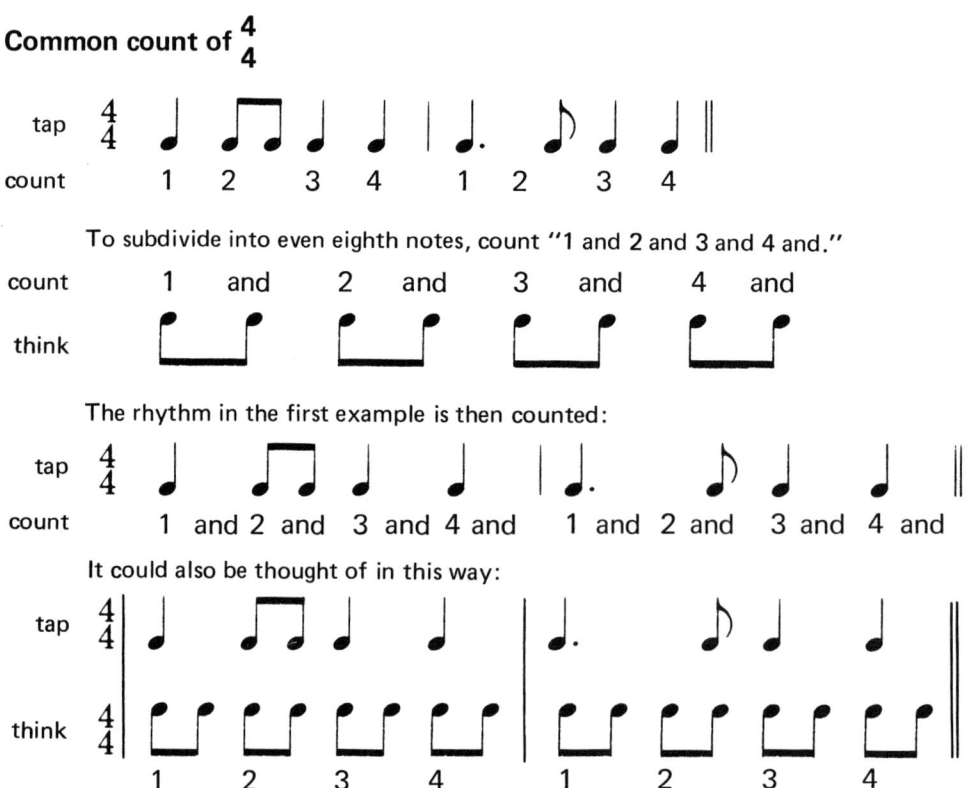

The subdivision provides a steady eighth-note pulse by which any note off the main beats may be correctly positioned.

1 Count these meters with the indicated basic pulse from the recordings:

1. Use *Basic Pulse: Fast Tempo* (S 7, B 2). ♪ is the pulse.

pulse 4/4
count   1 and 2 and 3 and 4 and   1 and 2 and 3 and 4 and

2. Use *Basic Pulse: Fast Tempo* (S 7, B 2). ♪ is the pulse.

pulse 3/4
count   1 and 2 and 3 and   1 and 2 and 3 and

3. Use *Basic Pulse: Moderate Tempo* (S 7, B 3). ♩ is the pulse.

pulse 2/4
count   1 and 2 and   1 and 2 and

4. Use *Basic Pulse: Moderate Tempo* (S 7, B 3). ♩ is the pulse.

pulse 4/4
count   1 and 2 and 3 and 4 and   1 and 2 and 3 and 4 and

5. Use *Basic Pulse: Slow Tempo* (S 7, B 4). ♩ is the pulse.

pulse 3/4
count   1 and 2 and 3 and   1 and 2 and 3 and

2 Listen to *Study I* (S 6, B 3). Observe the places where the chord in the top part falls **after** the beat. After listening a few times, tap the top part with the recording.

3 1. This is the rhythmic outline of *Study I*. Tap and count with the recording.

count 1and2and3and4and 1and2and3and4and 1and2and3and4and 1and2and3and4and

2. Repeat *Study I*, following this version, which uses a **tie** instead of a dotted note. The count is not subdivided. Tap and count:

count 1 2 3 4   1 2 3 4   1 2 3 4   1 2 3 4   1 2 3 4

4 Write the rhythm of the top part of *Study I* above this quarter-note pulse. Be careful to place the notes that fall after the beat in the correct places.

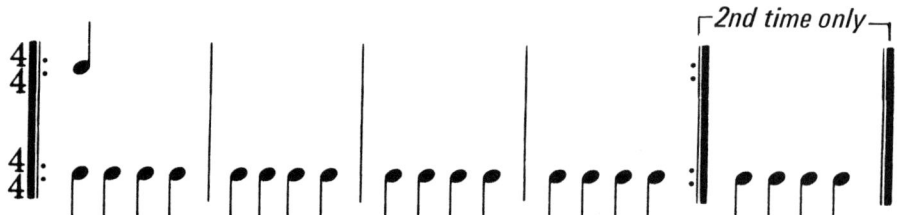

5 Above the subdivisions provided, write the three rhythms given below. Then speaking or thinking the subdivision, tap the rhythm. Remember that the subdivisions must be steady when you are counting or thinking a subdivided beat.

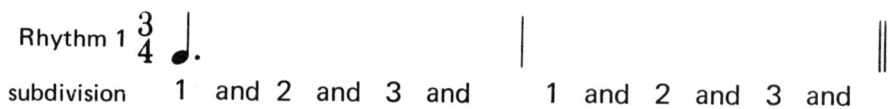

subdivision 1 and 2 and 3 and   1 and 2 and 3 and

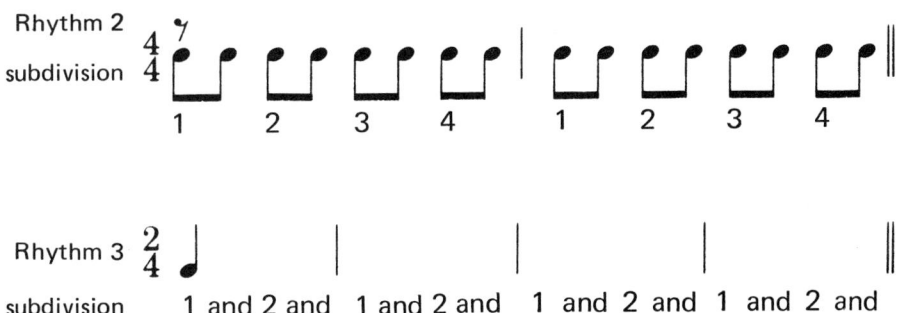

6 Play these exercises.

7 Choose from among these pieces in the *Scorebook* and tap the rhythms.

The Trees They Do Grow High (SB 1)

I Know Where I'm Going (SB 2)

The Riddle Song (SB 6)

Lullaby, by Brahms (SB 8)

Dona, Dona (SB 13)

Wayfaring Stranger (SB 15)

The First Noel (SB 32)

In the following, choose one part to tap out:

Remember, O Thou Man (SB 44)

The Young Convert (SB 42)

Willie, Take Your Little Drum (SB 43)

Dona Nobis Pacem (SB 37)

The Welcome Song (SB 39)

TERMS, SYMBOLS, AND CONCEPTS
Explain in your own words:
>subdivision
>methods for counting

CHAPTER 8

SUBDIVISION OF THE QUARTER NOTE INTO SIXTEENTHS

The quarter note can be further subdivided into four parts to help understand rhythms using eighth notes, sixteenth notes, and other notes of shorter duration. When speaking, accent "one" in each group of four.

6.

tap
count 1 2 3 4 1 2 3 4 1 2 3 4 1 2 3 4 1 2 3 4 1 2 3 4
         >   >   >   >   >   >

7.
tap
count 1 2 3 4 1 2 3 4 1 2 3 4 1 2 3 4 1 2 3 4 1 2 3 4

8.
tap
count 1 2 3 4 1 2 3 4 1 2 3 4 1 2 3 4 1 2 3 4 1 2 3 4

Repeat the rhythms above with the *Basic Pulse: Moderate Tempo* (S 7, B 3). The pulse equals the quarter note. Before you tap the rhythms, establish the pulse. The "1" of your count should coincide with the pulse on the recording.

2   Rewrite the rhythms in **1** below the appropriate subdivision. Write the stems **down**.

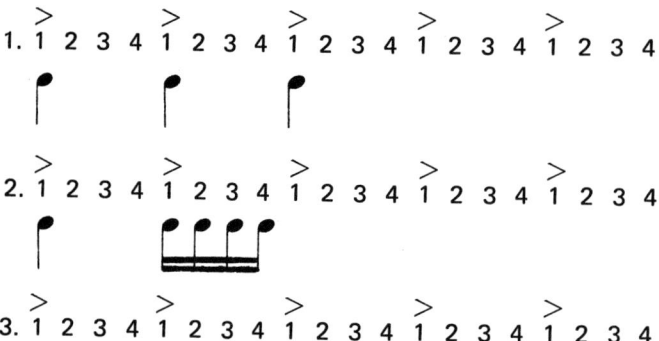

   >   >   >   >   >
1. 1 2 3 4 1 2 3 4 1 2 3 4 1 2 3 4 1 2 3 4

   >   >   >   >   >
2. 1 2 3 4 1 2 3 4 1 2 3 4 1 2 3 4 1 2 3 4

   >   >   >   >   >
3. 1 2 3 4 1 2 3 4 1 2 3 4 1 2 3 4 1 2 3 4

   >   >   >   >   >
4. 1 2 3 4 1 2 3 4 1 2 3 4 1 2 3 4 1 2 3 4

   >   >   >   >   >
5. 1 2 3 4 1 2 3 4 1 2 3 4 1 2 3 4 1 2 3 4

   >   >   >   >   >
6. 1 2 3 4 1 2 3 4 1 2 3 4 1 2 3 4 1 2 3 4

```
     >           >           >           >           >
7. 1 2 3 4   1 2 3 4   1 2 3 4   1 2 3 4   1 2 3 4

     >           >           >           >           >
8. 1 2 3 4   1 2 3 4   1 2 3 4   1 2 3 4   1 2 3 4
```

SUBDIVIDING INTO SIXTEENTHS, IN METER

When subdividing into sixteenths within a metered rhythm using the quarter note as the basic beat, the subdivision can be counted in this way: "one—ee—and—ee" (spoken slurred together with the accent on "one").

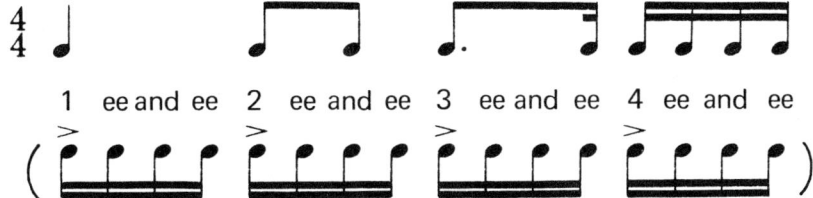

This method helps you keep track of the beat within the measure while still subdividing each beat into four parts.

3 Repeat **1**, using the "one—ee—and—ee" system.

4 Listen to *Study II* (S 6 , B 4). Tap the top part.

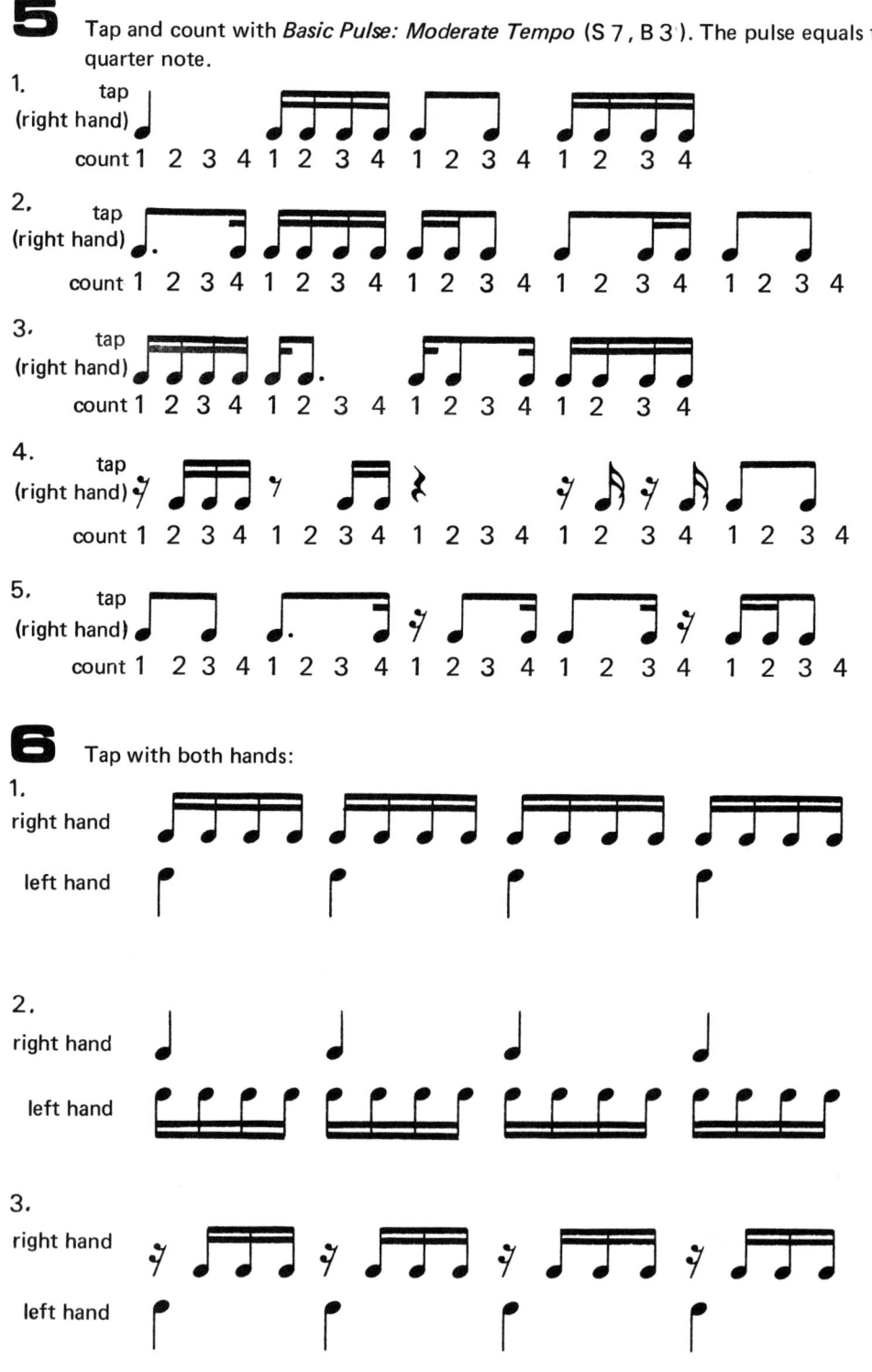

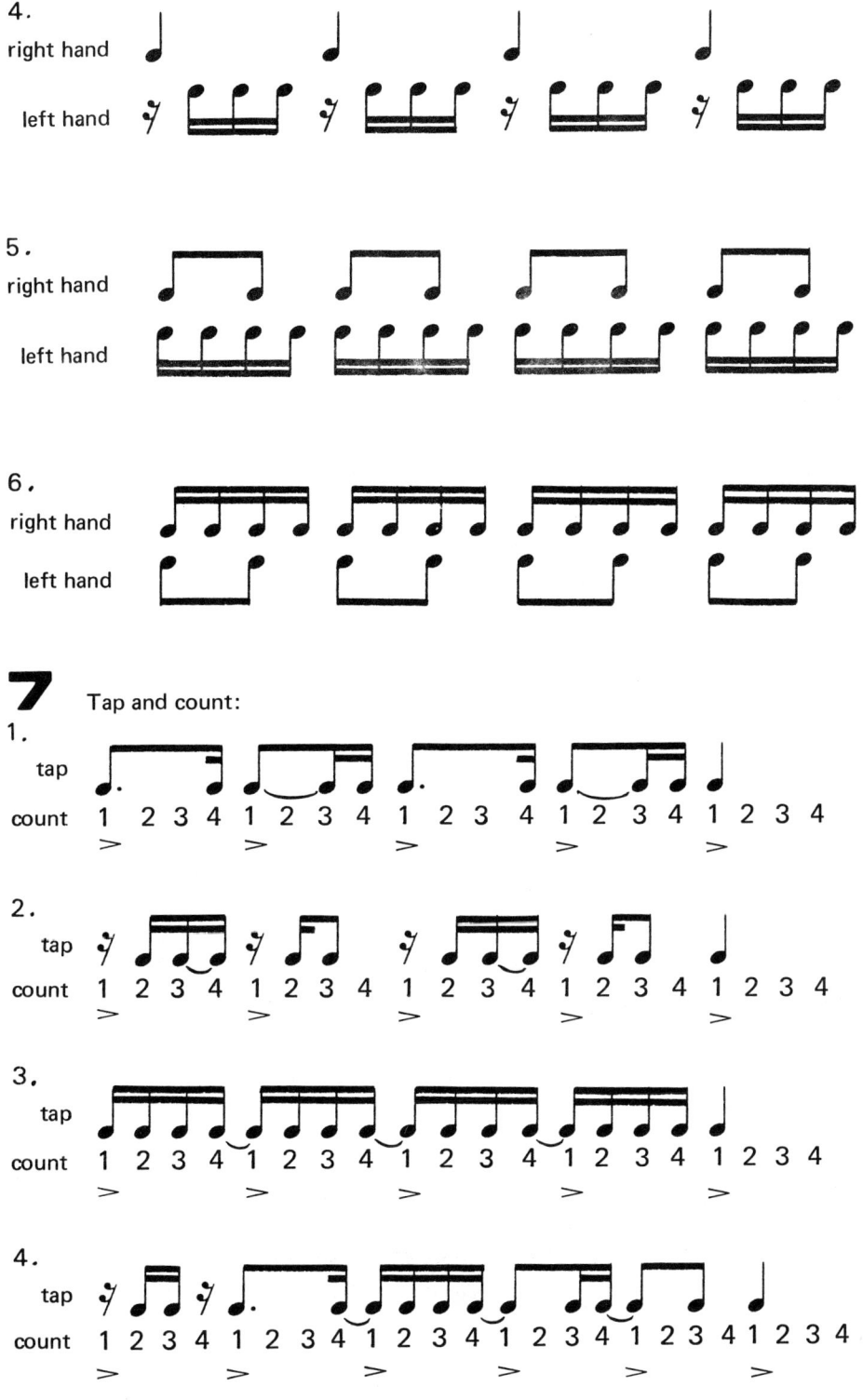

8 Play these exercises:

9 Play the following pieces from the *Scorebook*:

Alouette (SB 20)

This Old Man (SB 18)

Barbrie Allen (SB 9)

Listen to the Bach *Fugue* (SB 51, S 1, B 2). Tap out the first two measures, then follow the score to the end.

TERMS, SYMBOLS, AND CONCEPTS
Explain in your own words:

      subdivision into sixteenths

CHAPTER 9

TRIPLETS

The quarter note can also be divided into three equal parts. This is notated 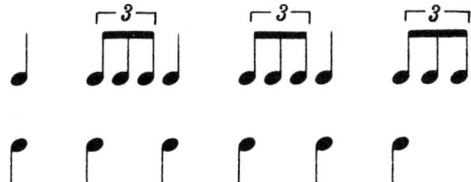 and each group is called a *triplet*.

1 Listen to *Study III*. Tap the top part with the recording.

2 Here is a rhythmic outline of *Study III*. Tap and count with the recording.

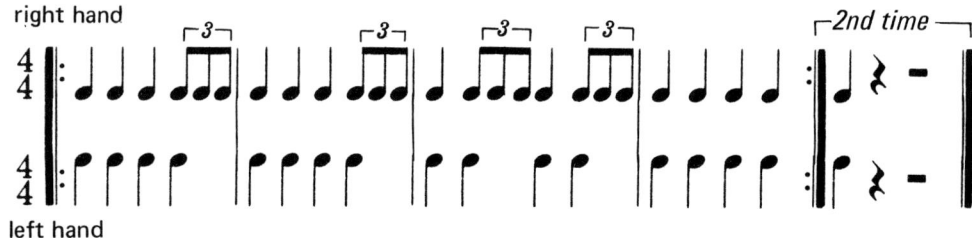

Observe how triplets are aligned on the rhythm spacer:

Compare the triplet with eighths:

Notice that only the use of a bracket and the number 3 (⌐—3—⌐) distinguishes eighth notes from triplets.

3 Align each pair of rhythms on the rhythm spacer, as indicated:

2. (a)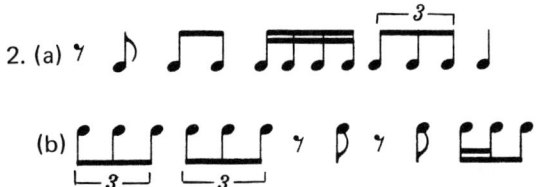

(b)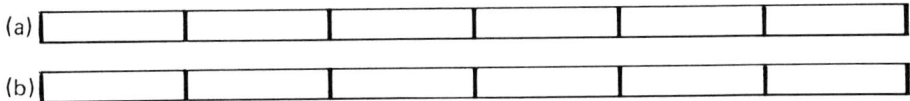

(a) | | | | | | |
(b) | | | | | | |

3. (a)

(a) | | | | | | |
(b) | | | | | | |

4. (a)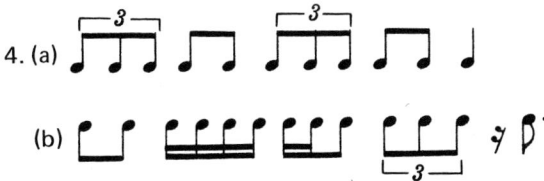

(b)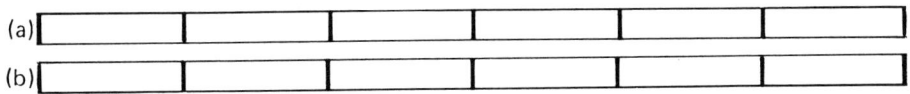

(a) | | | | | | |
(b) | | | | | | |

4 Tap the top part of *Study IV*. (S 6, B 6). Feel the difference between eighth notes and triplets.

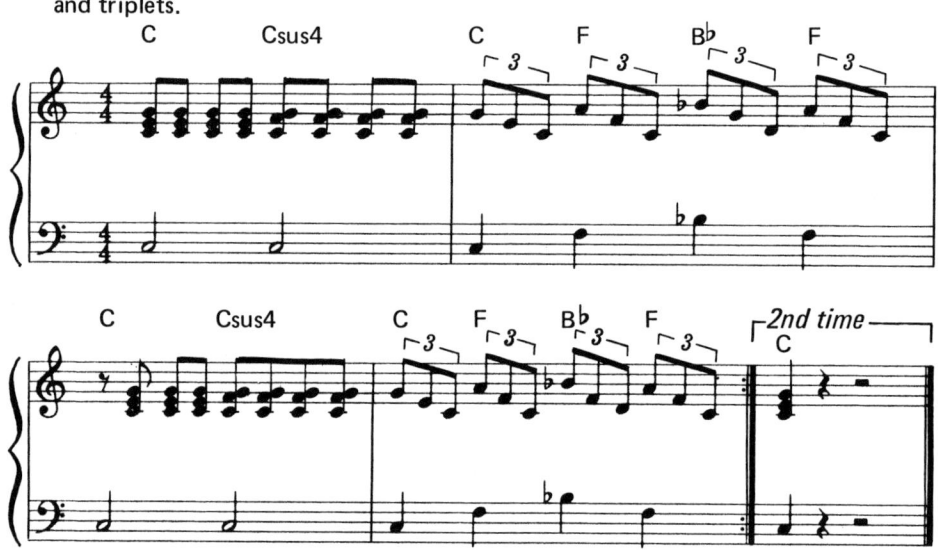

5 Here is a rhythmic outline of *Study IV*. Tap both hands with the recording.

COUNTING TRIPLETS BY SUBDIVISION

The quarter note was subdivided into **two** equal parts by counting "1 and 2 and." The quarter note can be subdivided into **three** equal parts by counting "1 and—a 2 and—a 3 and—a 4 and—a."

6 Tap and count with this rhythmic outline of *Study IV*.

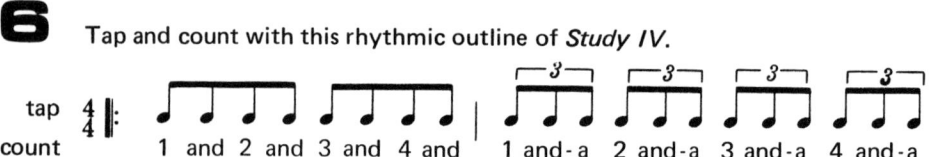

7 Count with *Rhythm 15* (S 8, B 4). In this exercise, the beat is subdivided into two, three, and four.

Rhythm 15

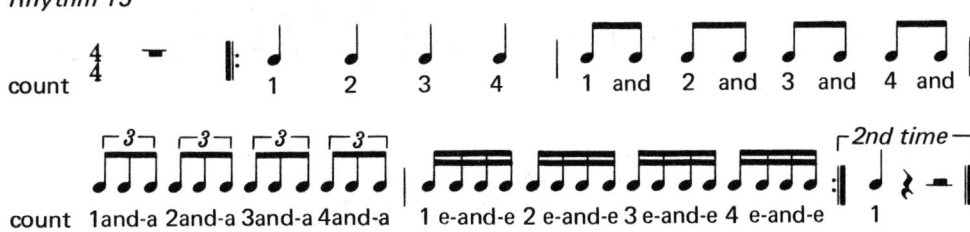

THE TRIPLET REST
When a rest occurs in the triplet subdivision, it is written like the eighth rest, but included within the triplet bracket.

8 Tap and count:

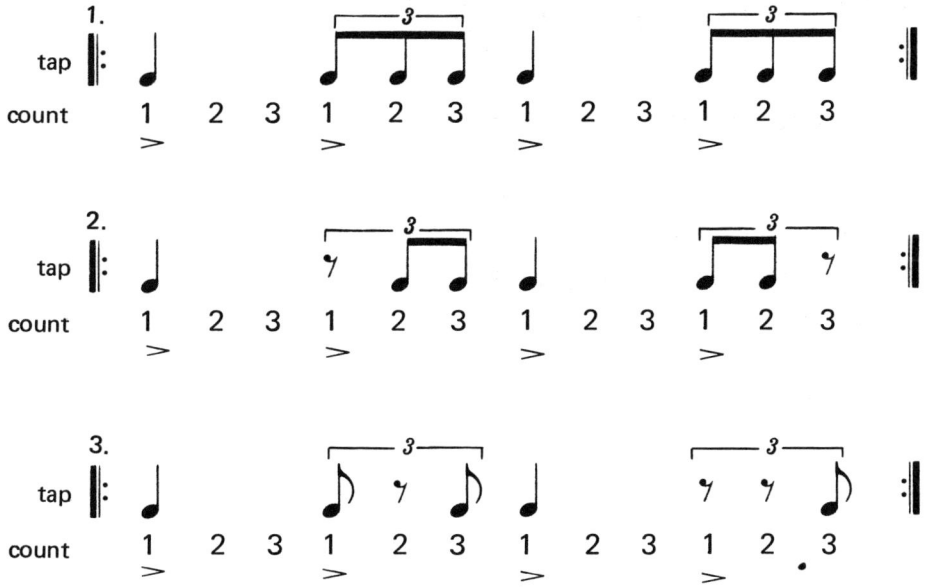

9 Tap the top part of the *Minuet* by Mozart (SB 48).

10 Play these exercises:

TERMS, SYMBOLS, AND CONCEPTS
Explain in your own words:

⎡─3─⎤

    comparing triplets to eighths

    subdivision of the pulse into 2, 3, and 4

    triplet rest

CHAPTER 10

COMPOUND METER

The meters we have studied so far have all utilized a basic pulse whose usual subdivision is two; such a meter is called a *simple meter*. In simple meter, the triplet is an irregular subdivision requiring a special type of notation. However, there are meters whose basic pulse regularly subdivides into three parts; such a meter is called *compound meter*.

Compound meters

Observe that in the compound meters, ♩. is the basic pulse.

1 Tap and count these rhythms:

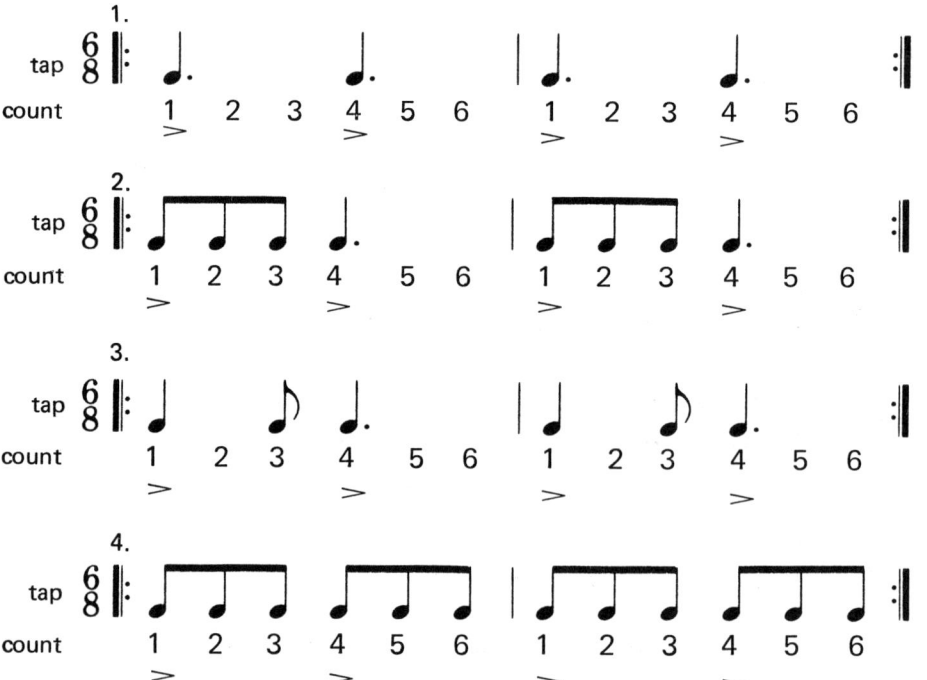

2 Tap and count these rhythms, first with the *Basic Pulse: Moderate Tempo* (S 7, B 3), then with the *Basic Pulse: Fast Tempo* (S 7, B 2). The pulse equals the eighth note subdivision (in this example, the subdivision [♪] is not to be confused with the **basic pulse**, which is ♩.). Count the basic pulse (♩.s).

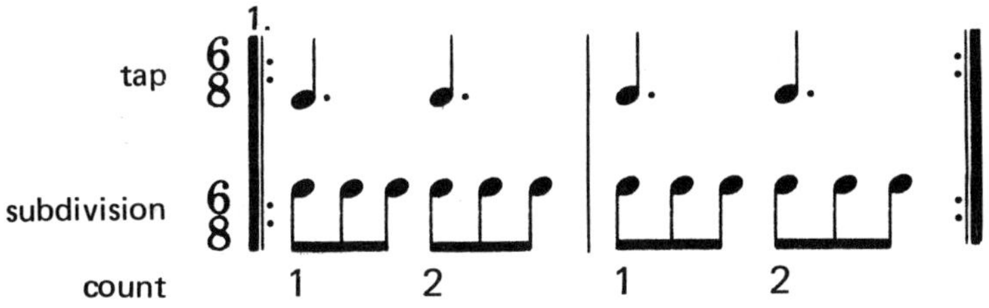

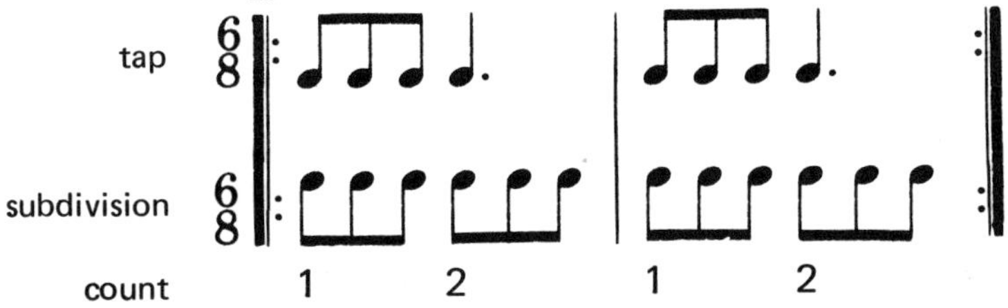

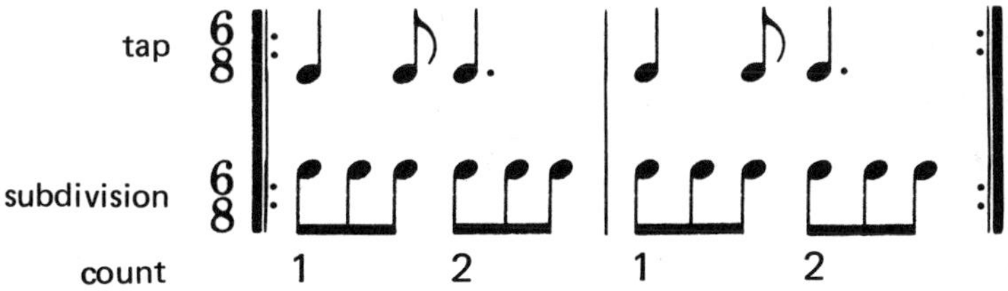

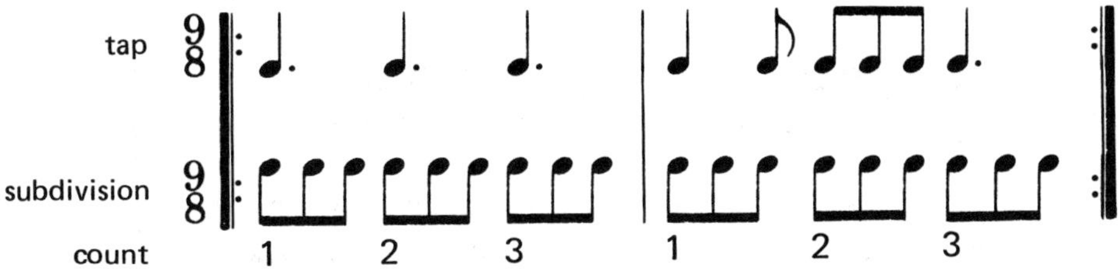

5.

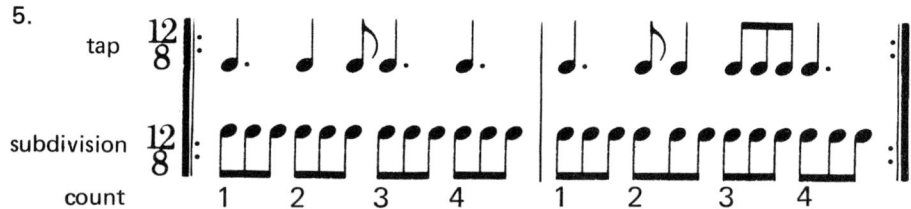

3 Listen to and follow the score of *Greensleeves* (S 5 , B 1 SB 3). Count it in two different ways: count the subdivisions (1 2 3 4 5 6) and count the basic pulse (1 2). After listening and counting a few times, tap the melody while following the score.

4 Sing *Silent Night*, following the score (SB 31) and tapping the subdivisions.

5 1. Take the first rhythmic figure of *Silent Night* and learn to tap it with your right hand against even eighth notes with your left. Singing it will help. Repeat until you have the rhythm right.

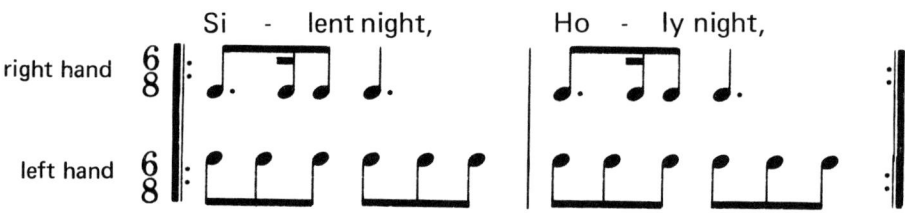

2. Tap with both hands:

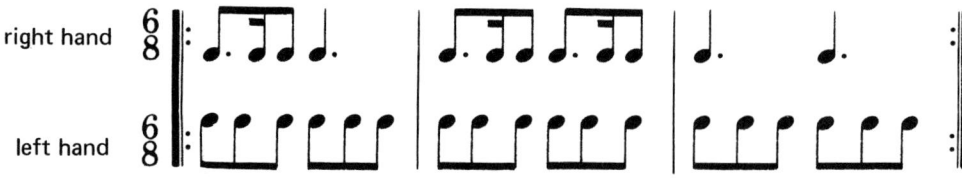

3.

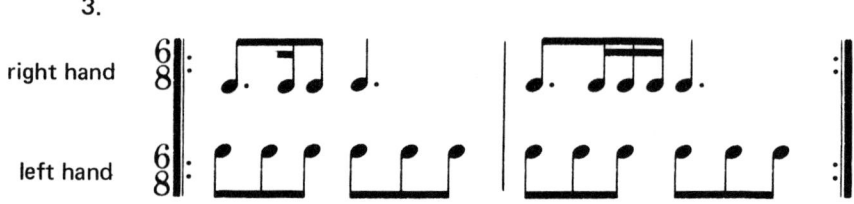

ANOTHER WAY OF COUNTING

If you want to count aloud in compound meter and indicate both the basic pulse and the subdivision, it can be done in this way:

6 Play these exercises:

7 Play these pieces in the *Scorebook*:

Drink to Me Only (SB 7)

Believe Me, If All Those Endearing Young Charms (SB 10)

TERMS, SYMBOLS, AND CONCEPTS

Explain in your own words:

    simple meter   subdividing compound meter

    compound meter   counting in compound meter

CHAPTER 11

1 Speak *Rhythms 16–19* with the recordings (S 8 , B 4 –5).

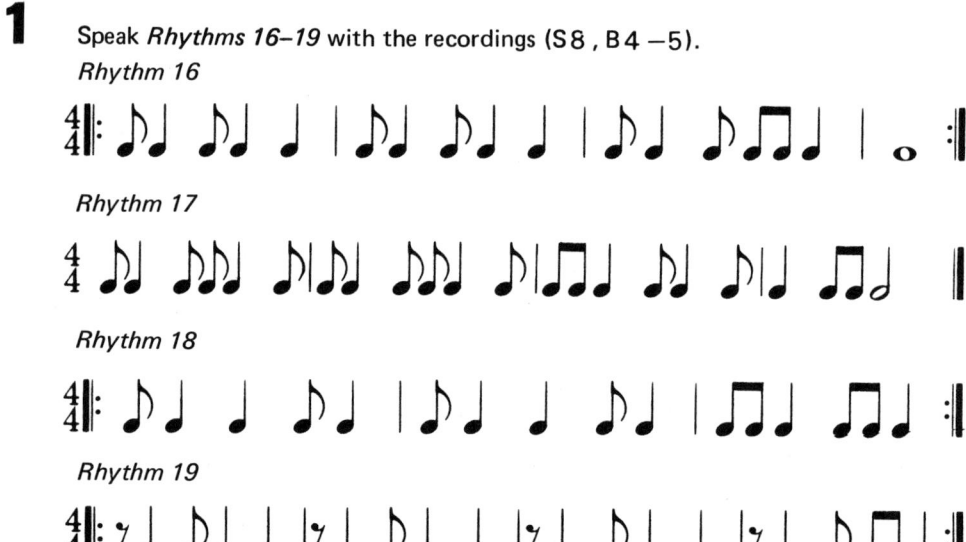

SYNCOPATED AND NONSYNCOPATED RHYTHMS
Notes can occur **on** the beat or **off** the beat.

On the beat

Off the beat

Rhythms which have accented notes off the beat are said to be *syncopated*. Rhythms 15–18 (on pages 55 and 63) are all syncopated.

Syncopated rhythm

Nonsyncopated

2 Line up these rhythms on the rhythm spacer:

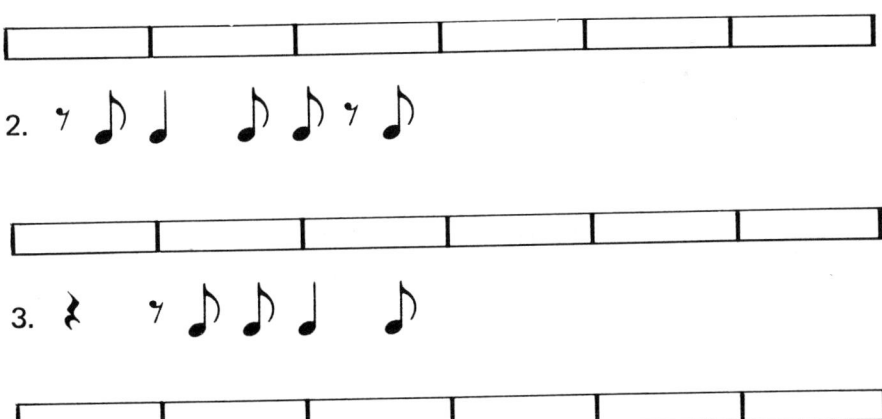

VISUALIZING WHERE THE BEAT FALLS
To understand a complex rhythm, you must be able to visualize where the beat occurs.

An easy way to indicate the beat is to draw a line where the basic beat occurs.

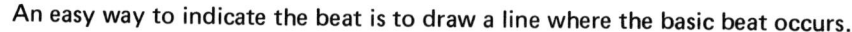

These marks locate the beat in the same way that the rhythm spacer does.

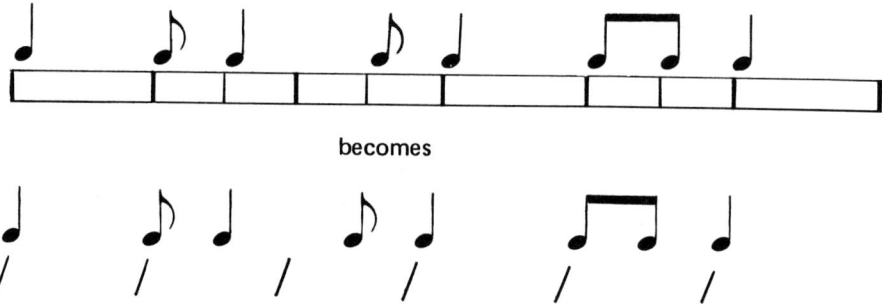

3 Mark where the quarter-note beat falls.
Example

1. ♩ ♩ ♫ ♩ ♩ ♫ ♩ ♩
2. ♩ ♩ ♫ ♫ ♫ ♫ ♩ ♩
3. ♫ ♩ ♫ ♩ ♩ ♩ ♩
4. ♫ ♫ ♫ ♫ ♫
5. ♩. ♫ ♫ ♩ ♩ ♫ ♩

6.

7.

8.

9.

4 Play the following pieces in the *Scorebook*:

Shoo Fly (SB 11)

The Riddle Song (SB 6)

Black, Black, Black (SB 14)

Wayfaring Stranger (SB 15)

TERMS, SYMBOLS, AND CONCEPTS
Explain in your own words:

    syncopation

       visualizing where the beat occurs

CHAPTER 12

ALTERNATING HANDS: DEVELOPING COORDINATION

1   1. Speak *Rhythm 1* with the recording (S 7, B 5).

2. Now speak and tap with the recording, using both hands. When the stems go up, use your right hand; when the stems go down, use your left hand. Remember, considerable practice may be necessary to master these exercises, since they combine understanding rhythm with physical coordination.

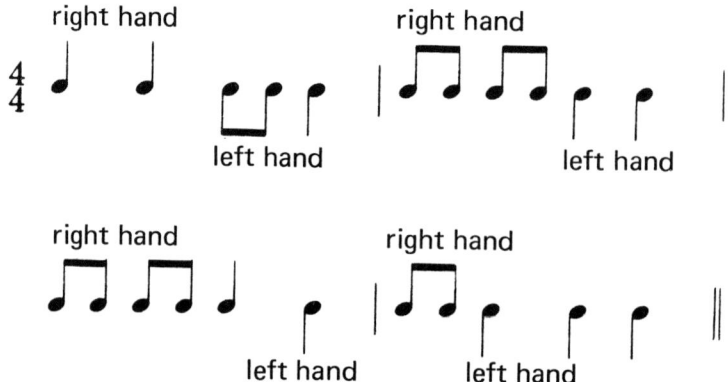

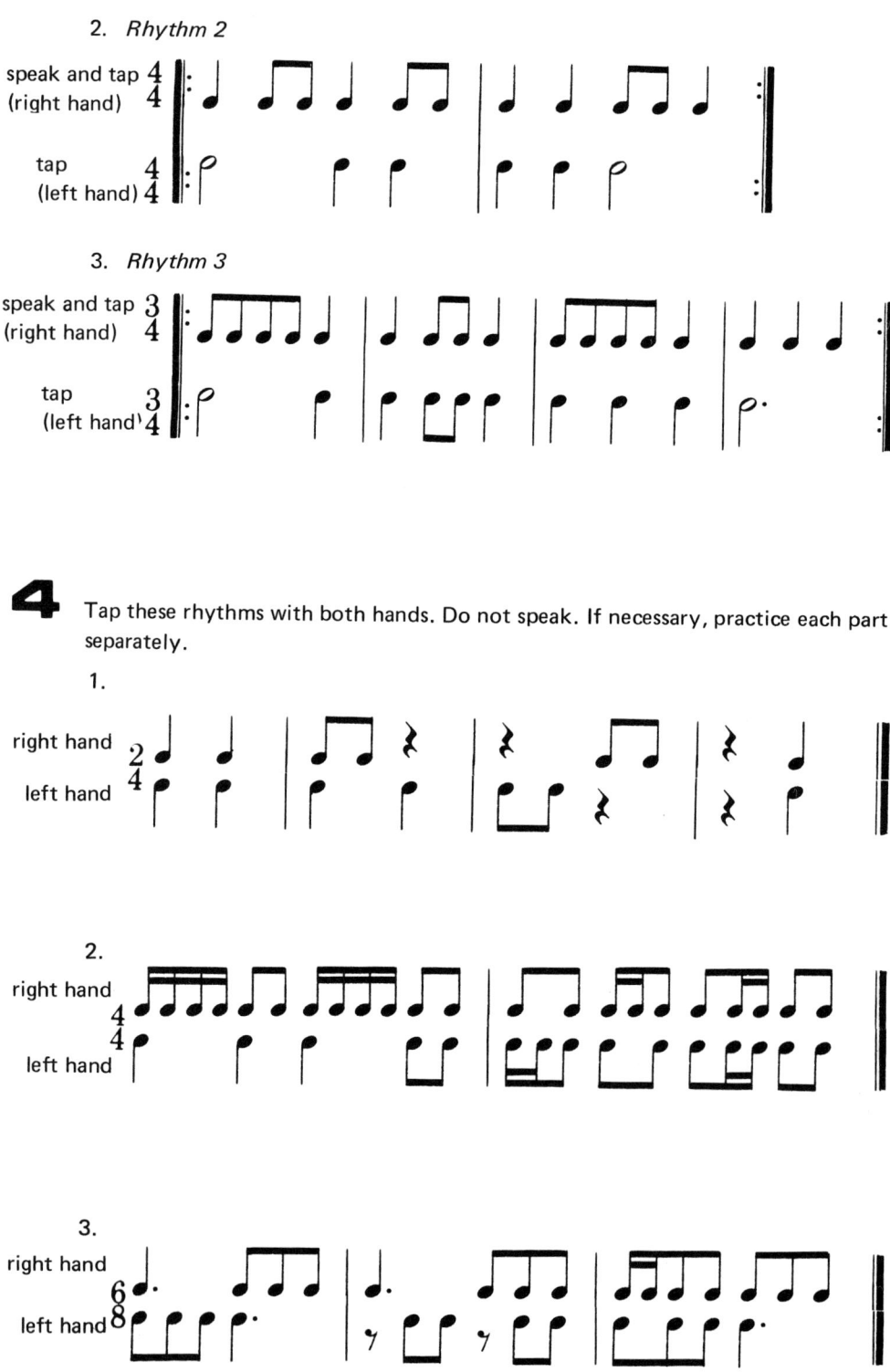

5 Tap the rhythm of *The Welcome Song* (SB 39) in the following manner: tap lines 1 and 2 together (line 1 with your right hand, line 2 with your left hand); then tap lines 2 and 3 together in the same way, and then lines 3 and 4.

CHAPTER 13

DIFFERENT VALUES OF THE BASIC PULSE
In the rhythms we have studied so far, the basic pulse has been represented by ♩ or ♩. Other rhythmic values can be used as the basic pulse, depending on the tempo, the historical period in which a piece was composed, or the whim of the composer. Observe these examples:

C AND ¢

C the symbol for common time, represents $\frac{4}{4}$.

¢ (*alla breve* sign) indicates a halving of the time values, thus changing **C** ($\frac{4}{4}$) to **¢** ($\frac{2}{2}$).

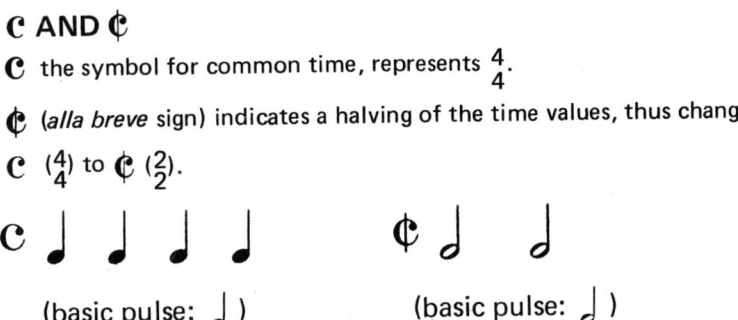

Changing the ratio of note values can go either way, as illustrated by this example:

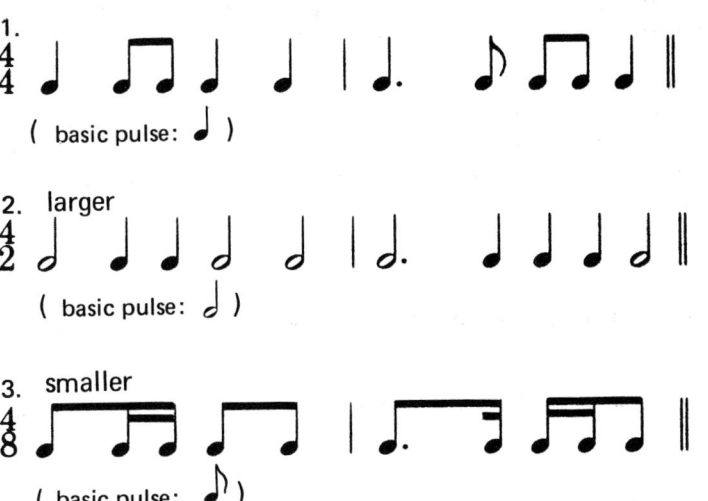

All three rhythms sound exactly alike, if the **tempo** (rate of speed) of the basic pulse is the same. Notice that example 2 is created by doubling the original quarter-note pulse, while example 3 is created by dividing the original quarter-note pulse in half.

1 Tap out *Study I* (S6, B3) with the recording, first in its original form, then in the two other versions.

2 Tap out *Study III* (S 6, B 5) with the recording three times, following these three versions.

3 Tap out the rhythm of *Greensleeves* (S 5, B 1) with the recording. Follow the original version (1) for the first verse. Follow the alternative notation (2) for the second verse.

4 Rewrite each of these rhythms in a different meter, as indicated.

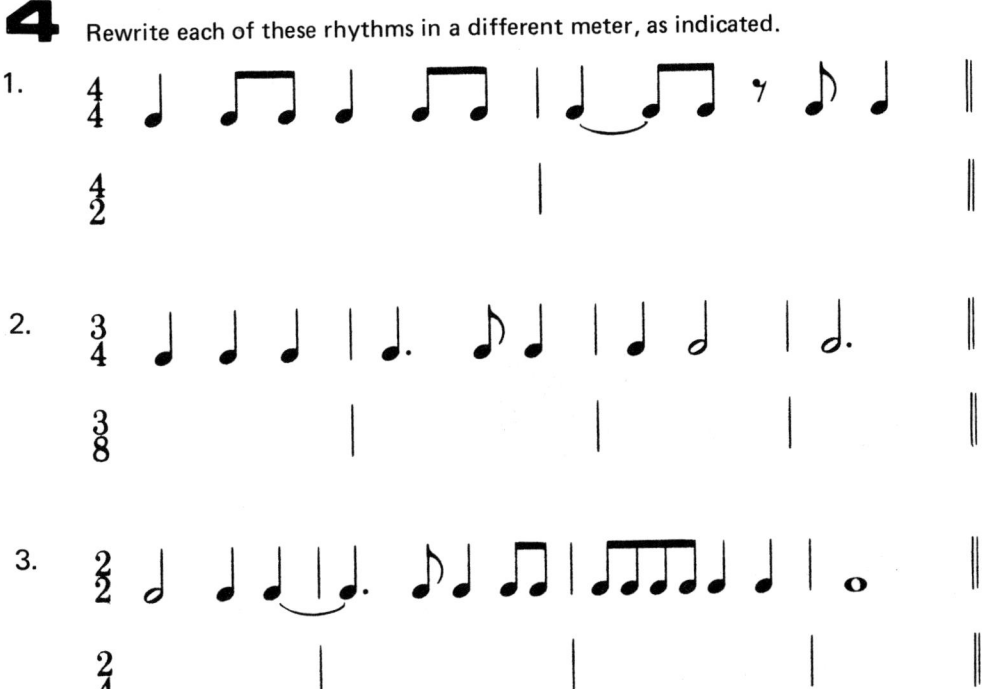

TERMS, SYMBOLS, AND CONCEPTS
Explain in your own words:

    using different note values for the basic pulse

    C and ¢

    doubling the value of the basic pulse

    dividing the value of the basic pulse

CHAPTER 14

CLEAR NOTATION
Rhythms must be written in a way that makes the basic pulse easy to locate. For example:

Confusing—does not show the basic pulse:

Clear—shows the basic pulse:

Because the beams begin on the beat, the basic pulse is easier to read in the second version. Sometimes the beat is not notated clearly because of other musical necessities, so it is important for you to be able to read rhythms in any version. However, when you write rhythms, try to represent the basic pulse clearly.

BEAMS
Beams usually begin on the beat unless there is a rest on the beat. Usually, no more than six notes are beamed together.

1 Rewrite these rhythms in a way that clearly shows the basic pulse.

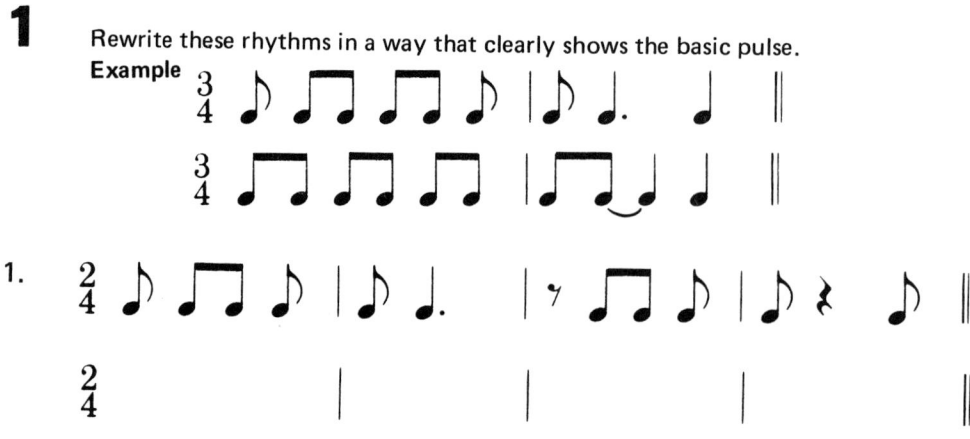

2.

3.

RESTS
Certain practices in writing rests are different from those in writing notes.

    1. The whole rest (▀) is used to represent a full measure of rest in any meter. It always hangs beneath the fourth line in the center of the measure.

Example

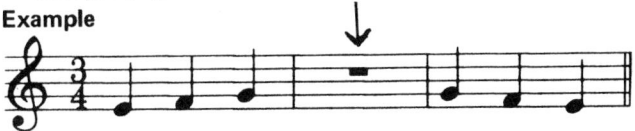

    2. Rests are not tied.

    3. Half rests (▄) always sit atop the third line. They are rarely used in $\frac{3}{4}$.

    4. Quarter rests (𝄽) and half rests (▄) are usually written **on** the beat, not **off** the beat.

ALIGNING TWO PARTS
Notes that sound together are written directly above or below each other. Correct spacing of two separate parts shows exactly where the notes occur. Observe the following example:

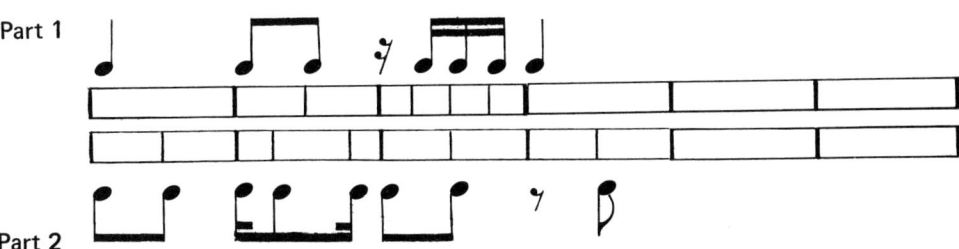

Correctly aligned:

Part 1

Part 2

2 Put each rhythm on the rhythm spacer. Then copy the two parts again, using the rhythm spacer as a guide for aligning them correctly, as in the example above.

1. 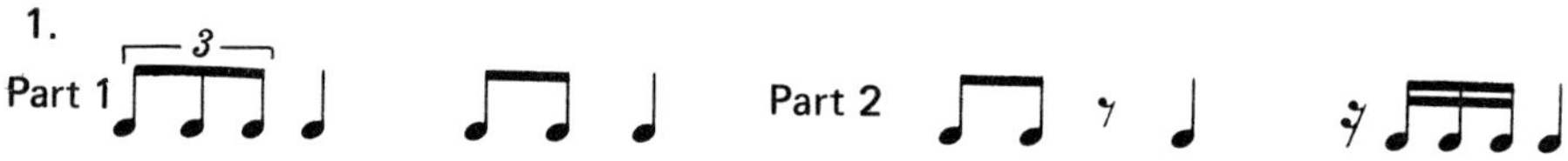
Part 1   Part 2

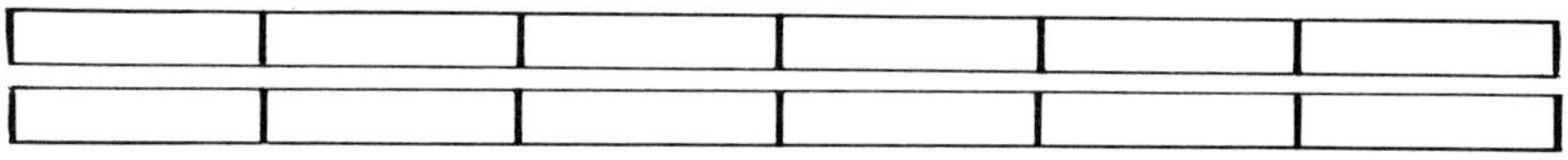

Part 1
Part 2

Part 1

Part 2

2. 
Part 1   Part 2

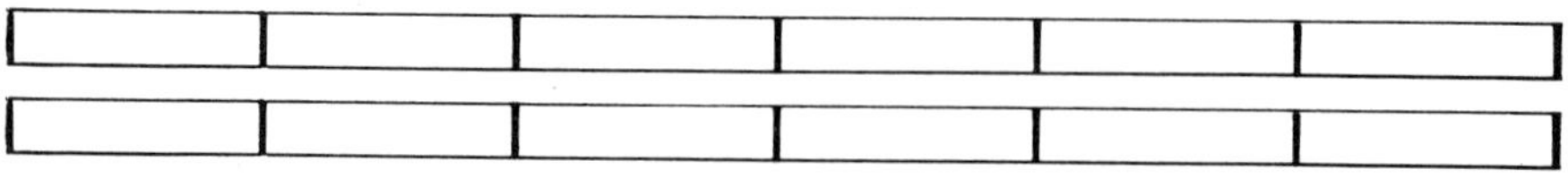

Part 1
Part 2

Part 1

Part 2

3.

4.

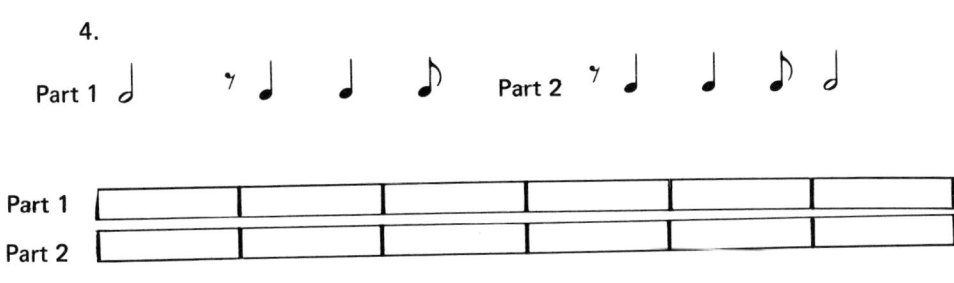

Part 1

Part 2

TERMS, SYMBOLS, AND CONCEPTS
Explain in your own words:

    clear rhythmic notation through the use of beams, ties, and rests

    proper use of rests

    aligning two parts

CHAPTER 15

TESTING YOUR RHYTHMIC SKILLS
Use this chapter as a test of your rhythmic skills. Prepare for each exercise by reviewing, if necessary.

1 Tap:

3 Tap with both hands:

Rhythm 17

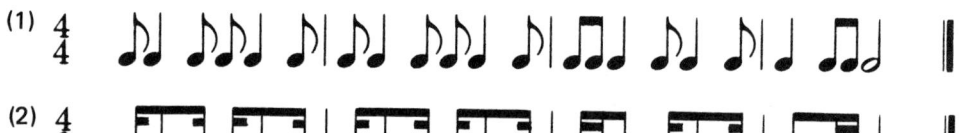

Rhythm 18

Rhythm 19

6 Play these pieces from the *Scorebook*:

Minuet for Lute (SB 46)

Minuet, by Purcell (SB 47)

Silent Night (SB 31)

Dona Nobis Pacem (SB 37)

Greensleeves (SB 3)

7 Play the *Dance of Zalongo* (SB 25). The rhythm is counted in this manner: